Advances in Personal Construct Psychology

Advances in Personal Construct Psychology
New Directions and Perspectives

edited by
Robert A. Neimeyer
Greg J. Neimeyer

PRAEGER

Westport, Connecticut
London

British Library Cataloguing in Publication Data is available.

ISBN: 0-275-97294-1

First published in 2002

Praeger Publishers, 88 Post Road West, Westport, CT 06881
An imprint of Greenwood Publishing Group, Inc.
www.praeger.com

Printed in the United States of America

The paper used in this book complies with the
Permanent Paper Standard issued by the National
Information Standards Organization (Z39.48–1984).

10   9   8   7   6   5   4   3   2   1

Copyright Acknowledgments

The author and the publisher gratefully acknowledge permission to use the following material:

Throughout text, extracts from George A. Kelly, *Psychology of Personal Constructs*, Routledge, 1991, originally published by W. W. Norton, 1955.

072402 - Galotti

Contents

Preface

Robert A. Neimeyer
Greg J. Neimeyer

In keeping with the inauguration of the new Praeger series, Advances in Personal Construct Psychology, we are pleased to open it with a forward-looking volume focusing on *Advances in Personal Construct Psychology: New Directions and Perspectives*. Originating in the pioneering work of the American psychologist George Kelly, personal construct theory has not only endured, but thrived in a diversity of contexts over the past half century. In compiling the present volume, we began with the notion of recruiting authoritative reviews of some of the major progressive programs of research in personal construct theory and kindred constructivist domains, and this emphasis is indeed reflected in the material between these covers. However, as the project evolved, the contents have also diversified to include deep-going critical appraisals of constructivist research methodology, as well as novel applications of constructivist concepts and methods to an impressive range of contexts, including counseling and psychotherapy, psychological problems, and cognitive psychology. Equally striking is the thorough reflexivity of the theoretical contributions to the volume, as contributors extend the implications of constructivist theory for such postmodern themes as the relational basis of identity, the narrative structure of experience, and the construction of the self. Thus, the chapters in this book advance the scope of personal construct theory, critiquing and augmenting its research methods, and deconstructing a number of problems typically construed under the rubric of "psychopathology."

Paralleling the intellectual diversity of contemporary personal construct theory is its remarkable internationality. Although American in origin, the theory increasingly has been taken up, applied, and stretched to accommodate the concerns of a broad coalition of researchers around the globe. The geographic reach of constructivist work is reflected well in the current volume, whose authors represent no less than six different countries that literally span the globe.

Where do these developments leave personal construct theory as it moves into its second half-century as a theory group? On the one hand, we are not so historically bound as to believe that the theory will survive in its original form—except in the history books—as it continues to mature and integrate new developments. On the other hand, this very mutability of the theory, its capacity to enter into transformative dialog with other streams of social and scientific discourse, strikes us as its greatest strength. Looking back at where personal construct psychology stood only a dozen years ago, the theory presently is more widely recognized and integrated, more methodologically diverse, and more broadly applied beyond the borders of the clinical domain that defined its original applications. As the field enters a new century, it is clearly engaged in the hurly-burly of exploring shifting alliances with other intellectual positions, and is becoming more self-critical, more social and contextual, and more boldly critical of psychological orthodoxy as a result. We trust that this both reflects and reinforces these developments, and represents an appropriate project to launch Praeger's series on Advances in Personal Construct Psychology.

part I

Theoretical Frontiers

Chapter 1

The Person As a Motivated Storyteller: Valuation Theory and the Self-Confrontation Method

Hubert J. M. Hermans

As a researcher in the field of personality I started, at the end of the 1960s, to construct tests for the measurement of achievement motivation and fear of failure (e.g., Hermans, 1970). Dissatisfaction, however, with the objectifying and impersonal nature of these tests, with the separation between assessment and change, and with the rather limited value range of such instruments, motivated me to search for alternatives. One of the authors who inspired me during this scientific exploration was George Kelly (1955), because in his work I found at least three elements that liberated me from the straightjacket of mainstream trait psychology: The personal and idiographic nature of his work, the relational approach in which the client is considered as a colleague, and his supposition that a multiplicity of building blocks (personal constructs in his case) are organized into a system and could be assessed using a grid methodology.

Now, almost 30 years later, I am still interested in my original field, human motivation, albeit in a quite different way from the period mentioned above. In the meantime, developments in the area of the psychology of the self in the line of William James and the recent upsurge of narrative psychology have stimulated me to investigate the construction of personal meanings or, using a more dynamic term, the process of valuation, in which the person is continuously involved. Moreover, my cooperation with Els Hermans-Jansen, a psychotherapist, and our common experiences with a variety of clients also have had a major impact on the work presented in this chapter. Finally, I came to realize that the most appropriate way to characterize the way in which people give form to their own lives is to phrase it in terms of the metaphor of the *motivated storyteller* (Hermans & Hermans-Jansen, 1995), which provides a fertile starting point for both theory and practice.

The several components of this metaphor, "story," "telling," and "motivation," are briefly addressed before elaborating on its theoretical, methodological, and practical implications.

THE NARRATIVE IMPULSE

Stories As the Organization of Events in Time and Space

People of all ages and cultures have used stories or narratives (myth, folklore, fairy tale, legend, epic, opera, motion picture, biography, novel, television play, personal anecdote, etc.) to give meaning to their environment and their own lives. Sarbin (1986), one of the main advocates of a narrative approach, views stories as a way of organizing episodes, actions, and accounts of actions in time and space. He suggests that narrative organizes our fantasies and daydreams, our unvoiced stories, our plans, our memories, and even our loving and hating.

Narratives or stories are for Sarbin part of the root metaphor of *contextualism* (Pepper, 1942). The central element of this metaphor is the historical event that can only be understood when it is located in the context of time and space. Sarbin (1986) argues that contextualism presupposes an ongoing texture of elaborated events, each being influenced by preceding and following episodes, and by multiple agents who engage in actions. There is a constant change in the structure of situations and in positions occupied by spatially located actors who are oriented to the world and toward one another as intentional beings. Often these actors have opposite positions, as though performing on a stage as protagonists and antagonists, entertaining relationships of love, hate, agreement, or disagreement. The thoughts, feelings, and actions of the protagonists can only be understood as emerging from their relationships with antagonists who, often unpredictably, coconstruct reality.

A large proportion of our experiences and actions receives a narrative structure, as McAdams (1993) has extensively argued. A concept that clearly demonstrates this structure is the so-called Quixote principle originally formulated by Levin (1970) and further developed by Sarbin (1990). This principle refers to identity shaping through reading or listening to stories. The reader is at first a participant in the story, identifying with one of the main characters. After the role of this character is enacted in the imagination, it is enacted overtly and guides the reader's behavior. The story of Don Quixote illustrates how a person forms an identity from reading fictional or historical tales and then proceeds to validate the newly acquired identity in daily life. Before he named himself Don Quixote, the lonely 16th-century Spanish nobleman, Alonzo Quesada, became impressed by heroic deeds of chivalry, as a result of intensive reading of the adventures of knights-errant. After creating silent fantasies in which he participated vicariously as actor or spectator in the stories he read, he took the step of acting on his imaginations and adopted an appropriately knightly name, Don Quixote. This name symbolized the heroship that he needed to transform the world into something better.

A historical case that exemplifies the Quixote principle is Goethe's novel, *The Sorrows of Young Werther*, published in 1774. The book was written in a time when death, especially death by one's own hands, had a romantic flavor. In the literature of that time there was even an aura of nobility and heroism about death and dying, especially if one composed one's own death scenario. Werther's struggle with rejection and his ultimate suicide were taken as guiding examples by young men of fashion, particularly by those who experienced unrequited love. A "Werther epidemic" followed the publication of the book. The typical suicide was performed in full Werther costume: blue tailcoat, yellow waistcoat, and boots. The pistol was aimed just above the eye (Sarbin, 1990, p. 55). The Quixote principle not only demonstrates the influence of imagination on action but also the cultural context of narratives.

Telling in Actual and Imaginal Relationships

When there is a story, there is always someone who tells the story to someone else. It is the dialogical reciprocity between teller and listener that makes storytelling a highly dynamic interactional phenomenon.

Two forms of dialog structure our daily experiences: imaginal and actual dialogs. In the lives of normal people these forms of dialogs are certainly not separated, but rather they exist side by side and even interwoven as part of our narrative construction of the world. In her book, *Invisible Guests*, Watkins (1986) argues that, even when we are outwardly silent, we find ourselves communicating with our critics, our parents, our consciences, our gods, our reflection in the mirror, with the photograph of someone we miss, with a figure from a movie or a dream, with our babies, with our pets, and even with our plants and flowers. When we plan to visit our friends, we "see" and "hear" them in our imagination before we actually meet them, and when we have left them, we reenact parts of the conversation. Imaginal interactions certainly have a pervasive influence on real interactions. Before I go to a meeting I imagine the people who will attend the meeting, and I have expectations of what they will say. During the meeting I imagine what the participants are thinking even if they are outwardly silent, and after the meeting I reenact what has been said, and I may inwardly criticize myself or others with the intention to act differently next time. In other words, imaginings are important factors influencing actual behavior.

Caughey (1984), a social anthropologist, has also studied the phenomenon of "imaginary social worlds." He did fieldwork on Fáánakker, a Pacific island in

Micronesia, and in the Margalla Hills of Pakistan and compared these cultures with North American culture. Caughey concluded that imaginal interactions are in no way restricted to non-Western cultures. He estimated that the "real" social world of most North Americans includes between 200 and 300 people (e.g., family, friends, acquaintances, colleagues). Moreover, their worlds are populated by a swarming throng of other beings, with whom no face-to-face contact exists. Caughey divides them into three groups:

1. Media figures with whom the individual engages in imaginal interactions (a suburban grandmother is described who had a lifelong "affair" with Frank Sinatra despite 40 years of marriage),

2. Purely imaginary figures produced in dreams and fantasies,

3. Imaginal replicas of parents, friends, or lovers who are treated *as if* they were really present.

Caughey argues, as did Watkins (1986), that imaginal dialogs and interactions exist side by side with actual interactions (e.g., "If my mother could see me now . . .").

Motivation, Plot Structure, and Story Themes

Stories are populated by motivated actors who are purposefully oriented to the world. The example of a detective story (Hermans & Kempen, 1993) may serve as an example. Confronted with a murder, the detective begins the task of finding the reasons or motives "behind" the deed. When detectives begin their investigations, and do not yet know the motive (e.g., revenge) behind the actions of the perpetrator, many observations may seem incoherent or even confusing. In this phase the detective is not yet able to determine whether a particular observation is "to the point." In the course of time, however, the imaginative detective may find out that many observations, hitherto incomprehensible, are part of an elaborate pattern of events that together form an insightful plot. The theme organizes the events so that a coherent plot structure emerges.

The example of the detective story reveals a more general feature of narratives: the dialectic relationship between event and plot. As Polkinghorne (1988) has argued, the meaning of a particular event is produced by the interaction between event and plot. Events do not dictate any plot, and not every plot is appropriate to any given set of events. In order to arrive at a meaningful plot structure, it is necessary to move back and forth between plot and events. According to the principle of "best fit," a proposed plot structure is compared with the events at hand, and revised accordingly. In this comparative process, a particular theme guides the selection of the events and the organization or revision of the plot. The theme allows the pulling together of the events as interrelated parts of a story.

Novels, movies, fairy tales, myths, program music, and other kinds of stories may be organized around a broad variety of themes, such as jealousy, revenge, tragic heroism, injustice, unattainable love, the innocence of a child, inseparable friendship, discrimination, and so forth. This thematic variety, however, does not exclude that culture provides us with a limited amount of basic themes that function as organizing frames for the understanding and interpretation of life events. There are different ways of classifying themes as structuring devices of stories.

Frye (1957) argued that themes in narratives are rooted in the experience of nature, and in the evolution of the seasons in particular. Spring has inspired comedy, expressing people's joy and social harmony after the threatening winter. Summer, representing abundance and richness, gives rise to romance, which depicts the triumph of good over evil, and of virtue over vice. (Note that for Frye, romance is not limited to attraction between people.) Autumn, representing the decline of life and the coming death of the winter, gives rise to tragedy. Finally, in winter, satire is born, because in this season comes the awareness of the fact that one is ultimately a captive of the world, rather than its master. In satire, people find an opportunity to criticize their own fate.

Whereas Frye's classification of story themes is based on the cyclical movements of nature, Gergen and Gergen (1988) have proposed a classification of a more linear type. They consider narratives as changing over time toward a desirable end state. A progressive narrative tells of increments toward an end state. An individual telling such a narrative might say, "I am learning to overcome my shyness and be more open and friendly with people." A regressive narrative is focused on decrements in the orientation toward a desirable end state. An individual might say, "I can't control the events of my life anymore." Finally, in a stable narrative the individual remains essentially unchanged with respect to the valued end point. Somebody involved in such a narrative might say, "I am still as attractive as I used to be."

The psychological motives of the actors may also be taken as a starting point for the classification of narratives. A classic example is Murray's (1938) system of needs and his use of the Thematic Apperception Test (TAT). A picture may invite subjects to tell stories with different themes (e.g., achievement, affiliation, dominance, sex, etc.). The underlying assumption is that the themes, expressed in the stories, reflect the subjects' more or less unconscious needs. Inspired by Murray, later investigators used TAT procedures to assess people's motives or needs; for example, achievement motive (McClelland, Atkinson, Clark, & Lowell, 1953), power (Winter, 1973), affiliation (Boyatzis, 1973), and the opposition of power and intimacy (McAdams, 1985). Such literatures reflect a close relationship between psychological motives and narratives.

In summary, three suppositions underlie the narrative approach presented in this chapter. First, stories acknowledge both the perception of reality and the power of imagination. Whereas stories combine fact and fiction (Sarbin, 1986), the telling of stories runs through real and imaginal dialogs (Caughey, 1984; Watkins, 1986). Second, space and time are basic components of storytelling. Stories always imply a temporal organization of events, and a plot structure that meaningfully relates past, present, and future. At the same time, stories are organized around actors who, as protagonist and antagonist, have opposite positions in a real or imaginal space (e.g., imagining what my father would say if he were still alive and was with us on the birthday of my child). Third, both the storyteller and the actors in the stories told are intentional beings who are motivated to reach particular goals that function as organizing story themes in their narratives. Story themes and psychological motives bring coherence and direction in events that are otherwise fragmented and dispersed over time and space.

VALUATION THEORY: PERSONAL MEANINGS IN THE SELF-NARRATIVE

Valuation theory (Hermans, 1987a, 1987b, 1988, 1989; Hermans & Hermans-Jansen, 1995) is based on the metaphor of the motivated storyteller. In this theory the three components (story, telling, and motivation) of the guiding metaphor are brought together as parts of an articulated conceptual system. (For a discussion of this theory and its methodology in the context of recent trends in constructivism, see Neimeyer, Hagans, & Anderson, 1998.)

Personal Valuation, Self-Narrative, and Self-Reflection

In agreement with such phenomenological thinkers as James (1890) and Merleau-Ponty (1945), the starting point of valuation theory is in the historical nature of human experience and in its spatio-temporal orientation. The individual lives in the present and is, from a specific point in space and time, oriented to past and future and to the surrounding world. The individual not only orients successively to different parts of his or her spatio-temporal situation, but also brings those parts together in an organized story or self-narrative.

The central concept, "valuation," refers both to the process of meaning construction and its product in which the events of a self-narrative are organized. A valuation has a positive (pleasant), negative (unpleasant), or ambivalent connotation in the eyes of the individual. Personal valuations, as subjective constructions of personal experiences, refer to a broad range of phenomena, such as a dear memory, a pleasant activity, a good talk with a friend, a disappointment in the contact with a significant other, a particular source of satisfaction in one's work, a physical handicap, an unreachable ideal, and so forth. During different periods of one's life, different valuations may emerge, because one's reference point is constantly changing. As a result of the act of self-reflection, different valuations are brought together into an organized valuation system in which one valuation is given a more prominent place than another.

The process term "valuation" is preferred rather then the more static term "value" because telling one's self-narrative requires a process of self-reflection. This process can be traced to James's (1890) classic distinction between *I* (the self-as-knower) and *Me* (the self-as-known) as the two main components of the self. The *I*, or the self-as-knower, continuously organizes and interprets experience in a purely subjective manner. Three features characterize the *I*: continuity, distinctness, and volition. The continuity of the self-as-knower is manifested by a "sense of personal identity" and a "sense of sameness" through time (p. 332). A feeling of distinctness, of having an existence separate from others, is also intrinsic to the *I*. A sense of personal volition is expressed by the continuous appropriation and rejection of thoughts by which the self-as-knower functions as an active processor of experience. Each of these features (continuity, distinction, volition) implies the awareness of self-reflectivity that is essential for the self-as-knower (Damon & Hart, 1982). In other words, the concept of "valuation" presupposes an *I* as an active processor of experience.

In defining the *Me*, or self-as-known, James (1890) was aware that there is a gradual transition between *Me* and *Mine*. In a famous statement, he identified the *Me* as the empirical self that in its broadest sense is described as all that the person can call his or her own, "not only his body and his psychic powers, but his clothes and his house, his wife and children, his ancestors and friends, his reputation and works, his lands and horses, and yacht and bank-account" (p. 291). These primary elements or constituents indicate for James a basic feature of the self, its extension. The incorporation of the constituents indicates that the self is not an entity, closed off from the world, and having an existence in itself, but, rather, extended toward specific aspects of the environment (Rosenberg, 1979). With this view on the extension of the self, James, in fact, transcends the strict boundaries of a self-contained, essentialistic self. Because the *Mine* (body, other person) belongs to the (extended) self, the self, in its broadest sense, is part of the environment, and the environment is part of the self. In terms of the present theory: The process of valuation presupposes an extending, spatially structured self.

Telling One's Self-Narrative

In valuation theory the notion of self-reflection is closely related to the notion of telling. When people narrate the events of their lives, they reflect at the same time upon themselves, taking the position of the listener into account. Of crucial importance for the relation between self-narrative and self-reflection is Sarbin's (1986) thesis that James, Mead, Freud, and others emphasized the distinction between the *I* and the *Me,* and their equivalents in other European languages, because of the narrative nature of the self. The uttered pronoun *I* stands for the author, the *Me* for the actor or narrative figure. In this configuration, the *I* can imaginatively construct a story with the *Me* as the protagonist. In such narrative construction the self as author can imagine the future and reconstruct the past (Crites, 1986).

Sarbin's (1986) translation of the *I–Me* distinction into a narrative framework has an important advantage. It presupposes an *I* that is involved in a process of telling something to someone else. The *I* is not only bound to the *Me* (I think about myself) but also to another *I* with whom the person is involved in a narrative relationship (I tell something about myself to you). The implication of this dialogical view of the self is that the content of the narration is dependent on the nature of the relationship in which the teller is involved. The *I* as telling or writing author has a public and tells and writes with this audience in mind. The audience then coconstructs the story and its content.

In everyday life, the context-dependent nature of one's self-narrative can easily be observed. People tell, at least to some extent, different self-narratives to different people and in different contexts. People may tell things to their friends that they do not tell to a stranger, and in their contact with a psychologist they may tell about confidential things, if they feel safe enough to do so. Different professional contacts also evoke different self-narratives. For example, in their contact with a medical doctor people may "somatize" psychological complaints (e.g., "I have stomach pain"), whereas in their contact with a psychotherapist the psychological or social nature of such complaints may receive more attention ("I have a conflict with my wife").

For the present theory, the context-dependence implies that there is no such thing as an "inventory of valuations," a supposedly fixed set of concerns that are waiting to be uncovered by the telling client or the examining psychologist. Rather, the psychologist as an active listener or probing interrogator significantly influences both the form and content of what the person tells. In other words, the process of valuation, as a context-dependent activity, is a co-construction of client and psychologist.

The Motivational and Affective Basis of Self-Narrative

People are not simply storytellers, they are passionate storytellers. That is, they tell those parts of their self-narratives in which they are affectively involved. They do not tell their stories like an "objective" historiographer who dispassionately relates events from a detached point of view. Rather, people tell their personal stories selectively and colorfully, placing emphasis on those events or combinations of events that have an affective meaning or that appeal to them emotionally.

In valuation theory it is assumed that each valuation, as a unit of meaning in one's self-narrative, carries an affective connotation and that basic motives are reflected in this connotation. That is, each valuation has a certain degree of personal involvement and reflects a particular set of feelings (a particular affective profile). When we know which types of affect are characteristic of a particular valuation, we know something about the valuation itself. This also implies that the affective meaning of a valuation cannot be separated from it. How does this conception of the self originate in James's work?

As already referred to, James (1890) defined the self as "the sum total of all he can call his." Having said this, James immediately went on to say: "All these things give him the same emotions. If they wax and prosper, he feels triumphant; if they dwindle and die away, he feels cast down, not necessarily in the same degree for each thing, but in much the same way for all" (pp. 291–292). In other words, James conceives of the self as extended to a *manifold* variety of things, and reacting with the *same* set of emotions. Similarly, we conceive of valuations as the phenomenological variety of narrative concerns relevant to an individual, associated with the same set of affective states (e.g., one may experience anxiety and anger in relation to both one's father and one's superior).

The phenomenological richness of personal valuations, which may vary not only between individuals but also within a single individual across time and space, represents the manifest level of the self (see Figure 1-1). At the latent level, however, a limited number of basic motives exist that are reflected in the affective component of the valuation system. Study of the affective component can, therefore, reveal which particular motive is active in a particular valuation and in the system as a whole. Note that the latent-manifest distinction poses the problem of generativity: How can humans generate on the basis of a finite set of experiences, an almost unlimited set of surface expressions? Both Freud and Chomsky answered this problem, each in their own ways and each using their specific terminology, by supposing a distinction between a latent and a manifest level (Freud) or between a deep and surface level (Chomsky), the deeper of which constitutes a limited set of basic motives or operations.

Two basic motives, in particular, have been taken into consideration to characterize the affective component of the valuation system: the striving for self-enhancement, or S motive (self-maintenance and self-expansion), and the longing for contact and union with the other, or O motive (participation with other people and the surrounding world). This distinction concerning the basic duality of human experience has been present in the writings of various authors: Bakan

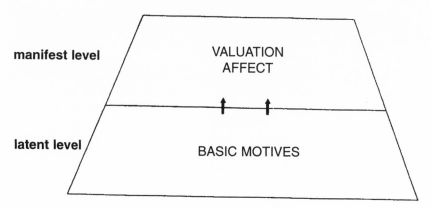

Figure 1-1. Relation between valuation, affect, and basic motives.
Source: Hermans & Hermans-Jansen, 1995.

(1966) viewed agency and communion as fundamental dynamic principles; Angyal (1965) relied on the concept of autonomy (or self-determination) and homonomy (or self-surrender); Klages (1948) considered Bindung (solidification) and Lösung (dissolution) to be two basic human motives; McAdams (1985) has distinguished power and intimacy as basic motives in a narrative context. Recently, the dimensions of individualism-collectivism and idiocentrism-allocentrism, again suggesting the basic character of the S and O motives, have been extensively discussed and investigated (Lau, 1992; Schwartz, 1990; Triandis, Bontempo, Villareal, Asai, & Lucca, 1988).

In valuation theory, it is assumed that the basic motives are reflected in the affective component of a valuation. This can be illustrated using two different valuations:

"At home I often get my way by pushing just a little bit."

"I feel fantastic when I paint a good picture."

Assuming that feelings of "strength" and "pride" are general indicators of the self-enhancement motive (S motive), the presence of these feelings in both of the valuations is evidence that they are expressions of the same underlying motive. Put differently, the valuations pertain to quite different aspects of the self (they differ on the *manifest* level), although they may be rooted in the same basic motive (they are similar on the *latent* level). In this theoretical construction, the affective component provides the bridge between motivation and valuation. The affect associated with a valuation can be considered as an expression of the basic motives from the *latent* level.

Some valuations representing the longing for contact and union with the other (O motive) follow:

"During the stormy weather on the North Sea, I felt a real bond with my brother: I felt lost in the elements, yet still remained standing without having to struggle to be strong."

"Singing in a group: The way I express most of my feelings."

Both of the valuations from the same client—although clearly different manifestations of the self—imply strong feelings of intimacy and love. If feelings of intimacy and love are assumed to be indicators of the O motive, then the two valuations can again be seen to differ on the manifest level but not on the latent level.

In close correspondence with S and O feelings, *well-being*, in the form of the difference between positive and negative feelings, plays a central role in valuation theory. The rationale is that obstacles are met on the path toward fulfillment of basic motives. People are purposefully oriented to the world, but obstacles often prevent the achievement of their goals, resulting in *negative* feelings. On the other hand, when something is achieved, or obstacles and hindrances successfully overcome, they are rewarded with *positive* feelings. It is supposed that each valuation is associated with a pattern of positive and negative feelings so that the emphasis of one of the two types of affect may give information about the extent to which basic motives are gratified.

Generalization and Idealization

Two concepts, generalization and idealization, particularly represent the emphasis on the organization of the valuation system and play a central role in the methodology presented in the following session. The more a particular valuation *generalizes* as part of the system, the more it determines the "general feeling" of the person under consideration. When one asks a person how he or she feels in general, it is highly probable that particular experiences color this general feeling more than others. For example, if the person is involved in a serious conflict in the work situation, there is a good chance that the feelings associated with this conflict are more likely to determine that person's general feeling in this period than, for example, his or her favorite sports team playing a winning game. The notion of generalization indicates that not all valuations are equally influential in the system. A valuation with a strong generalization in the system colors the way the person generally feels to a greater extent than a valuation with a weak degree of generalization.

Similarly, valuations may differ in the extent of *idealization*. The guiding idea is that certain valuations fit more with the way an individual ideally would like to feel than others. Valuations that color the ideal feeling are often different from those that influence the general feeling. In particular, this can be found when people are actually going through a period in which they are faced with personal problems that are associated with a significant degree of negative affect. In this case, the ideal feeling typically has an affective modality that is in contrast to the affective modality of the general feeling.

In summary, valuation theory is a narrative theory of the self based on the metaphor of the motivated storyteller. The notion of story is expressed in the central term "valuation" as a process of meaning construction. The concept of telling implies that the person, as an author relating about himself or herself as an actor, is part of a dialogical relationship in which the conversational partner (e.g., the psychologist) co-constructs the person's self-narrative. Clients are considered as experts in their personal meanings, whereas psychologists function as experts on theoretical and methodological issues and, moreover, have experience with a larger group of clients. The concept of motivation is based on the theoretical supposition that people as passionate storytellers focus selectively and colorfully on those events that are relevant from the perspective of basic motives. Two basic motives have received special significance in the theory: the striving for self-enhancement, and the longing for contact and union. From a narrative point of view, these motives correspond with two main types of stories in novelistic literature: hero and love stories. It is supposed that the basic motives are expressed in the affective component of a valuation and also determine which parts of the self-narrative are emphasized more than others. Two concepts are central in the affective organization of the self-narrative: generalization and idealization. The focus on the content and organization of the valuation system may shed some light on the complexity of the self. More specifically, the content and organization of self-narratives depend on two important influences: the *specific* context in which the story is told (audience, dialogical partner, setting, institution, culture), and basic motives as *general* story themes that are presumed to reflect basic psychological orientations present in people from different cultures and times. In this way, valuation theory presents a conceptual framework that brings together the particular and the general (for the integration of idiography and nomothesis, see Hermans, 1988).

THE SELF-CONFRONTATION METHOD:
VALUATIONS AND THEIR AFFECTIVE PROPERTIES

The self-confrontation method presented in this section is based on valuation theory, although it is not the only possible methodological device that can be derived from this theory. The method invites a person (subject or client) to perform a thorough self-investigation consisting of three parts: (a) the construction of a set of valuations; (b) rating each of the valuations using a list of affective terms; and (c) discussion of the results.

The valuations and affects are combined in a matrix, in which the rows represent the valuations and the columns the affect terms (see Table 1-1 for an example). The methodology first is explained and then is illustrated with an actual case.

Formulation of the Valuations

The valuations are elicited by a series of open-ended questions. The main questions, presented in Table 1-2, are intended to bring out units of meaning for the past, present, and future that are important in the eyes of the person. The questions are phrased in such a way that they invite individuals to reflect on their life situation and tell significant parts of their self-narratives. They are free to mention those concerns that they see as most relevant to them and to interpret the questions in any way they want. The subjects are instructed to phrase the valuations in their own terms so that the formulations are, as far as possible, in agreement with the intended meaning. The typical form of a valuation is a sentence, which is considered as the basic unit of text (James, 1890). In a sentence, the subjects bring together those events that they feel belong together as elements of a personal unit of meaning. There is no one-to-one relation between question and answer, and a quick response is not required. Each question leads to more than one valuation, and the subjects may mention as many valuations as come to mind. At the end of the interview subjects are asked whether the survey contains all of

Table 1-1
Matrix of Valuation x Affect: Raw Ratings of a Subject's Self-Investigation

							Affect Terms									
	1	2	3	4	5	6	7	8	9	10	11	12	13	14	15	16
1	1	1	1	5	1	1	5	5	5	4	1	1	5	3	2	0
2	0	0	0	5	0	0	5	0	5	0	0	0	5	0	5	0
3	1	0	1	5	0	0	5	5	4	5	0	1	5	0	4	0
4	0	0	0	4	0	0	0	0	5	0	0	0	4	0	4	0
5	5	1	4	2	1	4	4	5	1	4	3	4	1	4	1	5
6	0	0	1	4	1	0	3	1	5	0	0	0	2	0	4	0
Gen. feeling	1	0	1	4	0	1	4	4	4	1	1	1	5	1	4	0
Ideal feeling	4	5	4	0	4	4	4	5	0	4	4	3	0	2	1	5

(Left axis label: Valuationi Number)

Note: Rows represent valuations and columns represent affect terms used for the indices S, O, P, and N, where S = affect referring to self-enhancement, O = affect referring to contact with the other, P = positive affect, and N = negative affect. Affect terms: 1 = joy (P); 2 = self-esteem (S); 3 = happiness (P); 4 = worry (N); 5 = strength (S); 6 = enjoyment (P); 7 = caring (OP); 8 = love (O); 9 = unhappiness (N); 10 = tenderness (O); 11 = self-confidence (S); 12 = intimacy (O); 13 = despondency (N); 14 = pride (S); 15 = disappointment (N); 16 = inner calm (P). The numbers in the body of the table are the raw scores assigned by the client to each affect with respect to each valuation. The ratings are from the first self-investigation of Ann, the client that will be described in our case study later in this chapter.

the experiences they want to include in the investigation. If something is missing, they can add this. In special cases, the clinician or therapist may formulate additional valuations and propose that the client include these in the valuation system (see Hermans & Hermans-Jansen, 1995, pp. 64–67). At the end of the procedure the number of valuations may vary greatly, but in most cases it is between 20 and 40. Each valuation is written by the interviewer on a separate card and, in this concrete form, it is available for the second part of the investigation.

Affective Properties of the Valuations

In the second part of the investigation, the client is provided with a standard list of affect terms. Concentrating on the first valuation, subjects indicate on a 0–5 scale the extent to which they experience each affect in relation to the valuation (0 = *not at all*, 1 = *a little bit*, 2 = *to some extent*, 3 = *rather much*, 4 = *much*, and 5 = *very much*). In this phase of the investigation, the subjects work alone, rating each valuation with the same list of affect terms. This makes it possible for the different valuations to be compared according to their affective profiles. The list of affect terms is presented at the bottom of Table 1-1. This list provides a maximum amount of affective information with a minimum

Table 1-2
Main Questions of the Self-Confrontation Method

Set 1: The Past
These questions are intended to guide you in reviewing one or more aspects of your life that may have been of great importance to you:
• Has there been anything of major significance in your past life that still continues to exert a strong influence on you?
• Was there in the past any person or persons, experience, or circumstance that greatly influenced your life and still appreciably affects your present existence?

Set 2: The Present
This set also consists of two questions that will lead you, after a certain amount of reflection, to formulate a response:
• Is there anything in your present existence that is of major importance to you or exerts a significant influence on you?
• Is there in your present existence any person, persons, or circumstance that exerts a significant influence on you?

Set 3: The Future
The following questions will guide you to a response:
• Do you foresee anything that will be of great importance for, or exert a major influence on, your future life?
• Do you feel that a certain person, persons, or circumstance will exert a significant influence on your future life?
• Is there any future goal or object that you expect to play an important role in your life? You are free to look as far ahead as you wish.

---

number of terms. After the affective rating of the different valuations, a number of indices representing the motivational structure of the valuation system are calculated (for clinical use a more extended list is recommended, see Hermans & Hermans-Jansen, 1995, p. 277).

1. Index S is the total score of four affect terms expressing self-enhancement: Numbers 2, 5, 11, and 14 of Table 1-1.

2. Index O is the total score of four affect terms expressing contact and union with the other: Numbers 7, 8, 10, and 12 of Table 1-1. For each valuation, moreover, the S-O difference can be determined. When the experience of self-enhancement is stronger than the experience of contact with the other, S > O. When the feeling of contact with the other prevails, O > S. When both kinds of experience coexist, S = O.

3. Index P is the total score of four positive affect terms: Numbers 1, 3, 6, and 16.

4. Index N is the total score of four negative affect terms: Numbers 4, 9, 13, and 15. For each valuation, again, the P-N difference can be determined. This indicates the degree of well-being the person experiences in relation to the specific valuation.

Well-being is positive when P > N, negative when N > P, and ambivalent when P = N. (Note that the scores for each of the four indices S, O, P, and N range from 0 to 20 for each valuation.)

5. Index r represents the correspondence between the affective profiles for two valuations, calculated as the correlation between any two rows in the matrix. This correlation indicates any similarity between the affective meanings of two valuations expressed by the shape of the two affective profiles. The correlation often shows that valuations referring to quite different events (e.g., a remark by a teacher in the past and the experience of a present project) nevertheless have highly similar affective profiles in the same individual. Index r is also used for the measurement of the extent of *generalization* (Gen.) of a certain valuation within the system. This is done by asking the person, at the end of the valuation construction phase: "How do you *generally* feel these days?" This question does not ask for a specific valuation but is devised to assess "general feeling." The person answers directly with the same list of affect terms used for the characterization of the valuations. This pattern of scores is filled in as an additional row in the matrix (see Table 1-1). The product-moment correlation between the affective profile belonging to a specific valuation (any row in the matrix) and the affective profile of the "general feeling" is a measure of the extent of generalization of this valuation. The more positive the correlation, the more this valuation is expected to generalize within the system. For example, when a student is worrying about his study, then a valuation like "I think about my study all the time" will show an affective pattern that correlates highly with the affective pattern belonging to the "general feeling." The score profile of the general feeling can also be used to assess "general well-being." This is indicated by the P-N difference of the general feeling.

Similarly, the extent of *idealization* (Id.) of any valuation can be assessed by computing the correlation with the "ideal feeling." The ideal feeling is the affective profile provided as a response to the question "How would you like to feel?" This profile is filled in as the final row in the matrix. The idealization index (Id.) is the correlation of any valuation with the profile characteristic of the ideal feeling.

Finally, index r can be used to compare any valuation with any other valuation. A special technique, called a *modality analysis*, is used to compare a particular valuation with all other valuations. For a modality analysis, a particular valuation is taken as a pivot and correlated with all other valuations in order to search for an underlying theme. (For reliability and validity of the indices S, O, P, N, and r see Hermans, 1987a, p. 166 and pp. 169–171.)

Discussion with the Client

The discussion of the results usually follows 1 week after the self-investigation. During this week, the interviewer performs a qualitative analysis (studying the formulation of the valuations, with proper attention to their relation) and a quantitative analysis (calculation and interpretation of the indices in their combination).

The discussion aims to deepen the self-exploration of the client, stimulated by a profound dialog with the interviewer. Their discussion is based on the overall picture provided by the system as an integrative whole. In this system divergent valuations are contracted at one moment in time, so that new relations, hitherto hidden, can become visible. This overall view is very characteristic of a self-investigation. Whereas short talks and interviews are usually dispersed over time and therefore have a momentary quality, the total picture of a self-investigation provides a "bird's-eye view," permitting a perspective on the self *and its boundaries*. Subjects see what they value, and what they do not value. Moreover, they become aware of the lacunae in their valuation system. This confrontation with the content and organization of the valuation system benefits further from the explanation of the basic motives. The person can see in what valuations they are manifest and in what valuations they are lacking.

The discussion aims not only to develop insights but also to generate new ideas and to make plans. This is not necessarily confined to one session. It is even better to maintain it over successive sessions so that daily experiences can be compared with the content and organization of the valuation system. Here it becomes apparent that assessment proceeds gradually into change, because a thorough reflection on the organization of the system is the first step in a reorganization.

Second Self-Investigation

The second self-investigation, typically after some months, consists of the same stages as the first. There is, however, an important difference in the valuation construction phase. This time subjects do not start by formulating valuations. Instead, they are confronted by the statements constructed in Investigation 1. The interviewer rereads the questions with the person but, after each question, the interviewer now produces the statement that the person regarded as adequate in Investigation 1. Subjects are instructed to consider each valuation separately, whether they can still go along with its content; that is, whether in the new situation they would give the same answer to the questions. If this is not the case, there are various options available: An old valuation may be reformulated (*modification*); it may be replaced by a new one (*substitution*); it may be discarded altogether (*elimination*); or an entirely new valuation may be added (*supplementation*). This procedure guarantees that subjects have considerable freedom to point to the constant and changing parts of the valuation system.

ANN'S SELF-INVESTIGATION: ASSESSMENT, CHANGE, AND EVALUATION

Ann, a 40-year-old married woman with two adolescent children, contacted a psychotherapist (Els Hermans-Jansen) during a period in which she was having serious difficulties with her work. She had become involved in a conflict between the administration and her colleagues in the school where she taught. As a friend of the managing couple of the school, she became an "in-between" person, and, as a result of this position, was often approached both by the administration and by her colleagues in attempts to solve conflicts. When the administration finally left the school, her situation changed from bad to worse because she now had no mitigatory role to play. Moreover, she had to make the difficult decision of whether to stay in a nonsupportive job situation or give up her job. Unresolved past experiences, reactualized by the present problems in her work, brought this woman to a crisis point.

Ann related the following about her family background. She was raised in a Dutch middle-class family, the oldest of five children. She described her father as a very authoritarian person, who was in complete control of the situation at home. He had a strong normative attitude toward parent–child roles and gender roles. He required immediate obedience on the part of his children and would put them under "house arrest" when they broke any of the strict rules. Ann's mother took a very subordinate role in the family; she was often sick, and she suffered from asthma. As a result of her mother's physical weakness, Ann became a "second mother" in the family. Her father gave her special social responsibilities with regard to the family as a whole and her younger siblings in particular, often justifying this with the remark "You are the oldest and *therefore* the wisest." Family relations were further complicated by the parents' rather unhappy marriage. Ann described herself as living with the constant fear that her parents would separate, and as the oldest child she continually tried to "keep the peace" in the family. Her anxiety concerned not only the separation of her parents but also the breakup of the family and the danger of having to take sides: She had to avoid taking sides, she felt, because doing this or even giving the impression of doing so would lead to her parents' separation and the disruption of the family as a whole.

Ann performed two self-investigations, 9 months apart. In addition, an intermediate evaluation took place in order to check the direction of the initiated process of change.

First Self-Investigation

In the first session with the psychotherapist, the nature and aims of the self-confrontation procedure were discussed with the client and the expectations of client and therapist were made explicit. In the second session, the valuations were formulated (24 in total) and associated with the standardized set of affect terms as previously described. For illustrative purposes six valuations from her system are presented in Table 1-3, two referring to her past (1 and 2), two to her present (3 and 4), and two to her future (5 and 6).

When we compare the valuations referring to her past with those pertaining to her present situation, we see a reactualization of her past problems. It is suggested that the problem of being an "in-between person" (see valuation no. 4 in Table 1-3) was a confirmation of her past experience of being "between two parties" (see valuation no. 2 in Table 1-3).

Table 1-3
Ann's Valuations, General Feeling, Ideal Feeling, and Their Scores on the
Affective Indices at Time 1

Valuation	S	O	P	N	Gen.	Id.	No. 6
1. I've always had fear of losing people (my parents' marriage was no good; there was always tension); whenever possible I try to avoid conflict situations	6	15	3	17	.83	−.54	.62
2. I wanted to close myself off from the outside world whenever I was approached by my father or mother and didn't know what to do (between two fires)	0	5	0	20	.86	−.78	.92
3. I think it's a shame that my children won't go unaffected, that they also suffer from a problematic mother	0	16	2	18	.86	−.48	.66
4. In the conflict at school I feel like a buffer between two clashing parties	0	0	0	17	.74	−.91	.85
5. I hope I can calm down in the future (in my feelings)	9	17	18	5	−.30	.58	−.55
6. I'd like to appear on the outside as the person that I am on the inside, but have never let anyone see (above all, stronger and clearer)	1	4	1	15	.79	−.73	—
General feeling	2	10	3	17	—	−.67	.79
Ideal feeling	15	16	17	1	−.67	—	−.73

Note: S = affect referring to self-enhancement; O = affect referring to contact with the other; P = positive affect; N = negative affect; Gen. = generalization; Id. = idealization.

A conspicuous characteristic of Ann's system is the dominant role of the experience of unfulfilled love (see valuations nos. 1 and 3). Empirical research on this experience (Hermans & Hermans-Jansen, 1995; Hermans & Van Gilst, 1991) has shown a specific affective pattern in which this experience is expressed: low S, high O, low P, and high N. Looking at the formal structure of this experience, two components can be identified: (a) there is a loving orientation to another person or object (love, indicated by the 0 > S difference), and (b) there is an obstacle or boundary making this person or object unreachable (unfulfilled, indicated by the N > P difference). In theoretical terms, this structure represents the latent base of a great variety of personal valuations on the manifest level. Depending on the individual's history, the experience of unfulfilled love has various manifestations: the death of a beloved friend, an impossible love affair, an emigrant longing for his native country, an anticipated farewell, a Faustian longing for youth, or feeling close to somebody while at the same time feeling unable to express tenderness and sympathy.

In Ann's case, it can be seen that the affective profiles associated with both valuations 1 and 3 tend toward an affective pattern of unfulfilled love. This affective profile has a relatively strong generalization in the system as a whole. A clear indication of this is the affective pattern of the "general feeling" that also is associated with low S, high O, low P, and high N. Note also the high level of generalization (Gen.) of valuations 1 and 3 (Table 1-3). The dominance of the theme of unfulfilled love in the affective component of her valuations indicates that she feels strongly dependent on others.

Reorganizing the Valuation System

Although valuations indicative of unfulfilled love are, from a diagnostic point of view, influential in the valuation system, they did not play the primary role in the reorganization of the system. The valuation that played a crucial role in the reorganization of the system as a whole was no. 6: "I'd like to appear on the outside as the person that I am on the inside, but have never let anyone see (above all, stronger and clearer)." Ann explained that she saw really strong and clear behavior in *other* people but not in herself. For example, she related how her younger brother would talk back to their father and then added "I would never dare to." Because she didn't dare to be such a person," she associated this valuation (no. 6) with a very low level of self-enhancement and a high level of negative affect. At the same time, Ann was fascinated by strength and clarity and felt that a person with these characteristics was somewhere "deep down inside" herself. The psychotherapist suspected that the preceding valuation could perhaps function as an "entrance to change" and suggested that Ann concentrate on the affective significance of this valuation in the following session. This concentration was realized by taking valuation no. 6 as pivotal in a modality analysis.

In the *modality analysis,* the pivot valuation was correlated with all other valuations in the system (see the final column in Table 1-3 for the results). The valuations showing the highest correlations with the pivot were then examined for their common theme. Ann provided the following interpretations (proceeding from higher to lower correlations):

No. 6 x no. 2 (r = . 92): "When I was asked to do something and thought I was not strong enough, I would shut myself off."

No. 6 x no. 4 (r = .85): "The one party [the administration] overestimated me and the other party [colleagues] underestimated me . . . but I didn't show how I really felt. . . . When I could have manifested myself more. . . ."

After interpreting a number of other pairs of valuations in a similar way, the therapist invited Ann to summarize what she saw as the common theme underlying all of her interpretations. After some trials, Ann came up with the following: *"I have never had to fight for something for myself . . . nearly everything has always been arranged for me by others."* In other words, Ann had never had or taken the opportunity to obtain a minimal degree of self-enhancement as an independent person (see also the low level of S affect in Table 1-3). From a theoretical perspective, it can be concluded that this summary can be seen as a central theme in her self-narrative, and that this theme has been made explicit by taking the latent motivational base of the valuation system into account.

After this summary there was time for concentrated self-reflection and discussion about the pervasive influence of the basic theme. Ann went home in the knowledge that in the self-investigation she had confronted herself with an essential theme in her life. It made sense—for the period immediately following a thorough self-investigation—*only to look at what happens*; that is, Ann was invited to view from the perspective of the basic theme how her life was lived, and to watch from this perspective what happened between her and her environment.

As many psychotherapists have observed, the best strategy for encouraging change is not to stress the necessity or urgency of change but, rather, concentrate on the nature of one's *personal* experiences. Many people, eager for change and consciously striving for it, paradoxically fail to change because of increased feelings of stress and hurried disappointments that block the change process rather than promoting it. The change process requires serious self-reflection and concentration, *standing still for a while* and taking stock of the basic theme(s) in one's valuation system, even if it is painful.

Remarkably, the person in this state of concentrated self-reflection often *spontaneously* starts to take certain initiatives, explore alternatives, and experience a few trials and errors. These small changes are often probed with the awareness that "it can be different"; that is, the valuation system as it is currently formulated is not the last word, not a final "personality profile," not a fixed self. Rather, the individual's valuation system is a beginning, and in the context of the supportive relationship with the therapist the client begins the process of change—to retell parts of the self-narrative in a different light. This changing perspective is particularly apparent when some new events are *added* to the valuation system by the individual. This alteration of the valuation system indicates, in turn, the self-organizing capacity of the person. (For a more detailed and systematic procedure for stimulating change of the valuation system, see the attending-creating-anchoring cycle, Hermans & Hermans-Jansen, 1995, pp. 47–54.)

Intermediate Evaluation: Checking the Direction of Change

In accordance with the notion of self-instigated change, Ann began to take new initiatives, which were then discussed with the therapist on a weekly basis in close correspondence with the valuation system from the first self-investigation. These "initiatives" typically related to the assessed "gap" in her system: the low level of self-enhancement in the system. Some of these initiatives were prepared in the sessions with the therapist, whereas others occurred spontaneously and were later discussed with the psychotherapist. Some examples are as follows. When there was a misunderstanding at her daughter's school, she decided to write a letter to clarify things, although previously she would have left this to her husband. Ann heard that a neighbor had accused her of potential dishonesty, so she got in touch with the neighbor to explain her view, although previously she would avoid conflict at all costs. Similarly, in a conversation with a representative of an organization that invited her to give a self-description, she mentioned some "strong points" about herself, although earlier she would have considered this to be "boasting."

Three months after the first self-investigation, the therapist proposed performing a limited self-investigation in order to check the direction and nature of the change that was taking place. This was done simply by asking Ann what she thought to be the main changes since the initial investigation. These changes were formulated in the form of some valuations, and this small set of valuations was then rated with the standard list of affect terms. For evaluative purposes, the sessions with the psychotherapist, her own self-investigation, and the general feeling were also rated with the same set of affect terms.

Table 1-4 shows what Ann perceives to be the main changes formulated as three valuations (nos. 1, 2, and 3). A relevant feature of these change valuations is their *comparative* nature. The present is now perceived as *different* from the past. Although the content of the formulations suggests increased self-enhancement, the affective indices show that the O affect still tends to be higher than the S affect. This is also true for the general feeling, which is now more positive but still shows a rather low level of S affect.

A comparison of her affective ratings of the sessions with the psychotherapist and her own self-investigation shows that both are experienced as positive; clearly, these activities have found an "entrance" into the valuation system. The psychotherapy sessions tend to have more S affect than O affect, suggesting the sessions may be a forerunner to further valuation changes and a strengthening of the S motive.

To summarize, this intermediate evaluation shows the beginnings of change in the desired direction; namely, characteristics of the strong and clear-minded individual represented in valuation no. 6 (Table 1-3). The contours of increased self-enhancement are beginning to appear, although most of the change valuations themselves still show a predominance of affect referring to the contact motive.

Second Self-Investigation: Further Reorganization of the System

Nine months after the initial self-investigation, both Ann and psychotherapist felt that so much had changed in Ann's view of herself and the world that they

Table 1-4
Ann's Change Valuations, General Feeling, Sessions with the Psychotherapist, and
Self-Investigation during Intermediate Evaluation

Valuation	S	O	P	N	Gen.
1. I've become more sure of myself; I dare to do more things	8	12	10	5	.73
2. I am easier with myself; feel less burdened (by the problems of the administration and my mother)	6	11	10	4	.75
3. I do more what I want and don't mind too much about others' expectations; what others think I should do doesn't concern me	9	9	12	1	.65
Sessions with the psychotherapist	11	7	11	1	.19
My self-investigation	8	14	11	3	.69
General feeling	6	12	9	3	—

Note: S = affect referring to self-enhancement; O = affect referring to contact with the other; P = positive affect; N = negative affect; Gen. = generalization.

decided to perform a second self-investigation. The results are presented in Table 1-5, and the major changes are summarized below.

In the second investigation a breakthrough of self-enhancing valuations in the system can be seen. Valuations 1 and 2 at Time 1 have been modified, now expressing more self-confidence (no. 1) and more fighting spirit (no. 2) than at Time 1. This is also visible in the high levels of S affect. Some other valuations (nos. 4, 5, and 6) show clearly higher levels of S affect than O affect. This suggests that she feels able to put her interests before those of others when necessary (note that this type of valuation, S > O, was completely absent at Time 1). This reorganization implies that she has largely resolved her personal problems by finding strength within herself, and this increased strength and self-confidence has allowed her to decide to quit her job (no. 4). This removes a major burden from the valuation system and some stressful experiences that could be seen as reactualizations of her past in particular (e.g., no. 4 in Table 1-3).

The valuation that at Time 1 referring to her wish to be strong on the outside (no. 6) has assumed more realistic proportions at Time 2. When this valuation is correlated with all the other valuations (see final column in Table 1-5), high correlations with valuations mainly of type S > O are found (nos. 2, 4, and 5). This indicates that the potential force implied by valuation no. 6 has been integrated into the valuation system. (Note that the general feeling still has higher O than S, suggesting that the heightened level of S affect is not yet generalizing in the system.)

Summary of the Presented Case

Ann's case can be viewed as a self-narrative that originally showed a striking omission, the experience of self-confidence and self-esteem. Partly on the basis of collective values (her education as a woman) and partly on the basis of her individual history (oldest in a family with a sick mother; her parents' unhappy marriage), she developed the identity of an "in-between person," a person con-

Table 1-5
Ann's Valuations, General Feeling, Ideal Feeling, and Their Scores on the Affective Indices at Time 2

Valuation	S	O	P	N	Gen.	Id.	No. 6
1. I feel more sure of myself and accepted by others as being that way; I don't avoid conflict as much	11	13	16	5	.79	.76	.31
2. I fight more for my own interests	13	9	16	3	.68	.75	.57
3. We have all learned something from my difficult period; the fear that I would repel my children has not become a reality; in fact the opposite is true	14	16	9	1	.70	.68	.01
4. I'll quit my job; giving up my financial independence is better than going back to the old work environment where nothing is discussed	18	0	14	1	.21	.35	.75
5. I've gained some calmness	8	0	11	2	.11	.23	.81
6. I am in the process of coming out as the person that I am on the inside, but simply haven't let anyone see (above all, stronger and clearer)	13	2	16	4	.13	.26	—
General feeling	12	18	15	2	—	.96	.13
Ideal feeling	15	18	16	3	.96	—	.26

Note: S = affect referring to self-enhancement; O = affect referring to contact with the other; P = positive affect; N = negative affect; Gen. = generalization; Id. = idealization.

stantly caring for others and striving to maintain every relationship. As a consequence, she had no opportunities, or simply was not permitted, to develop an independent self. Nevertheless, Ann could clearly imagine herself as a strong, decisive, and assertive individual. This person was hidden "deep down inside" her but not, in her view, part of her actual behavior. Drawing on the possibilities she felt within herself and the support of a psychotherapist, however, she finally emerged from her crisis. Moreover, Ann's case shows that a crisis implies dangers *and* chances: She compensated for the original omission in her valuation system with her strength, which had been hidden until then. This resulted in a more extended and flexible valuation system and also allowed her to stop the recurrent cycle of imposed and normative caring.

This case study was presented to demonstrate how the assessment, change, and evaluative aspects of the self-confrontation procedure work in an optimal case. In this example, the three functions of the method (assessment, process promotion, and evaluation) were combined to realize a smooth transition between assessment and change. However, this is not always the case, and the transition may not always be so spontaneous and smooth. The transition is highly dependent on the (remaining) capacities and opportunities on the part of the person to reorganize the valuation system. For example, a client in a depressive state characterized by hopelessness and helplessness often feels unable to take the smallest initiatives, and even when such an initiative is taken it may be quickly swallowed up by the dominant and highly generalized feelings of hopelessness or apathy. In such a case there may be no spontaneous transition from assessment to change. A longer period may be needed to arrive at the point where reorganization can be attempted, and the patience, support, and engagement of the psychotherapist—perhaps using a broader array of techniques than those described in this chapter—may be crucial.

Types of Valuations

In the preceding sections, it was argued that the rich phenomenological variation of valuations is—on a more latent level—rooted in a limited set of basic motives. The self-confrontation method shows that these basic motives are typically expressed in the affective component of a valuation. Figure 1-2 summarizes the main types of valuation that can be found in the application of the self-confrontation method in research and practice (Hermans & Hermans-Jansen, 1995). They can be conceived of as major themes (though not the only ones) from the perspective of the basic motives. These themes can be compared with those formulated by the client as a result of the modality analysis. In Ann's case, her theme was phrased as "*I have never had to fight for something for myself* . . ." and, in the following process, her valuation system changes in the direction of valuations with a high degree of self-enhancement affect in combination with a high degree of positive affect. In fact, she made a movement from an emphasis on negative

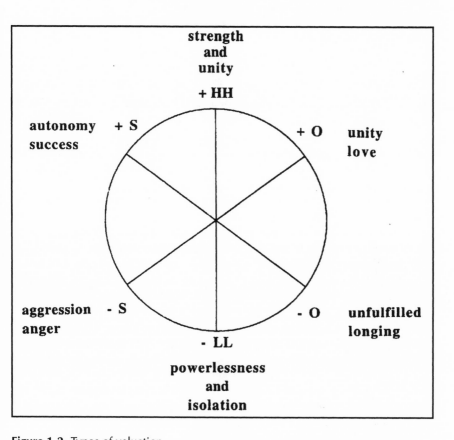

Figure 1-2. Types of valuation
+S, positive self-enhancement; –S, negative self-enhancement; +O, positive contact with others; –O, negative contact with others; +HH, positive combination of high self-enhancement and high contact with others; and –LL, negative combination of low self-enhancement and low contact with others. *Source:* Hermans & Hermans-Jansen, 1995.

longing for contact and union with the other (–O in Figure 1-2) at the first investigation toward a positive experience of self-enhancement (+S in Figure 1-2). In this way changes in the valuation system of a particular client can be depicted as movement of valuations on the circle. The localization of the main types of valuation and their frequencies helps psychologist and client to assess the biases of a valuation system at a particular moment and to clarify the direction the valuation process could take in the future.

ENRICHING THE VALUATION PROCESS: RESEARCH EXAMPLES

Over the years, valuation theory and the self-confrontation method have been applied to a diversity of research questions and problems in practice. In this section, some examples are presented that give, in Kelly's (1955) terms, an impression of the "range of convenience" of the theory.

Dreams As Pictorial Valuations

One of our projects combined valuation theory and Foulkes's (1978) program on dream research. In Foulkes's conception, the achievements of dreaming are ordinary rather than exotic, differentiated rather than unified, and, above all, expressible in words. Foulkes, therefore, suggested that it may be profitable to focus on the many strong structural parallels between dreams and ordinary, linguistically guided thinking. Like Foulkes, who conceived of a dream as a series of pictorial sentences, Hermans (1987a) analyzed a subject's dream as a series of pictorial valuations, which, combined, form a self-narrative. The dream was studied by comparing pictorial valuations (e.g., "I climbed a high ladder") with the ordinary valuations of everyday life, which usually have a more conceptual character (e.g., "I passed a difficult test"). It was supposed that the difference between the pictorial and conceptual valuations were but variations on a manifest level, and that both were rooted in a common motivational base on the latent level. Indeed, the findings showed strong affective parallels between particular dream symbols (central in the pictorial valuations) and the daily concerns of waking life (conceptual valuations), without the subjects being aware of these parallels. One person, for example, vividly described that she was walking quietly along a sandy wall in a small Dutch town, but suddenly, "The sand of the wall started to shift; I was not able to stop it and I became buried." When this sentence was included in her valuation system, the affective profile associated with this sentence showed a very high correlation with the affective profile of a conceptual valuation referring to the contact with her husband: "John is always able to let me know, nastily and pointedly, what he expects me to do, and I am not able to let him know that I can't or don't want to." Apparently, the two valuations had the same meaning from the perspective of the latent level.

It was found, moreover, that the dream symbols (e.g., "the burying sand"), that were initially separated from the waking valuations in the eyes of the client herself, were, after a period of self-reflection, meaningfully incorporated as parts of the waking valuation system, in a second self-investigation about 12 months later. In this self-investigation the client metaphorically described the relationship with her husband in this way: "Literally and figuratively, I don't have enough space with John." In fact, she used the metaphor of being buried by an external force in her dream (at Time 1) to express the lack of space in the contact with her husband (at Time 2). In general terms, dreams were found to be providers of symbols that were useful for the metaphorical expression of significant aspects of the subjects' life situation.

Themes in Collective and Individual Stories: Struggle and Love

In the tradition of research on psychological motivation and the storied nature of human experience (Bruner, 1986; Murray, 1938; Sarbin, 1986), our own work relates basic themes in collective stories to psychological motives in individual lives. The assumption is that there are two basic themes in collective stories—heroism and love—and that these themes are reflected in the psychological motives of individual people (self-enhancement and contact and union). In a study of Goya's serial painting, *The Capture of the Bandit El Maragato* (Hermans, 1988), it was observed that this painting expressed the polarity of winning versus losing, representing the theme of self-enhancement. It was found that the same theme was present in the self-narratives of individual clients: The experience of winning was expressed in such statements as, "My status is acceptable but not enough; I want to go a few steps further," or "My achievements were mine; they were valued (piano, sport, studying)" (type +S in Figure 1-2). The experience of losing was expressed in statements such as, "I have the feeling that John can be strong by keeping me weak" or "Violence and aggression have knocked me down" (type -LL valuations in Figure 1-2).

A similar procedure was followed in an investigation of the Narcissus myth (Hermans & Van Gilst, 1991). The central part of the myth, Narcissus looking into the water, was found to represent the experience of unfulfilled love (to be distinguished from the psychoanalytical dysfunction of narcissism), and can be considered as an expression of an existential longing for contact and union with other people and with oneself (expressed as valuations of type -O in Figure 1-2). On the basis of affective profiles derived from the central part of the myth, we explored whether similar profiles exist in the valuations of individual clients. It was found that the theme of unfulfilled longing was also present in specific statements such as, "I think it's a shame that I couldn't remove some of my mother's loneliness with my cheerfulness," or "First, I meant everything to him; now he means everything to me; the roles are now reversed." The Goya study and the Narcissus study suggest that basic themes, expressed in collective stories, are also present in the self-narratives of individuals.

The Personal Meaning of Psychosomatic Problems

Over time, we have studied a variety of psychosomatic complaints as parts of an organized valuation system. A typical finding has been that clients often have no idea about the psychological significance or origin of their complaints. One viable strategy, therefore, is to propose that the client include the complaint as a separate valuation so that it can be studied in the context of the valuation system as a whole. Clients then simply mention the existence of a problem (e.g., "pain in my stomach"), or they formulate a sentence that indicates nothing more than the frequency or degree of seriousness of their complaint (e.g., "I suffer from terrible pain in my neck"). In a further stage, the valuation referring to the psychosomatic complaint is correlated with the other valuations so that the affective commonality with other valuations can be made visible. The rationale is to actively link the "isolated valuation" with other parts of the system so that it becomes invested with personal meaning.

In one of our studies (Hermans, 1995), Alice, a 54-year-old woman, performed a self-investigation during a period of serious difficulties in her marriage relationship. Her husband, a playwright, had published a play in which his wife could be recognized as one of the main characters. This resulted in a irresolvable conflict for which they asked therapeutic assistance. Both partners performed a self-investigation as a starting point for a number of sessions in which they discussed their situation with a psychotherapist.

In one of her valuations Alice referred to "a pain in my neck and back of my head." In order to study the psychosomatic complaint in close relation with the other parts of the valuation system, the affective profile associated with the complaint was correlated successively with the affective profiles of all the other valuations of the system. In this analysis (called modality analysis, see preceding description of the self-confrontation method), it is supposed that the highest correlating valuations are of particular significance, because they have affective profiles similar to the complaint, and, therefore, share a similar affective meaning. By taking these highest correlating valuations into account, the personal meaning of a psychosomatic complaint (or any clinical problem) can be enlarged. In Alice's first self-investigation, two valuations showed very high correlations with the psychosomatic problem. One referred to her past: "My father: He avoided problems and used his children in his struggle against my mother: He always conformed to her authority and so he enforced our powerlessness as children." The second valuation referred to a problem in the contact with her husband: "In my husband's play, I don't recognize myself in the way he depicts me." Although correlations may not be interpreted in terms of causal relations, they suggest the existence of a common meaning in the pain and the problematic relationship with her father and husband.

The second self-investigation, 8 months after the first, again showed a high correlation between the same psychosomatic complaint and the modified valuation referring to the contact with her husband: "I regret that my husband has disclosed our problems in public before we had a chance to discuss them privately." As this formulation suggests, Alice's objections were more directly formulated against her husband. This formulation then led to a more articulated explicitness of the meaning of the complaint. After focusing on the highest correlating valuations in the first and second investigations, Alice was invited to phrase *in her own terms* the common meaning of the psychosomatic problem and the valuations with the highest correlations. This resulted in the following formulation, which reflects as a significant theme in her self-narrative:

My pain may be suppressed anger or resistance (the basic pattern of my behavior). I express my dissatisfaction in an indirect and, therefore, powerless manner. This means that a more direct resistance may relieve my pain.

Note that in this interpretation Alice not only interprets the affective commonality between her pain and the relationship with her husband, she also reflects on the direction in which her behavior should be changed. In this way, she gradually moves from assessment to change. (For more extensive treatments of the personal meaning of psychosomatic complaints and other clinical problems, see Hermans & Hermans-Jansen, 1995.)

Imaginal Figures As Contrasting Positions

Valuation theory is not a final theory, fixed forever. On the contrary, it is devised as an open framework in development that enables the researcher and clinician to investigate a diversity of psychological phenomena as a process of organization, disorganization, or reorganization of the valuation system. After the initial formulation of the theory, the notion of the multivoiced, dialogical self (Hermans, 1996a, 1996b; Hermans & Kempen, 1993; Hermans, Kempen, & Van Loon, 1992) stimulated its further extension. The essence of this extension is threefold. First, it is supposed that the self is composed of a multiplicity of voices, each able to formulate a specific valuation system. That is, different voices may reflect different memories about the past, different concerns about the present, and different goals and plans for the future. Second, it is supposed that the different voices and their corresponding valuation systems are on the manifest level of self functioning, and that these systems are influenced by the same basic motives on the latent level. Third, the different voices, producing different valuation systems from their specific perspectives, may exchange information and so influence one another in a dialogical fashion. Two examples that originate from the extended version of the theory are presented in the following: the contact with imaginal figures, and the phenomenon of multiple personality disorder.

In one of our research projects (Hermans, Rijks, & Kempen, 1993), the concept of the dialogical self was applied to the self-investigations of two women, each having had a long-lasting contact with an imaginal figure with a pervasive impact on their lives. One subject, Kathy, was a 31-year-old divorcee and had been brought up in a lower-class family. She had not graduated from high school, worked as a graphic designer, and had no psychiatric history. She participated in the self-investigation project because she was interested in exploring the role that her imaginal figure played in her life. She described this figure as "a guide who helps me to find my way in life," and said that she had been in touch with this figure since her early nursery school years. Kathy was invited to formulate, on the basis of open questions about her past, present, and future (see Table 1-1) a set of valuations from the perspective of her usual *I* position. Next, she was invited to formulate, on the basis of the same questions, a set of valuations from the perspective of her imaginal figure. The idea behind this investigation was that the guide had an individual story to tell and could do so in terms of a specific valuation system. It was found that the valuation systems for the two positions (Kathy and her guide) were quite different but not unrelated. For example, from her usual position, Kathy said about her past: "When I was alone, I constructed a fantasy world where I made myself a very strong person." From the perspective of her guide, she said: "As a child Kathy was quiet and reserved: I played with her in her own world." In addition, the guide said: "Sometimes I had to protect Kathy from her fantasies." As this example suggests, the guide was not only concerned about Kathy, but also corrected her when Kathy herself went too far in her fantasies. In this case, the guide is not simply a product of a dysfunctional mind, but, on the contrary, a constraint on Kathy's fantasy and a productive force in her self-organization.

The second subject, Liza, an unmarried woman 32 years of age, was brought up in a lower-class family. After the completion of her university studies 1 year prior, she was unemployed. She suffered from a mild, but chronic, depression and for that reason had attended some sessions with a psychiatrist. She participated in the self-investigation because she was interested in getting to know her imaginal figure, which she described as "a protecting father" who loved her and took care of her when she had serious problems. She said that she first became aware of this figure when she was 8 years old and sitting in a church. From her usual position Liza said, for example: "I never got protection from my [actual] father; I often had to protect him." The imaginal father seemed to have a compensatory function for Liza, and said: "I wanted to feel like she belonged and was of value." The two valuation systems (from Liza and her imaginal father) contrasted very strongly from an affective point of view. Liza herself formulated valuations that were very negative (more unpleasant than pleasant feelings), whereas the valuations from the imaginal father were very positive; that is, associated with much more pleasant than unpleasant feelings. This suggests that the imaginal figure was compensating for a felt deficiency.

Six months after the initial self-investigations, both Kathy and Liza performed a second investigation so that changes could be studied. The results of the second investigations suggested that Kathy had in the meantime increased her contact with her guide, and strengthened the interactional quality of the contact. Liza, however, did not profit very much from the contact with her imaginal father, and the valuations from her usual position did not show any improvement. These results suggest that there may be considerable individual differences between people in the quality of the contact with an imaginal figure, and that for the one person this contact may have a more beneficial influence on mental health than for the other.

Splitting of the Self: The Case of the Witch

The notions of "multiple personality," "dissociative disorders," and the recent notion of "dissociative identity disorder" (for reviews see Carson, Butcher, & Mineka, 1996; Kihlstrom, Glisky, & Angiulo, 1994; Putnam, 1993; Roberts & Donahue, 1994) are particularly relevant to our discussion, because they imply a serious reduction of the integration of the self that has become fragmented. As Watkins (1986) has argued, the main difference between (normal) imaginal dialogs and (abnormal) multiple personality is that in the latter there is a sequential monolog, rather than a simultaneous dialog. In the former, there is a simultaneity of positions among which the I is moving back and forth so that question and answer, agreement and disagreement, and an active process of negotiation between the several positions becomes possible. In the dysfunctional case, there are also several positions (e.g., "Eve White" and "Eve Black" in the famous case of Thigpen & Cleckly, 1954). However, a dialogical interaction between these positions is severely constrained or almost impossible. The client with a multiple personality can often tell something about the person in the other position, but does so in a rather objectifying manner. One example is the frivolous Eve Black who said about the decent Eve White, "When I go out and get drunk, she wakes up with the hangover" (Thigpen & Cleckly, 1954, p. 141). As the example suggests, there is little cooperation and interaction among the several positions, so that the person is doing in the one position things that are often beyond the control of the person in the other position.

As part of a comprehensive study on dysfunctional valuations (Hermans & Hermans-Jansen, 1995), we presented a detailed description of a client, Mary, who was, during the period of treatment, very close to suffering from a dissociative disorder. She had bad memories about her father, who was an alcoholic, and she was overwhelmed by disgust and panic when she saw any man who was drunk. In her adolescent years she joined a drug scene, which she remembered with the same panic and disgust, because she was sexually abused. She had great difficulties in telling how she was forced to have sex, sometimes even under armed threat. As a reaction to these experiences, she "protected" herself by always wearing a tampon. Moreover, she bathed excessively in order "to clean herself." The problems became acute when she married a man whom she loved very much. In strong contrast to her intimate feelings for this man, there were moments that she felt a strong disgust and aggression toward him that were entirely beyond her control. When her husband was sleeping, she felt an almost uncontrollable urge to murder him. There were times when she felt like a witch, an alien experience that frightened her, particularly because there were moments when the witch took almost total possession of her. She was scared to death, and felt sometimes literally strangled, by a power that was stronger than "herself."

After extensive discussion of her case, Els Hermans-Jansen, a psychotherapist, and I, a personality psychologist, decided to propose to her that she perform a self-investigation from the perspective of two positions, one from her usual position as "Mary," and the other from the position of "the witch." The rationale behind this proposal was that, given the split between the two positions (Mary and the witch), an improvement of her fragmented self was expected if (a) the two positions were to be clearly distinguished with regard to their specific wishes, aims, and feelings, and (b) a process of dialogical interchange could be established between the two positions, so that the witch could have the opportunity to say what she wanted. In this way, Mary could take the needs of the witch into account, without losing control of her vehement impulses.

We decided to invite not only Mary to rate the affective meaning of her own valuations, but also the witch to give her affective experience of Mary's valuations. For example, Mary said, "I want to try to see what my mother gives me: There is only one of me." This valuation was experienced by Mary in a very positive way. The witch, however, experienced the same valuation in a negative way and felt a fierce aggression toward the mother. The witch said, "With my bland pussycat qualities I have vulnerable things under my control, from which I can derive power at a later moment (somebody tells me things that I can use later to get what I want)." For the witch this valuation was associated with a large amount of self-enhancement affect and with a great deal of positive feelings. In relation to the same valuation, however, Mary felt a rather low degree of self-enhancement affect and a high amount of negative feelings. In other words, Mary and the witch demonstrated strongly contrasting affective responses regarding the same valuation.

On the basis of this self-investigation, we discussed with Mary two ideas that were based on our analysis of her twofold self-investigation. First, she was advised to exercise (e.g., by sport, cycling, or walking), in order to expand her imaginal space and to express the dammed up energy of the witch. Second, we proposed that she keep a diary in which she could write her daily observations, in order to sharpen her perception. In a later phase, she started to try out new actions. We give here, in her own words, an example of the type of strategy she developed to cope with the witch:

A few days ago Fred was sick in bed, with 104 degrees temperature, he even had blisters on his lips. I made breakfast for him and brought it upstairs. When I entered the room, and saw him lying on the bed, I loathed him, and I thought: "Don't think that I'm staying at home for you!" (I was planning to leave for a visit to friends in Amsterdam and to stay the night there). Standing by the bed I was thinking about this (with increasing venom), and became aware that the witch was coming up again. I left the tray with Fred, and left the house for a walk. During this walk I felt that I could discharge a part of the energy of the witch. At the same time I had the time to quietly reflect on the situation as it was: "He is sick, he needs me, and I want to care for him." I decided to buy a newspaper for him. When I came home, I explained to him that I would stay the night at home, and would go to Amsterdam the next morning. (So, I did not leave the decision up to him, but proposed it myself). Fred accepted this and the next morning I went out to visit my friends. (Hermans & Hermans-Jansen, 1995, p. 191)

As this passage suggests, Mary has not only made a clear perceptual distinction between the position of herself and the witch, but also develops a concrete strategy to deal with her opponent. This strategy includes that Mary does not split away from or suppress the witch, but rather tries to be as alert as possible to her appearance: When she comes, Mary decides to take a break, walks first (movement is important for the witch), and then makes a more balanced decision.

One year after the first self-investigation, Mary performed a second one in order to evaluate the changes. In the meantime, there were a limited number of sessions in which Mary discussed her daily experiences with the psychotherapist. In this second investigation, we found an increased similarity between the affective responses from Mary and the witch. Strikingly, the valuations that in the first investigation were formulated by the witch were, in the second investigation, reformulated in such a way that they were incorporated into Mary's system. For example, in Investigation 2 Mary said: "When this hard side comes and I recognize it, I get in touch. I can look at it and examine where the signal is from. Then I make good use of it." These findings suggested that a more dialogical relationship had developed between the two positions, and that Mary had been able to construct a more integrative valuation system.

CONCLUSION

Valuation theory is devised as an open and flexible theory for the study of a vast array of human experiences. The theory has been recently developed by taking into account the multivoicedness of the self and the possibility of dialogical relationships between its subparts. The theory provides not only a conceptual framework for distinguishing different positions in the self, it also offers a concrete strategy for assessment and change of the valuation systems associated with these positions. Instead of neglecting, suppressing, or splitting off incompatible positions, a procedure is followed in which the positions are taken up into a dialogical process. As part of this strategy, an incompatible position is not simply "cured" or treated as an undesirable symptom, but taken seriously as a partner with whom it is possible to meet "on speaking terms." The dialogical process, with dominance and struggle implied, is then a road to the integration of incompatible positions as part of a multivoiced self. Indeed, as a storyteller the person is motivated to keep the different voices together.

REFERENCES

Angyal, A. (1965). *Neurosis and treatment: A holistic theory.* New York: Wiley.

Bakan, D. (1966). *The duality of human existence.* Chicago: Rand-McNally.

Boyatzis, R. E. (1973). Affiliation motivation. In D. C. McClelland & R. S. Steele (Eds.), *Human motivation* (pp. 252–276). Morristown, NJ: General Learning Press.

Bruner, J. S. (1986). *Actual minds, possible worlds.* Cambridge, MA: Harvard University Press.

Carson, R. C., Butcher, J. N., & Mineka, S. (1996). *Abnormal psychology and modern life* (10th ed.). New York: HarperCollins.

Caughey, J. L. (1984). *Imaginary social worlds: A cultural approach.* Lincoln: University of Nebraska Press.

Crites, S. (1986). Storytime: Recollecting the past and projecting the future. In T. R. Sarbin (Ed.), *Narrative psychology: The storied nature of human conduct* (pp. 152–173). New York: Praeger.

Damon, W., & Hart, D. (1982). The development of self-understanding from infancy through adolescence. *Child Development, 4,* 841–864.

Foulkes, D. (1978). *A grammar of dreams.* Sussex, England: Harvester Press.

Frye, N. (1957). *Anatomy of criticism.* Princeton, NJ: Princeton University Press.

Gergen, K. J., & Gergen, M. M. (1988). Narrative and the self as relationship. *Advances in Experimental Social Psychology, 21,* 17–56.

Hermans, H. J. M. (1970). A questionnaire measure of achievement motivation. *Journal of Applied Psychology, 54,* 353–363.

Hermans, H. J. M. (1987a). The dream in the process of valuation: A method of interpretation. *Journal of Personality and Social Psychology, 53,* 163–175.

Hermans, H. J. M. (1987b). Self as organized system of valuations: Toward a dialogue with the person. *Journal of Counseling Psychology, 34,* 10–19.

Hermans, H. J. M. (1988). On the integration of idiographic and nomothetic research method in the study of personal meaning. *Journal of Personality, 56,* 785–812.

Hermans, H. J. M. (1989). The meaning of life as an organized process. *Psychotherapy, 26,* 11–22.

Hermans, H. J. M. (1995). From assessment to change: The personal meaning of clinical problems in the context of the self-narrative. In R. A. Neimeyer & M. J. Mahoney (Eds.), *Constructivism in Psychotherapy* (pp. 247–272). Washington, DC: American Psychological Association.

Hermans, H. J. M. (1996a). Opposites in a dialogical self: Constructs as characters. *Journal of Constructivist Psychology, 9,* 1–26.

Hermans, H. J. M. (1996b). Voicing the self: From information processing to dialogical interchange. *Psychological Bulletin, 119,* 31–50.

Hermans, H. J. M., & Hermans-Jansen, E. (1995). *Self-narratives: The construction of meaning in psychotherapy.* New York: Guilford Press.

Hermans, H. J. M., & Kempen, H. J. G. (1993). *The dialogical self: Meaning as movement.* San Diego, CA: Academic Press.

Hermans, H. J. M., Kempen, H. J. G., & Van Loon, R. J. P. (1992). The dialogical self: Beyond individualism and rationalism. *American Psychologist, 47,* 23–33.

Hermans, H. J. M., Rijks, T. I., & Kempen, H. J. G. (1993). Imaginal dialogues in the self: Theory and method. *Journal of Personality, 61,* 207–236.

Hermans, H. J. M., & Van Gilst, W. (1991). Self-narrative and collective myth: An analysis of the Narcissus story. *Canadian Journal of Behavioural Science, 23*, 423–440.

James, W. (1890). *The principles of psychology* (Vol. 1). London: Macmillan.

Kelly, G. A. (1955). *The psychology of personal constructs*. New York: Norton.

Kihlstrom, J. F., Glisky, M. L., & Angiulo, M. J. (1994). Dissociative tendencies and dissociative disorders. *Journal of Abnormal Psychology, 103*, 117–124.

Klages, L. (1948). *Charakterkunde* [Characterology]. Zurich, Switzerland: Hirzel.

Lau, S. (1992). Collectivism's individualism: Value preference, personal control, and the desire for freedom among Chinese in Mainland, China, Hong Kong, and Singapore. *Personality and Individual Differences, 13*, 361–366.

Levin, H. (1970). The Quixote principle. In M. W. Bloomfield (Ed.), *Harvard English Studies, 1. The interpretation of narrative: Theory and practice* (pp. 45–66). Cambridge, MA: Harvard University Press.

McAdams, D. P. (1985). *Power, intimacy, and the life story: Personological inquiries into identity*. Chicago: Dorsey Press. (Reprinted by Guilford Press.)

McAdams, D. P. (1993). *The stories we live by: Personal myths and the making of the self*. New York: William Morrow.

McClelland, D. C., Atkinson, J. W., Clark, R. A., & Lowell, E. L. (1953). *The achievement motive*. New York: Appleton-Century-Crofts.

Merleau-Ponty, M. (1945). *Phénoménologie de la perception* [Phenomenology of perception]. Paris: Gallimard; English trans. by Colin Smith (1962), *Phenomenology of perception*. London: Routledge & Kegan Paul.

Murray, H. A. (1938). *Explorations in personality*. New York: Oxford University Press.

Neimeyer, G. J., Hagans, C. L., & Anderson, R. (1998). Intervening in meaning: Applications of constructivist assessment. In C. Franklin & P. S. Nurius (Eds.), *Constructivism in practice: Methods and challenges* (pp. 115–137). Milwaukee, WI: Families International.

Pepper, S. (1942). *World hypotheses*. Berkeley: University of California Press.

Polkinghorne, D. (1988). *Narrative knowing and the human sciences*. Albany: State University of New York Press.

Putnam, F. W. (1993). Dissociative disorders in children: Behavioral profiles and problems. *Child Abuse & Neglect, 17*, 39–45.

Roberts, B. W., & Donahue, E. M. (1994). One personality, multiple selves: Integrating personality and social roles. *Journal of Personality, 62*, 199–218.

Rosenberg, M. (1979). *Conceiving the self*. New York: Basic Books.

Sarbin, T. R. (1986). The narrative as a root methaphor for psychology. In T. R. Sarbin (Ed.), *Narrative psychology: The storied nature of human conduct* (pp. 3–21). New York: Praeger.

Sarbin, T. R. (1990). The narrative quality of action. *Theoretical and Philosophical Psychology, 10*, 49–65.

Schwartz, S. H. (1990). Individualism-collectivism: Critique and proposed refinements. *Journal of Cross-Cultural Psychology, 21*, 139–157.

Thigpen, C. H., & Cleckley, H. (1954). A case of multiple personality. *Journal of Abnormal and Social Psychology, 49*, 135–151.

Triandis, H. C., Bontempo, R., Villareal, M. J., Asai, M., & Lucca, N. (1988). Individualism and collectivism: Cross-cultural perspectives on self-ingroup relationships. *Journal of Personality and Social Psychology, 54*, 323–338.

Watkins, M. (1986). *Invisible guests: The development of imaginal dialogues.* Hillsdale, NJ: Erlbaum.
Winter, D. G. (1973). *The power motive.* New York: Free Press.

Chapter 2

Insight: Transcending the Obvious

Christopher D. Stevens
Beverly M. Walker

If you go ahead and involve yourself, rather than remaining alienated from the human struggle, if you strike out and implement your anticipations, if you dare to commit yourself, if you prepare to assess the outcomes as systematically as you can, and if you master the courage to abandon your favorite psychologisms and intellectualisms and reconstrue life altogether; well you may not find that you guessed right, but you will stand a chance of transcending more freely those 'obvious' facts that now appear to determine your affairs, and you may just get a little closer to the truth that lies somewhere over the horizon. (Kelly, 1977, p. 19)

A hallmark of psychological constructivism is its treatment of human beings as proactive makers of meaning, as predicators as well as mediators of their psychological reality (Rychlak, 1990, 1991). The preceding quotation typifies the constructivist image of the person as creatively involved in the generation of meaning. Note, too, its emphasis on "emotional" and "motivational" states as a part of large-scale insights ("reconstruing life altogether"). Given these emphases, one might assume that the discussion of *insight* would be commonplace within constructivist writings. As it turns out, however, constructivists have not focused on insight, and most contemporary research is inspired by a fairly standard cognitive representationist/information processing perspective (Smith, Ward, & Finke, 1995; Sternberg & Davidson, 1995) in which insight is usually not understood as the product of proactive construction, but rather as the product of mechanistic, associationistic processes.

However, many of these cognitive approaches overreach themselves. Their findings sit more comfortably within a constructivist metatheory, featuring as they do emphases on high levels of abstraction and nonliteral, figurative construction, on the interplay of tacit and explicit mental processes, on the central role of a type of "emotional thinking," and on the social and pragmatic dimensions of insight. In this chapter, we briefly summarize these findings and compare them with what Kelly (1955) had to say about insight, particularly in relation to his Creativity Cycle. His constructivist approach is shown to be highly compatible with contemporary research. It is argued, however, that Kelly's account is insufficiently specified to help us adequately understand the processes involved in insight. An important aside is a discussion of emotion within personal construct psychology (PCP) and within contemporary research generally. It is proposed that a type of transcending affect is the "pivot" on which insight turns. To expand this proposal, Matte-Blanco's (1975, 1988) theorizing, particularly his notions of symmetrical and asymmetrical modes of thought, will be used to elaborate Kelly's account of loose and tight construing. It is proposed that this elaboration necessitates some qualifications of Kelly's theory. We further propose that insight experiences exhibit a nongrasping playfulness amid uncertainty that often results in a qualitatively different experience of self. Finally, we consider that insight reveals a looser anticipatory mode using a more associative, less discriminative logic. Such construing is not chaotic, but ideally is embedded in an awareness that does not "wait for" something expected, but "waits upon" the unknown.

FEATURES OF INSIGHT: CONTEMPORARY FINDINGS

Following the early terminology of Wallas (1926) and Hutchinson (1949a, 1949b, 1949c), most contemporary researchers have characterized insight in terms of four stages: Preparation, Impasse leading to "Incubation," a moment or period of Insight itself, and the Verification and Elaboration of the insight (Sternberg & Davidson, 1995). Generally speaking, there is a consensus that insight involves special processes or includes a qualitatively different mode of thought. The phenomenology of insight is taken to include sustained work on a problem until impasse is reached and the problem is set aside.

This marks the "incubation" stage, the resolution of which is variously explained by (a) the forgetting of misleading assumptions and approaches (Perkins, 1995; Smith, 1995a, 1995b; Ward, 1995), (b) the accidental encounter with the appropriate "solution" stimulus in the environment (Perkins, 1997; Seifert, Meyer, Davidson, Patalano & Yaniv, 1995; Weisberg, 1995), (c) a slow spreading activation that finally nudges the partly activated "solution" above the threshold for consciousness (Martindale, 1995; Yaniv & Meyer, 1987), and (d) the broadening of the number of elements and associated structures that can be simultaneously activated allowing for remote associations, analogies, and metaphors (Davidson, 1995; Gentner, 1983; Perkins, 1997).

The impending culmination of the "incubation" period is often marked by an intuitive, highly abstract "feel" that one is on the way to solution (Claxton, 1997; Ippolito & Tweney, 1995; Metcalfe & Wiebe, 1987). This intuitive stage is characterized by a general mental "playfulness" and tolerance of the absurd. Negative emotion is inimical to insight, especially at this stage, probably because insight requires a sustained "defocused" attention and a non–self-conscious, emotional calm (Csikszentmihalyi, 1990, 1996; Martindale, 1995). This calm or reverie is often achieved by the person engaging in trivial or recreational tasks, frequently just daydreaming. The occurrence of the "Aha!" experience is universally reported as enjoyable, even rapturous, and the experiencing person may lose awareness of the passage of time and of his or her immediate circumstances. Finally, a return to a more "rational," "logical," and less "tacit" self-consciousness marks the testing and elaboration of the insight.

There is much overlap in discussions and theories of insight, inspiration, creativity, and intuition. For our purposes they are distinguished as follows: *Creativity* is seen as a more embracing, longer-term combination of purposes, activities, and products, including insights (Gardner, 1993; Gruber, 1981, 1995). An important, arguably crucial, element within this larger creative process is the experience of *insight*. Thus a "creative" person may be expected to be someone who has the relatively frequent experience of insight. In similar fashion, *intuition* is here considered to be an important aspect or stage within the process of insight. The sense that one knows something in advance of one's capacity to articulate it appears to be crucial to insight. Finally, *inspiration* is distinguished from insight. *Insight* is considered as proactive understanding, whereas *inspiration* is often characterized as a more passive "reception" of ideas. This latter concept is derived from the ancient belief that insights into (spiritual) truths were "breathed" or "inspired" into the soul or mind by "spirits." Next, we summarize four important features of insight.

High Levels of Abstraction and Insight

The path to insight entails the use of high-level abstractions, variously described as metacognitions (Metcalfe & Wiebe, 1987), high-generality heuristics (Perkins; 1997; Ward, 1995), schematic anticipations (Mayer, 1995; Seifert et al., 1995), analogy and metaphor (Gentner, 1983; Gick & Holyoak, 1983; Smith, 1995a; Weisberg, 1995), themata (Briggs, 1990), failure indices (Seifert et al., 1995), and inceptions (Ippolito & Tweney, 1995). The defining feature of all these abstractive styles of thought is that they are superordinate, permeable structures allowing the person to simultaneously entertain a wide array of elements, ideas, and images. They are conducive to looser, imaginary associative play, and allow one to entertain unusual, even absurd, combinations of ideas and elements.

Remote analogies are rendered much more likely given the greater number of possibilities thus entertained (Ward, 1995). New chains of implications become possible as broad levels of abstraction entrain a much wider network of subordinate categories and ideas. Given the mastery of one's domain, or even better, given expertise in more than one domain (Simonton, 1993), this level of abstraction allows one to grasp connections between otherwise "irrelevant" conceptions.

Two Types of Mental Process: Tacit versus Explicit

Connected with higher levels of abstraction, a recurring finding is that insight reveals an alternation between different modes of thought. There is a near-universal emphasis of the role of intuition. This sensitivity to tacit understandings is present in most researchers' explanations of insight and is reflected in their theoretical constructs: "feelings of knowing" and "perceptual rehearsal" (Ippolito & Tweney, 1995), combinations in the "subconscious" (Csikszentmihalyi, 1996), "quasi-perceptual" and "imagistic" thinking (Seifert et al., 1995), "defocused attention" (Martindale, 1995), the ability for entering "flow" (Csikszentmihalyi, 1996), and playful "cross-modal" imaginings (Hunt, 1995). All these modes of knowing represent a type of "loosening" of the more familiar conscious processes of thought.

When confronted with complex and ill-defined problems that our habitual patterns of knowing cannot overcome, insight is needed to overcome the impasse. Verbalization and "thinking too much" are frequently counterproductive (Schooler & Engstler-Schooler, 1990), and a more divergent style of thought is required (Bowers, Farvolden, & Mermigis, 1995). A capacity for "omnivalence" or "Janusian thinking" (Briggs, 1990)—in which "normal" thought processes are suspended and contradictories can be held in mind simultaneously—is needed. Ippolito and Tweney (1995) proposed "inceptions" as a mode of guidance that underlies intuitive knowing. These are "sensory reconstructions" or high-generality imagery described as being somewhere between perceptions and symbolic thought, and, like Briggs's (1990) "themata," they represent a more aesthetically rich and personally "felt" mode of mental awareness. This recalls Langer's (1957) idea of a "presentational" mode of thought (as against the more discursive and conscious "representational" mode) as a collective term for all these types of tacit, figurative, and affectively nuanced mental processes.

One result of this "presentational" modality may be to bring about a different experience of self. It is widely reported that insight is experienced as both spontaneous or as "having a life of its own," and as exhibiting a quality of "exteriority," as if coming from outside oneself (Epel, 1993; Gardner, 1993; Gruber, 1995). The person commonly experiences a lack of self-awareness and self-concern and may lose track of time and surroundings. Typically, there is a suspension of one's usual judgment and evaluation processes. Indeed, attempting to articulate the process in words while in this stage seems to be counterproductive and disrupts the "flow" (Bowers, 1981; Schooler & Melcher, 1995).

The Social and Pragmatic Dimensions of Insight

Generally speaking, the cognitive literature underspecifies the social dimension of insight (Simonton, 1993, 1997), emphasizing instead its hypothesized intrapsychic mechanics. Wallace (1991) has argued that insight has a socially related, developmental facet—the "microgenetic" flash of insight being only one aspect of a larger and ongoing "macrogenetic," largely social, process. There also have been more "sociological" cognitive investigations (Csikszentmihalyi & Sawyer, 1995; Gardner, 1993; Gruber, 1981) that place insight within historical, cultural, professional, and interpersonal milieux. There is still a yawning theoretical gap, however, between the person's "inner" (mental) processes and the "outer" (social) forces acting upon them, and a paucity of explanations for how that gap is breached.

For example, Csikszentmihalyi and Sawyer (1995) argue that insight is socially structured. For these researchers the key component of insight is a "filtering mechanism" through which the unconscious is structured by socially informed, conscious learning. The discourses and practices of one's "domain" and the practitioners of one's "field" are the primary socializing influences. Through acculturation, mentoring, reading, and apprenticeship, a "subconscious filtering network" is built that organizes incoming information. Drawing on Minsky's (1985) notion of the "Society of Mind" and on the connectionist metaphor, many subconscious processing entities are described as acting simultaneously on incoming data, "testing hypotheses," and "generating hunches." But these hypothetical processes merely push the problem of explaining insight to vague inner reaches—effectively attributing these inner "minds" with the insightful properties we wish to explain.

Where these researchers are more informative is in their detailed attention to the pragmatics of generating insight. They describe in some detail the working lives of eminently insightful people. What emerges is an ongoing alternation between solitude and social interaction and between hard work and idle time. In accounting for their insights, respondents recognized how much a part of their field and the current *zeitgeist* their contributions were. All were keenly aware of the state of the current paradigm, the political considerations within their field(s) and the importance of conversations with respected colleagues—particularly in communicating and elaborating their insights with trusted peers. It is important to them that their insights "work" and are accepted. What emerges is not only cycles of creativity and insight, but larger cycles of (social) experience in which these insights are socially and pragmatically embedded.

The Role of Emotional Thought in Insight

The role of "emotional thinking"[1] in insight is of cardinal importance. This "feeling" intelligence implies a type of understanding that includes and goes beyond calculative, means-end thinking toward a more "meditative" form (Heidegger, 1978). It is marked by a receptive affective awareness and sensitivity. Such thinking responds to ill-defined problems, those we have little idea of how to approach methodically (Oatley, 1990). We argue here that the moods and affective qualities so characteristic, for example, of "flow" (Csikszentmihalyi, 1996) and of "themata" (Briggs, 1990) are *constitutive* of insight processes, not merely *consequent upon* insights.

Briggs (1990) and Goleman (1995) have summarized evidence that thoughts and memories may be coded or logged in the brain according to their emotional nuances or "feeling tones." In line with this, insight may be consequent upon an awareness and utilization of this orderly, affective "coding" and "predisposing" of our mental possibilities. Events and elements of understanding are grasped as comprehensible or as being within some orderly relationship, and this comprehensibility is *affectively* informed. In this way, affective "feelings" or intuitions are frequently experienced and acted upon *before* there is any conscious justification for such action (Bechara, Damasio, Tranel, & Damasio, 1997; Claxton, 1998). Accordingly, a "slowing down" of mental activity may be required if we are to escape our implicit, affective predispositions and perhaps make space for alternative possibilities.

Connected to "emotional thinking" is the experience of failure and disappointment. For example, when people are disappointed in their stymied attempts to solve a problem, they are much more likely to remember its elements—the "Zeigarnik Effect" (Reber, 1985). This phenomenon is probably ecologically advantageous, for our survival depends on our ability to anticipate and deal with the "problems" that life poses. It would be an advantage to recognize similar, perturbing situations more quickly than nonperturbing ones. "Primed" in this way, stray events or thoughts may subsequently provide the clue to the still-available "representation" of the problem, and insight may soon follow. Emotional "markers" may well perform this function (Damasio, 1994; Seifert et al., 1995).

Identity, particularly those aspects concerned with our survival, is also likely to be enmeshed with our ability to anticipate events successfully and, thereby, with emotional experience. Thus, failures to anticipate events would usually lead to anxiety. Doubts about our general *ability* to anticipate would be even more threatening. Consequently, it is "natural" for us to avoid situations of continuing uncertainty or impasse. Under conditions of threat and anxiety, thinking and behavior may become predictable and stereotyped and, thereby, unlikely to lead to insight (Amabile, 1990). Ironically, the capacity for insight, and for the flow of ideas and actions it entails, may therefore be tied to our capacity to deal with the anticipatory invalidation of impasse *without* our usual "ecologically advantageous," automatic affective responses. A tolerance for anxiety and threat, at least for a time, would appear to be useful. Conversely, the joy of insight may be tied to the renewed confidence in our capacity to anticipate events around us (Ippolito & Tweney, 1995). This return to anticipatory validation brings a welcome experience of "connectedness" with those events. Again, this points to a type of emotional intelligence or ability that affords us a certain serenity, mental playfulness, and "looseness," even in the face of failure and confusion. In the following discussion, we see how these broad findings fit within the constructivist psychology of George Kelly.

A READING OF PERSONAL CONSTRUCT PSYCHOLOGY

Before we see what Kelly has to say about insight, it is important to clarify what type of reading of Kelly we use. This is by no means straightforward. Reactions to Kelly's earliest writings within a PCP framework have linked his views with diverse, seemingly contradictory, psychological positions ranging from behaviorism to existentialism, with others in between. Even within constructivism, disagreement exists concerning its nature and alignment with other constructivisms (Chiari & Nuzzo, 1996; Mahoney, 1995; Neimeyer, 1995; Stam, 1998; Warren, 1998). Furthermore, Kelly's practice was eclectic and, although this may be a major strength clinically, it can lead to confusion theoretically.

At least part of the explanation for this lack of agreement arises because of the development of Kelly's theory between the early 1950s and his last papers in 1966. As Mair (1989) put it, "his is a psychology itself in motion." The contrast between the first volume of the *Psychology of Personal Constructs* (1955) and Kelly's numerous papers, which were in many cases subsequently published (most notably Kelly, 1969), has been remarked on by a variety of writers.

To illustrate, Mair (1989) contrasted the relative conventionality of Kelly's earlier theorizing and its focus on how experience is structured, with the more radical perspective of his later work in which the mode of his presentation modeled the kind of psychology he seemed to be reaching toward. That latter psychology gave "invitations for participation in psychological realities shaped by the manner and style of his telling, by a rhetoric of humor and disrespect, tradition and innovation, that he employs to speak a frame of mind into life" (Mair, 1989, p. 4).

But the characterization of the earlier Kelly that is most relevant here concerns its relatively individualistic focus, a focus more amenable to a cognitive reading (Butt, 1995, 1998; Radley, 1977). By this we mean that "cognitive" interpretations tend to reify constructs as something people "have" rather than as something they "do" and, hence, use a mechanistic metaphor for the person (Kirkland & Anderson, 1990). Thus, constructs are often treated as internal processes that are causes of (subsequent) behavior. When we opt for extension or definition of our system (the Choice Corollary), the cognitive interpretation would consider this choice as a type of prediction based on introspective knowledge of the (internal) construct system. An alternate reading would emphasize construing as anticipation within situated action (Butt, 1998; Radley, 1977). This alternate view would tend to see the "elaborative choice" as a post hoc judgment, as a way of understanding people's choices, made (mostly) unself-consciously amid the flurry of life's events. It is this approach that is consistent with Kelly's later writings. Choice is then understood as pragmatically codetermined by the exigencies of the situation, its discourses and resources, and by the position and nature of the person within that situation. From such a viewpoint, most construing emerges within action without conscious prediction or forethought (Butt, 1995).

This reading sits more comfortably with Kelly's insistence that PCP was not a cognitive theory and with his repeated rejection of the assumed necessity to distinguish cognition, affect, and behavior in certain philosophical and psychological traditions. It is also consistent with his proposal that behavior be considered as an independent, not a dependent, variable. The later Kelly (1966b, 1966c, 1977), and even the Kelly of the second volume (1955), tended to write about behavior as a question, rather than as a test of a construction. Notably, one of his last papers was a reworking of his "Autobiography of a Theory," titled "Behavior Is a Question" (1966a).

Arguably, this later approach is much more compatible with the emphasis in the insight literature on tacit and unconscious awareness and on the attendant uncertainty and emotionality of insight processes. We agree with Butt (1998) and Radley (1977), who rejected the dualist image of the person who construes and *then* behaves, or who predicts and *then* finds out. Although important dimensions of our construing may fit this pattern, most is more tacit and more affectively charged in terms of our pressing interests. We believe that such an interpretation of personal construing is more amenable to an understanding of the genesis of insight.

Kelly and Insight: Relevant Contrasts

The "Negative" Pole

Most of Kelly's references to insight are negative in tone. Indeed, the majority of his uses of the term "insight" are in "scare quotes," sometimes expressing skepticism, at other times outright disdain. His strongest disapproval is reserved for (presumably psychodynamic) therapists who see their job as providing insights for the client to internalize: "*Insight*, as we see it, is too often applied by clinicians only to those clients who adopt the clinician's pet constructs" (Kelly, 1955, p. 359). Clearly, therapist-centered "insight" of this type was to have no place in PCP. But of course clients will not be bereft of their own insights. For Kelly, however, there are problems here too. These "insights" may be the result of an overdilated perceptual field—in which the client believes his or her every thought is a wonderful insight. Kelly (1955) lampoons this as the "I-see-it-all-now type of reconstruction" (p. 842).

Kelly's concern is not only that an "insight" may be trivial. If it is indeed a "comprehensive construction of one's behavior" (1955, p. 917), Kelly's definition of a "new insight," then he warns that it "can be extremely threatening. It may throw a client into a state of panic" (p. 917). When discussing the *Generalization of Insight* in the context of a "hostile" client,[2] Kelly sounds a dire warning to overzealous therapists:

If therapy is "deep," there will come a time when the therapist will expect the client to see that his hostility is more widely diffused than he realized during the early weeks of treatment. If the therapist is impatient to pass this landmark, he may wake up some morning to find that his prize therapy case has ended up in suicide or in a psychotic break. (1955, p. 891)

More generally, Kelly believed that brilliant therapy room insights may actually block future movement by locking the client into the past or into fatalist constructions. "The client finally has a satisfactory formulation of 'how he got that way,' but his 'insights' are not sufficiently permeable to carry implications as to 'what he can do about it'" (1955, p. 1091).

The "Positive" Pole

That insight was not a goal of psychotherapy, however, did not mean it was unimportant in the therapeutic process. Indeed, he discussed favorably the nature of "new insight" (1955, p. 917), and his entire therapeutic project could be characterized as an attempt to assist the client to come to just such insights. Considering his theory's philosophical basis in "constructive alternativism," whereby it is assumed that "all of our present interpretations of the universe are subject to revision or replacement" (Kelly, 1955, p. 15), it could reasonably be expected that reconstruing and seeing matters in a fresh light would receive Kelly's unambiguous support. In fact, there is some support for this expectation: "Only when new events are unexpectedly brought into the display is it likely that *genuinely new insights* can be instigated" (1959, p. 24, emphasis added). So here we see that "genuine" insight is possible. Compare the positive tone of the following passage to those presented earlier:

A genuinely new insight does what all experienced therapists have long known that it does; it changes not only the way a particular problematic event is seen, but also the way many others are seen. It changes them so that the client often refers to them as if they all had somewhat different identities now. (Kelly, 1959, p. 24)

Kelly obviously has in mind here the positive potential of genuine insight. He went on to say that such a burst of insight must be tested against future events; that it may fail to "point as sharply to subsequent events as it should" (1955, p. 44). Nonetheless, the context also makes it clear that there is no thoroughgoing therapeutic movement without this type of insight. When one considers PCP, the capacity to build new constructs and to change with a changing world (Creativity Cycle), to extend and define one's system of constructs (Choice Corollary), to never be boxed in by circumstances but always to have the relative freedom of reconstrual (Constructive Alternativism)—in fact, nearly everywhere one looks—there is room for the fresh outlooks that insight implies.

Insight and Reconstruction in PCP

Because insight marks a change in a person's understanding, the ways in which Kelly conceptualized reconstruction promise to be a useful place to start. The purpose of personal construct therapy is reconstruction; that is, to assist clients in changing their active anticipations of themselves and of their world. Kelly, on a number of occasions (1955, pp. 941, 945), described three types of reconstruction. Where the client (a) reconstrues without altering constructs or the existing construct system, (b) reconstrues by reorganizing the construct system, and (c) reconstrues by developing new constructs.

"Noninsight" Reconstructions

The first two reconstructions above are "noninsight" reconstructions. For example, each construct, being bipolar, offers the possibility of contrast reconstruction or "slot rattling," as Kelly (1955) called it. That is, the person reconstrues an event by merely using the opposite pole of the construct. As such, there is no new dimension of understanding formed, only the utilization of resources inherent in the construct. Alternatively, the person can reconstrue by surveying his or her repertoire of relevant constructs (Circumspection), by choosing one (Preemption), and choosing the most "elaborative" pole of the construct (Control). This CPC cycle (Circumspection-Preemption-Control) does not create new constructs or new insights.

In similar fashion, Controlled Elaboration (1955, pp. 938–939) is reconstruction in which the hierarchies of the system are reorganized (often superordinate constructs are tightened) in order to better integrate constructs. This internal consistency leads to more certainty, and this experience may be (rashly) labeled "insight." Kelly warned that controlled elaboration may be overvalued by those who believed therapy should aim for verbal consistency, which often entails a sort of false "insight" wherein the client merely agrees with the therapist. Finally, the reduction of constructs to impermeability may limit the use of a problematic construct by tying it tightly to specific elements, or by tying it to the past. Although there is no substantial change to the conceptual basis of the construct, this process often leads to the development of a new construct that better deals with the elements now excluded from the original construct.

Reconstruction Involving Insight

It is the third type of reconstruction, the development of new constructs, that repeatedly earned Kelly's highest praise (1955, pp. 134–135, 187, 586, 941) and that is most relevant to our interest in insight. Kelly considered the development of new constructs as central:

In addition to producing superficial movement, or seesaw movement, in some instances, and using the method of controlled elaboration in others, the psychoclinician's role is most fundamentally one of helping the client to *revise constructs*. (1955, p. 586)

The development of new constructs allows for new understandings, for understandings not possible within the existing construct system. There are two main avenues to new insight: (a) new elements applied to old constructs, and (b) new constructs applied to existing elements.

New Elements Applied to Old Constructs

Developing new constructs may be achieved by increasing the range of convenience of a construct, making it more permeable. This makes it applicable to more events and may, thereby, lead to a need *to alter the construct's conceptual basis* and, thus, to experiencing new insights. Take, for example, a person who may, somewhat simplistically, consider that people who are religiously active are either "dogmatic" or "spiritual." If this construct is causing the person problems, the therapist may introduce new, challenging elements for the client in an effort to encourage more differentiated construing in this regard.

The therapist may help the client to see, for example, that what he or she has been labeling "dogmatic" might also include an experience-based, thoughtful conviction in the wisdom of central doctrines of one's faith. On the other hand, some behavior that has been seen as "spiritual" may be understood to include a person who practices a nonreflective, preemptive (i.e., dogmatic) rejection of all religious dogma. To incorporate these new elements, Kelly (1955) speculated that the construct axes must be "rotated," which would have the effect of bringing the construct into a new relation with the rest of the person's system of constructs. The label of the construct ("religious people") may remain the same, but the discrimination at the heart of the construct may be quite different, and it may come under the regnancy of different (perhaps more permeable) superordinate structures.

In the preceding case, the "dogmatic" pole may be replaced by a notion of "unthinking inflexibility," whereas the "spiritual" pole may now reflect "genuine religious experience" (independent of whether any particular dogma is professed). The reigning superordinate construct may now be a more permeable (perhaps more abstract) one from the person's repertoire, something like "close-mindedness"–"openness," for example. Because these new elements have brought about a "rotation" of the construct, further new elements, once not relevant, are also now within the range of convenience of the revised construct and allow for further new insights. This revised construct will represent new behavioral implications, some welcome, some problematic. In other words, new insight emerges progressively from series of Creativity Cycles as the person "fine-tunes" the developing construct dimension(s).

New Constructs for Old Elements

Another strategy the therapist may use in developing construct revision is helping the client "impose new constructs upon old elements" (1955, p. 939). Normally, constructs introduced by the therapist in this way are relatively incidental. That is, they apply noncomprehensively to elements and people not central to the person's identity and core experience. In terms of the previously mentioned "religious person" construct, a new construct of "closemindedness–openness" may be "provided" by the therapist and applied to specific people quite removed from the person's day-to-day life (perhaps by way of an analogy, fable, or story). Gradually, as the construct allows the person to better anticipate reality, it may be applied to more and more familiar people and perhaps, finally, to the client's self. As this happens, the old construct of "dogmatic"–"spiritual" can be reduced to relative impermeability and confined to the particular people and incidents that occasioned its formation. The new construct "takes over" many of the old elements, and the "same" events are now seen in an entirely different light.

The Creativity Cycle: Producing New Insights

Construct revision and replacement is facilitated by series of Creativity Cycles. These cycles are characterized by alternating sequences of *loose* and *tight* construing:

Loosening is defined as characteristic of those constructs leading to varying predictions, while a tight construct holds its elements firmly in their prescribed contexts. Under loose construction, an element classified at one pole of a construct on one occasion is envisioned at the contrast pole on another. (1955, pp. 1029–1030)

Such a loosened construct is elastic, shifting the allegiance of elements to its poles (as in dreams). Thus in a dream a person may appear, for example, to be male. Then, without any apparent sense of contradiction, the person changes into a female. Kelly considered such loosening "a necessary stage of creative thinking" (1955, p. 1030). Loosening can lead to more construct *permeability*. That is, it can develop constructs that more easily admit newly perceived elements into their contexts. If such (permeable) constructs are superordinate enough, they open up a whole field of further, subordinate construct variations, including an openness to new experiences. When the tightening phase of the creativity cycle is reached, one may experience new insight, as the newly formed construct allows one to "see" things in ways not possible before. This is why large-scale insights can be alternatively so liberating, or so threatening: being superordinate, they can carry great implications for the person.

Kelly (1955) described loosened construction as a type of rubber template cast over events. Because the person allows for approximate results, or nonexactitude, previously rejected elements may now be subsumed by constructs, or existing elements may even be placed at the opposite ends of the construct concerned. This can only mean that the discriminative function or contrast implied by the construct is weakened at the expense of its sameness function. Later in the chapter, we return to this idea in our speculations linking symmetrical and asymmetrical thought (Matte-Blanco 1988; Rayner, 1995) with Kelly's Creativity Cycle. An example may help. Using a bipolarity "gentle–violent," I may understand my friend as a gentle person today and as violent tomorrow, and perhaps gentle again the next day—even given relatively similar contextual conditions.[3] Loosening, therefore, is a description applied to construing, which operates amid this type of shifting of elements. It may also reduce anxiety by not exposing prediction to exact test. An awareness that my friend "really" is violent may be quite threatening or guilt-provoking, so loosening-up the meaning of "gentle–violent" may help one avoid these discomforts. The difference between "gentle" and "violent" is allowed to blur. In quite loose construing, almost any experience can fit one's anticipation. Even if predictions appear to be disconfirmed (to an onlooker), the loosely construing person may say, "that is practically what I said" (Kelly, 1955, p. 854). But even in the loosest of construing, Kelly asserts there is always some discriminative structure.

A construct does not exist in isolation. It is a summary term for an act of discrimination, an awareness operating within a system of associated meanings. The particular rules of association Kelly defined were ordinal, operating in terms of superordinate structures determining subordinate ones. Loosening, therefore, is simultaneously a description of the altered relations of a (subordinate) construct *and* of the hierarchies that subsume that construct. Loosening involves the operation of superordinate hierarchies that do not highlight what we might normally consider to be illogicalities. Rather than operating within strict ordinal relations, loose construing may involve more "lateral" associations, invoking more than one chain of construct implications either at a time or in succession. This also may help account for the expanded range of convenience of loose constructs.

One effect of loosening is to help us tolerate ambiguity while we experiment with ideas. On initial tightening, this experimentation is often rejected in the face of relevant evidence. On the other hand, the new construct may prove anticipatory; it may enable the person to understand or "fit" with events in a new, perhaps improved way. That is, tightening sometimes leads to new insights. Nonetheless, for Kelly, these new insights must be tested and integrated into the construct system before they earn the title of "genuine new insights."

The Experience Cycle: The Path to Genuine New Insights

The Experience Cycle represents the pathway to optimal psychological functioning in PCP, and it is where insight, for Kelly, finds its proper home. Roughly, the cycle is as follows: construal within a situation, imaginative involvement or commitment, affirmative anticipation in action, assessment of outcomes, and, finally, reconstrual. Or, as Kelly put it:

Imagination, once stirred, often leads to initiative, and initiative to action, and action produces something unexpected for men to contemplate and experience, and, finally, the newest experience throws the recollections of prior experiences into fresh perspective. (1980, p. 8)

Kelly seemed to use a narrow definition of "insight," one that was restricted to the "Aha!" experience where loosened construction is provisionally tightened. Thus, he viewed the "new constructs which arise out of loosened construction, not as the "true thoughts" or "insights" of the person, but as new hypotheses which still must be tightened up and tested before they are to accepted as useful" (1955, p. 530). But this view fits perfectly with the insight literature's emphasis of the profligacy of insight (Perkins, 1995; Simonton, 1997) and of the universal need to verify and elaborate the "Aha!" experience—for it to be integrated within the person's broader matrix of meanings. That is, this type of Kellian emphasis on pragmatic criteria is found in most contemporary accounts of insight. A PCP understanding of the integration of new constructs should, therefore, contribute to an understanding of the nature and experience of insight.

A direct parallel between the traditional stages of insight and Kelly's Experience Cycle (1955) can be made. With the exception of an incubation period, these stages of experience match the classic stages of Wallas (1926):

1. Preparation	Construal, involvement, commitment
2. Impasse	Unexpected events, invalidation, perhaps hostility
Incubation	No clear match
3. Insight	Stirred imagination; affirmative participation
4. Elaboration and Verification	Assessment and reconstrual

This process exemplifies Kelly's definition of a "genuine new insight" as a "comprehensive construction of one's behavior" found to be permeable enough to anticipate or fit with new events. Our invented constructs must be supported by discovery, by pragmatic results. New constructs need to be devised and revised, not because any construct is as good as another, but because of their relative efficacy. Indeed, the world and the person are cospecified in our construals and, within validated (viable) construing, person and world merge. Within invalidated (nonviable) construing, the person "bumps" into the world, experiencing this as a perturbation to the smooth flow of living or anticipation. When one no longer anticipates or fits with one's world, separateness (anxiety) is born. Reconstrual likely follows in an attempt to restore our sense of connection with our world, especially with others, even if it were via "hostility" or denial.

It seems to be in the "incubation" period that crucial work toward an experience of insight is undertaken. It is probably here that construct axes are (somewhat vaguely) "rotated" as cycles of loosening and tightening are undertaken.

The term "incubation," suggesting as it does "sleep," betrays our cultural biases toward verbalizable, conscious experience, but this period is unlikely to be a period of mental inactivity—whatever that might mean for a living person. Kelly's account of insight is underspecified in exactly this phase of awareness. One looks in vain in Kelly's writings for an account of loosening (and tightening) beyond descriptions of its effects or of methods for its manipulation. This is extraordinary, given the importance of these processes within his therapy. In a recent PCP-list discussion (October 20, 1998), Fay Fransella, a prominent PCP practitioner and author, recalled that Kelly repeatedly said he considered "loosening–tightening" his most important theoretical construct. Yet these processes are not built into the assumptive structure of his theory. As Bell (1996) has indicated, apart from the detailed treatment of loosening and tightening as *practical strategies* in therapy, they seem to fulfill an *ad hoc theoretical role* of accounting for psychological phenomena, such as fragmentation and perhaps construct revision, that are poorly accounted for by his formal fundamental postulate and corollaries.

Insight as a Means to Therapeutic Ends

The contents of insights are secondary, for Kelly, to the person's overall psychological adjustment and to the requirements of the construct system as a whole. Mastery of the Creativity Cycle, although an essential skill to be learned in therapy, is not sufficient for therapeutic success. The client must, in addition, learn to sort the wheat from the chaff, as it were, in relation to his or her insights.

The therapist seeks only to have the client work through a series of stages of "insight," partly so that he will attain a particular better mode of adjustment, partly so that he will learn *a way* to develop better and better modes of adjustment. The therapist teaches the client how to be creative in reconstruing his life. (1955, p. 1085, emphasis added)

It is evident that Kelly was interested, not in producing particular insights, but in engendering *a way* of dealing creatively with the world, of generating insights in an ongoing fashion. Each client was to be trained as a "constructive alternativist." Arriving at ever-fresh visions of what is worthwhile (Kelly, 1980) is a goal that one never quite attains; it extends beyond the therapy room into the person's future ventures. Developing the skill to generate and to integrate selected insights is a major goal of Personal Construct therapy. One has to learn how to become open to new elements in the context of one's constructs and how to "try on" new constructs and weave them into one's system of constructs.

Although therapy is not our focus here, Kelly's emphasis on enabling clients to develop their ability for creativity and insight is most relevant. In this regard, important questions remain. By what specific processes do we produce these new insights? How does a construct become more permeable or accommodate new elements within its purview? How do we assimilate a new construct, adjusting it and weaving it into the fabric of our system? In the next section, we try to answer these questions by analyzing Kelly's descriptions of loose and tight construing and by moving into a more speculative (loose) phase of our inquiry.

How to Generate Insights

Loosening Construing

There were four therapeutic strategies for inducing loosening in a client described by Kelly (1955, pp. 1033–1050). Loosening can be brought about by relaxation, by chain association, by recounting dreams, and by the therapist's uncritical acceptance of the client. Kelly (1955) does not explain how and why such processes lead to loosening, except to simply say that relaxation produces loosening and "because the [loose] structure is more resilient, [it is] often less likely to be shattered into anxiety" (p. 1034). More is said later about why such strategies might be conducive of loosening, but to indicate the path we wish to tread, being relaxed or feeling accepted and unthreatened are characterized *as a form of construing*, as a type of "transcending affect." It is characterized as a capacity to dwell in a nonanxious way within multiplicity, openness, and uncertainty. It may be that the normal implicative links to self and core constructs are suspended for a time to facilitate this.

The effects of therapeutic loosening are varied. Because certain elements are no longer "logically" ruled out, "forgotten" events might now be recalled. In addition, preverbal constructs may now be allowed to have approximate form in words or in figurative and nonverbal expression. Ideas can be combined in novel, experimental ways and, finally, the loosening of a preemptive construct by the inclusion of new elements may lead to the application/fashioning of other constructs relevant to the elements at hand.

But what happens during loosening apart from the (vague) "rotating" of the construct axis? Kelly suggested new elements come into one's field of attention, not now being "ruled out by logic-tight construction," and new experiences are thereby generated, including different responses from one's associates. The looseness generally extends the range of convenience of the construct and can make it more permeable to new experience. In addition, a loosened construct, when it starts to tighten, "begins to fall into place under some new forms of superordinate construction" (1955, p. 1050). This allows for new patterns of implication, for new possibilities in meaning as the new superordinating structure takes over, or subsumes, the remaining old elements in the changed construct while introducing its own range of elements. But Kelly does not explain *how* or *why* this loosening comes about, content as he was to describe its general features and therapeutic manipulation.

Kelly identified in loosening part of what he referred to as "schizoid" thinking. There is ample evidence that excessive loosening, that is loosening not subsumed within adequately permeable superordinate structures, can lead to considerable anxiety, even to a diagnosis of schizophrenia and thought disorder (Kelly, 1955, p. 497, see also Bell, 1996; Winter, 1992). Nonetheless, it is clear that loosening is neither inherently adaptive or maladaptive:

"Schizoid" thinking takes place, on occasion, in almost everyone; that it is characteristic of transitional stages in one's mental development; that it is even characteristic of the transitional stages in solving an ordinary problem; that it appears in the course of creative production; and that it may appear in some degree in any far-reaching adjustment. (1955, p. 866)

We see here the positive potential for creativity and insight that loosening provides. A crucial feature is that loose construction ("schizoid thinking") is a characteristic of *transition* within the construct system, and this introduces the topic of emotion in PCP.

Loosening and Emotion

One of Kelly's many original theoretical contributions was to characterize what normally goes under the title "emotion" in transitional terms: emotion as an awareness of change in one's propensity for anticipation. For example, "anxiety" was reconceptualized as an awareness that events were somewhat outside one's capacity to anticipate. "Threat" was defined as an awareness of imminent comprehensive change to one's core structures. Thus "emotion," in Kelly's terms, *is* a type of construing (consistent with his rejection of the tripartite division of mental life into cognition, affect, and conation). It is construing characterized by an awareness of the vicissitudes of construction and reconstruction and, because it frequently involves changes in constructs, it is intimately intertwined with cycles of loose and tight construction. McCoy (1977, 1981), in elaborating Kelly's "emotional" scheme, reasoned that positive emotion is generally related to awareness of the success of one's anticipations, whereas negative emotions are related to an awareness of one's unsuccessful attempts to anticipate. It is noteworthy that the content of a "positive" emotion need not be pleasurable, only that anticipation was successful. As construct systems are dynamic processes always in transition, emotionality is potentially always present within construing—its intensity varying with the implications judged to flow from the incipient changes. Construing may be "nonemotional" to the extent that its content does not include awareness of the validational fortunes and incipient changes within our construct system.

Of particular interest here, in our inquiry into insight, is what occurs after impasse. We have noted that impasse is frequently characterized by denial or "hostility," as Kelly defined it. That is, the problem-solver cannot see beyond previously invalidated solutions, because these ways of being have worked in "similar" situations in the past, or because the implied changes to constructs are too threatening, or both. But what occurs when/if hostility is abandoned? Perhaps the person will constrict, thus cutting off potential reconstruction as well as the awareness of any need for change. Or if the person is confident in these matters of impasse and insight, loosening may be a deliberate "metacognitive" and "aggressive" strategy, one learned from previous breakthroughs. Alternatively, anxiety may lead to loosening of construing as the person defensively attempts to defocus his or her "inadequate" construing. This implies that within loose construing, we experience *less* emotion. When one attempts to be aware of, to validate the implications of the now-tightening construct, "emotional" experience occurs. And this brings us to the question of tightening.

Tightening Construing

Tighter construing, on the other hand, is brought about by a wide variety of techniques. These include time, place, person and word binding, judging or evaluating one's constructions, the client or therapist verbally summarizing the constructions concerned, using historical explanation, relating one's thinking to others, the therapist asking for explanation or clarification, the therapist challenging the construction, enacting one's constructions, forming clear concepts, and asking for validating evidence. The effects of tightening include defining or making explicit what the person is predicting or anticipating, stabilizing construction so that the person's behavior is less capricious, facilitating the organization of ordinal relationships within the construct system, reducing some constructs to impermeability, and encouraging specific experimentation based on clear hypotheses. And we might add to these that it is often when we tighten up loose construing that we may experience "emotion." That is, when we become aware of the implications for our construct system of the construing that is being tightened up, we can be said to be construing "emotionally."

The basic operation within tightening is placing the construct more firmly within a structure of ordinal (hierarchic) relationships and implications. As Kelly said: "When one construes loosely and his constructs are not bound by superordinate structures, he may be 'experiencing' only. When one construes tightly, it becomes possible, though not inevitable, for his constructs to be fitted into a system" (1955, p. 1068). The more explicit the placement of elements within a construct, the more "tightly" it can be subsumed within a hierarchical structure, allowing for consistent implication and more explicit anticipation. This implies that loosening corresponds to the relative undoing of this hierarchic, implicative structure—a loss of structure normally associated with anxiety. But perhaps deliberate loosening within superordinate "emotional assessments" of nonthreat, or of one's overall anticipatory competence, allays potential anxiety. This reflects the role given to "metacognitions," in the cognitive insight literature, that frame what is happening, making difficulties and frustration meaningful, even subjectively "positive."

Tightening and Emotion

At an emotional level—in terms of an awareness of the anticipatory fortunes of our construing process—such a "fitting into a system" of a newly formed construct would be experienced as "positive" (McCoy, 1977, 1981), even if, further down the track, the implications prove threatening or anxiety-provoking in other areas of the system. Thus, Kelly was cautious about preemptively embracing moments of insight in therapy. Nonetheless, here we see a plausibly simple account of the joy and positive affect universally associated with the moment of insight. In particular, the type and degree of positive affect is related to whether core or peripheral constructs are involved, and whether comprehensive or incidental change is at stake. For example, comprehensive validation of core structures can lead to an experience of "love" (McCoy, 1977), whereas similar partial validation is related to "happiness" and "joy"; or "contentment" is related to an awareness of the adequate anticipatory function of one's system, and so on. Such emotional states seem to be ubiquitous in insight experiences.

Alternatively, when loose construing is tightened and does not fit into a system of implications (leads to confusion or contradiction), anxiety may be experienced due to the lack of anticipatory structure. This can lead to further loosening and to distortions of thought and perception (Bell, 1996) and to an inability to predict and make sense of events. Or, again, if the superordinate system under which one tightens construing is open to creativity, ambiguity, and experimentation, then initial anticipatory failures may be taken in the person's reconstructive stride. Further "aggressive" Creativity Cycles may then be undertaken.

PCP AND THE INSIGHT LITERATURE: COMPARISONS AND CONTRASTS

It is now time to see what concordances and differences exist between our reading of insight, in PCP terms, and the four general findings of the insight literature reported earlier.

High Levels of Abstraction

Kelly's account of loosening and tightening required that more permeable, superordinate structures "take over" the loosened construct and allow new elements and new implications to be related to it as it takes form. This movement to alternative superordinate (abstract) structures begins with the weakening of the discriminative power of the relevant construct(s). This looseness parallels the typical insight literature finding of a tolerance for ambiguity, a capacity to entertain "contradictories" (omnivalence) and the sort of "metacognitive" processes (construing one's construing) that provisional tightening could represent. This shift to other construct subsystems builds a bridge across which creative analogies and metaphors may be found. As suggested earlier, however, Kelly provides little explicit description of how and why this shifting between systems comes about—a matter we return to in a later section.

Two Types of Mental Processes: Tacit versus Explicit

Kelly (1955) considered that construing is not exclusively, or even primarily, a conscious experience. Rather, it takes place at various levels of cognitive awareness. Tacit or intuitive understandings are as much construing as are highly conscious, verbalized constructions. Kelly (1955) gave a number of reasons for construction to be tacit. There may be a lack of viable structure in which the discrimination can be presented for conscious reflection (submergence, suspension, extreme looseness), or it may simply be "preverbal"—a catch-all term Kelly (1955) used to describe construing not symbolized in words. Generally speaking, verbalizing construing tends to make it tighter (though not all tight construing need be verbalized/verbalizable). Thus, as reported in the general insight literature, verbalizing tends to be destructive of more fluid, tacit constructive processes.

Parallels can be drawn between loose construction and tacit awareness, and between tight construction and more explicit, conscious understanding. Loose construction need not be tacit or unconscious, though it has this tendency because of its characteristic, fluid discriminative structure. The looser the construing, the less likely it will be at a high level of awareness.[4] Tight construing, on the other hand, being well integrated within ordinal structures of implication, is more often available to conscious reflection. The alternation between loose and tight construing is directly comparable to the typical, ongoing alternation between tacit and explicit mental processes in the insight literature. In addition, the techniques Kelly devised to elicit loose and tight construction mirror those working activities reported by eminently creative people (Epel, 1993; Gardner, 1993; Gruber, 1995).

Although Kelly is full of praise for adventurousness, for ceaseless curiosity and openness to change, we do not find in his writings the insight literature's emphasis on abstract imagery, of reverie or flow, of feelings of knowing, and so on. Nor does Kelly mention a qualitatively different experience of self within the insight experience—especially of the often-reported sense of "connectedness" or "oneness" with one's world. We have seen that he had pragmatic reasons for his emphases, being much more interested in the verification and integration of insights. Nonetheless, we may find in a further exploration of such "transpersonal" phenomena clues not only to the genesis of insight, but to an expanded way of being that it represents. This is a way of being that inspired Kelly to encourage us to "transcend the obvious," to dare to alter even our fundamental assumptions. Significantly, this requires pragmatic commitment, daring, and courage, not an abstract separation from the world.

Social and Pragmatic Dimensions of Insight

This chapter began with Kelly's impassioned entreaty to immerse ourselves in the world, to embrace the pragmatic nature of our anticipations. Pragmatism emphasizes the interrelatedness of mind and world—especially our social world.

We are constrained by, and a part of, the environing "other." The personal, social, and pragmatic are inextricably intertwined as our psychological world is, arguably, firstly interpersonal and only later apparently "private." For example, Walker (1996) has written of the misleading implications drawn from the word "personal" in the title Kelly gave his theory. Indeed, Kelly (1955, p. 179) admits to entertaining the term "Role Theory" for his approach, thereby positioning sociality in particular as central to his whole theory. Both the pragmatic (Stevens, 1998; Warren, 1998) and social (Butt, 1998; Kalekin-Fishman & Walker, 1996; Stam, 1998; see also chapter 3 by Stojnov & Butt in this book) implications of PCP are of current research interest. There is much to be done in elaborating these aspects of PCP, but space precludes and this must wait for another occasion.

Although Kelly (1955) did not spell out the social and pragmatic dimensions of insight, his approach is thoroughly concordant with the insight literature findings in this regard. What is clear is the parallel already drawn between the stages of insight and the stages of the Experience Cycle. The person goes through characteristic alternations: between abstract processes and concrete action; between solitude and social interaction; between silence and conversation; between tight, well-practiced understandings and looser, more fluid processes. Thus, Kelly sets out in some detail how to manage loose and tight construing, especially in Volume 2 of his grand opus (1955), and this is in close concordance with the reported day-to-day practical engagement of eminently creative people. Moreover, the whole thrust of his therapy is to integrate new understandings within the person's life, to test and validate, to reconsider, to test again, to reconstrue, and so on. At a deeper level, this approach to insight views it as something one does, as a type of situated action. Insight processes are a pragmatic coupling with one's environing "other"—be that people, the physical world, discourses, and so on. Later, we suggest how this is experienced as an altered sense of self within insight processes.

The Role of "Emotional Thought" in Insight

We have seen that insight is constituted as much by "emotional" as "cognitive" processes, and we have also seen that Kelly (1955) characterized construing in similar terms. He did not so much banish emotional experience from his theory (see Bruner, 1956; Rogers, 1956) as offer a new way of conceiving of it. Emotions are presented as forms of awareness, and gone is the ancient opposition of irrational emotion and logical reason (Bannister, 1977; Warren, 1998). Our "rational" being is not separate from the "lived equivalence-difference patterns" that define us, including, for example, the facial expressions, racing heartbeat, sweaty palms, and short sharp breaths of panic.

Our elaboration of insight in PCP terms has posited a central role for "emotional thinking." Emotion frequently arises as we turn our attention to newly emerging constructs. Kelly (1955) underspecified this affective role in his explicit account of insight. Generally, he considered that the construct system was designed to be "anxiety-tight," but in insight, we see the possibility for another motivational vector: the contrasting positive emotional experiences. Fortunately, McCoy (1977, 1981) has elaborated Kelly's "emotional" scheme, supplementing his definitions with complementary "positive" emotions. To explain the phenomenology of insight, this is absolutely essential. As we have seen, negative emotions are inimical to insight, whereas a state of evenly hovering, equanimous attention is conducive of creative thought. This recalls McCoy's (1977) definitions of "contentment" and "satisfaction" as reflecting a subjective faith and security in one's anticipatory abilities. Creative practitioners of all kinds have reported their deliberate cultivation of this attitude in pursuit of insight (Csikszentmihalyi, 1990). Herein is a paradox at the heart of creativity: We are born to anticipate events (Kelly's Fundamental Postulate), yet Kelly (1977) encourages us to abandon even our "favorite" understandings, muster up daring, and expose ourselves to uncertainty—even to "reconstrue life altogether."

Within PCP, as with the insight literature, emotional experiences and challenges are constitutive of insight. Calmness and relaxation, which we have conceived of as a style of superordinate construing, allow for subordinate loosening. Self-consciousness (related to core construing) is backgrounded, and there is a slowing down of thought, a flow of construction guided by subjective "feel" rather than critical judgment. This is reminiscent of a more "meditative thought" (Heidegger, 1978), which allows for the suspension of judgment so widely reported in insight research as a prelude to breakthrough. We then proposed that provisional tightening of loose construing, a type of "affective assessment" (Rychlak, 1968, 1977), either confirms the frustration of impasse or leads to the relief and joy of insight.

EMOTION AND MIND:
SOME CONTEMPORARY PROPOSALS

Contemporary theorizing about the relation of emotion and mind promises to move us forward in our inquiry. Neurophysiological evidence, for example, suggests that emotionality is involved in the ordering of our thinking (Bechara et al., 1997; Damasio, 1994; Goleman, 1995; LeDoux, 1995). Similarly, within PCP, "emotional" construing is involved in modulating changes within the construct system, and Kelly encourages "provisional" tightenings within the Creativity Cycle. That is, we believe he urges a type of nonurgent, playful, affective awareness that alternates with, and permits again, loose understandings.

Primary and Secondary Emotions: An Important Distinction

It is not just any sort of emotion that can effectively enable people to take uncertainty in stride. We mentioned earlier a distinction between emotion and affect we borrowed from Rychlak's Logical Learning Theory (1968, 1977, see note 1). Essentially, this is that whereas "emotion" is a general term—which may include more-or-less instinctive or innate responses—"affect" implies a psychological "assessment." It affirms one possibility, one meaning in an event, aware at the same time that "it could have gone another way." But what of pan-cultural, "wired-in" emotional responses, the evidence for which has expanded and consolidated considerably since Kelly's day (LeDoux, 1995; McCoy, 1977; Tomkins, 1962)? The fear response and its accompanying physiological changes, for example, do not seem to depend on personal constructions. It is unlikely we all happened to construct the same basic emotional patterns. Rather, it seems we begin with a basic subconstructive repertoire that is endlessly elaborated and refined. But the basis appears to be given.

This distinction between innate and constructed emotions is considered to be paralleled in the physiology of two proposed "emotion" pathways in the brain. The first is a very fast, "instinctive" path utilizing the "old brain" through a single synapse from the thalamus to the amygdala—the latter operating as a type of emotional "sentinel" for experience (Goleman, 1995). The second, slower, and more "reflective" path (the "standard route") runs from the thalamus via a much larger projection of nerves to the prefrontal lobes (implicated with "working memory") and thence to the neocortex generally (Goleman, 1995; Le Doux, 1995). In this second "emotional" pathway, much more sensory "information" is argued to be available and, crucially, the prefrontal area appears to be able to enhance or inhibit the response of the amygdala. That is, the prefrontal cortices have "links to every avenue of motor and chemical response available to the brain" (Damasio, 1994, p. 181). In short, secondary affective constructions are proposed to have a certain capacity to inhibit and activate innately provided emotional pathways.

Most of the brain's activity is concerned with intrabrain "communication." The psychological counterpart of this is that memories and so on can also stimulate activity in the amygdala and the limbic system, engendering emotional experience independently of sensory "input." In this way, the basic emotional range is added to, refined, expanded exponentially, and thoroughly interlaced with thought. This leads to a distinction between "primary" and "secondary" emotions (Damasio, 1994; Goleman, 1995). Constructed, emotionally coded "pathways" are thought to be "hooked into" the amygdala-related emotional complex, leading to the well-documented findings that decision-making and intuitive preferences are often "faster than thought" (Claxton, 1997, 1998; Zajonc, 1980).

To this extent we can, therefore, divide emotions into relatively involuntary and voluntary processes, each mediated by different neurological networks but both emanating from the amygdala (LeDoux, 1995). At least in relation to fear, some fascinating implications follow from this. People demonstrate individual differences in their capacity to have insight into their emotions. For whatever reason (genetic or experiential, or both), people may vary in the degree to which "lower-order" pathways or "higher-order" pathways are capable of triggering emotional experience. Moreover, LeDoux (1995) points out that memories associated with the amygdala appear to be indelible. This reflects the well-known therapeutic experience that, for example, traumatic emotional memories tend to transcend time and never seem to be completely erased. One implication is that extinction of such memories involves inhibition (submergence or suspension in Kelly's terms), not erasure, and "the role of therapy may be to allow the cortex to establish more effective and efficient synaptic links with the amygdala" (LeDoux, 1995, p. 229). This implies not only that we may be able to inhibit indelible emotional responses, but also that we may be able to modulate and utilize emotional pathways generally.

It is possible that very fast, nonconsciously mediated emotional responses are forms of "primitive" construing (Katz, 1984). Such ecologically programmed survival responses would be highly superordinate, constraining large-scale networks of subordinate construction. For example, Damasio's (1994) "somatic markers" are special feelings generated from "secondary" emotions. Through constructive experience, primary feelings and emotions become connected to anticipated events, highlighting various options and eliminating others. According to this idea, intuition would be an example of covert somatic markers in which there is a very fast preselection of options carried out according to biologically informed preferences or "values." Contemporary theorists (Claxton, 1997; Goleman, 1995; LeDoux, 1995) have suggested that such emotional processes are "quick and dirty" appraisals that predispose us toward certain actions and decisions, and away from others.

Neuroanatomical development seems to suggest that very early memories may be "emotional" ones, because the networks subserving declarative conscious memories do not mature sufficiently until the second or third year (LeDoux, 1995). The development of early constructs, especially dependency constructs[5], could be built on the basis of an innate predisposition to divide experience into positive and negative emotional construals. It is not that we have direct, "objective" access to these body-based emotional patterns, that they directly determine our thinking. Rather, we find converging evidence for the idea that there are universal, innate, survival-related emotional processes that constrain and abide in our constructions. They are in just as much need of construal as anything else in the world. Indeed, being able to "place them within a system," to tighten them up as it were, may be one of our most pressing life tasks and linked to our highest achievements.

This leads directly to the proposal that emotion preceded reason both in evolutionary terms and in each person's ontogenesis and that it forms the basis of thought. Langer (1972) argued that symbolic thought emerged from the human being's highly active emotionality, from the "values" thereby imposed on experience. Rational decision-making is inoperable without such inherent preference mechanisms (Bechara et al., 1997; Zajonc, 1980) that predispose us to certain affirmations and steer us away from others. "Normal" thinking seems to require recourse to "emotional" pathways in the brain. "Gut feelings" and intuitions may well use the same predisposing neural mechanisms as the innate emotional responses.

Passive and Active Emotions

One way of understanding the point being made here is to map it onto a distinction made by the 17th-century philosopher Spinoza (1967) between "passive" and "active" emotional states (Warren, 1987, 1998). Passive emotions, or "passions," are those that lack adequate ideas to explain one's state, and these occasion "pain." Active emotions are of the "intellect" and contribute to one's anticipation of events, thereby engendering "pleasure." All emotions are seen as partly constituted by the thoughts associated with them. Spinoza's third primary emotion was desire, or "conatus" as he more generally called it. Warren (1987) describes this as a tendency to self-preservation that underpins our anticipatory efforts. The parallel to Kelly's (1955) Fundamental Postulate—"A person's psychological processes are chanellized by the ways in which he anticipates events"—is obvious. This is Kelly's version of the "conatus." And McCoy's (1981) distinction between positive and negative emotion corresponds to Spinoza's distinction between active and passive emotion, respectively.

Spinoza alerts us to the importance of transcending the "passions," not by an emotionless reason, but by a transcending affective stance. "Passions" arise from more-or-less unconstrued responses following contact with the external world (or changes within the body). This relative passivity means such emotions are often contrary to the person's "conatus." Active emotions, however, constitute the ability to proactively anticipate events while recognizing oneself as the source and ground for one's emotions. That is, in the grip of negative (passive) emotion one is (ideally) obliged to reconstrue.

A PROVISIONAL TIGHTENING:
KELLY, INSIGHT, AND EMOTION

We have posited a type of transcending affect that, depending on its permeability and degree of comprehensiveness, can modulate primary emotional responses. In construing this way, the person can utilize some of the features of "primary" emotional processes. One such feature is the making of broad, quick-and-dirty "appraisals," viewing multiple possibilities very quickly, screening out many, predisposing us to others. In the face of ill-defined problems, such a skill is essential given the vast combinatorial possibilities that may confront the problem-solver (Perkins, 1997). Such a transcending affective stance also allows for a slowing down of "normal," highly practiced, propositional thought (Claxton, 1997). This superordinate affective stance is a relatively loose form of construing that "allows" subordinate discontinuities, even absurdities (i.e., from a tightly construed vantage point).

We have seen that Kelly's account of insight illuminates the four major findings of the insight literature:

1. The importance of shifts in levels of abstraction,
2. The alternation between explicit and tacit levels of awareness,
3. The social and pragmatic dimensions of insight, and
4. The role of "emotional" thought.

But along the way we have noticed certain gaps in Kelly's account. First, we noted that there was no account for how loosening and tightening allows us to shift between apparently "unrelated" constructs. We also found little that reflected the literature's emphasis on abstract imagery and reverie that often leads to a profoundly different sense of self. Connected with this latter sense is "emotional" construing. We suggested Kelly underspecified the role of affective construing in insight. We then introduced McCoy's (1977) elaboration of Kellyan emotions and connected the provisional tightening of loose construing with a transcending affective assessment (Rychlak, 1968).

But more was needed. We undertook an analysis of current research into emotion, because the evidence concerning insight and emotion was pointing outside Kelly's definitions of emotion. We drew the distinction between primary and secondary emotions. Spinoza helped us to view the gradations of emotion—from relatively innate response patterns to abstract, rationally structured affective assessments—in terms of the adequacy of the ideas that informed them. But why does emotion have the capacity to open up possibilities, to engender creativity and make for quantum jumps in understanding? We are in need of other conceptual dimensions that can carry us further in our quest for insight into insight. It is to Matte-Blanco's (1975, 1988) distinction between *asymmetrical* and *symmetrical* thinking that we now turn to look at how these complementary processes may deepen our understanding of loose and tight construing.

MATTE-BLANCO AND THE SYSTEM UNCONSCIOUS

Bell (1996) argued that loose construing best matches the five main features of Freud's (1911) unconscious and of primary process thinking. These features are (a) the absence of mutual contradiction, (b) condensation, (c) timelessness, (d) displacement, and (e) replacement of external by internal reality. Bell was interested in how cognitive-perceptual disorders are related to loose construing, and he turned to Matte-Blanco's (1975, 1988) account of the system unconscious, and of conscious thought, to help explicate loosening and tightening. We, too, consider that Matte-Blanco's account may provide an understanding of insight beyond Kelly's explanation of the creativity cycle.

Asymmetrical and Symmetrical Processes

Matte-Blanco (1975, 1988) proposed that conceptualization can be thought of in terms of sets[6] that can be related in two ways: asymmetrically and symmetrically. Asymmetrical relationships are based in difference, are "rational," and are hierarchic, whereas symmetrical relationships are based on sameness, are "irrational," and are equivalent. Applying this to the framework of PCP, as Bell (1996) does, asymmetrical relationships function as do ordinal relationships between constructs as set out in the Organization Corollary. That is, they operate in terms of transitive "If . . . Then" implications, allowing for prediction of the following kind:

If A, . . . then B.

If B, . . . then C.

Given A, . . . therefore C.

It follows that the converse of an asymmetrical relation is not equivalent. Thus, "John is taller than Mary" does not equal "Mary is taller than John." If "Mary is taller than Anne," it also follows that "John is taller than Anne," and so on. Symmetrical relationships, on the other hand, demonstrate relations of sameness and of reversibility. This appears illogical to highly conscious, asymmetrical thinking. For example, "Mary is taller than John" can, under "symmetrization" of thought, be held to be equivalent to "John is taller than Mary."

Matte-Blanco (1975, 1988) suggested that symmetrical thought shares some of the properties of infinite sets. A (mathematical) property of infinite sets is that each element can stand in one-to-one relation with a part or subset of its set. An example of this is given in Rayner (1995) concerning the relationship between the set of natural numbers and the set of even numbers. It appears there will be twice as many natural numbers as even numbers. But because every natural number is exactly one half of its corresponding even number, then *each* element (natural number) can be related to a subset of its elements (even numbers). A subset can, in some loose fashion, be *identified* or equated with the whole set.

Set of natural numbers: {1, 2, 3, 4, 5, . . .}

Set of perfect squares: {2, 4, 6, 8, 10, . . .}

Although notions of size and equality are problematic within infinite sets, it is clear that the "normal" rules and comparisons of sets break down under the appearance of infinity. Matte-Blanco believed that conceptualization in the unconscious operates in analogous, symmetrical fashion. Thus, in symmetrical thought, elements flout classical laws of (asymmetrical) logic and can be identified with the whole set and, thereby, in deeper levels of symmetry, to all the elements within the set. Symmetrical thought, where only sameness is recognized, is pervasive in the unconscious and influential in emotional states.

Dimensions of Awareness

Matte-Blanco (1975, 1988) also argued that asymmetrical and symmetrical thought differed in terms of their dimensionality. Asymmetrical thought is confined to the three spatial dimensions plus time, whereas symmetrical thought (including strong emotion) operates within a higher dimensionality. It is this characteristic of symmetrical thought that keeps it relatively "unconscious," only entering full consciousness indirectly by way of figurative, metaphorical, and nonverbal expression. Matte-Blanco (1988) compared the types of mathematical distortions that occur when we try to represent something of higher dimension in terms of fewer dimensions with attempts to translate unconscious contents into conscious thoughts. Typically, distortions appear where elements are repeated. The more the dimensional reduction, the greater the repetitions and distortions (see Bell, 1996, and Rayner, 1995, for discussions). Such (consciously recognized) distortions and contradictions are ideally "contained" within asymmetrical thought flexible enough to accommodate the "contradictories." This would be an example of bimodal thought.

Bimodal Thought

Symmetry tends to reign in the unconscious, whereas asymmetry is characteristic of (though not confined to) conscious, "rational" thought. Matte-Blanco (1988) makes it clear that optimal mental functioning involves *both* principles working in harmony. In such *bimodal* thought, all levels of consciousness are felt. The symmetrical aspects create a felt depth and dimensionality to one's awareness, but do not override consistent, asymmetrical inference. The registration of sameness or symmetry is a necessary component of "rational" thought:

when abstraction occurs in logical thought, and identity (symmetry) is discovered; but it is immediately circumscribed by awareness that there are a great many properties that *distinguish* from each other the items under scrutiny. (Rayner, 1995, p. 78)

This is bimodality. The symmetrical is bounded by asymmetry, and consistent inference is maintained. In rich and emotionally evocative imagination, the two logics work in harmony. Insight may reflect this harmony as a bringing into awareness of a dimensionality and a sense of infinity unavailable by asymmetrical means alone. Moreover, Matte-Blanco (1988) considers the "indivisible mode" (symmetry) to be the ground or basis of all consciousness.

Bilogic

Of course not all thinking operates so ideally. It is when asymmetrical and symmetrical processes alternate or occur simultaneously, but not in concert, that cognitive-perceptual distortions appear. This is called *bilogical* thought. Within bilogic, we may become aware of the intransitivity and illogicalities of our awareness, and this can be anxiety- or threat-provoking. Because symmetrization is the process of ignoring asymmetrical relationships and implications, in this state object and subject may not be discriminated and it can be close to an experience of just Being. Abstracted conceptions, attributes, or intuitions ("loveliness," "evil," "niceness") are floating relatively free of specific relations. Rayner (1995) refers to bilogical structures as manifesting "looseness." Within the looser, symmetrical awareness, we may not be aware of the inconsistencies—which, of course, parallels the suggestion made earlier that we may loosen construing to avoid awareness of anticipatory failures. Awareness of inconsistencies, and often negative affect, occurs upon the return to asymmetrical thought.

Levels of Consciousness

Matte-Blanco outlined five levels or strata of consciousness. At the fifth level, symmetrization reaches a logical limit where everything is identified with everything else. In contrast, at the first stratum, analytical rational distinction-making (asymmetrical thought) reigns. Within the "lower" (third to fifth) strata, anxiety and threat may not be experienced because there is little access to invalidation in the form of a more asymmetrical awareness of contradictions and inconsistencies. The unconscious is unconscious because its higher dimensionality cannot be grasped within conscious thought. For example, emotion (which is found in relatively asymmetrical form at the second stratum and in more "unconscious" symmetrical form in the third stratum) is characterized by "a greater number of dimensions than that which our self-awareness is capable of dealing" (Matte-Blanco, 1988, p. 91).

In support of Matte-Blanco's scheme, there is emerging evidence (Gilhooly, Keane, Logie, & Erdos, 1990) that concepts and emotional schemas tend to be processed differently. For example, there is a lack of differentiation in the processing of phobic stimuli in favor of fast activation of highly cohesive prototypes (Watts, 1990). That is, this type of emotional experience tends to work in terms of similarity judgments or resemblances (symmetry) rather than distinctions and differences (asymmetry). Emotional thought tends to be associative and simultaneously activates clusters of similar concepts and schemas.

MATTE-BLANCO, PCP, AND INSIGHT: SOME IMPLICATIONS

We now suggest some parallels between what Matte-Blanco was saying about the system unconscious and the nature of personal construing.

Tight and Loose Construing and Bipolarity

Bimodal thought can be seen as "textbook" bipolar construing where a construct is defined as a simultaneous awareness of sameness-yet-difference. Take, for example, the following definition of bimodal thought:

When classification works with a two-valued logicality, different members of a class remain distinct individuals but are seen as similar though different; they have some class-defining quality or attribute in common. (Rayner, 1995, p. 47)

Tight constructs tend toward asymmetry as they are characterized by both consistency of inference and are based on a clear distinction between their contrasting elements. Loose construing is akin to symmetry or sameness where the basis for the bipolar distinction of the elements within a construct's range begins to dissolve and contradictories (to the tightly construing mind) can be held in mind simultaneously. Loosening reveals that construct membership may at times be fuzzy. That is, elements may no longer clearly belong at one pole or another (or even inside or outside the construct's range of convenience). This is contrary to Kelly's (1955) Dichotomy and Range corollaries, whereby elements are viewed as either at one pole or another of a construct (or not within the construct at all).

Symbolization and Ordinal Relations

Kelly (1955, pp. 297–299) gives an example of symbolization wherein "mother" can be both an element in a construct (set of elements arranged in sameness–difference relations) and may also, for the construing person, stand as the name or symbol for the entire set. This opens the possibility for the identification of "mother" with all elements in the construct—including the elements of the contrast pole. This is directly analogous to the relations observable in infinite sets, in which elements can come to stand for the whole set (a symmetrical relationship). This "raising" of an element to a symbolic status opens up unusual implicative possibilities, especially with other constructs sharing a number of similar elements. Specifically, this can help us account for the "lateral" (associative or based on sameness) shifting to other trains of implications so ubiquitous in accounts of insight. It begins with an abstractive move "up" the ordinal ladder as it were, but progresses by a "descent" utilizing other "nonrelated" or "illogical" trains of implication. That is, there is a type of symmetrical, associative logic that alternates with asymmetrical construing—making what appears to the conscious mind (to strictly asymmetrical or tight construing) as "quantum jumps."

This, of course, has implications for Kelly's Organization Corollary. We propose that in loose construing, shifts between ordinal levels can occur "illogically" (not in terms of superordinate and subordinate relationships) because various constructs sharing similar elements can be activated simultaneously. This multi-dimensionality, or simultaneous activation of multiple trains of implication, could reflect the massively parallel nature of brain activation, most of which does not reach consciousness. Perhaps loosening construing allows for a more widely spread, simultaneous, activation of multiple constructs containing similar elements—making for more fluctuating, "fuzzy" anticipations.

Martindale's (1995) connectionist theory of insight suggests just this. In "normal" focused attention, only the most practiced neural networks would be sufficiently activated to push them above the threshold for consciousness. Such a "steep association gradient" leads to fewer, more stereotypical responses. In defocused attention, however, the activation is spread widely, activating many more networks—a "shallow association gradient" that maximizes the possibility for remote associates and creative analogies. In this regard, electroencephalographic (EEG) measures indicate that "creatives" show the same increases in cortical activation in solving well-defined problems as "normals," but, in fact, show *less than their baseline* cortical activation when involved in ill-defined creative tasks (Csikszentmihalyi, 1990), thus suggesting an empirical measure for focused and defocused attention.

Bell (1996) has, in fact, shown that many construct relations are symmetrical. About 20% of construct relations in standard grids and 30% in implications grids are mutually implicative, rather than ordered hierarchically. As such, they stand outside the formal assumptive structure of the theory (e.g., the Organization and Modulation Corollaries). In similar fashion, Butt (1995) has found that construct hierarchies often loop back again. Interestingly, this symmetricality helps to explain one of Kelly's (1955) corollaries, the Fragmentation Corollary, which allows for inferential incompatibility (intransitivity) between constructs. That is, some of the relations between constructs are more strongly based on similarities or sameness rather than on ordinal differences.

Emotion: A Pivot to Insight

Emotion is the mother of all invention. (Matte-Blanco, 1988, p. 98)

Matte-Blanco felt emotion occupied a kind of creative hinterland between symmetry and asymmetry, and here we find echoes of Kelly's (1955, p. 866) claim that "schizoid" thinking, or the loosening of construing, is always present in "creative productions." Rayner (1995, p. 123) described "a level of optimal emotionality that will allow infinite and finite to meet for those mysterious and fruitful moments of a quantum leap." This represents an optimal balance between looseness and tightness, playing the "edges" of emotionality. Too little asymmetricality and the loosening runs away with itself into distortions of thinking and perception. Too much asymmetricality and our thinking is shallow and brittle, without recognition of pattern or regularities, and vulnerable to new experience.

Here we find further grounds for a useful cross-fertilization between Matte-Blanco and Kelly.

Emotion, as defined by Kelly, can be seen as belonging to the second stratum or level of consciousness, where emotionality is more or less conscious and where there are reasonably distinguishable and separate elements within a class or construct. This more or less corresponds to Kelly's definition of loose construing in that there is still identifiable structure within a weakened bipolarity. Why should emotional construing be akin to looser construing? Recall the recent research into emotion. Emotions are described as "quick-and-dirty," holistic appraisals of inner and outer reality in the service of one's maintenance processes. Emotional awareness operates in terms of organismically based values: Does this impede my coupling with my world, or enhance it? Such an awareness has system-wide access, both neurologically and psychologically. When we appraise emotionally, we are not interested in small detail or distinctions. We take a global perspective, a panoramic view, discounting local contradictions and incompatibilities in favor of the big picture. And our emotional appraisals are not always consistent. They can change from day to day, even from hour to hour. In Kellyan terms, they are often superordinate, permeable, and comprehensive structures, and are relatively loose. Consider "threat," the awareness of imminent comprehensive changes to one's core construing. Such an awareness must take an overview of some of the system's most superordinate and comprehensive constructions.

Granting this, emotions are often moves toward a "higher" complexity of awareness because they are of a higher dimensionality. This makes them more difficult to capture in consciousness. Using Martindale's (1995) metaphor of defocused attention and shallow association gradients (see earlier discussion), emotional thought is a style of construing that activates many concepts in parallel. And this perfectly matches Matte-Blanco's definitions of symmetrical thought, involving simultaneous chains of implication that can be expressed often only symbolically and figuratively.

Bilogic, Negative Emotion, and Invalidation

If negative emotion occurs following unsuccessful anticipation, usually the construct system will tighten up. The person will constrict his or her perceptual field and may construe in hostile fashion and become angry if challenged. Or, if this no longer seems possible, he or she may continue loosening, moving into more and more symmetrical realms, and avoiding provisional tightening and the testing of anticipations. Distortions of perception and cognition can result. The person may reenter asymmetrical or tighter construing and may experience very strong negative emotion, becoming aware of the expanding intransitivities and illogicalities in his or her thinking. This is the experience of bilogic. In Spinozan terms, such a person is in the grip of passive emotion, where one's ideas cannot "capture" or "channel" one's experience. One's anticipatory capacity is in tatters. In deepening symmetrization, each time one tries to tighten construction, *every-*

thing is seen as outside one's capacity to construe. This was Kelly's (1955) concern about overzealous therapists who were impatient for their clients to realize how widespread their hostilities were. Such clients can end up in a psychotic state, because they do not have sufficiently permeable and comprehensive superordinate structures to accommodate the burgeoning implications.

Positive Emotion and Bimodal Thought

Positive emotion is the likely concomitant of bimodal thought—where symmetrical thought is in harmony with one's asymmetrical awareness. Being in a more meditative or defocused state of attention, such as that induced by dream reporting, relaxation, word association, uncritical acceptance, and meditation, may encourage one to stay within looser construing long enough for nonhabitual patterns of inference to be explored. In a way, it is using one's innate emotional capacities voluntarily, deliberately. Herein lies the possibility for new insight. One has to learn to trust one's intuitions and feelings when tighter construing fails.

Within the Creativity Cycle, provisional tightening is the crucial moment, the pivot on which insight may turn. The person remains in an optimal level of looseness or symmetricality, and does not tighten too much. One may undergo gentle modulations between associative then discriminative processes, rocking back and forth until something looks promising. This is a transcending affective state in which there is a balance between open possibility and structured distinction-making. This ongoing (emotional) appraisal of the anticipatory implications of the tightening construct is an instance of our innate tendency, our intuitive sensitivity, to our viability or fit in our world. Incipient invalidation "feels bad" and is avoided. Incipient validation is felt before it is consciously understood.

A Different Sense of Self

One of the intriguing findings in the insight literature is the oft-reported experience that one's sense of self is altered within the process of insight. People report a loss of the sense of time and of place (defining features of symmetrical awareness), and they sense that the insight is flowing spontaneously but not being directed by themselves (Epel, 1993). The positive emotion intrinsic to insight casts everything in its hues. All is united and connected (a positive symmetrical experience) and this sets the person at peace, allowing for sustained defocused attention and mental playfulness. In contrast, it is well known that self-consciousness, performance anxiety, or even just offering people rewards (Amabile, 1990) inhibits creativity and insight. This self-orientation is inimical to spontaneity generally.

This is reminiscent of Heidegger's (1966) "meditative thought," which "waits upon" rather than "waits for" something. Martindale's (1995) notion of shallow association gradients suggests that there may be many trains of thought and implication operating simultaneously, all somewhat evenly activated. In states of superordinate emotional calm and security, the normally highly superordinate and self-oriented, survival-based construing may be in relative quiescence. The "self" is a focus for much of our psychic life, and consciousness is intimately tied to self-consciousness. The world is filtered through our affective assessments: Is this good or bad for me? But when we feel safe and secure, the self may move out of the focus of attention and one may entertain less censored processes. The system's resources are freed up. There is little distraction, little background static, and an evenly hovering, receptive attention can allow first one train of implication then another to gently rise into conscious awareness (provisional tightening). And just as gently, this awareness can allow that discrimination to fade until the next comes of its own accord. This would correspond to a profoundly different sense of self in which the characteristic superordinancy of self-oriented anticipation is in relative abeyance. It may also account for the overall lower than usual levels of cortical activation found when thinking creatively.

Here is a distinction between prediction and anticipation that we think is important. Prediction has more a connotation of "looking for" something, where we know roughly what we are looking for. Anticipation, however, particularly in its tacit dimensions, has more of an openness to "wait upon" what arrives, for what, we know not. It recalls Warren's (1994) "objective attitude," an attitude that allows the world to be as it is, not how we want or even expect it to be. Such meditative thought and "releasement" allows for a sense of space and openness, a slowing down of the mind (Claxton, 1998). If tightening is kept in abeyance long enough, a type of psychic "vacuum" is created that attracts a flurry of new possibilities. If "nature abhors a vacuum," then it seems the asymmetrical mind "abhors openness."

It is usually retrospectively that people realize their insight experiences were enjoyable. That is, upon tightening or a return to asymmetry, self-awareness returns. This is possibly so because during insight we are less concerned about maintenance and core processes and the anticipatory fortunes of our construing. We are "lost" in our thoughts. This seems to be a qualitatively different state of being, symmetrically infused and shepherded in by looser, abstract superordinate structures of greater flexibility and permeability.

This is not irrelevant to the terrors of the mystic who, it seems, must pass through the "dark night of the soul," must "lose oneself" first, in order to experience oneness with existence—a sense of indivisibility and unity redolent of Matte-Blanco's (1988) deeper levels of the unconscious. There are common themes here of connectedness and non–self-consciousness. Somewhat paradoxically, when one's core or identity-related anticipatory structures are validated, McCoy's (1977) definition of "love," one becomes less self-conscious. In the deeper transpersonal and altered states of consciousness, such experiences of absorption and being one with the universe are ubiquitous (Hunt, 1995). Ironically, the freedom from self-consciousness flows from comprehensive validation of one's self.

CONCLUSIONS: TRANSCENDING THE OBVIOUS

A useful way to consider insight is as follows: First, there are the normal, probably implicit processes of anticipation and navigation of our physical and social world. Much of this passes unnoticed (tacit "knowing how") as our system encounters no perturbation and "fits" or "couples" with our world. Usually, however, we run up against the world in the form of invalidation. Tighter, more asymmetrical thought is called into play to examine the situation, using its repertoire of understandings and strategies to solve the "problem." Not infrequently, even this direct approach, this hard work on the problem, ends in frustration. We find ourselves at an impasse, repeatedly using trusted approaches that nonetheless do not solve this "ill-defined" problem (hostility). If we can afford to, we put the problem aside, allowing ourselves to relax, either purposely or by default, and we attend to other matters. Occasionally we return to it and we "see" the solution. The moment of insight arrives unexpectedly (if it does) with a subjective sense of certainty or solution. We examine the "solution" and either find with joy that it is the awaited answer, or see with some resignation that it was a false hope.

How did this all happen? Whether by intention or by accident, the person enters into a period of defocused, more symmetrical awareness. Such a "presentational" mode is characterized by an "aesthetic" attitude, by a "felt sense" of what one considers, and by a more abstract and figurative style of thought. Above all, it tends to dwell in the affective "feel" of things as against a more intellectual, judging rationality. Whereas in tighter asymmetrical construing, we may be disturbed by such "illogicality," in this mode of consciousness, which is more dreamlike and more playful, it is the broader context and dimensionality of events that is embraced rather than a more narrow focus on distinctions and hierarchic relations. This more affective style of thought moves us into symmetrical relations whereby the distinctions and differences between elements become fuzzy, less distinct. This facilitates more abstractive thought as events and things once seen as contrasting are now seen in terms of their similarities. Constructs sharing some elements are now more likely to be related as construct axes are "rotated" and the "quantum jumps" to "nonrelated" chains of inference become possible.

The implications for PCP and for research are multiple. We have seen that not all construing is neatly bipolar, nor does it always operate in strictly transitive or hierarchical fashion. Constructs and their relations can be fuzzy. Our analysis of loosening and tightening in terms of Matte-Blanco's ideas has introduced a looser, more associative, and multidimensional style of thought that can, ideally, operate in tandem with tighter ordinal construing. Available to us, therefore, is the possibility of entering into a more adventurous mode of construing—the awareness of which will help us understand and value our more tacit or unconscious anticipatory processes. Related to this, we have proposed some ideas concerning "emotional construing" and outlined the latter's possible role in construct revision and insight. A transcending affective stance may be crucial in backgrounding self-concern, allowing for non–self-conscious absorption and movement into creativity and insight. In discussing insight, we have attempted to enter into the adventurous frame of mind of the later Kelly, a frame of mind that invites us to take risks, to entertain the preposterous, and to innovate in order to transcend the obvious.

NOTES

1. We distinguish between emotion and affect following Rychlak (1977). The term "affect" is here meant to emphasize a personal predication or assessment process, whereas "emotion" is here used as a more general and inclusive term covering relatively instinctive, preconceptual reactions and action tendencies all the way through to highly refined, affective nuances (see also Spinoza, 1967, for a similar distinction between passive and active emotions). In these terms, animals clearly experience primitive (passive) emotions analogous to human fear, satiation, and so on, but it is by no means clear as to whether they generate affective experience such as confidence, dread, or amusement.

2. In Kelly's terms, "hostility" refers to the nonacceptance of invalidation and to the distortion of the evidence to fit one's anticipations.

3. This differs from "slot rattling," because in slot rattling the discrimination inherent in, for example, "gentle—violent," stays the same, but in loosening the construct meaning must change to accommodate the shifting of elements within its range. It is also significant to note that this shifting of discrimination may not be disturbing to me but may be quite alarming for those around me (particularly my "friend").

4. It is noted, however, that one may be aware of the implications and apparent "illogicalities" of preverbal or tacit construing. But this is a successive or subsequent phenomenon. Such an awareness is likely to be experienced emotionally as the intransitivities or the "fragmentation" in thought is recognized. Later, we relate this to what Matte-Blanco (1988) has called "bilogic."

5. Those linking people to their survival or "maintenance processes."

6. Personal constructs can be usefully represented as sets (Caputi, 1986; Chiari, Mancini, Nicolo, & Nuzzo, 1990) and Bell (1996) has proposed that, given this, Matte-Blanco's ideas can also be usefully applied to construing.

REFERENCES

Amabile, T. (1990). Within you, without you: The social psychology of creativity, and beyond. In M. A. Runco & R. S. Albert (Eds.), *Theories of creativity* (pp. 61–91). London: Sage.

Bannister, D. (1977). The logic of passion. In D. Bannister (Ed.), *New perspectives in personal construct theory* (pp. 21–378). London: Academic Press.

Bechara, A., Damasio, H., Tranel, D., & Damasio, A. R. (1997). Deciding advantageously before knowing the advantageous strategy. *Science, 275,* 1293–1294.

Bell, R. (1996). How can personal construct theory explain disorders of perception and cognition? In B. M. Walker, J. Costigan, L. L. Viney, & W. Warren (Eds.), *Personal construct theory: A psychology of the future* (pp. 153–171). Melbourne, Australia: APS Imprint.

Bowers, K. S. (1981). Knowing more than we can say leads to saying more than we can know: On being implicitly informed. In D. Magnusson (Ed.). *Toward a psychology of situation: An interactional perspective* (pp. 171–194). Hillsdale, NJ: Erlbaum.

Bowers, K. S., Farvolden, P., & Mermigis, L. (1995). Intuitive antecedents of insight. In S. M. Smith, T. B. Ward, & R. A. Finke (Eds.), *The creative cognition approach* (pp. 27–51). Cambridge: MIT Press.

Briggs, J. (1990). *Fire in the crucible.* Los Angeles: Tarcher.

Bruner, J. S. (1956). A cognitive theory of personality. *Contemporary Psychology, 1,* 355.

Butt, T. (1995). Ordinal relationships between constructs. *Journal of Constructivist Psychology, 8,* 227–236.

Butt, T. (1998). Sociality, role and embodiment. *Journal of Constructivist Psychology, 11,* 105–116.

Caputi, P. (1986). *Representing grids symbolically.* Paper presented at the 3rd Australasian Personal Construct Psychology Conference, Lincoln School of Nursing, Victoria, Australia.

Chiari, G., Mancini, F., Nicolo, F., & Nuzzo, M. L. (1990). Hierarchical organisation of personal construct systems in terms of the range of convenience. *International Journal of Personal Construct Psychology, 3,* 281–311.

Chiari, G., & Nuzzo, M. L. (1996). Personal construct theory within psychological constructivism: Precursor or avant-garde? In B. M. Walker, J. Costigan, L. L. Viney, & W. G. Warren (Eds.), *Personal construct theory: A psychology for the future* (pp. 25–54). Carlton South, Victoria: Australian Psychological Society.

Claxton, G. (1997). *Hare brain tortoise mind: Why intelligence increases when you think less.* London: Fourth Estate.

Claxton, G. (1998). Investigating human intuition: Knowing without knowing why. *The Psychologist, 11,* 217–220.

Csikszentmihalyi, M. (1990). *Flow: The psychology of optimal experience.* New York: Harper Perennial.

Csikszentmihalyi, M. (1996). *Creativity: Flow and the psychology of discovery and invention.* New York: Harper Perennial.

Csikszentmihalyi, M., & Sawyer, K. (1995). Creative insight: The social dimension of a solitary moment. In R. J. Sternberg & J. E. Davidson (Eds.), *The nature of insight* (pp. 329–363). Cambridge: MIT Press.

Damasio, A. R. (1994). *Descartes' error: Emotion, reason, and the human brain.* New York: Putnam's.

Davidson, J. E. (1995). The suddenness of insight. In R. J. Sternberg & J. E. Davidson (Eds.), *The nature of insight* (pp. 125–155). Cambridge: MIT Press.

Epel, N. (1993). *Writers dreaming.* Melbourne, Australia: Bookman Press.

Freud, S. (1911/1961). Formulations of the two principles of mental functioning. In *The standard edition of the complete psychological works of Sigmund Freud* (Vol. 12). London: Hogarth Press.

Gardner, H. (1993). *Creating minds: An anatomy of creativity seen through the lives of Freud, Einstein, Picasso, Stravinsky, Eliot, Graham, and Gandhi.* New York: Basic Books.

Gentner, D. (1983). Structure-mapping: A theoretical framework for analogy. *Cognitive Science, 7,* 155–170.

Gick, M. L., & Holyoak, K. J. (1980). Analogical problem solving. *Cognitive Psychology, 12,* 306–355.

Gilhooly, K. J., Keane, M. T. G., Logie, R. H., & Erdos, G. (1990). *Lines of thinking* (Vol. 2). London: Wiley.

Goleman, D. (1995). *Emotional intelligence*. New York: Bantam Books.

Gruber, H. E. (1981). On the relation between "Aha experiences" and the construction of ideas. *History of Science, 19,* 41–59.

Gruber, H. E. (1995). Insight and affect in the history of science. In R. J. Sternberg & J. E. Davidson (Eds.), *The nature of insight* (pp. 397–431). Cambridge: MIT Press.

Heidegger, M. (1966). *Discourse on thinking* (J. M. Anderson & E. H. Freund, Eds.). New York: Harper & Row.

Heidegger, M. (1978). *Basic writings: From Being and Time (1927) to The Task of Thinking (1964)* (D. F. Krell, Ed.). London: Routledge and Kegan Paul.

Hunt, H. T. (1995). *On the nature of consciousness: Cognitive, phenomenological, and transpersonal perspectives*. New Haven, CT: Yale University Press.

Hutchinson, E. D. (1949a). The nature of insight. In P. Mullahy (Ed.), *A study of interpersonal relations: New contributions to psychiatry* (pp. 421–445). New York: Hermitage Press.

Hutchinson, E. D. (1949b). The period of frustration in creative endeavor. In P. Mullahy (Ed.), *A study of interpersonal relations: New contributions to psychiatry* (pp. 404–420). New York: Hermitage Press.

Hutchinson, E. D. (1949c). Varieties of insight in humans. In P. Mullahy (Ed.), *A study of interpersonal relations: New contributions to psychiatry* (pp. 386–403). New York: Hermitage Press.

Ippolito, M. F., & Tweney, R. D. (1995). The inception of insight. In R. J. Sternberg & J. E. Davidson (Eds.), *The nature of insight* (pp. 433– 462). Cambridge: MIT Press.

Kalekin-Fishman, D., & Walker, B. M. (1996). *The construction of group realities: Culture, society and personal construct theory*. Malabar, FL: Krieger.

Katz, J. O. (1984). Personal construct theory and the emotions: An interpretation in terms of primitive constructs. *British Journal of Psychology, 75,* 315–327.

Kelly, G. A. (1955). *The psychology of personal constructs*. New York: Norton.

Kelly, G. A. (1959/1989). The function of interpretation in psychotherapy. Series of three lectures given to Los Angeles Society of Clinical Psychologists in Private Practice (B. M. Walker & F. Fransella, Eds.). London and Wollongong: The Centre for Personal Construct Psychology and The Wollongong Personal Construct Group.

Kelly, G. A. (1966a). *Behavior is a question.* Paper prepared for presentation at the 10th Inter-American Congress of Psychology, Lima, Peru, April 3–7.

Kelly, G. A. (1966b). Behavior is an experiment. In D. Bannister (Ed.), *Perspectives in personal construct theory* (pp. 255–269). London: Academic Press.

Kelly, G. A. (1966c). Ontological acceleration. In B. Maher (Ed.), *Clinical psychology and personality: The selected papers of George Kelly* (pp. 7–45). New York: Krieger.

Kelly, G. A. (1969). *Clinical psychology and personality: The selected papers of G. A. Kelly*. New York: Krieger.

Kelly, G. A. (1977). The psychology of the unknown. In D. Bannister (Ed.), *New perspectives in personal construct theory* (pp. 1–19). London: Academic Press.

Kelly, G. A. (1980). A psychology of the optimal man. In A. W. Landfield & L. M. Leitner (Eds.), *Personal construct psychology: Psychotherapy and personality* (pp. 18–35). New York: Wiley.

Kirkland, J., & Anderson, R. (1990). Invariants, constructs, affordances, analogies. *International Journal of Personal Construct Psychology, 3*, 31–39.

Langer, S. K. (1957/1971). *Philosophy in a new key: A study in the symbolism of reason, rite, and art.* Cambridge: Harvard University Press.

Langer, S. K. (1972). *Mind: An essay in human feeling* (Vol. II). London: John Hopkins University Press.

LeDoux, J. E. (1995). Emotion: Clues from the brain. *Annual Review of Psychology, 46,* 209–235.

Mahoney, M. J. (1995). Continuing evolution of the cognitive sciences and psychotherapies. In R. A. Neimeyer & M. J. Mahoney (Eds.), *Constructivism in psychotherapy* (pp. 39–67). Hyattsville, MD: American Psychological Association.

Mair, M. (1989). Kelly, Bannister and a story-telling psychology. *International Journal of Personal Construct Psychology, 2,* 1–14.

Martindale, C. (1995). Creativity and connectionism. In S. M. Smith, T. B. Ward, & R. A. Finke (Eds.), *The creative cognition approach* (pp. 327–335). Cambridge: MIT Press.

Matte-Blanco, I. (1975). *The unconscious as infinite sets: An essay in bi-logic.* London: Duckworth.

Matte-Blanco, I. (1988). *Thinking, feeling, and being: Clinical reflections on the fundamental antinomy of human beings and the world.* London: Routledge.

Mayer, R. E. (1995). The search for insight: Grappling with gestalt psychology's unanswered questions. In R. J. Sternberg & J. E. Davidson (Eds.), *The nature of insight* (pp. 3–32). Cambridge: MIT Press.

McCoy, M. M. (1977). A reconstruction of emotion. In D. Bannister (Ed.), *New perspectives in personal construct theory* (pp. 93–124). London: Academic Press.

McCoy, M. M. (1981) Positive and negative emotion: A personal construct theory interpretation. In H. Bonarius, R. Holland, & S. Rosenberg (Eds.), *Personal construct psychology: Recent advances in theory and practice* (pp. 105–113). London: St. Martin's Press.

Metcalfe, J., & Wiebe, D. (1987). Intuition in insight and noninsight problem solving. *Memory and Cognition, 15,* 238–246.

Minsky, M. (1985). *The Society of the Mind.* New York: Simon & Schuster.

Neimeyer, R. A. (1995). Limits and lessons of contructivism. *Journal of Constructivist Psychology, 8,* 339–361.

Oatley, K. (1990). Do emotional states produce irrational thinking? In K. J. Gilhooly, M. T. G. Keane, R. H. Logie, & G. Erdos (Eds.), *Lines of thinking* (Vol. 2, pp. 121–155). London: Wiley.

Perkins, D. N. (1995). Insight in minds and genes. In R. J. Sternberg & J. E. Davidson (Eds.), *The nature of insight* (pp. 495–533). Cambridge: MIT Press.

Perkins, D. N. (1997). Creativity's camel: The role of analogy in invention. In T. B. Ward, S. M. Smith, & J. Vaid (Eds.), *Creative thought: An investigation of conceptual structures and processes* (pp. 523–538). Washington, DC: American Psychological Association.

Radley, A. (1977). Living on the horizon. In D. Bannister (Ed.), *New perspectives in personal construct theory* (pp. 221–249). London: Academic Press.

Rayner, E. (1995). *Unconscious thinking: An introduction to Matte Blanco's bi-logic and its uses.* London: Routledge.

Reber, A. S. (1985). *The Penguin dictionary of psychology*. London: Penguin.

Rogers, C. R. (1956). Intellectualized psychotherapy. *Contemporary Psychology, 1,* 357–358.

Rychlak, J. F. (1968). *A philosophy of science for personality theory*. Boston: Houghton Mifflin.

Rychlak, J. F. (1977). *The psychology of rigorous humanism*. New York: Wiley.

Rychlak, J. F. (1990). Kelly and the concept of construction. *International Journal of Personal Construct Psychology, 3,* 7–19.

Rychlak, J. F. (1991). The missing psychological links of artificial intelligence: Predication and opposition. *International Journal of Personal Construct Psychology, 4,* 241–249.

Schooler, J. W., & Engstler-Schooler, T. Y. (1990). Verbal overshadowing of visual memories: Some things are better left unsaid. *Cognitive Psychology, 22,* 36–71.

Schooler, J. W., & Melcher, J. (1995). The ineffability of insight. In S. M. Smith, T. B. Ward, & R. A. Finke (Eds.), *The creative cognition approach* (pp. 97–133). Cambridge: MIT Press.

Seifert, C. M., Meyer, D. E., Davidson, N., Patalano, A. L., & Yaniv, I. (1995). Demystification of cognitive insight: Opportunistic assimilation and the prepared mind perspective. In R. J. Sternberg & J. E. Davidson (Eds.), *The nature of insight* (pp. 65–124). Cambridge: MIT Press.

Simonton, D. K. (1993). Blind variations, chance configurations, and creative genius. *Psychological Inquiries, 4,* 225–228.

Simonton, D. K. (1997). Creativity in personality, developmental, and social psychology: Any links with cognitive psychology? In T. B. Ward, S. M. Smith, & J. Vaid (Eds.), *Creative thought: An investigation of conceptual structures and processes* (pp. 309–324). Washington, DC: American Psychological Association.

Smith, S. M. (1995a). Fixation, incubation, and insight in memory and creative thinking. In S. M. Smith, T. B. Ward, & R. A. Finke (Eds.), *The creative cognition approach* (pp. 135–156). Cambridge: MIT Press.

Smith, S. M. (1995b). Getting into and out of mental ruts: a theory of fixation, incubation, and insight. In R. J. Sternberg & J. E. Davidson (Eds.), *The nature of insight* (pp. 229–251). Cambridge: MIT Press.

Smith, S. M., Ward, T. B., & Finke, R. A. (1995). Paradoxes, principles, and prospects for the future of creative cognition. In S. M. Smith, T. B. Ward, & R. A. Finke (Eds.) *The creative cognition approach* (pp. 327–335). Cambridge: MIT Press.

Spinoza, B. (1967). *Ethics*. London: Everyman Edition, J. M. Dent.

Stam, H. J. (1998). Personal construct theory and social constructionism: Difference and dialogue. *Journal of Constructivist Psychology, 11,* 187–204.

Sternberg, R. J., & Davidson J. E. (1995). *The nature of insight*. Cambridge: MIT Press.

Stevens, C. D. (1998). Realism and Kelly's pragmatic constructivism. *Journal of Constructivist Psychology, 11,* 281–306.

Tomkins, S. A. (1962). *Affect, Imagery, Consciousness*. New York: Springer.

Walker, B. M. (1996). A psychology for adventurers: An introduction to personal construct psychology from a social perspective. In D. Kalekin-Fishman & B. M. Walker (Eds.), *The construction of group realities: Culture, society and personal construct theory* (pp. 7–26). Malabar, FL: Krieger.

Wallace, D. B. (1991). The genesis and microgenesis of sudden insight in the creation of literature. *Creativity Research Journal, 4,* 41–50.

Wallas, G. (1926). *The art of thought.* New York: Harcourt Brace Jovanovich.

Ward, T. B. (1995). What's old about new ideas? In S. M. Smith, T. B. Ward, & R. A. Finke (Eds.), *The creative cognition approach* (pp. 157–178). Cambridge: MIT Press.

Warren, W. G. (1987). *Personal construct theory and "the cognitive": A philosophical investigation.* Institute of Behavioral Sciences, University of Newcastle, Australia.

Warren, W. G. (1994). Subjecting and objecting in personal construct psychology. In *European perspectives in PCP: Selected papers from the Inaugural Conference of European Personal Construct Association.* York, England: European Personal Construct Association, 1992.

Warren, W. G. (1998). *Philosophical dimensions of personal construct psychology.* London: Routledge.

Watts, F. N. (1990). The cohesiveness of phobic concepts. In K. J. Gilhooly, M. T. G. Keane, R. H. Logie, & G. Erdos (Eds.), *Lines of thinking* (Vol. 2, pp. 145–155). London: Wiley.

Weisberg, R. A. (1995). Prolegomena to theories of insight in problem-solving: A taxonomy of problems. In R. J. Sternberg & J. E. Davidson (Eds.), *The nature of insight* (pp. 157–195). Cambridge: MIT Press.

Winter, D. A. (1992). *Personal construct psychology in clinical practice: Theory, research and applications.* London: Routledge.

Yaniv, I., & Meyer, D. E. (1987). Activation and metacognition of inaccessible stored information: Potential bases for incubation effects in problem solving. *Journal of Experimental Psychology: Learning, Memory, and Cognition, 13,* 187–205.

Zajonc, R. B. (1980). Feeling and thinking: Preferences need no inferences. *American Psychologist, 35,* 151–175.

Chapter 3

The Relational Basis of Personal Construct Psychology

Dusan Stojnov
Trevor Butt

Different approaches to constructivism (at least in the realm of psychotherapy) have been characterized as a "fuzzy set with indistinct boundaries, whose members manifest considerable diversity and even occasional contradiction" (Neimeyer, 1993, p. 224). However, one common denominator in constructivist theories seems to be implied in almost every discussion of the basic tenets of constructivism. Personal, radical, social, and any other constructivist theory all seem to advocate some form of antirealist position, opposing the view that there is a real world "out there" and that theoretical statements of science are true in terms of their correspondence with that reality. Therefore, broadly speaking, all constructivist theories have somehow challenged the idea of a mind-independent reality.

A closer scrutiny reveals that, just as there are many forms of constructivism (see Botella, 1995, and Chiari & Nuzzo, 1996, for detailed discussion), there are also many types of realism. Furthermore, some forms of constructivism seem to be congruent with certain types of realism. This possibility further frays the rather thin thread binding the diversity of constructivist perspectives together in what we call "constructivist metatheory."

The realism-antirealism debate seems to push into the background another equally important issue—essentialism. The aim of this chapter is to explore this ontological position advocating the inner essence of things on the one side, and its antithesis, which we term *relationism,* on the other. It is our contention that all constructivist theories in psychology, even if they do not deny the existence of a true reality "out there," all share an anti-essentialist perspective that favors an epistemological view granting the ontological primacy of relations over essences. We think that this is also the case with personal construct psychology (PCP), which has always presented a challenge to classification. Some voices have been raised claiming a realist position of PCP (Mahoney, 1988; Neimeyer, 1993; Noaparast, 1995; Warren, 1985). There is also the interesting recent debate about whether PCP is cognitive, constructivist, constructionist; an individual or a social theory (Burkitt, 1991, 1996; Butt, 1996; Mancuso, 1996, 1998; Stam, 1998). We argue that PCP and other salient constructivist theories unequivocally oppose essentialism. Furthermore, we propose that PCP, like the majority of constructivist theories, advocates the primacy of relations over essence in its view of personality. We also advocate a reading of Kelly that emphasizes the social and relational aspect of PCP, as well as the social origins of personality.

We first address the issue of realism and its compatibility with PCP. Our contention is that the complexity of realist positions makes any simple contrast with constructivism difficult. Second, we discuss the issue of essentialism versus relationism, and here we assert the unambiguous opposition to essentialism in constructivism. Finally, we outline a reading of PCP that draws both on its roots in pragmatism and existential phenomenology to promote its status as a relational approach to personality.

DIFFERENT REALIST VIEWS: ANOTHER FUZZY SET?

Realism is an ontological position that claims that the external world is a reality, and not a figment of our imagination, which can be known independently of observers and independently of the processes of knowing and perceiving. Such a view further implies objectivity in the sense that what is known would be real whether or not it was known. It has been claimed that this philosophical thesis is shared and accepted by "both scientific realists and traditional empiricists, and indeed by most ordinary folk, including children above the age of two" (Greenwood, 1994, p. 16).

Unlike Greenwood, we think that realism is not so easily shared even among realists themselves—not to mention children over 2. For, just as there is a multiplicity of constructivist perspectives, there exists a multiplicity of adjectives attributed to realism nowadays: "ontological," "epistemological," "ethical," "modal," "intentional," "strong," "weak," "radical," "critical," "convergent," "scientific," "naïve," "traditional," "regressive" —to name but a few.

Besides the common Aristotelian tradition, probably the most influential realist position recently proposed is critical scientific realism. It assumes that science is about reality that exists independent of observers. In principle, and "contra Kant, this reality is knowable, though normally only in a symbolic and distorted way" (Toumela, 1977, p. 2). Although we cannot be directly aware of the material objects in the world, our perceptions nevertheless do give us some kind of knowledge of them. It is not just objects in the physical world, but also objects in the social and psychological worlds that exist and have properties independent of our theoretical concepts of them and theoretical discourse about them. Knowledge about reality is primarily obtained by means of scientific theorizing and observation, and this knowledge always remains corrigible. A central feature of this view is that there exist objects and properties, which are not observable or capable of experience at all. We need special theoretical concepts and a theoretical discourse to speak about this nonsensible (nonempirical) part of reality.

The idea of the corrigibility of our observation and theorizing forms the core difference between traditional and critical realism. For if it turns out that certain theories that claimed to represent the real world can prove to be incorrect and need some refinement and correction, it seems worth questioning what they were representing in the first place. Even some important advocates of critical realism (Bhaskar, 1989; Toumela, 1977) agree that the supposed "asymptotic unification of the picture" given by different scientific theories, or the idea of "final truth" about the world is something mythical. At present, we are not in the position to know how the final picture of the world will look, once our scientific inquiries are successfully completed. So, the greatest possible heuristic emphasis should be made upon theoretical *approximations* that will lead us to discover this final picture. Therefore, we are left with our conceptual and empirical efforts to investigate it, although these efforts do not jointly exhaust the "real." Critical realism insists that the empirical is only a subset of the actual, which is itself a subset of the real. This further introduces another distinction between depth realism and shallow realism, or "actualism."

It seems that antirealist theories are not the only meaningful contrast to realism. There are various contrasts within realist ontology, making it as "fuzzy" a set as one may detect in constructivist metatheory. Every philosophy may be construed as some kind of realism: Berkeley is realist about sensations, Plato about forms, Bradley about the Absolute. Therefore, the first question that may arise when talking about realist doctrine is: which realism? And the second: are some realisms more realist than others? An attempt to answer these questions is beyond the scope of this chapter; nevertheless, the mere act of their asking may serve the purpose of revealing an aura of "fuzziness" and fragmentation in the "realist camp."

Although two opposite ontological positions—realism and antirealism—appear mutually exclusive, it seems possible to anticipate some threads of convergence between them. On the consequential level, it is difficult to establish the difference between hypothetical constructs on the one hand, and pragmatic constructs on the other. Hypothetical constructs are confirmed in many different research designs and, therefore, are not fictions, but veridical statements reflecting "true" reality that can be usefully applied in psychology (because what is not "real" cannot function or work in practice). Pragmatic constructs (personal or common), are "fictions" that have been confirmed by their meaningful and frequent use in praxis (because they function, they are "real"). It seems that the difference lies only in the emphasis and syntax of the words in the same sentences (What is "true" functions versus what functions is "true"). In the case of the first sentence, in keeping with realism, neither confirmation nor refutation is possible, because it is saturated with a much stronger metaphysical charge (because final truth about the world is not yet discovered, we cannot know if it functions or not). In the second sentence, "truth" is based on pragmatic criteria and much more appropriate to a constructivist way of thinking. Therefore, it seems appropriate to infer that the foundations of realism rest on a nontestable, unscientific, and fictional, or, to put it in one word—metaphysical assumption.

PERSONAL CONSTRUCT PSYCHOLOGY:
A CASE OF (CRITICAL) REALISM?

We hope that this discussion sets the stage for our argument that a sharp, black-and-white distinction between realist and antirealist positions is not viable when applied to the realm of constructivist psychology. Although a majority of constructivist authors deny both the linguistic and epistemic objectivity of theoretical descriptions of "real" objects, some recent articles reject the realist-antirealist classification as a form of oversimplification (Efran & Heffner, 1998; Neimeyer, 1995; Noaparast, 1995). Furthermore, Neimeyer (1995) classifies himself "as neither realist nor antirealist, but *arealist*, someone for whom term has little meaning" (p. 342, emphasis in original).

On the other hand, positioning constructivist metatheory on its ontological grounds reveals an unambiguous tendency to contrast it with realism. This embraces the view that no external realities exist apart from our knowledge or consciousness of them. It denies that our knowledge is a direct perception of reality. On the contrary, it might be said that we all construct our own versions of reality and respond to them as if they are "real." This is obviously the case with Bateson's (1979) dictum that the map is not the territory; shared by Gergen's (1985) view that discourse about the world is not a reflection or map of the world but an artifact of communal exchange, and Kelly's (1955) opinion that PCP is not identical with traditional realism, "since man can erect his own alternative approaches to reality" (p. 17).

But while stating his ontological convictions, Kelly (1955) also says that "We presume that the universe is really existing" (p. 6); also "that it is a real world we shall be talking about, not a world composed solely of the flitting shadows of people's thoughts" (p. 6); and finally "it is real world and not a figment of our imagination" (p. 7). Furthermore, he asserts that:

A person may misrepresent a real phenomenon, such as his income or his ills, and yet his misrepresentation will itself be entirely real. This applies even to the badly deluded patient: what he perceives may not exist, but his perception does. Moreover, his fictitious perception will often turn out to be a grossly distorted construction of something which actually does exist. Any living creature, together with his perceptions, is a part of the real world. (Kelly, 1955, p. 8)

Kelly concludes that life itself, to his way of thinking, is characterized by its essential measurability. Thus, reality is subjected to the measure of the person as scientist, and this brings Kelly on an ontological level very close to the motto of scientific realism: *Scientia mesura*! Searle (1995) claims that "realism is the view that there is a way that things are that is logically independent of all human representations. Realism does not say how things are but only that there is a way that they are" (p. 155). "Things" in the previous two sentences does not refer to material objects or even objects. It is, like the "it" in "It is raining," not a referring expression. This is why Mahoney (1988) and Neimeyer (1993) talk of Kelly as a "critical realist" or a "critical constructivist"; why Noaparast (1995) argues that his theory is compatible with "sophisticated realism," and why Warren (1985) claims compatibility between a realist position and personal construct theory.

There is no doubt that Kelly was postulating an outer reality. On the other hand, it is also clear that he was opposing realism. But the facet of realism Kelly opposed was a view that reduced events to some of their aspects. Accordingly, the universe is an ongoing affair that we understand by anticipating it. Therefore, what we deal with in PCP are our anticipations, and not material objects, which exist independently of our sense of experience. For our knowledge of reality is not constrained by the essence of what is to be known independently of our process of anticipation, but from the imaginative capacities of our minds, for "all of our present interpretations of the universe are subject to revision or replacement" (1955, p. 14). So, postulating an independent reality, which can be reached only in terms of personal constructs, and implying that it exists independently of our constructs, does not imply that we know what it is outside the frames of reference of our constructs. Kelly did not deny the world, he just asserted (in a way strikingly similar to Goodman, 1978) that we cannot claim to know a world beyond our experience. This did not prevent him from building a 1218-page-long frame of reference for dealing with our frames of reference!

PROPERTIES OF THINGS: INNER ESSENCES OR RELATIONS?

But what is it that we are dealing with under the frame of reference? Is it a way that things really are, belonging to the realm of their inherent properties; or a way that we think they are, on the basis of how we relate with them? The first view implies transphenomenality, or going beyond appearances in that knowledge may be not only of what appears, but of some deeper underlying structures that can even contradict appearances; the second makes the whole universe in some sense dependent on the relation between mind and what is to be known. The doctrine of essentialism advocates the view that "objects (including people) have an essential, inherent nature which can be discovered" (Burr, 1995, p. 184); the alternative is termed *relationism* and favors an epistemological view granting the ontological primacy of relations over essences.

From an essentialist perspective, the "best" and "truly scientific" theories seek to describe the essences or the "essential nature" of things—the realities that lie behind the appearances. Such theories are neither in need of, nor susceptible to further explanation. They are themselves ultimate explanations (and, thus, definitely opposed to Kelly's constructive alternativism), and to find such theories is the ultimate aim of the scientist. The doctrine of essentialism thus pertains to science, whose aim is not to describe our ordinary world of common experience (or "appearances"), but to discover hidden essences of things. It attempts ultimate explanations, which are in no need of any further explanation, or constructive revision. Explanation such as this is, thus, not dependent on the mind of the perceiver; it reveals an inner essence or an inherent property of what we are trying to explain.

However, the opposite position to essentialism—a disbelief in the existence of inner essences of things—does not automatically mean not believing in the existence of those things themselves. The relationist perspective present in constructivist metatheory denies not the existence of a real world "out there," but, rather, our incapability to know it in an objective way. Knowledge, thus, aims not at discovering the inherent properties of things or their essence, but at the way they reveal themselves to the constraints of our knowledge apparatus in a certain relation. This is altogether another ontological debate, and we try to show, in the remaining text, that PCP and other constructivist approaches favor an epistemological view in which ontological primacy is granted to relations, rather then individual entities with inherent properties of relations over essence. Of course, constructivist ideas did not originate in an intellectual vacuum, without historical precedent.[1] Because a detailed historical overview of relational doctrine in philosophy is too big a project, we do not deal with it in this chapter (for a detailed account of relational doctrines, see Henninger, 1989).

Nevertheless, there is another, less remote, relationist work worth referring to: John Macmurray, a Scottish philosopher whose work was thoroughly based on a relational perspective, influenced Kelly during his years at the Edinburgh.[2] Macmurray (1961) cogently states the primacy of relational being in his account of personhood. We are first persons, and our personality is not achieved in isolation at the expense of the others or by the development of certain faculties such as reason or by conscious social acceptance of the others. Macmurray (1957) proposes a complete change of standpoint from the primacy of the *cogito*, to the primacy of the self as agent and constituted by one's relationship with another person. This is an entirely different way of envisaging the person, rooted as we are in equating the person with the individual self. Instead, the person is conceived as primarily an agent, as constituted by personal relations.

Macmurray gives an example of what it is to be constituted a person by other persons in the simple relationship between mother and a child. In taking an example of the mother and child, he also takes a tilt at the Aristotelian tradition, which suggests that the human infant is, first, an animal organism that acquires personality as it grows up. Macmurray (1961) says:

From the outset the relationship between mother and child is personal; in the human infant—and this is the heart of the matter—the impulse to communicate is his sole adaptation to the world in which he is born. Implicit and unconscious it may be, yet it is sufficient to constitute the mother-child relation as the basic form of human existence, as a personal mutuality, as "You and I" with a common life. For this reason the infant is born a person and not an animal. . . . If we did not know there are other persons we could literally know nothing, *not even that we ourselves existed.* (p. 60; emphasis added)

Saying that we are, first, persons means that we are constructed to be directed outward in intentional activity to mutuality or friendship or communion (all used by Macmurray to describe the state of relational being). Other people are no longer there to be feared or dominated but rather to sustain and constitute us in mutual relations and be sustained and constituted in return. Macmurray's views have considerable implications for a world in which we lament a selfish individualism that destroys human community rather than individualism or collectivism, with all that that implies for social ethics. Whatever our anthropology, as far as Macmurray is concerned, the expression "individual intelligent being" seems to be void of meaning.

The influence of Macmurray's relational perspective on personhood, especially his view of the constitutive role that other people play in our constitution, is probably most obviously present in Kelly's (1955) definition of the term *person*:

Presumably the child, as he initially structures his social world, depends more upon figures than upon constructs. But is not a figure itself a matter of construction? Does not the child's mother, for example, become a person in his world to the extent that she represents the intersect of certain personal construct dimensions which he sets up? Some of these dimensions are no more than minor discriminations of what has taken place versus what has not taken place. Yet their point of intersection becomes, in the child's eyes, the Mother figure. (p. 297)

Therefore, "From the standpoint of the psychology of personal constructs a person is perceived as the intersect of many personal construct dimensions" (p. 298). Finally,

When we say that a person is the intersect of many subjective dimensions, we mean, of course, that a person, as constructed by someone such as ourselves, is a unique combination of dichotomous categorical interpretations. (p. 300)

For the sake of clarity, it should be noted that for Kelly, person *per definitionem* is not an inner essence, or an intrinsic property of the individual. If the *other person* is construed (and thus produced) in our eyes, *we* are also produced in the eyes of the other. That places the position of a person *between* self and others, in the realm of mutual relations. *My* person cannot exist as an essence of a person residing inside of *my* body, if there is no perceiver "out there" who will offer *his* or *her* construing system to constitute *my* personality. The construction of this other as a *person* is, in return, heavily dependant on my construing of that person, and not on his or her inherent qualities, which are provided by the inner essence of that person. It is not just that we produce constructs whose intersection constitutes the figure of others; at the same time, when we construe others, we are construing a necessary condition for our own constitution—and that is *other as a person*. Simply speaking, for the construction of our own mode of being as persons, *we need another person as much as we need ourselves!* Therefore, for both Kelly and Macmurray, the person is seen as being produced in mutual relations. Consequently, it is our deep belief that personal construct systems are not situated "in the head," but *between* people. It seems that Kelly made the person a "crossroads" of interacting human individuals. It is *not* located *within* individuals, as in the view of substantionalists, and conceived as an integumented and "unified entity that persists through change, binding changes together but itself unchanging" (Bertocci, 1965, p. 296). The *realm of mutual relations between people seems to precede the realm of personhood* and acts as a social fabric of personal becoming.

Congruent with Macmurray's and Kelly's understanding of the person as something being produced in relations between people is the meaning of the concept "person" in recent philosophical inquiries (for a cogent analysis of concept of person, see McCall, 1990). In common everyday speech, we use the adjective "personal" to denote something private, belonging to us, that we do not necessarily have to or want to share with others. However, within the boundaries of philosophy, this concept has an altogether different meaning. The term *person* refers to what is cognized of the individual by others. The individual, recognized as a person, is a public entity; in this sense, the person is a third-person entity. Whatever is known, attributed, or thought of the individual constitutes that individual as a person. Thus, the identity of an individual as a person is what is determined by third persons, as this mode of understanding of individuals encompasses that which is attributed to an individual by others. Both what constitutes a person—personhood—and the conditions for identifying persons—personal identity—are to be found in the public domain. Persons are social beings, created and constituted, and found only in society. Thus, individuals can only exist as persons in social situations. Furthermore, the social situation is not determined by essential properties of individuals who enter in it, but is formative of individuals themselves: it is the relations between people, their interrelatedness, that forms the basis of personal features ascribed to others.

Besides having a life of their own in philosophy, essentialist ideas have had an important impact on psychology, especially influencing personality theories. They have set the scene for a view that proposed an inner essence or inherent quality of personality that determined how people act in different situations, as well as how their relations with different people are affected by this essence they "carry" in each and every relation they enter. We now summarize the essentialist view in psychology represented by trait psychology, and then contrast it with the constructivist alternative, which we think is representative of relationism.

IMPLICATIONS OF ESSENTIALISM IN PSYCHOLOGY

Although the history of psychology is full of disputes between incongruent, often mutually exclusive views, for a relatively long period orthodox psychologists achieved consensus that the location of personality was in some way "inside" the person. Although personality was not visible, the majority of scientists and practitioners in the field inferred its existence somewhere inside their subjects or clients—or under the skin—as Allport (1937, 1961) proclaimed in his seminal book on personality. For a long time to come, the *trait*, as the basic unit of personality analysis, was given dominant attention in the area of personality research, as well as in the area of clinical and educational psychology. In this section, we elaborate on the basic features of this essentialist approach, mainly in the field of personality psychology.

In the opinion of the majority of authors researching personality traits, personality is considered an essence constituted by personality traits, abilities, and features that can be measured. The trait is something real:

A personal disposition is a generalized neuropsychic structure (peculiar to the individual), with the capacity to render many stimuli functionally equivalent, and to initiate and guide consistent (equivalent) forms of adaptive and stylistic behavior. (Allport, 1961, p. 373)

In reviewing the conditions for an adequate theory of personality, Allport is unambiguous about the place where personality resides. He stresses the overall importance of integumentation—that is, personality as centered within the organism, and not in the relations between people, or in the "eye of the beholder":

Human personality has a locus—within the skin. . . . The reason that I stress the criterion of integumentation is that both psychological and philosophical personalists need to rescue human personality from the clutches of those who confuse it with the impression a man makes on others, with his reputation, with his "social stimulus" value. . . . The "biosocial" view takes your personality to be what other people think and do about you, not what you yourself think and do. . . . The biophysical view, unlike the biosocial, would hold that Robinson Crusoe in solitude has "as much" personality before as after the advent of his man Friday. (Allport, 1960, pp. 20–21)

Allport's dread of the option that what makes human personality are the impressions about that person made by others is understandable. He was obviously threatened with the alternative of losing the personality as solid properties and accepting the alternative that makes personality dependent on the frequently whimsical opinions of the others. That would make any personality utterly inconsistent and unpredictable, because it would have to change whenever and wherever opinion about it is changed.

Kelly's (1955) view on self is surely not substantionalist:

The self is, when considered in the appropriate context, a proper concept or construct. It refers to a group of events which are alike in certain way and, in the same way, necessarily different from other events. *The way in which the events are alike is the self.* That also makes the self an individual, differentiated from other individuals. The self, having been thus conceptualized, can now be used as a thing, a datum, or an item in the context of a superordinate construct. The self can now become one of the three things—or persons— at least two of which are alike and different from at least one of the others.

When the person begins to use himself as a datum in forming constructs, exciting things begin to happen. He finds that the constructs he forms operate as rigorous controls upon his behavior. His behavior in relation to other people is particularly affected. Perhaps it would be better to say that his behavior in comparison with other people is particularly affected. *It is, of course, the comparison he sees or construes which affects his behavior.* Thus, much of his social life is controlled by the comparisons he has come to see *between* himself and the others. (p. 131; emphases added)

But what Kelly presents as an alternative to biophysical view is not the threat of losing the solid ground for the predictions about ourselves, as implied in Allport's statement. Equating the person with her constructions *of* others is not the same as equating her with constructions *by* others, which is what Allport is arguing against.

One of the most important arguments of PCP, in relation to development of self-construing, would seem to be that we develop our picture of ourselves by construing *others' construction of us.* Self is understood in comparisons of others, in terms of meanings that have been developed *between* people to explain the nature of personhood, and using as the evidence our interaction with others and their response to us (either accepting or rejecting).

This is to say that we give a meaning to other people's views on us through our view on them. We need the view of others to find out what *we* are:

It is through our active exploration of others and not through contemplation of our own navels that we come to understand ourselves. The classic Robinson Crusoe figure would suffer from an increasingly impoverished sense of self, since only his fading history and his anthropomorphic response to his island's animals, would serve to paint his portrait. It is out of our life with, against, and through other people that we come to understanding of what we were and are and would become. (Bannister, 1983, p. 385)

Allport was aware that personality is not a given entity and that it has to develop; hence, the name of one of his books, *Becoming* (1955). But considering his concerns with biosocial views on personality, what he failed to admit was that in order to become, we need to become *through the eyes of the others*. Otherwise, it is hard to believe that Robinson Crusoe, if he grew up in solitude on a desert island, could become a person at all.

For Burkitt (1991), Allport's approach to personality is an example of Leibnizian monadology, with its idea that the biological organism is a stable and self-contained system, separated spatially from all other people. Besides being "monadic," this view could also be addressed as "foundationalism," because it refers to personality firmly founded within the organism. But above all, Allport's definition of personality is what Burkitt calls "essentialist," in that "personality is the dynamic organization within the individual of those psychophysical systems that determine his characteristic behavior and thought" (Allport, 1937, p. 28). Furthermore, traits are the basic units of its description.

Traits may be individual or general, superficial or nuclear, constitutionally inherent or acquired (Allport, 1937; Cattell, 1966; Eysenck, 1953; and more recently Costa & McCrae, 1992). A person's conduct in this view is thought to be largely determined by the combination of traits he or she possesses. These traits will outweigh the influence of specific situations surrounding the person. This is the image of personality present in the theory underlying personality tests and inventories that aim to measure individual differences in specific traits, such as extraversion or introversion, and record the precise patterning and combination of traits within a particular individual.

The assumptions on which trait theory is based reflect what Trilling (1974) has called the "honest soul" approach to personality. This approach views people as if they simply are their dispositions, or the sum of their traits: honest, dishonest, lazy, industrious, or whatever. An established list of someone's traits provides a sufficient account for his or her actions, as a possession of certain traits as underlying "essences" will be a sufficient reason to explain certain actions. It would be extremely difficult to see honest soul or trait theory persons as acting out a part of "managing" the impression given to others, as they are entirely synonymous with their disposition and completely identified with it. The "extravert" cannot act as an introvert—he or she cannot help but be extraverted, because this is determined by the underlying disposition or essence. For this reason, from the standpoint of trait psychology it would be meaningless to talk about an identity crisis: Honest souls have only one identity, not many, because they have one essence, not many. They are either what they are (the sum of their traits) or they are not. Therefore, there is no distance or separation within the person to enable certain inner conflict or fragmentation. It also appears as out of the range of possibilities of honest souls to wonder if they are being authentic to their "true" nature, because they are always that nature.

Critics (Mischel, 1968) have noted the weaknesses and limitations of trait theory. It ignores the inconsistency in human behavior, an issue that Kelly (1955) addressed in his fragmentation corollary. Trait theorists draw sophisticated inferences about personality traits on the basis of their personality tests. However, these inferences are of little value in nontest situations, where the explanation of "trait-driven" nature ceases to predict conduct. The uncomfortable fact is that behavior is a good deal more situation-specific than is allowed in trait theories. Furthermore, people are social beings playing different social roles requiring different manifestations of personality: parents, children, teachers, politicians, and others.

We can see the antithesis of trait theory in the role theory of Dahrendorf (1973), where social role is defined as sets of activities, qualities, and styles of behavior that are associated with social positions. The position the individual occupies in society, or the role he or she plays, determines personality. As opposed to trait theory, in role theory people are not "natural" characters, they become performers, social characters, much more in line with principal characters in a theater play than with minor characters in the novel. In this theory, drama and theater provide more appropriate metaphors of personality (Goffman, 1959). Like the actor on the stage, someone's actions are not expressive of unique personality, but expressive of his or her role. The role-player thus has two characteristics that honest souls lack: one is a social insincerity, and the other is a multiple set of possibly incongruent identities. This introduces individual fragmentation, because different roles may require different selves, and the person may be divided among many responses, experiencing conflict alien to the model of the person presented in trait theories.

Although role theory can avoid the critique aimed at trait theories, it still represents a species of essentialism, in that all objects, including people, retain an essential, inherent nature that can be discovered. The difference is in that the main emphasis is moved outside of personality, toward the "true" structures, which also "really" exist, although residing outside the individual, in society. In the case of trait theory, it is the essence of an inner quality; in the case of role theory, it is the essence of society. In both cases, however, personality is seen as a product of an underlying essence that determines behavior.

THE RELATIONAL ALTERNATIVE

The essentialist view of human nature seeks to explain the behavior of people across different situations by referring to physiologically grounded dispositions to react. Thus, what people actually do in different relations is, by and large, determined by underlying traits, which guide "consistent forms of adaptive and stylistic behavior." The constructivist alternative, which we outline in this section, opposes this view in that it claims that dispositions to react are not essences determining relations. Instead, personality traits are constructs produced in relations between people, in a socially and culturally mediated process whereby an observer (or a person as scientist) imposes a meaning on what Kelly calls an "event" (in this case, a particular way that someone behaves). What one has in mind when talking about the personality traits of some other person ceases to be the source of knowledge about the person being perceived. Despite Allport's (1960) warning that "unless we rid ourselves of all definitions that place our personalities in other people's minds, we shall never have a secure enough locus for a theory of personality as a system" (p. 21), Kelly has done exactly that. He located the personality of an actor in the perceiver's mind. Therefore, without a relation between perceiver and perceived person, the whole realm of human personhood would not exist. Human individuals are constituted as persons in the network of interrelations.

FRAGMENTATION REVISITED

When we see joint action as preceding individual action and a relation as the ground on which construing emerges, new light is thrown on the problem of the inconsistency in behavior. Kelly confronted this issue in his Fragmentation Corollary, which proposes that "a person may successively employ a variety of construction subsystems which are inferentially incompatible with each other" (1955, p. 83). He defines inconsistency in terms of incompatible anticipations: "Do the wagers one lays on the outcome of life cancel each other out or do they add up?" (1955, p. 87). Kelly proposed that although these wagers may be inconsistent at a subordinate level in our day-to-day behavior, at a superordinate level, consistency is the rule. He believed in an order imposed from the top down in a hierarchical construct system, which is the property of the person. The person seeks self-consistency because an integrated construct system is vital to his or her anticipatory endeavors. Kelly accepted the notion of determinism in behavior to the extent that subordinate action is determined by superordinate core structure: "In his role as the follower of his own fundamental principles, he finds his life determined by them" (1955, p. 78).

This does not appear to square with the primacy of construing in action, which occurs at a relational level between and not within people. Is a person's conduct determined by some internal gyroscope, in the form of superordinate core structure, or does it arise prereflectively between them, being the property of their relationship? There is a paradox in our experience that we can feel ourselves to be both integrated people, the same person today that we were yesterday, and at the same time a plurality of different roles. It was to deal with this paradox that Mair (1977) suggested that we think of ourselves not as unities, but as communities. This metaphor allows for both the donning of various social masks and roles that may be "inconsistent" with one another, while preserving the existence of a core structure: "a sensitive center of experience . . . a prince in the encampment" (Mair, 1980, p. 114). Here, construing in action is allowed, in the form of the performance of social roles, but is relegated to a superficial rule-following level of existence. There is a distinction between being oneself and playing a role. Or perhaps some roles are more "central" to us than are others. We might find that the behavior called out of us in our various roles—say, as teacher, daughter, and politician—do not "add up," but there still exists a vitally important core theory—we may as well call it the self—that lends an order to any incidental chaos.

And, although Kelly has placed the person between people, both Mair and the Kelly of 1955 preserve an inside/outside split in the person. There is a personal world "in here" and a social world "out there." But what is also undeniably clear is that certain behaviors are not seen as the features of personality themselves, they are construed as such. This is not to say that personality does not exist, that it is not "real." Constructivism does not deny any sense of agency, but, rather, claims that there are different ways of construing it. Furthermore, even if we postulate an inner essence, which is determining behavior, we can never tell what it is "really" like. And this does not apply to personality, only.

REALITY EXISTS, BUT WHAT WE KNOW OF IT IS WHAT WE DO TO IT

Saying that we cannot know what the world "really" looks like is not the same as claiming that the real world does not exist. Constructivism does not deny the existence of objects in the world, just as it does not question the existence of the world itself. If there is no real computer on our desk, and if it is not really there, how on Earth can we write a real article and submit it to be judged by real reviewers and read by real public? Is the community of apparitions in our heads the only alternative left to deal with? This issue was at the center of von Glasersfeld's assertion that there is no simple argument to justify the distinction between experiential reality and ontological reality:

I have never said (nor would I ever say) that there is no ontic world, but I keep saying that we cannot know it. . . . We do not make claim of knowledge that exists "in itself"; that is, without an observer or experiencer. I, for one, am talking about what we know or can know. And as far as our knowledge (not God's knowledge) is concerned, I claim that we cannot even imagine what the word "to exist" might mean in an ontological context, because we cannot conceive of "being" without the notions of space and time, and these two notions are among the first of our conceptual constructs. (von Glasersfeld, 1991, p. 17)

There is simply no privileged rock bottom out there somewhere that we can appeal to in order to find out what events (things and people included) are "really" like outside of our heads. But this does not mean that human knowledge is contained within the boundaries of individual consciousness. Von Foerster (1981) dismisses the danger of labeling constructivism as another solipsist doctrine. Solipsism, the most extreme form of subjectivism, argues that a person can only know about his or her own consciousness. But, at the same time, each person, although insisting that he or she is the sole reality, is capable of imagining other persons not being unlike himself or herself. To carry this argument further, that person could concede that the other imagined persons can also insist that they are the sole reality and that their imaginative universe is populated by apparitions, one of which may be the person who is imagining that he or she is the sole reality. Now, how can this paradox of double existence—being a creator of the sole reality, and at the same time the apparition of the sole reality created by another person—be reconciled? Von Foerster's solution to the danger of solipsism is to apply the principle of relativity: "A hypothesis that holds for A and holds for B will be rejected if it does not hold for A and B together" (1981, p. 308). However, the principle of relativity is not a hypothesis; it cannot be proved to be either true or false. It is a postulate that one assumes to be true. Thus, it is a matter of choice:

If I reject it, I am the center of the universe, my reality is my dreams and my nightmares, my language is monologue, and my logic monologic. If I adopt it, neither I nor the other can be the center of the universe. As in the heliocentric system, there must be a third that is the central reference. It is the *relation between Thou and I,* and this relation is identity: reality = community. (von Foerster, 1984, p. 60; emphasis added)

To get back to our real computer, and real article, and real public metaphor, this does not mean that "real" or "ontic" objects have to be there before one has seen them as computer, article, and public, respectively. This means that in our experiential realm, there is a kind of raw material, which affords certain constructions. In von Glasersfeld's view,

Concepts are not like picture postcards against which one matches experiential material; rather, they are pathways of action or operation. . . . Concepts have no iconic or representational connection with anything that might "exist" outside the cognizing system; and the raw material out of which concepts are composed or coordinated cannot be known to have any such connection either. (1991, p. 18)

This is similar to Kelly's (1955) assertion that constructs are not mere representations, but guidelines for action, or grounds for prediction (p. 12). Basically this means that perception is coimplicative with action: If an object is construed as a glass, one will drink from it; however, if it is construed as a vase, one will use it to put flowers in. Its "real" nature will be determined by our actions (i.e., our relation toward it), not by its essence.

Kelly's view on the importance of relational primacy appears unambiguously clear when he opposes the essentialist approach to aggression, and talks about disorders of transition, including hostility:

From the standpoint of the psychology of personal constructs, it is this basic principle of *interactive relationship* between aggression and hostility which accounts for the phenomena which, under other psychological systems, are described traitwise as "intolerance of ambiguity" or "the authoritarian personality." As we have already claimed, and hope to have demonstrated partially, the psychology of personal construct is more concerned with *interactive* psychological principles than with traits, types or grouping of persons. (Kelly, 1955, p. 882; emphasis added)

This point deserves further clarifying. We cannot have a representation of something we do not have direct access to. In a way, we are "sentenced" to the "artifacts" of our sensory and synaptic systems, just as the methodologist is sentenced to the artifacts of mathematics or stochastic methods he or she uses. It is not possible to avoid the mediation of our nervous system with all of its sensory receptors and neural cells. We cannot just walk out of our synapses, see whatever is there to see, and report directly to the cortex how the "outside" reality "really" looks: "We cannot step outside the domain specified by our body and nervous system. There is no world except that experienced through those processes given to us and which make us what we are" (Varela, 1984, p. 320). The "real" world "out there" is only the sum of constraints within which the organism operates, and it is only "when actions or operations fail that one can speak of 'contact' with the environment" (von Glasersfeld, 1987, p. 234). This means that we acquire stable and reasonable knowledge of the world "out there" through stabilizing our actions and mental operations—or our relations toward what is basically a closed system. In Maturana's opinion,

A closed neuronal network does not have input or output surfaces as features of its organization. . . . [G]iven a closed system, inside and outside only exists for an observer who beholds it, not for the system. . . . The environment where the observer stands acts only as an intervening element through which the effector and sensory neurons interact, completing the closure of the nervous system. (1978, p. 42)

For the constructivist, there is no simple distinction between what is "inside" and "outside" in our experience. Von Foerster illustrates this point with a clarifying example of an infant playing with a rattle:

For the child there is no toy; there is only a stable sensorimotor behavior. The child only has access to what is represented on the retina and sensory tactile sensations arising from the operations on the rattle. But since the child can control the rattle, it can anticipate and make predictions about the rattle. Sensorimotor competence may now have a name, and the easiest way to name it is to call it a rattle. (cited in Segal, 1986, p. 139)

This approach to knowledge as a process of reality representation as opposed to reality computation seems to be congruent with Gergen's distinction between an exogenic perspective of knowledge as copy or mirror the actualities of the real world versus an endogenic perspective regarding the origins of knowledge depending on processes endemic to organism: "Humans harbor inherent tendencies, it is said, to think, categorize, or process information, and it is these tendencies (rather than features of the world in itself) that are of paramount importance in fashioning knowledge" (Gergen, 1985, p. 269). This sounds strikingly similar to Piaget's statement that "Intelligence . . . organizes the world by organizing itself" (1937, p. 311). Furthermore, "Knowledge does not begin in the I, and it does not begin in the object; it begins in *interactions*" (1973, p. 20; emphasis addded).

RELATIONS AS THE SOURCE OF PERSONALITY

What we say about someone or something does not reveal some hidden properties independent of our relating with him or her and independent of our efforts to give it certain meaning:

When I say Professor Lindzey's left shoe is an "introvert," everyone looks to his shoe as if this were something his shoe was responsible for. Or if I say that Professor Catell's head is "discursive," everyone looks over at him, as if the proposition had popped out of his head instead of mine. Don't look at his head! Don't look at that shoe! Look at me; I'm the one who is responsible for the statement. (Kelly, 1969c, p. 72)

Exploring the metaphorical and hermeneutic nature of selfhood, Shotter (1985) also refers to the ontological primacy of relation over substance in emphasizing that the "whatness" of a "you" appearing to an "I" cannot be exhausted, because it is being constructed in interaction between people:

While I can encounter, perceive, and know you in many ways, you as such are never exhausted by what I perceive, encounter and know; there is always more of you to come, for what you will be is now indeterminate. This does not mean . . . that there is another you that stands hidden, behind the you that I encounter, a you that is totally inaccessible to me. (Shotter, 1985, p. 184)

This means that our effort to know what is the true "essence" (of things, ourselves, or other persons) will be always preceded by our relations toward it and mediated by our knowing apparatus, making epistemology and ontology inseparably interwoven in a common process of constructing meaning. Taylor (1971) took this point even further, claiming there is a crucial epistemological difference between natural and social sciences, because

Man is a self-defining animal. With changes in his self-definition go changes in what man is, such that he has to be understood in different terms. But the conceptual mutations in human history can and frequently do produce conceptual webs which are incommensurable, that is, where the terms can't be defined in relation to a common stratum of expressions. . . . The success of prediction of natural sciences is bound up with the fact that all states of the system, past and future, can be described in the same range of the concepts . . . . Only if past and future are brought under the same conceptual net can one understand the states of the latter as some function of the states of the former, and hence predict. (Taylor, 1971, p. 49)

What we are trying to show is that a relationist perspective present in constructivism emphasizes the epistemological impossibility of grasping a "real" or "true" essence of things, because what we usually refer to as an essence is gradually being produced and reproduced in relationship. If two observers have two differing perceptions of the "real" essence of the third person, this contributes to that person's self. This is what von Foerster (1981) calls ontology of the observer and emphasizes in his distinction of scientific objectivity and constructivist postobjectivity. In the former, the properties of the observer do not enter in the description of the observation, but in the latter, the description of the observation reveals the properties of the observer. Therefore, "the logic of the world is the logic of the description of the world" (p. xviii). In other words, what I say about you actually reveals something about me, and my self could not be constituted without some relation toward the other person's self and relation of the other person's self toward me.

For Gergen, language also does not represent the reflection of an objective essence of the external world waiting to be discovered. Rather, samples of language are integers within patterns of relationship:

Language derives its significance in human affairs from the way in which it functions within patterns of relationship. . . . Propositions do not derive their sense from their determinant relationship to a world of referents. At the same time, we find that the semanticist view can be reconstituted within a social frame. Following the treatment of reference as a social ritual, with referent practices as sociohistorically saturated, the semantic possibilities for word meaning are brought into being. It must be underscored, however, that semantics thus becomes a derivative of social pragmatics. It is the *form of relationship* that enables semantics to function. (Gergen, 1994, p. 52; emphasis added)

For a constructionist, the process of thinking is not in itself a venture of putting thought in words (thought presumably being a corresponding representation of the external world imported through the senses). As Shotter (1997) suggests, presenting a new dialogical or relational paradigm, people do not simply put their ideas into words. In their attempt to coordinate their activities, they construct different kinds of living social relationship, forming a dynamically sustained context from which "what is talked about" gets its meaning. Although Shotter talks about constructed relations, he approaches them from the standpoint of their linguistic and conversational reality. Following Bakhtin, Shotter (1993a) emphasizes that words, as such, lack any specific meanings in themselves; they are interindividual:

given the practical, socio-relational nature of language, what matters in a tradition of argumentation, is the terms within which the arguments within it are conducted: to argue in relational rather than individualistic terms, is to attempt to interrelate ourselves to each other in a relational rather than an individualistic fashion, to begin to "socially construct" a relational society. (p. 182)

Even a self, so far construed as the most private experience we have an access to, for Gergen cannot be seen as a reflection of an inner essence, but a relation:

As belief in essential selves erodes, awareness expands of the ways in which personal identity can be created and re-created in relationships. . . . We may be entering a new era of self-conception. In this era the self is redefined as no longer an essence in itself, but relational. In the postmodern world, selves may become the manifestations of relationship, thus placing relationships in the central position occupied by the individual self for the last several hundred years of Western history. (Gergen, 1991, pp. 146–147)

We hope that this discussion has given solid arguments to support the thesis that the constructivist approach, including PCP, presents an alternative to the essentialist position claiming that what we call "traits," "personality," or "character" (and, indeed, all our knowledge) is produced in relations, and not the product of some inherent properties of things that can be discovered. Furthermore, those relations do not have to be placed solely in the head of persons as scientists: they exist between people, and people together are responsible for creating, choosing, abandoning, or recreating them.

THE PRIMACY OF THE INTERPERSONAL REALM

Even if we read Kelly's work as an example of a relational approach favoring the view of the ontological primacy of relations over inherent properties of individuals, his theory has been developed mainly as a mentalistic psychology, at the expense of an interpersonal approach to the person. In this section, we look at the reason for this direction of elaboration. We then go on to examine the possibility of an alternative elaboration of PCP, which draws on the thought of Mead (1934) and Merleau-Ponty (1962). In "invitational mood" (Kelly, 1969b), we focus on what is going on between people rather than within them. The issue of fragmentation is then examined from this perspective.

By calling the development of PCP "mentalistic," we mean that construct theorists have been concerned with employing the penetrating and frequently clinically useful techniques offered by the theory to uncover "construct systems," which are thought of as the property of individuals. Although grids have been used to discover the relationship between constructs, laddering and pyramiding have been seen as showing the hierarchical nature of individual construct systems. The explanation of individuals' conduct is thought of as residing in some way "inside" the person. Implicit in this approach is a separation of the person and the world; an inside/outside distinction. It is only a short step to seeing "constructs" as cognitive structures. Even if these do not cause persons to act as they do in any simple way, constructs regulate behavior rather in the same way that "efficacy beliefs" do in social learning theory (Bandura, 1977). Construct theorists may claim that the reification of construing in this way is nothing more than a way of talking about construing; that, following Kelly (1955), they fully recognize the folly of separating cognition from behavior. Nevertheless, it is surely the case that our language shapes and even imprisons our thinking, a point emphasized not only by Wittgenstein (1972) and the social constructionists (Burr, 1995), but also by Kelly (1969b) in his cautions against the indicative mood.

Perhaps the reason for this search for individuals' construct systems, core structures, and superordinate constructs is best understood when we appreciate the clinical focus of PCP:

The focus of convenience that we have chosen for our own theory-building efforts is the psychological reconstruction of life. We are concerned with better ways to help a person reconstrue his life so that he need not be the victim of his past. If the theory we construct works well within this limited range of convenience, we shall consider our efforts successful, and we shall not be too much disturbed if it proves to be less useful elsewhere. (Kelly, 1955, p. 23)

Because psychotherapy is seen as chiefly an individual enterprise, the idiosyncrasy of the person and the power of personal agency are underlined. Kelly constantly emphasized that we have it in our power to change our lives, that we can reconstrue that which we cannot deny. "Man can enslave himself with his own ideas and then win his freedom again by reconstruing his life" (1955, p. 21). He can be read as saying that we can think our way out of trouble, perhaps in the fashion of the cognitive therapists who had yet to come onto the therapeutic scene (Beck, 1976; Ellis, 1962).

But while the Individuality Corollary asserts that "persons differ from each other in their construction of events" (Kelly, 1955, p. 55), the Commonality Corollary allows that "to the extent that one person employs a construction of experience which is similar to that employed by another, his psychological processes are similar to those of the other person" (1955, p. 90). Constructions can be individual or communal. Surely, the reason why Kelly emphasized the individual nature of construction, why this should be the "default" position for the psychologist, was because it is a pragmatic clinical heuristic device. Volume 2 of *The Psychology of Personal Constructs* is replete with cautions for clinicians to avoid constellatory and preemptive construing of their clients. They should maintain a "credulous approach," not assume one schizophrenic is like another, and never assume they know what things mean to the client. It is better for the clinician to view everybody as unique, as well as to emphasize what power people do have to alter their situations. Kelly recognized both the commonality of construing and the situated nature of freedom (Kelly, 1969a). His "individualism" constitutes advice to clinicians on what to avoid in their practice.

This, indeed, is the view of Hinkle (1970), who goes on to suggest that one of Kelly's objectives in devising PCP is manifest in the Sociality Corollary. This corollary states that "whatever one does in the light of his understanding of others' outlooks may be regarded as his role" (Kelly, 1969f, p.178). Hinkle argues that there is a hidden moral agenda to PCP, which Kelly did not emphasize in his efforts to make his theory acceptable and scientific to his audience of psychologists. Perhaps this should not surprise us, given Kelly's admiration for Dewey, whose moral agenda was quite explicit (Dewey, 1929/1993). Bannister and

Fransella (1971) agree that the Sociality Corollary was of central importance to Kelly, and offers an opportunity for the elaboration of a social psychology through his concept of role.

In his advice for analyzing self-characterization sketches, Kelly (1955) suggests rereading the whole sketch as if it were an elaboration of each sentence. Perhaps, then, it might be useful to look at PCP as if it were an extension of the Sociality Corollary. Stringer and Bannister (1979, p. xiii) contend that social psychology probably has a stronger claim on PCP than any other subdivision in psychology. Let us consider what a more social construct theory would look like. This first involves setting PCP in the context of pragmatism.

PCP and Pragmatism

Support for the validity of reading of PCP in a way that privileges the relations between people rather than an intrapsychic reality comes from an examination of the tradition of American pragmatism in which Kelly was steeped. Kelly always underlined the differences between PCP and other psychologies (Kelly, 1969e, p. 216). However, he paid tribute to the pragmatism of Dewey, "whose philosophy and psychology can be read between many of the lines of the psychology of personal constructs" (1955, p. 154). Joas (1997) lists the defining features of pragmatism as (a) antifoundationalism, (b) the fallible nature of truth, (c) pluralism, (d) the importance of inquiry, and (e) the social nature of the self. It is clear that PCP has drawn on all of these features, although the last remains to be developed. Kelly's philosophical position of constructive alternativism (1955) incorporates the first three. The person as scientist model, which stresses humankind's forward movement and inquiry, also comes from Dewey:

Even with his best thought, a man's proposed course of action may be defeated. But in as far as his act is a truly a manifestation of intelligent choice, he learns something—as in a scientific experiment, an inquirer may learn through his experimentation, his intelligently directed action, quite as much, or even more, from a failure, than from a success. (Dewey, 1929/1993, pp. 133–134)

Above all, the pragmatists held that progress depended on questioning received wisdom, not accepting the dichotomies that have been handed down to us like theory/practice, mind/body, stimulus/response, and self/other (Mounce, 1997). Here we can see the origins of personal constructs that may both restrict and facilitate psychological movement. We can see the pragmatist Kelly rejecting the dichotomies of, for example, cognition/behavior and freedom/determinism as constructions of the world rather than representations of it. He also approaches the self/other issue skeptically in his examination of role in the therapeutic relationship (Kelly, 1969e). The construct "man versus the environment is a somewhat fuzzy notion. . . . We must keep it clearly in mind that we invented this construct and must hold ourselves responsible for it" (1969e, p. 217). The boundary between one person and another belongs not to the world of events, but is a construction to be judged not in terms of its truth, but its usefulness.

Mead's Philosophy of the Act

It was this dichotomy of self/other, which most preoccupied Dewey's friend and colleague, George Mead. Farr (1996, p. 65) quotes Jane Dewey saying that Mead had as much influence on her father as did William James. In particular, Mead socialized Dewey's work on the philosophy of the act, the focus of his seminal paper on the reflex arc (a paper that very probably influenced Kelly, as it emphasizes the anticipatory and questioning nature of behavior). Just as Mead socialized Dewey's work, so it may have influenced Kelly's. For both Dewey and Mead, the meaning of an act cannot be understood from the perspective of either the actor or observer alone. Dewey emphasized how the behaviorist cannot capture the actor's perspective from an external vantage point. Mead's social behaviorism underlines that the reflective consciousness of the actor requires a social history, a starting point in interactionism from which this consciousness emerges.

Instead of starting, in effect, with an Individuality Corollary, Mead (1934) proposed that sociality precedes individuality. Rather than starting with individual consciousness and trying to explain social interaction, Mead's proposition was that consciousness (mind) was an emergent property, one that has evolved through the interactions we have with each other. "Mind arises through communication by a conversation of gestures in a social process or context of experience—not communication through mind" (Mead, 1934, p. 50). As a convinced Darwinian (Farr, 1996), Mead argued that we can see this conversation of gestures in other animals. Using the example of two dogs preparing to fight, he observes that they do not mimic one another, but adopt complementary gestures, anticipating the moves of their opponents. What Mead saw as our distinctive humanity comes from our consciousness of ourselves (self). This emerges from our ability to take the role or perspective of the other, through reflecting on our action. Taking the perspective of the other then, occurs initially in relation—a "conversation of gestures"—through a behavioral dialog with others, and later through a "conversation of symbols," that is, through shared language. So "mind" and "self" were not intrapsychic entities for Mead, but processes that were essentially relational.

When Mead talked of taking the role of the other, he was not referring to those "sociological" versions of role from which Kelly (1955) distanced himself. Mead was not claiming that people fit into preordained roles laid down by society. To take the role of others is to see your own action from their position, to act in view of the other's perspective. Indeed, both Holland (1977) and Ashworth (1979) have noted the similarity between Mead and Kelly in their versions of role. This congruence is even more striking in Kelly's redefinition of role: "whatever one does in the light of his understanding of others' outlooks may be regarded as his role" (Kelly, 1969f, p. 178).

This emphasis on the relational in no way denies the existence of a private world of reflection. What it stresses is that our private worlds are constructed out of the public world. In deciding to stay in and write rather than to go out and play tennis, I may ponder the pros and cons of each course of action, and decide that what is primarily at issue is meeting a deadline before making my decision. What Mead's work underlines is that this process of circumspection, preemption, and choice (Kelly, 1955) takes the form of a conversation with myself. As James (cited in Billig, 1987) asserts, we can only deliberate because we have witnessed arguments between people. What goes on "in our heads" is always derived from what goes on in the social world. The relational precedes the intrapsychic; sociality preceded individuality.

Neither does the essentially prereflective nature of intersubjectivity deny our ability to deliberate and decide on a particular course of action. We clearly can and do consciously choose to act in one way rather than another. However, conscious deliberation preceding choice is the exception rather than the rule in human action. Kelly (1969c) affirms that our behavior is chosen and not motivated, yet such choice is normally not the focus of the person's awareness. In everyday life, a person's behavior is not usually the result of deliberation, although it is nonetheless intentional. An intersubjective perspective on this prereflective activity sees action not simply as the property of any particular individual; not something that can necessarily be traced back to the plan inside a particular participant. Instead, people together spontaneously produce joint action (Blumer, 1969; Shotter, 1993b). Action becomes social action, or praxis (Radley, 1979). Shotter (1993b) describes this as knowing from within a situation, a type of knowledge he distinguishes from "knowing how" and "knowing that."

For Mead, people are primarily prereflective; they act, and reflection is an emergent property, the product of language that they may later use to deliberate on their actions. However, theorists who have developed from Mead have not elaborated the prereflective conversation of gestures. It is the conversation of symbols that has been emphasized by the sociological school of symbolic interactionists (Blumer, 1969). In the view of contemporary commentators on Mead (Farr, 1996; Joas, 1997), this has been at the expense of the preverbal conversation of gestures. The concentration on social meaning and language has ignored Mead's emphasis on preverbal impulse behind action. The symbolic interactionists' stress on interpretation and reflection places too much weight on deliberation, as it were, inside individuals. We can, however, turn to the phenomenology of Merleau-Ponty (1962) here.

Elaboration of the Relational Realm in the Existential Phenomenology of Merleau-Ponty

The bringing together of the existential phenomenology of Merleau-Ponty and the pragmatism of Mead does not present a clash of paradigms. Rorty (1982, 1989), the current standard-bearer of pragmatism, claims that although existentialism and pragmatism differ in tone, they share antifoundationalism as a basis for their view of the person. Rosenthal and Bourgeois (1991) and Crossley (1996) both emphasize common visions of Mead and Merleau-Ponty on the primacy of the intersubjective and relational origins of the person.

Merleau-Ponty (1962, 1964, 1993) addressed the problem of the recognition of other selves in an attempt to combat what he saw as the solipsism of Sartre (1958). The basic unit of analysis for Merleau-Ponty is intention, a relational concept that denotes the person's connectedness with the world. Individual consciousness and the world are always connected; we are always scared of something, thinking about something, desiring for something. Fear, thought, and desire do not exist in a vacuum. When we perceive other persons, we do not see their behavior and infer their inner state. Reflection and cognition are not necessary in communication. We read their intention directly and prereflectively. When I greet old friends and see them smile, wave, and come toward me, I do not infer friendliness from their behavior. Friendliness *is* this configuration of posture, gesture, and expression. It is their friendliness as intention that I perceive.

My own conduct is then drawn from me prereflectively in this joint action. Of course, my friend and I may mislead each other. It is open to us to try to manage our expression. To say that we read intention directly is not to say that we always read it correctly. Processes "internal" to the person may intervene in our interaction, but in everyday life, this is not normally the case. Here we see Mead's conversation of gestures. The term "gesture" itself implies intentionality—gestures are made to someone, about something. "Behavior," the term preferred by psychologists, bleaches the meaning and intention out of gesture.

Like Mead, Merleau-Ponty (1962) sees individuality as being forged out of sociality and commonality. Drawing on Piaget's developmental studies, Merleau-Ponty (1962, p. 355) notes that when an adult playfully prepares to bite one of a baby's fingers, the baby spontaneously mimics a biting action with its mouth. It also naturally responds to a smiling face with a smile of its own. How can an infant respond like this to the actions of another? How do they translate the intentions and movements of another into actions they themselves make? Merleau-Ponty contends that the dualist argument by inference and analogy—"I feel this when I do such and such so s/he must as well"—is unconvincing, because the infant at this stage cannot recognize its own image in a mirror. In fact, this explanation has to assume a common world—that which it is attempting to explain. Where Piaget concludes that the child grows out of its egocentrism, the belief that others see the world as it does, Merleau-Ponty argues that its acquired recognition of different perspectives has to be built on an essential commonality and a reading of each others' intentionality. There could be no communication between people if they did not potentially share the same horizons.

In adult life, we take for granted our ability to perceive from within a relational situation. The widespread belief that there is a mind inside each body leads us to believe that a complicated process of inference based on an internal cognitive structure precedes our action. Construing is seen as the property of individuals and not residing in relational social action. Merleau-Ponty uses conversation as an example of joint action. In a dialog between two people, the perspectives of the participants merge into a single fabric, where each contribution is elicited by the interaction:

I am freed from myself, for the other person's thoughts are certainly his; they are not of my making, though I do grasp them the moment they come into being, or even anticipate them. And indeed, the objection my interlocuter raises to what I say draws from me thoughts which I had no idea I possessed. . . . It is only retrospectively, when I have withdrawn from the dialogue and am recalling it that I am able to reintegrate it into my life and make it an episode in my private history, and that the other recedes into his absence. (Merleau-Ponty, 1962, pp. 354–355)

So, although we reflect on our action, it is prereflective joint action on which we reflect. This prereflected joint action is intentional; it makes sense in terms of the situations in which we are participants and are immersed. Construing, then, takes place in action and not "in our heads." It is gesture, or behavior, that is the person's "independent variable" that owes nothing to sequential explanation originating in an internal construct system (Kelly, 1969d). The boundary between the inside and the outside of the person indeed becomes "fuzzy" when as Ihde (1984, p. 47), paraphrasing Merleau-Ponty, put it: " I am outside myself in the world of my project."

This mirrors Kelly's definition of a person as an intersect of many subjective dimensions as constructed by someone such as ourselves. The intersect of many subjective dimensions that makes *your* personality is located in *my* head. Although what I say about you reveals more about me and my criteria of construing certain dimensions, without the relation (of me and you, but also of any other persons) there would not be a person to be construed and a person to construe. My personality is thus located "outside the skin," because it needs human interrelatedness to become, to be knitted in the fabric of the human being. The realm of relations provides this fabric. Therefore, I am outside of myself and equally in yourself, as much as you are outside yourself and inside myself.

Furthermore, this discussion points to the problem of boundaries. If personality is completely mind-dependent and does not have some extra mental being, we may say (and this would hold not just in the realm of personality psychology but in the whole universe) that no two things would be actually distinct prior to the mind's activity and all would be one, as if we were living in one undivided universe. This reflects Kelly's idea of an "integral universe," which exists as a single unit going on all the time. Take for example this quotation (Kelly, 1955):

Man looks at his world through transparent patterns or templates, which he creates and then attempts to fit over the realities of which the world is composed. The fit is not always very good. Yet without such patterns the world appears to be such an *undifferentiated homogeneity* that man is unable to make any sense out of it. (p. 9, emphasis added)

Stated simply, we have to watch the universe through the transparent patterns we produce, because otherwise it would not make any sense to us. But this statement also implies that distinctions among the things in the universe, or boundaries between "separated" things, personality included, are dependent on the mind's activity! Borders between people are the products of human conceptual activities happening in a shared meaning system produced in social relations. They are the artifact of mind and *not* the way world "really" exists.

CONCLUSION

Emphasizing the primacy of relations over essences presents a challenge for the science of psychology. For if there is no hidden essence to be discovered and to be held responsible for the conduct of individuals, psychology will have to divest itself of all those IQ and personality tests that assume essential human attributes. It will not be easy to convince orthodox psychologists to abandon those foundations that appear to have conferred on it a scientific status. It might also prove difficult to persuade those construct theorists who search for internal construct systems, core structures, and indeed, constructs "inside" the person.

Nevertheless, it is our contention that an elaborated understanding of human responsibility and capability bids us look between people as well as at what they have made out of what is between them. A personality is not something that we fashion on our own, but is produced in joint action in the context of social relations and afforded by the materials available to us. We change as our social contexts allow us to. Human responsibility and psychological reconstruction become extremely complex issues. But, if we can be forgiven for indulging in some wordplay, this is the reality of human existence.

NOTES

1. Cappadoccian triadology seems to be the first organized attempt to base a relational paradigm of human existence (and, thus, a remote ancestor of a constructivist thought, a point taken by von Glasersfeld, 1991). As far back as in the fourth century A.D. in Byzantium, eastern Christian theologians known as Cappadoccian fathers (St. Basil the Great, St. Gregory of Nyssa, and St. Gregory Theologian) developed their views of triadology, or the doctrine of the Holy Trinity. As God lives in the tropersonal triadic community (consisting of Father, Son, and the Holy Spirit), so people live in personal community with their fellows. God's mode of being is actually an ontologically fundamental paradigm for people, thus giving Cappadoccian theology wider philosophical relevance. Cappadoccian personology developed from their triadological doctrine and is founded on their highly pondered concept of *shesis*, a Greek word that means interrelation. This basically means that whatever God is, actually presents the effect of the interrelations in his tropersonal community. This doctrine is opposed to the better known triadological doctrine of St. Augustine, in which God's essence is not the effect of mutual relations in the Holy Trinity, but their cause (for comprehensive explanation, see Torrance, 1988).

2. The ideas of Macmurray reviewed in this chapter are based on the concept of person, as given in Macmurray's Gifford lectures delivered in 1953–1954, entitled "The Self As Agent" and "Persons in Relation" (Macmurray, 1957, 1961). These lectures are the fruition of Macmurray's philosophical career at Manchester, Johannesburg, Oxford, London, and Edinburgh Universities. We hope that this explains how Kelly could have known Macmurray's work, published in 1957 and 1961, prior to writing his own two volumes, published in 1955.

REFERENCES

Allport, G. (1937). *Personality: A psychological interpretation*. London: Constable & Company.

Allport, G. (1955). *Becoming: Basic considerations for a psychology of personality*. New Haven, CT: Yale University Press.

Allport, G. (1960). *Personality and social encounter*. Boston: Beacon Press.

Allport, G. (1961). *Pattern and growth in personality*. London: Holt, Reinhart & Winston.

Ashworth, P. (1979). *Social interaction and consciousness*. Chichester: Wiley.

Bandura, A. (1977). Self-efficacy: Towards a unifying theory of behavior change. *Psychological Review, 84*, 191–215.

Bannister, D. (1983). Self in personal construct theory. In J. Adams-Webber & J. Mancuso (Eds.), *Applications of personal construct theory* (pp. 379–387). Toronto, Canada: Academic Press.

Bannister, D., & Fransella, F. (1971). *Inquiring man*. Harmondsworth, England: Penguin.

Bateson, G. (1979). *Mind and nature*. London: Flamingo.

Beck, A. (1976). *Cognitive therapy and the emotional disorders*. Harmondsworth, England: Penguin.

Bertocci, P. (1965). Foundations of personalistic psychology. In B. Wolman & E. Nagel (Eds.), *Scientific psychology: Principles and approaches* (pp. 293–316). New York: Basic Books.

Bhaskar, R. (1989). *Reclaiming reality*. London: Verso.

Billig, M. (1987). *Arguing and thinking: A rhetorical approach to social psychology*. Cambridge: Cambridge University Press.

Blumer, H. (1969). *Symbolic interactionism*. Englewood Cliffs, NJ: Prentice-Hall.

Botella, L. (1995). Personal construct psychology, constructivism and postmodernism. In R. Neimeyer & G. Neimeyer (Eds.), *Recent advances in personal construct psychology* (Vol. 3, pp. 3–36). New York: Springer.

Burkitt, I. (1991). *Social selves: Theories of the social formation of personality*. London: Sage.

Burkitt, I. (1996). Social and personal constructs: A division left unresolved. *Theory & Psychology, 6*, 71–77.

Burr, V. (1995). *An introduction to social constructionism*. London: Routledge.

Butt, T. W. (1996) PCP: Cognitive or social psychology? In J. Scheer & A. Catina (Eds.), *Constructivism in Europe*. Giessen, Germany: Psychosozid Verlag.

Cattell, R. B. (1966). *The scientific analysis of personality theory*. Chicago: Aldine.

Chiari, G., & Nuzzo, L. (1996). Psychological constructivisms: A metatheoretical differentiation. *Journal of Constructivist Psychology, 9*, 163–184.

Costa, P. T., Jr., & McCrae, R. R. (1992). Four ways five factors are basic. *Personality and Individual Differences, 13,* 653–665.

Crossley, N. (1996). *Intersubjectivity.* London: Sage.

Dahrendorf, R. (1973). *Homo sociologicus.* London: Routledge & Kegan Paul.

Dewey, J. (1929/1993). Philosophies of freedom. In D. Morris & I. Shapiro (Eds.), *John Dewey: The political writings* (pp. 133–141). Indianapolis, IN: Hackett.

Efran, J., & Heffner, K. (1998). Is constructivist psychotherapy epistemologically flawed? *Journal of Constructivist Psychology, 11,* 89–105.

Ellis, A. (1962). *Reason and emotion in psychotherapy.* New York: Lyle Stuart.

Eysenck, H. J. (1953). *The Structure of Human Personality.* London: Methuen.

Farr, R. (1996). *The roots of modern social psychology.* Oxford, England: Blackwell.

Gergen, K. J. (1985). The social constructionist movement in modern psychology. *American Psychologist, 40,* 266–275.

Gergen, K. J. (1991). *The saturated self: Dilemmas of identity in contemporary life.* New York: Basic Books.

Gergen, K. J. (1994). *Realities and relationships: Soundings in social construction.* Cambridge: Harvard University Press.

Goffman, E. (1959). *The presentations of self in everyday life.* Harmondsworth, England: Penguin.

Goodman, N. (1978). *Ways of worldmaking.* Indianopolis, IN: Hackett.

Greenwood, J. (1994). *Realism, identity and emotion.* London: Sage.

Henninger, M. G. (1989). *Relations: Medieval theories 1250–1325.* Oxford, England: Oxford University Press.

Hinkle, D. (1970). The game of personal constructs. In D. Bannister (Ed.), *Perspectives in personal construct theory* (pp. 91–110). London: Academic Press.

Holland, R. (1977). *Self in social context.* London: Macmillan.

Ihde, D. (1984). *Experimental phenomenology.* Albany: State University of New York Press.

Joas, H. (1997). *George Mead: A contemporary re-examination of his thought.* Oxford, England: Blackwell.

Kelly, G. A. (1955). *Psychology of personal constructs.* New York: Norton.

Kelly, G. A. (1969a). The autobiography of a theory. In B. Maher (Ed.), *Clinical psychology and personality: The selected papers of George Kelly* (pp. 46–66). London: Wiley.

Kelly, G. A. (1969b). The language of hypothesis: Man's psychological instrument. In B. Maher (Ed.), *Clinical psychology and personality: The selected papers of George Kelly* (pp. 147–163). London: Wiley.

Kelly, G. A. (1969c). Man's construction of his alternatives. In B. Maher (Ed.), *Clinical psychology and personality: The selected papers of George Kelly* (pp. 66–94). London: Wiley.

Kelly, G. A. (1969d). Ontological acceleration. In B. Maher (Ed.), *Clinical psychology and personality: The selected papers of George Kelly* (pp. 7–45). London: Wiley.

Kelly, G. A. (1969e). The psychotherapeutic relationship. In B. Maher (Ed.), *Clinical psychology and personality: The selected papers of George Kelly* (pp. 216–223). London: Wiley.

Kelly, G. A. (1969f). Sin and psychotherapy. In B. Maher (Ed.), *Clinical psychology and personality: The selected papers of George Kelly* (pp. 165–188). London: Wiley.

Macmurray, J. (1957). *The self as an agent.* London: Academic Press.

Macmurray, J. (1961). *Persons in relation.* London: Academic Press.

Mahoney, M. (1988). Constructivist metatheory I: Basic features and historical foundations. *International Journal of Personal Construct Psychology, 1,* 125–137.

Mair, J. M. M. (1977). The community of self. In D. Bannister (Ed.), *New perspectives in personal construct theory* (pp. 125–149). London: Academic Press.

Mair, J. M. M. (1980). Feeling and knowing. In P. Salmon (Ed.), *Coming to know* (pp. 113–127). London: Routledge.

Mancuso, J. (1996). Constructionism, personal construct psychology, and narrative psychology. *Theory & Psychology, 6,* 47–70.

Mancuso, J. (1998). Can an avowed adherent of personal-construct psychology be counted as a social constructionist? *Journal of Constructivist Psychology, 11,* 205–219.

Maturana, H. (1978). Biology of language: The epistemology of reality. In G. A. Miller & E. Lenneberg (Eds.), *Psychology and biology of language and thought: Essays in honour of Eric Lenneberg* (pp. 27–63). San Diego, CA: Academic Press.

McCall, C. (1990). *Concepts of persons.* Aldershot, England: Avebury.

Mead, G. (1934). *Mind, self and society.* Chicago: University of Chicago Press.

Merleau-Ponty, M. (1962). *Phenomenology of perception.* London: Routledge. (Originally published 1945.)

Merleau-Ponty, M. (1964). The child's relations with others. In J. Edie (Ed.), *The primacy of perception* (pp.96–158). Evanston, IL: Northwestern University Press.

Merleau-Ponty, M. (1993). The experience of others. In K. Hoeller (Ed.), *Merleau-Ponty and psychology* (pp. 33–66). Newark, NJ: Humanities Press.

Mischel, W. (1968). *Personality and assessment.* New York: Wiley.

Mounce, H. (1997). *The two pragmatisms.* London: Routledge.

Neimeyer, R. A. (1993). An appraisal of constructivist psychotherapies. *Journal of Consulting and Clinical Psychology, 61*(2), 221–234.

Neimeyer, R. A. (1995). Limits and lessons of constructivism: Some critical reflections. *Journal of Constructivist Psychology, 8,* 339–361.

Noaparast, K. B. (1995). Towards a more realistic constructivism. In R. A. Neimeyer & G. J. Neimeyer (Eds.), *Advances in personal construct psychology.* Greenwich, CT: JAI Press.

Piaget, J. (1937). *La construction du reel chez enfant* [The child's construction of reality]. Neuchatel, France: Delachaux et Niestle.

Piaget, J. (1973). *Jean Piaget, the man and his ideas* (R. I. Evans, Ed.). New York: Dutton.

Radley, A. (1979). Construing as praxis. In P. Stringer & D. Bannister (Eds.), *Constructs of sociality and individuality* (pp. 73–90). London: Academic Press.

Rorty, R. (1982). *Consequences of pragmatism.* New York: Harvester Wheatsheaf.

Rorty, R. (1989). *Contingency, irony and solidarity.* Cambridge, England: Cambridge University Press.

Rosenthal, S., & Bourgeois, P. (1991). *Mead and Merleau-Ponty: Towards a common vision.* Albany: State University of New York Press.

Sartre, J. P. (1958). *Being and nothingness.* London: Methuen.

Searle, J. (1995). *The construction of social reality.* Harmondsworth, England: Penguin.

Segal, L. (1986). *The dream of reality: Heinz von Foerster's constructivism.* New York: Norton.

Shotter, J. (1985). Social accountability and self specification. In K. J. Gergen & K. E.

Davis (Eds.), *The social construction of the person* (pp. 167–191). New York: Springer-Verlag.

Shotter, J. (1993a). *Conversational realities*. London: Sage.

Shotter, J. (1993b). *Cultural politics of everyday life*. Buckingham, England: Open University Press.

Shotter, J. (1997). The social construction of our inner selves. *Journal of Constructivist Psychology, 10*, 7–25.

Stam, H. (1998). Personal construct theory and social constructionism: Difference and dialogue. *Journal of Constructivist Psychology, 11*, 187–203.

Stringer, P., & Bannister, D. (1979). *Constructs of sociality and individuality*. London: Academic Press.

Taylor, C. (1971). Interpretation and the sciences of man. *Review of Metaphysics, 25*, 3–51.

Torrance, T. F. (1988). *The Trinitarian faith*. Edinburgh, Scotland: T. & T. Clark.

Toumela, R. (1977). *Human action and its explanation*. Dordrecht, Germany, and Boston: D. Riedl.

Trilling, L. (1974). *Sincerity and authenticity*. London: Oxford University Press.

Varela, F. J. (1984). The creative circle: Sketches on the natural history of circularity. In P. Watzlawick (Ed.), *The invented reality* (pp. 309–325). New York: Norton.

von Foerster, H. (1981). *Observing systems*. Seaside, CA: Interesystems Publications.

von Foerster, H. (1984). On constructing a reality. In P. Watzlawick (Ed.), *The invented reality* (pp. 41–63). New York: Norton.

von Glasersfeld, E. (1987). *The construction of knowledge*. Seaside, CA: Interesystems Publications.

von Glasersfeld, E. (1991). Knowing without metaphysics: Aspects of the radical constructivist position. In F. Steier (Ed.), *Research and reflexivity* (pp. 12–30). London: Sage.

Warren, W. G. (1985). Personal construct psychology and contemporary philosophy: An examination of alignments. In D. Bannister (Ed.), *Issues and approaches in personal construct theory* (pp. 253–267). London: Academic Press.

Wittgenstein, L. (1972). *Philosophical investigations*. Oxford, England: Blackwell.

part II

Methodological Advances

Chapter 4

Textual Analysis of Therapeutic Discourse

Manuel Villegas

Since 1973, when Labov and Fanshell published their paper on "Therapeutic discourse: Psychotherapy as conversation" a great deal has been published on this topic. For some writers, the object of the analysis of therapeutic discourse is the communicative interaction between therapist and client (Stiles, 1992, 1993a, 1993b). For others, it is rather the content of the client's discourse that has to be analyzed; for example, eliciting his or her system of constructs (Feixas, 1988; Feixas & Villegas, 1991, 1993), identifying the client's evaluations through the extensive use he or she makes of the language (Caro, 1994), extracting the characteristics of the narrative structures of different pathologies (Gonçalves, 1995; Pubill, 1994; Villegas, 1995, 1997, 1998), or making explicit the implicit matrices of any discourse manifestation of the client (Villegas, 1992).

Although each has a different objective, all of these procedures and many others are no doubt legitimate and useful when it comes to studying therapeutic discourse. The method we propose here is taken from textual linguistics (Van Dijk, 1977), and it differs from the others in at least one of the following three characteristics:

1. It is not centered in the meaning of singular words, as are different forms of content analysis, but in the meaning of the text as a whole.
2. It implies the analysis of superficial and deep structures, using different linguistic tools such as cohesion, connection, coherence, and macrostructures.
3. It always refers to the context of production (i.e., to the pragmatic conditions in which it is produced), regardless of the typology of the text.

This method is called *textual analysis,* because the unit of analysis is always a text. Although analysis of discourse is specifically a hermeneutic operation (Ricoeur, 1986), textual analysis permits the realization of this operation by means of a linguistic technique that aims at disclosing the discursive matrix, bearing in mind that any text is one of the possible actualizations of that same matrix. According to Van Dijk (1998), in different approaches to the concept of discourse we encounter three main dimensions in which several disciplines are involved: the use of language (linguistics, pragmatics, semiotics); communication of beliefs (psycholinguistics, cognitive psychology); and interaction in social situations (ethnography, ethnomethodology, social psychology).

From a constructivist point of view, we understand discourse as being the "communication of thought (system of constructs) by speech, talk or conversation." In this way, we approach discourse analysis in psychotherapy with a clearly defined cognitive psychological focus, given that the client's ideological or discursive matrix constitutes the object of our analysis, although the method (the textual analysis) is, of course, linguistic. To this end, we distinguish between *discourse analysis*—what one intends to say (intentionality)—and *textual analysis*—the analysis of what is actually said (literality). For the moment, we are not interested in either social interactions or conversational modalties that are no doubt produced by the verbal exchanges between the client and the therapist, because we are, in fact, interested in the semantic content of this particular discourse. This semantic content is, of course, manifested through the dialog in the therapeutic interview, but may show itself in many other ways, including conversations and written documents (McTavish & Pirro, 1990), such as self-characterizations, letters, diaries, poetry, memoirs, autobiographies (Villegas, Feixas, & López, 1990), or in any other kind of personal documents (Allport, 1942). We consider all of these forms of discursive expression to be texts that can be analyzed using the methodology proposed in this chapter, that is, textual analysis.

This kind of analysis requires that oral discourse be transcribed. According to McTavish and Pirro (1990), by "text" we mean a "transcript of naturally occurring verbal material." Consequently, we use the term *text* to refer to any written record of a communicative event, whereas we reserve the term *discourse* to refer to the interpretation of the communicative event in context, which thus implies a hermeneutic activity.

Since the very beginnings of psychotherapy, the psychotherapist's task has been described as the interpreter of the client's discourse. Within this framework, the psychotherapeutic interaction presupposes the task of interpretation (hermeneutics) in which the therapist (addresee), using textual analysis (method), tries to comprehend the client's (addresser) discursive matrix (intention) manifest in the text (object). This structure is represented graphically in Figure 4-1.

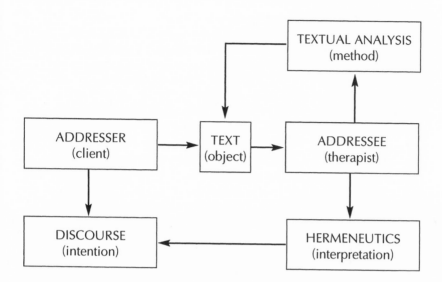

Figure 4-1. Structure of therapeutic interaction as hermeneutic interpretation of client discourse.

TEXT AND DISCOURSE

Although the terms *text* and *discourse* are frequently used as synonyms in different languages, we establish a clear distinction between each of them based on the literal conditions of the first and the intentional aspects of the second (Levelt, 1989).

The existing relationship between the text and the discourse can be, in some way, compared with that which Christian theology (inspired by neoplatonism) establishes between "Verbum" ($\Lambda o\gamma o\sigma$) and "Caro" ($\sigma\alpha\rho\xi$), the text being the manifestation or the *epiphany* of the word (discourse). In this way, in completing the analogy, we can say that the text is the incarnation of the discourse. The discourse accounts for the relationship between the intentions of the transmitter (*addresser*)—speaker or writer—and the intentions of the receiver (*addressee*)—listener or reader—implies the correlative processes of production and comprehension, and is the object of hermeneutics. The *text*, on the other hand, refers to the transmission itself; the message, insofar as the message is an ostensible product—both oral and written—becomes the object of the textual analysis. The text comes to life when both the author (in the process of *production*), and the addressee (in the process of *interpretation*), bring the discursive *dynamic* into play. With the introduction of this dynamic, the text is no longer a *static* product but is, rather, the place where the negotiating actions of the addresser and the addressee meet, as can be seen in Figure 4-2.

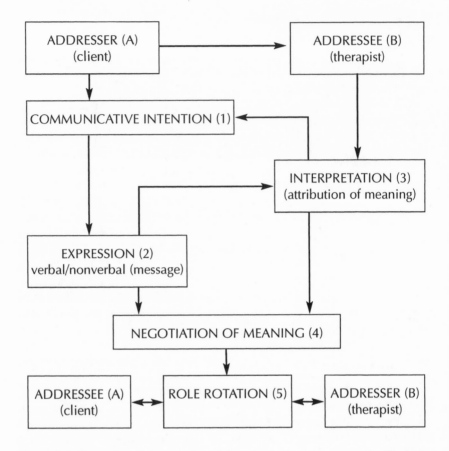

Figure 4-2. Dynamic of interpretation of therapeutic texts in communicative inter-action between client and therapist.

Subject *A,* whom we consider the addresser, given that he initiates the com-munication, wishes to transmit (1) some idea or information, express some kind of emotional state, or obtain some kind of benefit from subject *B,* who is the receiver or addressee of *A*'s action. To do this, addresser *A* verbally or nonver-bally emits (2) a message that contains, more or less explicitly, an intention. Subject *B* receives the message and attempts to decipher its content not just at an immediate significance or literal level, but also at an intentionality level. To achieve this, *B* must interpret it (3) by attributing a contextualized meaning to the message according to what he or she knows about the transmitter, *A,* the moment that the message was transmitted and the reactions that it provoked. The inter-pretation consists of both deciphering the messsage's semantic content as well as comprehension of the final pragmatics expressed. Often, the addressee does not achieve a satisfactory interpretation of the intentionality of the transmitter, and a large part of the time consumed by the initial transmissions is taken up by negotiating activity (4). The addressee, having taken the negotiating initiative, assumes the role of transmitter, and the transmitter the role of addresssee, and so on. This phenomenon is known as *role rotation* (5), and it is the basis of ordinary conversation, in general, and in therapeutic dialog, in particular.

Addresser and addressee exchange their intentions through the text, whose analysis allows the reconstruction of the discursive matrix that generates it and converts it in the *transactional* object of the communication (Brown & Yule, 1983). The producing subject elaborates the text, bearing in mind the presence or absence of the addressee and his or her specific characteristics as a receiver who is incorporated as a collaborator in the production of the text. The presence of the receiver is guaranteed by the relationship with a specific or ideal addressee—the model reader—who determines the success or failure of the communicative act.

This relationship also constitutes the pragmatic as well as the production *context*. These contexts are not usually present in the text or are present in a solely inferential fashion, so that they are only intelligible with reference to the communicative intention or the interactive situation elaborated under its influence, as we shall see later, when we consider the processes of discourse production. The *extratextual references* that are in the minds of the speakers do not appear, even though they form part of the discourse. Such references may or may not be textually actualized, depending on the information that is considered *relevant*. The assessment of what is considered *relevant* arises, in turn, from the *negotiation* or *cooperation* among the interlocutors, something that, as some authors have observed, schizophrenics fail to do (Belinchón, 1991; Belinchón, Rivière, & Igoa, 1992; Rochester & Martin, 1979; Villegas, 1985).

Thus, text and discourse cannot be used as synonyms, in the first instance because all texts refer to a discourse, whereas not all discourse is actualized in the text. In fact, the discourse does not always acquire an external or observable form—as in a soliloquy—neither does it always encounter circumstances that favor its production or, indeed, the production can be interrupted due to the adressee's lack of collaboration. Consequently, discourse preexists and transcends the text insofar as the text is no more than one of its infinite possible actualizations. Second, text and discourse contain different linguistic considerations. In fact, discourse is free of having to succumb to the rules of the linguistic system: It is reduced to the macrostructural organization and condensed into a macropropositional synthesis. In a certain way, it captures predominantly predicative and agrammatical interior language characteristics (Vygotsky, 1934/1962), but it is not equivalent to an internal monolog such as those offered by literature (Siguan, 1985), which has a textual entity, even if it is not well-informed. The text, for its part, is expanded along microstructures and gramatically conditioned micropropositional realizations. It is abundant in redundancies, which develop the theme or topic of the discourse, which is in turn regulated, in its construction, by the use of different kinds of connectors that establish functional relations of coordination or subordination, as well as by morphosyntatic harmony markers. This distinction between text and discourse is similar to that made by Belinchón et al. (1992), who defined discourse as a "set of semantic, pragmatic, and grammatical representations and as cognitive and linguistic processes which underline the planning and transmission of coordinated series of announced linguistics or texts with communicative purposes in a conversational context" (pp. 633–634). The reference to semantic-pragmatic representations, and to the processes implied in the production as contrasting with the resulting product, characterizes, from our point of view, the distinction between discourse and text. It is not necessary, under any circumstances, to postulate a conversational surround for the proceedings of a discourse or text. This is no more than a type of text, characterized by its dialogic nature, produced by an interactive situation or a *communicative exchange* (Edmonson, 1981; Werth, 1981). Leaving aside the question of processing aspects that affect discourse production and comprehension, Figure 4-3 helps to sum up some formal characteristics that differentiate text and discourse.

The distinction between text and discourse is central in our approach. On the one hand, such a distinction implies and explains that the text refers to the discourse, but on the other, it does not always represent it. In other words, everything that is said refers to what one means (intentionality) but what one says (literality) does not always represent what one means. This phenomenom is characteristic of certain particularities of human language present at both a semantic and a pragmatic level. For example, consider the following dialog between a young woman and her work colleague:

X: "What a downpour!"

Z: "Don't worry, I'll walk you home."

Here, the communicative intention (a plea to be walked home) is not expressed in the words of the young girl's (X) sentence, but is correctly interpreted in the colleague's (Z) sentence. The pragmatic dimension of the expression (X) is inferred from the knowledge that (X) and (Y) have of the situation, of the needs of (X), and of the type of interaction that exists between (X) and (Y). This is a common situation when it comes to human interactions and constitutes the wide field of pragmatics.

In semantics, the lack of coherence between literality (text) and intentionality (discourse) is also a frequent occurrence, as can be seen in the use that human thought and language makes of metaphors and analogies as a means of constructing and expressing experience. One of its most spontaneous and autonomous manifestations can be found in dreams, which according to Lakoff (1998) are structured around processes of metaphorization of experience. Their comprehension requires the interpretation of the literality of the text in accordance with the existential context in which they are produced (Villegas, 1998),

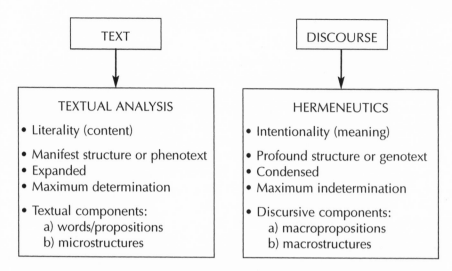

Figure 4-3. Differences between text and discourse.

wherein lies the key to their meaning. For example, consider the following dream of an Italian patient who began to develop agoraphobic symptoms after having fixed a wedding date with his betrothed.

I'm driving along in a car dragging a newspaper stand behind me as if it were a caravan. Suddenly, an open-topped sports car comes up on me at full speed, and in it are two of my old drinking buddies with two absolutely stunning blondes in miniskirts.

Here, the caravan represents a slow and heavy method of transport, completely the opposite of his drinking friends' sports car. These are the friends with whom he used to go to bars before becoming engaged. The dream shows the opposition between the contracted matrimonial ties and the bachelor's freedom that he has felt obliged to renounce: "I cannot run, I cannot escape; I am condemned to everyday life" (in Italian the word "newspaper" is *quotidiano* or *giornale;* from "every day"). The metaphorical text dealing with the cars on the roadway refers to the discourse on the sensation of a loss of freedom linked to marriage.

In this way, a text is no more than one of many ways of manifesting or actualizing a particular discourse or discursive matrix (genotext), which can be expressed in many differrent ways (texts) on many different occasions (contexts), although never in a completely satisfactory manner. The permanent lack of satisfaction produced by the operation of transforming the preverbal thought into an articulate and manifest text leads to pondering the nature of the pathways the discourse follows in such a transformation, that is, from a thought to the word.

THE DISCURSIVE MATRIX: CONDITIONS AND
MODALITIES OF EXPRESSION

The basis of a discursive conception of psychology lies in understanding any human act as an expression or act of personal, and at the same time shared, meaning (Bruner, 1990) that contributes to creating the discursive world in which we live.

The gestation of each significant expression (see Figure 4-4) has its origins in individual or collective life experience (*Lebenswelt*) (1). The mental representation of the meaning of an experience configures the ideological matrix or vision of the world (*Weltanschauung*) (2), which becomes the discourse's matrix or vertebrating axis. Any pretext (3), event, or active internal or external circumstance will suffice to produce a verbal or nonverbal expression (4) of the discursive matrix, called text. In fact, providing that subjects emit a message, then they are expressing something of themselves or at least something that is coherent with themselves.

Although *latu senso,* any signlike or semiotic product could be thought of as text (Eco, 1990) insofar as these codes constitute the actualization of a discourse,

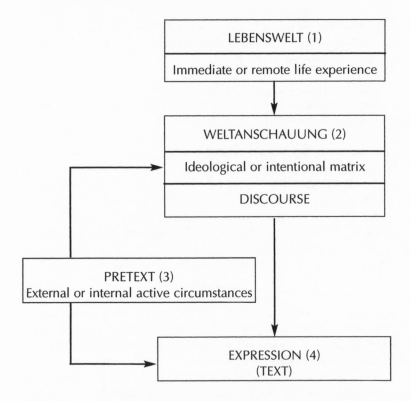

Figure 4-4. Conditions of expressive production.

for the purposes of this chapter, we reserve the term *text* for those productions that use only linguistic code (Villegas, 1992), regardless of the typology—oral, written, dialogic, or monologic—with which it is adorned. Likewise, in this sense, and despite the legitimate ethnomethodological perspective to which we have already referred, we take *conversation* as being text, and not as discourse, given that even though it can be spoken, listened to, recorded, or transcribed, it constitutes a linguistic product (Van Dijk, 1977) and not a process.

CONDITIONS OF TEXTUALITY AND CONTEXTUALITY

A text is comprehensible or interpretable only if it meets the conditions of textuality and contextuality. The textuality refers to the internal regularities of the text; for example, agreement and coherence, based on the *diaphoric* elements (anaphora and cataphora), which, situated within a text, relay earlier or later elements of the same text with which they are coreferenced and constitute the basis of the text's internal coherence. Semantic contextuality implies a semantic isomorphism; that is, equivalence across the textual world (intratextual context) and the referential world (extratextual context). This equality creates a semantic isotopy that defines or delimits one of the narratively infinite "possible worlds," thus creating a *semantic framework,* which permits the identification and relational comprehension of its components. The contextuality refers to the set of production conditions, reception and interpretation, external to the text; that is, to the real or ideal *communicative framework.* Discourse is, therefore, carried out as a pragmatic act, along with all its psychological and sociological implications.

Textuality

Given that the comprehension of a text requires a reconstruction of its deep structure, according to the connection between narrative statements, their order, and lexical realization, for the time being we set aside phenomena that affect only the superficial structure of a text, in order to limit ourselves to the study of those that contribute to its deep structure. The word "text," given its etymology, refers to textile. Textile is composed of many interwoven threads that bestow unity to the material: the texture (Halliday & Hassan, 1976) or textuality (De Beaugrande, 1979, 1980). The threads are woven in two directions: horizontal (weft) and vertical (warp).

These directions are the same as those that mark the lines of the text. The horizontality is achieved, above all, by the cohesion of microstructures. The verticality is achieved by the connection between these. The connection between microstructures leads to the formation of macrostructures whose entire set makes up the phenotext. The recovery of the genotext or discursive matrix is achieved through analyses of redundancy and coherence. All text transmits a message or information. The nucleus of this message is the *theme* whose expansion gives way to the *rheme*. Part of this expansion is due to the *redundancy* (i.e., to the informative reiteration), which can be maximum, medium, or minimum. Maximum redundancy is achieved by interrelating homogenous elements (reiteration, equivalence, definition, possession). Minimum redundancy is achieved by interrelating heterogenous elements (conjunction, disjunction, opposition). Finally, medium redundancy is achieved by relating homogenous with heterogenous elements (inference, condition).

Generally, a text contains both homogenous and heterogenous information. Homogeneity is self-explanatory and constitutes the initial information given (intratextual references). Sentences that contain homogenous information facilitate comprehension but hardly contribute to theme expansion. Heterogenous information is obtained by differentiating or opposing the information given earlier, thus constituting new information (Clark & Havilland, 1977), which is opposed to or distinguished from the old information. Anaphora, cataphora, and deictics, using various forms of pronominalization and lexical cohesion, constitute the most usual linguistic markers of *redundancy*. The *endophoric* (*anaphoric* and *cataphoric*) elements, situated within a text, relay earlier or later semantic elements of the same text with which they are coreferenced. They powerfully contribute to producing the isotopic effect of the text as a whole.

A microstructure is made up of groups of sentences strongly linked together by means of *redundancy*. The connection between the various microstructures gives *coherence.* A text is coherent if it establishes noncontradictory isotopic relations between the various microstructures in the text. These relations can be inferential, causal, temporal, parallels, oppositions, and so on, and are often functionally established through *connectors*—functional words—but can also be established semantically by lexical words (lexical cohesion) or even indicated by modal or temporal morphemes.

Semantic Contextuality

The combination of redundancy and coherence forms an important set that generates the semantic context or world of reference. This has more of a macrostructural character insofar as it constitutes the *frame of reference* from which the text acquires its meaning. The concept of frame is essential for textual coherence; it refers to the intratextual contexts created by the text itself: for example, the word *statue* can be introduced without any other reference if we create a frame with reference to a church, museum, bridge, or monumental square. The references are sometimes internal to the text insofar as the text explains itself. We are then referring to intratextual context. At other times, the references are external and have to do with an encyclopedic or general knowledge, which is not explained in the text but is supposed to be shared by the addresser and the addressee. Here, we are referring to extratextual context.

The sensation of comprehension of a text, as a result of the combination of many levels of intra- and extratextual coherence, adheres to a phenomenon that Greimas (1966) called *isotopy*, which has been defined as "the permanence of a classmatic base," "redundant set of semantic categories," or "a permanence which, throughout the discourse, refers to the same bundle of categories which justify a paradigmatic organization." With that, Greimas wished to designate the *iterativity* along a syntagmatic chain of contents that assures the homogeneity of the discourse. One isotopic disjunction can clash with a homogenous text, something that often underlines the humor or the punchline of a joke.

Pragmatic Contextuality

Finally, it must not be forgotten that the text is produced as a social act (Halliday, 1978; Halliday & Hassan, 1980) within a personal interactional framework (Goffman, 1967), where text is received and produced (pragmatic context). In this case, the knowledge of the relational characteristics that unite the addresser and the addressee, the kind of situation that they are in, and the adequacy of the objectives pursued in their communication, is essential in order to understand the text.

The idea that coherence is not an intrinsic property of texts, but is actually dependent on the conditions defined by the knowledge and expectancies of the participants, is present in both classic (Morris, 1938) and current interpretations of coherence. Van Dijk (1993), for example, states that discourses and conversations will be coherent insofar as they are *interpretable*. Sperber and Wilson (1986, 1987), to this end, believe that human communicative interaction is governed by the principle of *cognitive economy,* which supposes that the speakers attempt to produce maximum *relevance* using the minimum possible effort, while at the same time underlining the discursive activity's utmost dependence on the central cognitive processes, such as those of inference (see Belinchón et al., 1992).

However, this interpretability of discourse can be reduced neither to the sole competence of the speakers nor to their mental operations, but rather is mediated by the texts, given that, as we have repeatedly indicated, these are the object of *communicative exchange.* This object has certain autonomous characteristics that both restrict and facilitate communicative interaction. Such characteristics are linguistic in nature and mark the structure of the text. Some of them do so superficially, others at a more profound level. Among the first kind, we find all of the elements we have underlined in the coherence analysis, which are absolutely necessary to preserve the autonomy of the text. The condition of necessity, however, does not imply sufficiency. In actual fact, the text moves not only on a plane of superficial cohesion but also on a level of profound coherence that refers to the discursive matrix that generates it and is transparent only at a macrostructural level. This coherence is not, however, held in an arbitrary construction of the interpreters mind but is based on the markers that the author himself has left in the *text*. These markers should, in an equal fashion, be the object of a *textual analysis*.

TEXTUAL ANALYSIS

All texts, whatever their nature, are born from a discursive matrix whose essence should be understood by the listener or reader if interpretation is to be made. This matrix or discursive nucleus can be synthesized in a macroproposition or deep macrostructure, which generates the different microstructures in the text as well as their overall coherence and integration. Therefore, the aim of textual analysis is the reproduction of the discursive synthesis, where the semantic (ideological, informative, emotional, pragmatic) nucleus is condensed, which is expressed across the different structures in the text. Apart from relations of cohesion, these structures also maintain relations of meaning, which are the structures identified by comprehension.

Textual analysis is a linguistic technique used to deconstruct the process of discourse production in an attempt to comprehend its semantic matrix and structure. In order to carry out this operation, it is necessary to follow a systematic procedure, which can be summed up in the following flow diagram:

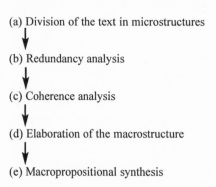

(a) Division of the text in microstructures

(b) Redundancy analysis

(c) Coherence analysis

(d) Elaboration of the macrostructure

(e) Macropropositional synthesis

Division of the Text in Microstructures
(Different Units of a Text)

We can consider microstructures to be those units of text that have, among themselves, a certain homogeneity that distinguishes them from the other textual units. The methods for textually indicating microstructures are varied, but we can basically underline two: segmentation and connection. By *segmentation* we mean the more or less explicit thematic division the text establishes. Thus, in the text of a stutterer (see Figure 4-5), the division into microstructures is relatively easy, given that the microstructure {0}, which serves as an introduction, lists the various types

Microstructure {0}

The most complete point in my self-analysis is the issue of relationships with others. I can distinguish between four groups of people with whom I normally have relations: relatives {1}, first- and second-class friends {2}, and girls {3}. Naturally, this subdivision is not quite so black and white but rather gives way to overlapping areas that give rise to friends who are relatives, girls who are friends, and so on. . . .

Microstructure {1}

Since about a year ago, my family relations have been more relaxed, I don't get irritated any more. . . .

Microstructure {2}

With my friends I am quite okay. However, I get especially nervous with some of them. . . .

Microstructure {3}

As far as girls are concerned, absolutely nothing is going well. Partly this is because I am very demanding. . . .

Figure 4-5. Division of the text in microstructures (text taken from a 26-year-old stutterer).

of "interpersonal relationships" (the theme), which will later be developed into successive microstructures {1}, {2}, {3} . . ., which are put in brackets {}.

By *connection*, on the other hand, we mean various structural links that are established between one microstructure and another, which take various forms: causal, temporal and so forth. At the same time as these links join microstructures together, they can also differentiate them. In the text spoken by Benjamin Constant, which we shall analyze later (see Figure 4-10), the division criterion is clearly marked by the connectors "before/now," which follow the initial microstructure {0} and introduce the microstructures {1} and {2}.

Microstructural division is very useful to enable us to get to the bottom of the nuances of the text and to uncover their internal structural relations. Some texts, such as the following rabbinical tale, present a structure clearly marked by connectors—temporal connectors in this case: {1} When, {2} Later, {3} Later still, {4} Then, {5} [Connector 0] God created man . . . (see Figure 4-6).

In this text, the division into microstructures does not offer any difficulty, as all of them, excluding the fifth, have the same structure. All of them have an equivalent subject (rabbi), they all describe the same situation (disaster), and in all of them the same action is developed (rituals) with the same results (miracle). The only difference refers to the different abilities/incapacities of the different rabbis in each

Microstructure {1}

When the great Rabbi Israel Baal Shem Tov saw that some disaster threatened the people of Israel, he would go to a certain place in the forest where he could meditate, light a fire, and say a special prayer. In this way a miracle would happen and the disaster would be averted.

Microstructure {2}

Later, when the occasion arose, his disciple, the famous Magid of Mezricht, with the same motive of interceding with the heavens, would also go to the same place in the forest and say: "Oh Lord of the Universe, Listen to me! I do not know how to light a fire but I can still recite the prayer." And the miracle occurred once again.

Microstructure {3}

Later still, the Rabbi Moshe-Leib of Sasov, with the intention of saving his people once again, went into the forest and said, "I do not know how to light a fire, neither do I remember the prayer, but I do know the place in the forest and that should be enough."

Microstructure {4}

Then, the Rabbi Israel of Ryshin found himself obliged to confront disaster. He sat in his armchair, with his head in his hands he addressed God saying, "I cannot light a fire, neither am I able to remember the prayer nor can I find the place in the forest. The only thing that I can do is tell the story and that should be enough," and indeed it was enough.

Microstructure {5}

God created man because he loves stories.

Figure 4-6. The structure of a rabbinical tale.

microstructure. The parallelism of the first four microstructures is also underlined by the temporal connectors that initiate each of them. The fifth microstructure is so different that it stands out from the others. Compared to the first four, it is not introduced by any connector, it is shorter, and it has a causal composition. The subject has changed, and it introduces a totally new topic: the creation of man.

Redundancy Analysis

The theme of a text and its expansion—rheme—arise from redundancy. This is what enables us to say what is being talked about in the text. In a certain way, the redundancy analysis is the same as a content analysis, although it does not follow the quantitative criteria of the latter. The advantage of a redundancy analysis is that it includes not only synonyms, but also hyponyms and antonyms. Moreover, the redundancy analysis is not governed by quantitative criteria but rather by textual criteria, which not only respects the text but also helps to create and preserve the context.

If the theme of a text is indicated by reiteration (e.g., the succession of disasters that affected the Jewish people in the rabbinical tale, and the miracles with which God remedies the situation), the rheme is characterized by its expansion. This is carried out by the successive microstructures. In this way, each microstructure constitutes a similar unit of redundancy, but at the same time new and different to the preceding one, which makes way for the next one. In the example of the rabbinical tale, each of the first four microstructures present the same theme albeit in different successive points in time with different leading characters (rabbis) in a dynamic of progressive forgetfulness. In this way the specification of the units of redundancy are equivalent to the identification of the microstructures (see Figure 4-7).

By talking about the characteristics of textuality, we have already widely referred to the different types of redundancy that may characterize each of the microstructures. Let us now have a look at how the elements of redundancy in a given microstructure are marked in the text, using as an example the microstructure $\{0\}$ in the text spoken by the stutterer.

In it, the words that constitute redundancies are shown, and the coincidences between them are indicated by a numerical subindex. Articles, prepositions, and other semantically empty forms are systematically discarded, as are adverbial markers and conjunctions. The redundant elements are made up of words with semantic content, as shown by the following indices:

1. Personal pronouns: I/MY/ME;
2. Nominal and verbal forms of the word "relation": RELATIONSHIPS and to HAVE RELATIONS;

The most complete point in my self-analysis is the issue of relationships$_2$ with others$_3$. I$_1$ can distinguish$_4$ between four$_5$ groups of people$_3$ with whom$_3$ I$_1$ normally have relations$_2$: relatives$_3$, first-$_5$ and second$_5$-class friends$_3$, and girls$_3$. Naturally, this subdivision$_4$ is not quite so black$_6$ and white$_6$ but rather gives$_7$ way to overlapping$_4$ areas that give$_7$ rise to friends$_3$ who are relatives$_3$, girls$_3$ who are friends$_3$ and so on. . . .

Figure 4-7. Identification of redundancy/microstructures in text.

3. Hyperonym: OTHERS → hyperonym: PEOPLE → and cohyponyms: RELATIVES →
   FRIENDS → GIRLS;

4. Syntopics: DISTINGUISH → SUBDIVISION → OVERLAPPING AREAS;

5. Numerical cohyponyms: FOUR, cardinal: FIRST and SECOND;

6. Reiterations: TYPE/TYPE;

7. Reiterations: GIVES/GIVES.

The redundancy of this microstructure is made clear by the fact that the words with a higher presence index refer unequivocally to the world of relationships (the sum of the indices 1, 2, and 3 is equal to 12/24, 50% of the set of redundancy elements present in this microstructure).

Coherence (Analysis of Logical Connection between Different Microstructures)

There exists a certain possibility of overlapping between the redundancy and coherence analysis, given that the latter is often achieved through lexical cohesion (synonyms, antonyms, etc.), which is, at the same time, a form of redundancy. In order to avoid duplicities in the classification, we have used the following criteria: Redundancy is considered as that type of lexical cohesion that is produced in the interior of a microstructure, whereas coherence is considered to be the type of lexical cohesion that is produced between microstructures at a macrostructural level. For example, in the rabbinical tale, the word "*disaster*" is an element of redundancy in the interior of the microstructure {1} and of coherence between the microstructures {1} and {4} (see Figure 4-8). In this way, redundancy and coherence are distinguished but not opposed. Therefore, the same word can be both an element of redundancy and an element of coherence at the same time.

The redundancy analysis shows the theme with which a text is dealing; however, it does not underline the structural relationships that articulate that theme. That is the task of coherence analysis. For that reason, the coherence analysis corresponds more to the vertical lines of a text than to the horizontal ones.

A theme can be developed along a text with hardly another articulation but the successive enumeration of its components. If this is the case, then what we are dealing with is coherence by juxtaposition, temporal succession, agreement, homogeneity, and so on. For example, in the rabbinical tale, the coherence is achieved by the reiteration of the same elements from one microstructure to another, even though these elements are portrayed in successive historical moments, by different rabbis on each occasion, and with different levels of ritual competence. This rabbinical tale is an extremely redundant text in which the different lexical elements are repeated from one microstructure to the other. These redundant elements are represented in capital letters in the different microstructures.

Microstructure {1}

WHEN {1,2} the great RABBI {1,2,3,4} Israel Baal Shem Tov saw that some DISASTER {1,4} threatened the PEOPLE OF ISRAEL {1,3}, he WOULD GO TO A CERTAIN PLACE IN THE FOREST {1,2,3,4} where he could meditate, LIGHT A FIRE {1,2,3,4}, and SAY A SPECIAL PRAYER {1,2,3,4}. In this way A MIRACLE WOULD HAPPEN {1,2} and the DISASTER {1,4} would be averted.

Microstructure {2}

LATER {2,3}, WHEN {1,2} the occasion arose, HIS DISCIPLE {1,2,3,4}, the famous Magid of Mezricht, with the same motive {1,2,3,4} of interceding with the HEAVENS {2,4,5}, WOULD ALSO GO TO THE SAME PLACE IN THE FOREST {1,2,3,4} and SAY {2,3,4}: "OH LORD OF THE UNIVERSE {2,4,5}, Listen to me! I DO NOT KNOW HOW TO {2,3,4} LIGHT A FIRE {1,2,3,4} BUT {2,3} I CAN {2,4} STILL {2,3} RECITE THE PRAYER" {1,2,3,4}. And the MIR-ACLE {1,2} OCCURRED {1,2} once again.

Microstructure {3}

LATER {2,3} STILL {2,3}, the RABBI {1,2,3,4} Moshe-Leib of Sasov, with the intention of saving HIS PEOPLE {1,3} once again, WENT INTO THE FOREST {1,2,3,4} and SAID {2,3,4}, "I DO NOT KNOW HOW TO {2,3,4} LIGHT A FIRE {1,2,3,4}, NEITHER DO I REMEMBER {2,3,4} the PRAYER {1,2,3,4}, BUT {2,3} I DO KNOW {2,3,4} THE PLACE IN THE FOREST {1,2,3,4} and that should be ENOUGH {3,4}."

Microstructure {4}

Then, the RABBI {1,2,3,4} Israel of Ryshin found himself obliged to con-front DISASTER {1,4}. He sat in his armchair, with his head in his hands he addressed GOD {2,4,5}, SAYING, {2,3,4}: "I CANNOT {2,4} LIGHT A FIRE {1,2,3,4}, neither am I able to REMEMBER {2,3,4} the PRAYER {1,2,3,4}, nor CAN {2,4} I find the PLACE IN THE FOREST {1,2,3,4}. The only thing which I CAN DO {2,4} is tell the STORY {4,5} and that should be ENOUGH {3,4}," and indeed it was ENOUGH {3,4}.

Microstructure {5}

GOD {2,4,5} created man because he loves STORIES {4,5}.

Figure 4-8. Coherence analysis of a rabbinical tale.

The coherence between the microstructures is guaranteed in this text through the intense coreferentiality (isotopy), based on a strong lexical cohesion that characterizes this text and that is indicated after each word with the number of the microstructure where it appears between brackets {}. The purely successive temporal connection between microstructures increases the textual coherence.

In the text, some elements clearly appear in in the first four microstructures: RABBI (or disciple), PLACE IN THE FOREST, and PRAYER appear equally, even though the reason {2} for the rabbis' intercession with GOD {2,4,5} is expressed in different ways, which is none other than the petition of his intervention to perform a MIRACLE {1,2} and thus avert DISASTER {1,4} for the PEOPLE OF ISRAEL {1,3}. It is interesting to note that this last reference disappears in the last microstructure {4} in order to pave the way for a less particular and more universal concept in {5}: that is, man. The succesive degradation of the rabbis' memory with respect to the rituals leads, finally, to the fact that the STORIES {4,5} prevail over them given that God prefers them to the rituals.

The question of the entire coherence of the text is put at stake in the fifth microstructure, which apparently has nothing to do with the previous ones. The coherence is saved by hanging onto only one word, STORIES, which stands as the coherent element with the fourth microstructure and thus with the others. There is another lexical element, GOD, which in an explicit or implicit fashion is present in all the previous microstructures, not as addressee of the rituals, however, but rather as agent OF MIRACLES.

Macrostructure (Organizing Plan of the Text)

The analysis of the coherence allows us to understand the macrostructure or discursive matrix of the text. A macrostructure is a graphic representation of the coherent structural relationships by which the text is organized. These can be based on relationships of similarity, opposition, condition, causality, inference, and so on. In Figure 4-9, a graphic representation of the rabbinical tale's macrostructure is proposed.

This text is displayed in two unequal blocks as far as length is concerned, but they are equal in their significant force. These two blocks are displayed in a contrasting fashion. Rabbis are on one side, and God is on the other. Rabbis overcome misfortunes, interceding with Heaven through different rituals (searching for the place in the forest, lighting a fire, saying a special prayer), although they are not able to perform some of them. Finally, the rabbis can only tell stories, and that is sufficient for miracles to be accomplished, because God loves stories. Stories, not rituals, are what make miracles possible.

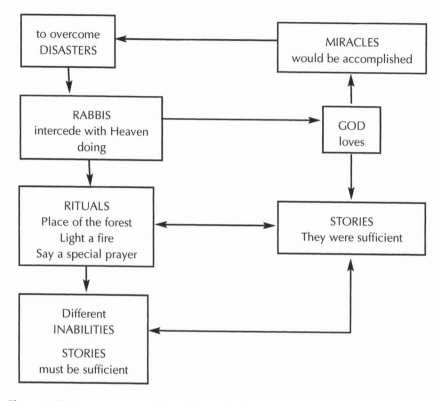

Figure 4-9. Macrostructure of the rabbinical tale.

Macroproposition (Discursive Synthesis)

A macroproposition is a discursive synthesis. It is made up of a sentence or proposition that maximally condenses the meaning of the text being analyzed with reference to the genotext or discursive matrix from which it proceeds. It constitutes the final step in the process of textual analysis and implies a certain degree of discursive interpretation: it is focused more on what is meant by the text (intention) than on what it actually says (literality). Macropropositional syntheses are not uncommon in ordinary language, as is demonstrated by the use of popular proverbs and the formulation of morals at the end of fables and oriental stories.

Any macroproposition is inevitably an interpretation or reading of a text. Without doubt many readings of a text are possible, but as Eco says (1992), not all of them are legitimate. For example, the macroproposition that sums up the discursive synthesis in the text from the rabbinical tale could be the following: "God prefers stories to rituals." Given that the coherence element of this text is the word *stories,* this has to be the *core* of any macropropositional synthesis.

Besides, it will have to bear in mind the opposition between the rabbis and the divine will. Thus, a possible and legitimate macropropositional synthesis could be the following one—"God loves stories, not rituals"—or the one we have used previously—"Stories, not rituals, are what make miracles possible."

It is evident that other possible formations of the same idea exist; there is even room for the possibility of focusing the macroproposition on other aspects. However, in any case, a macroproposition must meet the following conditions: (a) it must be plausible and coherent with the text; (b) it must be as synthetic and take on as much as possible; (c) it must express in sentence form the discursive nucleus as shown in the macrostructural analysis. In this way, when two or more possible macrostructures compete, the preferred one should be that which best meets these three requirements. Thus, for example, when confronted with two macropropositions of the following kind—(1) "God prefers stories to rituals" and (2) "When faced with disaster, Rabbis turned to God in search of a miracle, carrying out various rituals,"—the first one should be preferred because, although both meet the condition (a), the first is briefer and more synthetic than the second (b) and, above all, the first expresses much better the discursive nucleus (c) than the second, which remains on the literal or anecdotal surface of the text without referring to macrostructural opposition between rituals and stories, which is the leitmotiv of the tale. The text we have just analyzed has more of a religious character than a psychological one, but in any case the method we have developed can be applied to any type of discourse. Therapeutic discourse, in fact, is not exempt from the linguistic rules of production and interpretation of texts.

According to the techniques of text analysis, therapeutic discourse is made up of a series of themes that are articulated and connected to each other through the logical semantic knots that constitute their macrostructure. The identification of these structural knots, which link the episodic events narrated by the patient, is a necessary condition for their deconstruction.

METHODOLOGICAL APPLICATIONS

To apply these analysis procedures is not difficult, and it is entertaining in the beginning. In reality, it is a systematic reading procedure that mainly bears in mind the semantic structure of the text. With a little practice the procedure can be automated, providing us with very rich and structured information about the text. At first glance, this systematic reading does not appear to add anything to an intuitive reading; however, as one advances with it, one discovers semantic and contextual implications that would otherwise pass totally unnoticed, at the same time as they reveal the macrostructural organization of the text. Moreover, the systematic search for redundancy and coherence implies making explicit the semantic and pragmatic contexts of text production. Finally, this can be compared with other texts from the same author (intertextual analysis), which contributes even more to the configuration of the discursive matrix.

ADOLPHE: A CASE DEMONSTRATION

Textual Analysis: Procedure

We continue our demonstration with a brief text taken from *Adolphe*, a novel written by Benjamin Constant (1985), which was published for the first time in 1816. In Figure 4-10 the same text is reproduced twice. In the upper half of the figure, the text can be read without any kind of methodological manipulation. In the lower half, the same text can be seen as it was left after being divided into microstructures, illustrating the elements of both redundancy and coherence.

Three microstructures have been identified in the text. The first, corresponding to the number {0}, has an introductory character. In it **FREEDOM** and **DEPEN-DENCE** are opposed. This contrast, on the other hand, runs through the entire text and is the basis for coherence at a macrostructural level. In actual fact, the microstructure {1} is devoted to the development of the theme of dependence (DEPENDED {0}), whereas the microstructure {2} focuses on the consequences of freedom (FREE {0}).

With the sparse data at our disposal, we can already say that Benjamin Constant's discourse has a theme of confrontation between dependence and freedom. However, it could be a political, philosophical, or ideological confrontation. In actual fact this is not the case: What we are dealing with, as we will later see, is an affective confrontation. This opposition generates clashing sentiments. In fact, the redundancy in this microstructure is achieved by the oppositional lexical cohesion between "**heavy**" and "**longed for**" on the one hand and between "had . . . **desired**" and "had **rebelled**" on the other. **FREEDOM** and **DEPEN-DENCE** also have an oppositional lexical cohesive role to play here within the introductory microstructure as well as at a macrostructural level. Finally, the repetition of "**HOW/HOW**" is clearly a redundant factor.

The microstructure {1} is initiated with the connector *BEFORE,* which constitutes a marked contrast with *NOW* in the microstructure {2}. Both connectors are connective elements on a macrostructural plane and constitute the semantic context. The microstructure {1} is devoted, as mentioned earlier, to DEPEN-DENCE and, therefore, develops the declared theme in the second sentence of the microstructure {0}. This dependence is understood as a subordination of all acts as a means to an end and of all movements to the approval of an observing eye. The end in question is to "save misfortunes" and to "provoke merriment," expressions united by oppositional lexical cohesion. "Misfortunes" and "merriment" are also lexically related to "happiness,"—synonymous with the latter term and antonymous of the first term. MOVEMENTS {1} are entrances and EXITS {2}, which are controlled by A FRIENDLY EYE and executed in the presence of ANOTHER person. This other person is the observing eye, which observes his movements, the destiny of acts geared toward obtaining happiness. However, this presence is annoying and results in "complaining upon" and "impatience." In this

ADOLPHE (by Benjamin Constant)

"How heavy upon me this freedom which I had so much desired! How my heart longed for the dependence which oftentimes I had rebelled against! Before, all of my acts were to one end; I was sure, with each of them, of saving a misfortune or of fostering some merriment. I complained upon it then; I grew impatient if a friendly eye observed my movements, if the happiness of other people depended on them. Now no one observed them; they are of interest to no one; no one with me would dispute neither my time nor my hours; no voice would reclaim me when I went out. I would be free, in truth, I would be no longer loved; I would be a stranger to the entire world."

DIVISION INTO MICROSTRUCTURES
ANALYSIS OF REDUNDANCY AND COHERENCE
Microstructure {0}

How$_0$ heavy$_1$ upon ME$_2$ {0,1,2} this **FREEDOM**$_3${0/1/2} which$_3$ I$_2$ {0,1,2} had so much **desired** $_4$!

How$_0$ MY$_1$ {0,1,2} heart longed for$_2$ the **DEPENDENCE**$_3$ {0/1/2} which$_3$ oftentimes I$_1$ {0,1,2} had **rebelled**$_4$ against!

Microstructure {1}

BEFORE$_0$ {1/2}

all of MY$_1$ {0,1,2} **acts**$_2$ were to one end; I$_1${0,1,2} was sure, with each of **them**$_2$, of **saving a misfortune**$_3$ or of **fostering some merriment**$_3$. I$_1$ {0,1,2} **complained**$_4$ upon it then$_0$; I$_1$ {0,1,2} grew **impatient**$_4$ if **A FRIENDLY EYE**$_5$ {1/2} OBSERVED {1/2} MY$_1$ {0,1,2} **MOVEMENTS**$_2$ {1/2}, if the happiness$_3$ of **OTHER PEOPLE**$_5$ {1/2} DEPENDED {0/1/2} on **THEM**$_2$ {1/2}.

Microstructure {2}

NOW {1/2}

NO$_0$ **ONE**$_1$ {1/2} OBSERVED$_2$ {1/2} THEM$_3$ {1/2} (now); THEY$_3$ {1/2} are of **interest**$_2$ to **NO**$_0$ **ONE**$_1$ {1/2}; **NO**$_0$ **ONE**$_1$ {1/2} with ME$_4$ {0,1,2} would **dispute**$_2$ neither$_0$ MY$_4$ {0,1,2} **time**$_5$ nor$_0$ MY$_4$ **hours**$_5$; **NO**$_0$ **VOICE**$_1$ {1/2} would **reclaim**$_2$ ME$_4$ {0,1,2} when I$_4$ {0,1,2} WENT OUT {1/2}. I$_4$ {0,1,2} **would be**$_5$ FREE$_6$ {0/1/2}, in truth, I$_4$ {0,1,2} **would be**$_5$ no longer loved$_6$; I$_4$ {0,1,2} **would be**$_5$ a STRANGER$_6$ {1/2} to the **ENTIRE WORLD**$_1$ {1/2}.

N.B.: The numerical indices that follow the words written in bold type with numerical reference in lower case indicate the terms between which relationships of synonymity, antonymity, hyponymity, and so on, are established within the same microstructure: e.g. **misfortune**$_2$, **merriment**$_2$, **happiness**$_2$ {1}

Figure 4-10

microstructure then {1}, the redundancy is obtained mainly by opposition and equivalence.

The microstructure {2} begins with the connector *NOW,* whose macrostructural function has already been underlined. The threads of coherence let loose in the preceding microstructures are recovered in a conclusive fashion no later than in the first line of the microstructure {2}. "NO ONE OBSERVED THEM," as lexical elements of cohesion with the microstructure {1}. "OBSERVE" is a repetition of the same word present in the microstructure {1}; "THEM" has "MOVEMENTS" as an antecedent in the first microstructure {1}; and "NO ONE" {2} as a contrast, which is therefore an item that is lexically cohesive with "a friendly eye" and with "another person," also from the first microstructure {1}. "NO ONE" is the most repeated word in this second microstructure {2}; indeed, it is repeated on three occasions, to which we can add the synonym "NO VOICE," which has "the entire world" as its antonym. The insistence produced by these pronouns and adjectives is reiterated by the repetition of the negative adverbs/pronouns: "of interest to *no* one," "*neither* my time *nor* my hours," "*no longer* loved." This redundancy effect does not end there: "interest, dispute, reclaim" are all equal terms used to refer to the effects that the subject's "acts" and "movements" could provoke in the absent "voice" and "eye." This absence makes FREEDOM possible, but the price is to be "no longer loved," to be "a stranger to the entire world."

These last two sentences also constitute a redundancy insofar as they are present as definitions of what it is to be FREE. To be free means to be dependent on no one, but at the same time implies not being loved by anyone, being a stranger to the entire world. The theme of freedom brings the textual coherence cycle to a close insofar as it refers to the first sentence, "How heavy upon me this freedom" from the introductory microstructure {0}.

Finally, an observation in relation to the semantic context. The context refers to the narrator and his relationship with another person. From the rest of the novel, it is deduced that this other person is a woman named Eleonor; Adolphe first attempts to conquer her, then achieves this goal, and finally abandons her. "Eye," "voice," and "person" are the semantic contextual references that the text gives us in reference to her. The references to the narrator are more explicitly manifest. In this way, we can say that the subject *I* is permeating the entire discourse; moreover, his textual representation is achieved by using the pronoun that corresponds to the first person singular "I," the objective pronoun "me" and the possesive pronoun "my."

Discursive Synthesis: Procedure

Until now, the work of analyzing the text of *Adolphe* has been carried out according to the methodological guidelines described for textual analysis. Let us now try to formulate a macroproposition using successive syntheses, which represent the discursive nucleus of the text written by Benjamin Constant.

Microstructure {0} (synthesis):

• Contrast between: Freedom (desired) versus dependence (rebellion)

Microstructure {1} (synthesis):

• Context: Before the presence of a friendly eye

• Contrast between: Happiness/love versus presence/control

Microstructure {2} (synthesis):

• Context: Now absence of friendly voice

• Contrast between: Freedom/absence versus love/dependence

From a structural point of view, the text presents a coherence based on opposition. This opposition takes place at a transcendental level between freedom and dependence. Freedom is understood as the absence of an external control. Dependence is understood in terms of an inevitable effect of love. It is evident that the association between love and dependence or control is not necessary but is only possible. The discursive nucleus developed in the pages of *Adolphe*, Benjamin Constant's novel, is mainly composed of this incompatibility/contrast between freedom and love. The entire text is no more than one of the infinite possible actualizations of this transcendental discourse.

However, discourse is usually expressed not by abstract or transcendental formulation, but rather in a concrete fashion, sequenced and embedded in everyday life. One of the principal vertebrating axes of human experience is time. And time is exactly the category that defines the division of Benjamin Constant's text into two central microstructures, which refer to the past (*BEFORE*) and to the present (*NOW*). Both temporal dimensions are equally marked by a confrontation of emotions, affects, actions, and reactions. Before, Adolphe felt loved, but he rebelled against dependence and love in favor of freedom. Now that the price of not being loved means he does not depend on anyone, he longs for that dependence, and his freedom weighs heavy upon him. In Figure 4-11, an attempt is made to illustrate this conflict that constitutes the discursive nucleus not just of the text but of Benjamin Constant's entire (autobiographical?) novel.

It is clear that the theme of this text is the dialectic between attachment (love/dependence) and freedom. This theme is developed in many pages of the novel. Expressed in textual form, the theme can be summed up in the following macroproposition: *"Freedom and love are (lived as) incompatible."*

"Lived as" has been placed in parentheses and put in lower case because this is precisely the difference that separates a life experience ("I cannot *find* a way of making love and freedom compatible") from a belief ("There *is* no way of making love and freedom compatible").

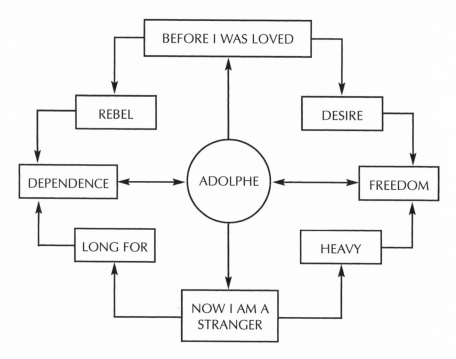

Figure 4-11. Macrostructure of *Adolphe's* text.

The text written by Benjamin Constant was deliberately chosen because of its brevity and clear structure. It corresponds precisely to what Castilla del Pino (1993) calls a well-formed discourse (WFD): It includes an introduction, a plateau, and a clearly defined ending. Not all texts are as transparent, but all can be subjected to this method of analysis (Villegas, 1992).

A TEST FOR THE READER

At this point, readers are encouraged to attempt the analysis of a larger text. The text in question (see Figure 4-12) is the response of a 26-year-old male patient to the first picture of the Thematic Apperception Test (TAT). The reason for consultation is a serious breakdown in the patient's study behavior. Readers will find the text unaltered at first without any kind of analytical-textual manipulation so that they can rehearse the method if so desired "without the presence of a friendly eye who observes their every move." Using the subsequent pages, readers can follow the different steps involved in the analysis and can check on their process of self-learning. If readers consider the moment to be too premature, they can, of course, wait and carry out the excercise with other texts considered

---

CONTEXT

The following is the response of a 26-year-old patient (male) to the first picture from the Thematic Apperception Test (TAT). The subject's motive for consulting the psychologist was the fact that he had seriously fallen behind in his studies.

TEXT

This child can no longer bear to play the violin, because he is obliged to do so. He experiences a few moments of discomfort while he thinks of other, more pleasant, things to do with which he could occupy his time. He cannot take it any longer. He stares obnoxiously at the violin.

I can identify with him, because I also must do things that I do not want to do. But it has always been like that: There are always, and always will be, things to do that you do not like. I feel a kind of impotence: Life pits you up against things that you do not want to do because you have other projects, projects that you cannot carry out because you must do the other things (those from life).

Figure 4-12

later in the chapter. Readers should remember that the first step that must be carried out is the division of the text into microstructures.

COMMENTARY

In the text, the semantic isotopy is regulated by the theme offered in the picture, which is then interpreted according to the author's apperceptions. The author's discourse develops along a script based on the first, albeit ambiguous, picture in the series. The process usually begins by referring to the characters appearing in the pictures and moving toward the actual projections. In order to understand the structure of the discourse, it is necessary to divide the text up into various microstructures (see Figure 4-13).

Commentary on Microstructures and Redundancy Analysis

Four microstructures were found in this text. The divisions were formulated as follows:

• The first microstructure {1}, which opens the text, refers to the child in the picture who is staring at the violin. It is written in the third person and in the present tense.

- The second microstructure {2} begins with a change in the subject, who becomes the first person thanks to the connector "also," which establishes the I/child comparison.
- The third microstructure {3} is characterized once again by a change in the subject, which has now moved toward the impersonal, thus opening up a much more generic and abstract discourse as shown by the insistent repetition of the adverb "always."
- Finally, the fourth microstructure {4} returns the subject to the first person "(I) feel" and, after the colon, takes up the discourse on impotence with maximum linguistic redundancy to define that person as a confrontation between the obligations imposed on him by life and his personal projects.

The redundancy analysis shows a very reiterative text (bear/bear; more/more; violin/violin; do/do; always/always; life/life), some synonyms: (cannot bear/cannot take it; things/projects), and antonyms (discomfort/pleasant).

- The first microstructure evolves by way of a linguistic redundancy that is half introduced by the connector "because," which describes the reason for the child's discomfort.
- The second microstructure establishes the comparison ("I also") between the child and the author, with a medium redundancy that gives his reasons for identifying himself with the child ("because").

Microstructure {1}

This $child_0$ can no $longer_1$ $bear_2$ to play the $violin_3$, because he_0 is obliged to do so. He_0 experiences a few $moments_4$ of $discomfort_5$ while he_0 thinks of other, more $pleasant_5$, things to do with which he_0 $could_6$ occupy his_0 $time_4$. He_0 $cannot_6$ take it_6 any $longer_1$. He_0 stares $obnoxiously_2$ at the $violin_3$.

Microstructure {2}

I_0 can identify with him, because I_0 also must do_1 $things_2$ $that_2$ I_0 do not want to do_1.

Microstructure {3}

But it has $always_1$ been like that: There are_2 $always_1$, and $always_1$ will be_2 $things_2$ to do_3 that you do not like.

Microstructure {4}

I feel a kind of $impotence_1$: $life_2$ pits you_3 up against $things_4$ that you_3 do not want to do_5 $because_6$ you_3 have other $projects_4$, $projects_4$ $that_4$ you_3 $cannot_1$ carry out_5 $because_6$ you_3 must do_5 the other $things_4$ ($those_4$ from $life_2$).

Figure 4-13. Microstructural divisions and elements of redundancy.

- The third microstructure contains a maximum redundancy that defines the meaning of "always be like this" in the text, that is, there will always be things to do that we do not like.

- The fourth microstructure is also a definition, a maximum redundancy, with respect to what the author feels; that is, impotence at not being able do what he wants to because of life's obligations. In Figure 4-14 the coherence analysis of the preceding text (the response to the first picture of the TAT) is made.

Commentary on Coherence Analysis

The microstructures {1} and {2} establish a comparison between the author and the child using: "I can identify with him (the child)." The author, therefore, refers to the child in both the first and second microstructures as a pretext for talking about himself (I also). This comparison refers to the "obligation" {1/2/3/4} of having to "do things that you do not like," among which is having

---

{1} This child$_1$ CAN {1/2/4} no LONGER$_2$ {1/2} bear$_3$ to play the violin$_4$ BECAUSE {1/2/4} he$_1$ is OBLIGED {1/2/3/4} to DO$_5$ {1/2/3/4} so. He$_1$ experiences a few MOMENTS$_6$ {1/3} of discomfort$_7$ while he$_1$ thinks of other, more PLEASANT$_7$ {1/3/}, THINGS {1/2/3/4} to DO$_5$ {1/2/3/4} with which he COULD$_8$ {1/2/4} occupy his$_1$ TIME$_6$ {1/3}. He$_1$ CANNOT$_8$ {1/4} take it any LONGER$_2$ {1/2}. He stares at the violin$_3$ obnoxiously$_2$.

{2} I$_1$ {2/4} CAN {1/2/4} identify with HIM {1/2/}, BECAUSE {1/2/4} I$_1$ {2/4} also MUST {1/2/3/4} DO$_2$ {1/2/3/4} THINGS$_3$ {1/2/3/4} that$_3$ {1/2/3/4} I$_1$ {2/4} do not WANT {2/4} to DO$_2$ {1/2/3/4} any LONGER {1/2}.

{3} But it has ALWAYS$_1$ {1/3} been like that: There ARE$_2$ {1/2/3/4} ALWAYS$_1$ {1/3}, and ALWAYS$_1$ {1/3} WILL BE$_2$ {1/2/3/4}, THINGS$_3$ {1/2/3/4} to DO {1/2/3/4} THAT$_3$ {1/2/3/4} YOU {3/4} do not like {1/3}.

{4} I {2/4} feel a kind of IMPOTENCE$_1$ {1/2/4}: Life$_2$ {2/4} pits YOU$_3$ {3/4} up against THINGS$_4$ {1/2/3/4} to DO$_5$ {1/2/3/4} THAT$_4$ {1/2/3/4} YOU$_3$ {3/4} do not WANT {2/4} to DO$_5$ BECAUSE$_6$ {1/2/4} YOU$_3$ {3/4} have other PROJECTS$_4$ {1/2/3/4} THAT$_4$ {1/2/3/4} YOU$_3$ {3/4} CAN-NOT$_1$ {1/2/4} CARRY OUT$_5$, BECAUSE$_6$ YOU$_3$ {3/4} MUST {1/2/3/4} DO$_5$ the OTHERS$_4$ {1/2/3/4} (THOSE$_4$ {1/2/3/4} from life$_2$).

Figure 4-14. Coherent elements.

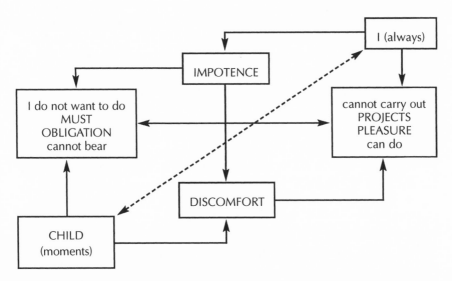

Figure 4-15. Macrostructure of TAT response.

to "play the violin." However, the violin is really a concrete example of a more abstract phenomenon: that is, having to "do things that you do not like" {1/2/3/4}, which is the reason why the violin does not have elements of coherence in the other microstructures, whereas its substitution, the word "thing," appears in all of the microstructures.

The third microstructure is connected to the first by virtue of the temporal theme "always" {3}, which is understood as something invariable, in contrast to the variable characteristic "moment" {1}. It is also related to the first microstructure {1} by the pleasure theme {1/3} (pleasant/like). The idea of the obligation is underlined by the expression "things to do," which is repeated in the fourth microstructure {4}.

This last microstructure {4} is connected to the first {1} through the theme of *"impotence"* ("you/he cannot"); it is also connected to the second {2} by the theme of *"will"* ("do not want to do"). All microstructures are permeated by the "obligation" theme {1/2/3/4}, which impedes us from carrying out our life projects. On the grounds of these elements of coherence, we can then represent the macrostructure of the text graphically (see Figure 4-15).

Commentary on Macrostructure

The text is composed around a *diagonal* vector or axis that establishes the projective comparison; that is, "*I (just as) the child.*" There is a similarity between them both with respect to a conflicting nucleus (on the horizontal axis) between obligations/musts and projects/pleasures, which are seen as incompatible. In contrast, the reactions on the *vertical* axis are different, just as one might expect from an adult and a child. The child experiences a *moment* of discomfort with respect to the violin but may be able to do other, more pleasant, things in other moments. It is not necessarily always the same. The adult author, on the other hand, feels a kind of impotence when faced with the impossibility of carrying out his projects because of life's obligations. The child is submerged in a heteronomous conflict (the obligations imposed on him from the outside), whereas the adult is engaged in an autonomous one (the musts, internal, fixed in his own conscience). It is logical that the patient will experience a serious mental block with regard to his studies if these enter into conflict with life's musts, if they form part of both his obligations or his projects.

The *diagonal* axis corresponds to the conditions that this test, in particular, produces and refers more to the pretext (the pictures of the TAT) than to the discourse, which is why we have represented it with a dashed line. The *horizontal* axis, on the other hand expresses the discursive nucleus in itself, the contrast between duties and projects. From this, we can extract the discursive synthesis or, indeed, the *macroproposition* generated by it: "in this life it is impossible to make projects compatible with duties." The *vertical* axis gives us the reason for the motivational block: the feeling of impotence when faced with this impossibility. Although the discursive nucleus (ideological matrix) can be produced indifferently, in general, it will be represented along the horizontal axis and the symptomatic, affective, and emotional reactivity on the vertical axis.

ANALYSIS OF AN ORAL SELF-INTRODUCTION WITHIN A THERAPY SESSION

One area of special interest for the psychotherapist is the analysis of oral manifestations produced within a therapy session. If the patient consents to an audio recording of the sessions, then it is possible to transcribe them entirely or to select particularily important parts of them with a view to later analyzing the written version. The following text, for example, is from a self-introduction of a patient at the beginning of a session as published by Castilla del Pino (1974) (the analysis of which follows in Figures 4-16, 4-17, 4-18, and 4-19).

The text offers a new opportunity for readers to practice their textual analysis skills if they so wish. Each of the figures represents a different step in the process, which allows the reader to rehearse, step by step, every operation necessary to carry out a textual analysis.

Commentary on Macrostructure

The macrostructure is organized around a complaint: "I am not feeling well; I am not like I was before; I am bored." This complaint is born from a lack of being happy and is expressed using the contrast "being happy about everything versus not being interested by anything" / "having everything versus not having anything to talk about." The axis that explains these contrasts, underlain by the polarities constituted by the absolute opposition *everything* versus *nothing,* are the temporal changes produced between "*before* the birth of the son" and "*after* the birth of the son"; changes that are not made explicit and should be explored. Whatever these changes may be, the current moment is characterized by boredom and ill health (a quasi-depressive state) for which no apparent or justifiable reason exists ("I don't know what I am complaining about" versus "although I know why I say it" versus "she [her sister] does not know why she is complaining"). Although it does not appear justifiable, there is a way for the woman to exonerate herself by attributing the lack of communication to her husband, exemplified in his interest in the sports pages, which drives her *crazy* versus while he is so *relaxed*. The semantic opposition between the woman and her husband (which occupies the vertical axis) can also be perceived in the type of verbs used to describe the attitudes of each person: whereas the verbs used by her are ideational (to think), phatic (to say, to tell, to shut up), affective (interest, love), moody (to be, to feel), reactive (to be happy, to get bothered, to be bored), the type verbs he (her husband) uses are enactive (to want) and active (to leave, to arrive, to come).

Yes, I am married and I have three children: one boy, the little one, and two girls. My husband is an engineer, and he works for an electrical machinery firm. He did not come because he did not want to ask for leave, nor did he want to say what it was for. I'm glad, because I don't know how to tell him that I prefer to come alone. If I would have come with him, I would have been more inhibited. The truth is that I don't think that I have anything to hide from him, but it is always better like that. Don't you think so? . . . I am not feeling well since a few months after the birth of my son. I am not like I was before; I am bored. Before, I was happy about everything. How little things interest me now, my husband, the children, everything! It's not that I don't love them, but they also bore me. What a life! . . . I don't know what I am complaining about, really. I have everything; we are fine. . . . But it's just that a woman, what does she have to do? . . . You will say that you've never had a patient so stupid, because now I was about to tell you something stupid: that now everything my husband does bothers me. Not everything; but, for example, before, when he arrived home from the factory, I was happy, but now, I told him already, we don't have anything to talk about. Is it possible that he doesn't have anything to say to me? He says that he is tired, that he just wants to relax, and he starts to read the paper. He likes football very much and that drives me crazy. The fact that he wants to leave work to come home to read the sports pages. I told my sister: "Look, cut out the nonsense, you think that marriage is one thing and then it's something very different." When she told me that she didn't know what I was complaining about, I shut up. She will know why I said it soon enough.

Figure 4-16. An oral self-introduction.

Microstructure {0} (Self-presentation)

{0} Yes, I am married and I have three children: one boy, the little one, and two girls. My husband is an engineer, and he works for an electrical machinery firm.

Microstructure {1} (Justification)

{1} He did not come because he did not want to ask for leave, nor did he want to say what it was for. I'm glad, because I don't know how to tell him that I prefer to come alone. If I would have come with him, I would have been more inhibited. The truth is that I don't think that I have anything to hide from him, but it is always better like that. Don't you think so?

Microstructure {2} (Problem definition: complaint)

{2} I am not feeling well since a few months after the birth of my son. I am not like I was before; I am bored. Before, I was happy about everything. How little things interest me now, my husband, the children, everything! It's not that I don't love them, but they also bore me. What a life! . . .

Microstructure {3} (Self-criticism)

{3} I don't know what I am complaining about, really. I have everything; we are fine. . . . But it's just that a woman, what does she have to do? . . . You will say that you've never had a patient so stupid, because now I was about to tell you something stupid: that now everything my husband does bothers me. Not everything; but, for example, before, when he arrived home from the factory, I was happy, but now, I told him already, we don't have anything to talk about.

Microstructure {4} (External attribution)

{4} Is it possible that he doesn't have anything to say to me? He says that he is tired, that he just wants to relax, and he starts to read the paper. He likes football very much and that drives me crazy. The fact that he wants to leave work to come home to read the sports pages.

Microstructure {5} (Generalization)

{5} I told my sister: "Look, cut out the nonsense, you think that marriage is one thing and then it's something very different." When she told me that she didn't know what I was complaining about, I shut up. She will know why I said it soon enough.

Figure 4-17. Microstructural divisions.

{0} Yes, I$_0$ AM {0/2} MARRIED$_1$ {0/5} and I$_0$ HAVE {0/1/2/3/4} three$_2$ CHILDREN$_3$ {0/2}: one$_2$ BOY$_3$ {0/2}, the little one, and two$_2$ GIRLS$_3$ {0/2}. MY$_0$ {0/1/2/3/4/5} HUSBAND$_1$ {0/1/2/3/4} is an engineer, and he$_1$ WORKS {0/4} for an electrical machinery FIRM {0/3}.

{1} HE $_0${0/1/2/3/4} did not COME$_1$ {1/4} BECAUSE {1/3/5} he$_0$ did not WANT$_2$ {1/4} to ask for leave, nor did he WANT$_2$ {1/4} to SAY$_3$ {1/3/4/5} what it was for. I$_4$'m glad, BECAUSE {1/3/5} I$_4$ don't KNOW {1/3/5} how to TELL$_3${1/3/4/5} HIM$_0$ {0/1/2/3/4} that I$_4$ {0/1/2/3/4/5} prefer$_2$ to come$_1$ alone$_6$. If I$_4$ {0/1/2/3/4/5} would have come$_1$ with$_6$ HIM$_0$ {0/1/2/3/4}, I$_4$ would have been more inhibited. The truth is that I$_4$ don't$_0$ THINK$_7$ {1/5} that I$_4$ HAVE {0/1/2/3/4} ANYTHING {1/2/3/4} to HIDE {1/3/4/5} from HIM$_0$ {0/1/2/3/4}, BUT {1/2/3} it is ALWAYS {1/3} better like that. Don't YOU{1/3} THINK$_7${1/5} so$_6$?

{2}I$_1$ am not {0/1/2/3/4/5} feeling$_2$ WELL {2/3} since a few$_3$ months after$_4$ {2/3} the birth of my SON$_5$ {0/2}. I$_1$ AM$_6${0/2} not like I$_1$ was$_6$ BEFORE$_4$ {2/3}, I$_1$ am$_2$ BORED$_7$ {2/3}. BEFORE$_4$ {2/3}, I$_1$ {0/1/2/3/4/5} WAS {0/2/3/4} HAPPY$_7$ {2/3} about EVERYTHING$_8$ {1/2/3/4}. How$_9$ {2/3/5} little$_3$ things INTEREST$_7$ {2/3} ME$_1$ {0/1/2/3/4/5} NOW$_4$ {2/3}, my HUSBAND {0/1/2/3/4}, the CHILDREN$_5$ {0/2}, EVERYTHING$_8$ {1/2/3/4}! It's not that I$_1$ don't love THEM$_5$ {0/2}, BUT {1/2/3} they$_5$ also BORE$_7$ {2/3} ME$_1$ {0/1/2/3/4/5}. WHAT$_9$ {2/3/5} a life! . . .

{3} I$_1$ {0/1/2/3/4/5} don't KNOW {1/3/5} WHAT$_2$ {2/3/5} I$_1$ {0/1/2/3/4/5} am COMPLAIN-ING$_3$ {3/5} ABOUT, really. I$_1$ HAVE$_4$ {0/2/3/4} EVERYTHING$_5$ {1/2/3/4}; we$_1$ are FINE {2/3}. BUT$_6$ {1/2/3} it's just that a woman$_7$, WHAT$_2$ does she$_7$ have to do$_8$? . . . YOU$_9$ {1/3} WILL SAY$_{10}$ {1/3/4/5} that you$_0$'ve NEVER$_0$ {1/3} had$_4$ a patient so STUPID$_{11}$ {3/5}, BECAUSE {1/3/5} NOW$_{12}$ {2/3} I$_1$ was about to TELL$_{10}$ {1/3/4/5} YOU$_9$ {1/3} something STUPID$_{11}$ {3/5}: that NOW$_{12}$ EVERYTHING$_5$ {1/2/3/4} my$_1$ HUSBAND$_{13}$ {0/1/2/3/4} does$_8$ BOTHERS$_3$ {3/4} ME$_1$ {0/1/2/3/4/5}. Not EVERYTHING$_5$ {1/2/3/4}; BUT$_6$ {1/2/3}, for example, BEFORE$_{12}${2/3}, when HE$_{13}$ {0/1/2/3/4} ARRIVED {3/4} HOME$_{14}$ {3/4} from the FACTORY$_{14}$ {0/3}, I$_1$ {0/1/2/3/4/5} WAS {0/2/3/4} HAPPY$_3$ {2/3}, BUT$_6$ {1/2/3} NOW$_{12}$ {2/3}, I$_1$ TOLD$_{10}$ {1/3/4/5} HIM$_9$ {1/3} already: we$_1$ don't HAVE$_4$ {0/3/4} ANY-THING$_5$ {1/2/3/4} to TALK ABOUT {1/3/4/5}.

{4} Is it possible that he$_1$ doesn't HAVE {0/3/4} ANYTHING {1/2/3/4} to SAY$_2$ {3/4} to ME$_3$ {0/1/2/3/4/5}? HE$_1$ {0/2/3/4} SAYS$_2$ {1/3/4/5} that HE$_1$ {0/2/3/4} is tired$_4$, that HE$_1$ {0/2/3/4}just WANTS$_5$ {1/4} to relax$_4$, and he$_1$ starts$_6$ to read$_7$ the paper. HE$_1$ {0/1/2/3/4} likes$_5$ football$_8$ very much and that drives$_6$ ME$_3$ {0/1/2/3/4/5} CRAZY$_4$ {3/4}. The fact that HE$_1$ {0/1/2/3/4} WANTS$_5$ to leave$_9$ WORK$_{10}$ {0/4} to COME$_9$ {1/3/4} HOME$_{10}$ {3/4} to read$_7$ the sports$_8$ pages.

{5} I$_1$ {0/1/2/3/4/5} TOLD$_2$ {1/3/4/5} my$_1$ sister$_3$: "Look, cut out the NONSENSE {3/5}, you$_4$ THINK {1/5} that MARRIAGE {0/5} is one thing$_5$ and then it's something$_5$ very differ-ent." When she$_3$ TOLD$_2$ {1/3/4/5} ME$_1$ {0/1/2/3/4/5}that she$_3$ didn't KNOW$_6$ {1/3/5} WHAT {2/3/5} I$_1$ {0/1/2/3/4/5} was COMPLAINING {3/5} ABOUT, I$_1$ {0/1/2/3/4/5} shut up. She$_3$ will KNOW$_6$ {1/3/5} why I$_1$ {0/1/2/3/4/5} SAID$_3$ {1/3/4/5} it soon enough.

Figure 4-18. Redundancy and coherence analysis.

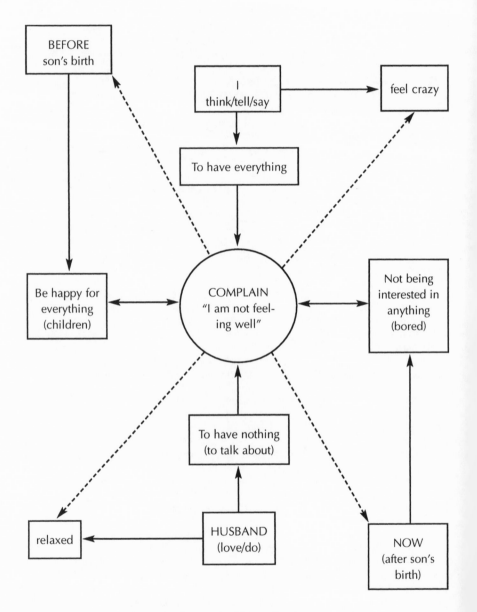

Figure 4-19. Macrostructure of an oral self-introduction.

Observations

Rhetorical style:
* Questions (Is it possible that he does not have . . . ?, what does she have to do?)
* Admirations (What a life! . . .)
* Pragmatic incursions (Don't you think so? . . . , you will say . . . , I've already told him)
Use of connectors:
* Temporal connectors: before, now (after the son's birth)
* Causal connectors: because (explain and ask)
* Adversative: but (oppose, contradict, qualify)
Generalizations:
* Quantifiers: everything versus nothing
* Temporal: always versus never

Macroproposition

"After the birth of my last child I lost the happiness in my marriage; my husband no longer takes any notice of me."

INTERTEXTUAL ANALYSIS

The *intertextual analysis* applications that can be carried out are as diverse as the variety of texts that our imagination will allow. A particularily useful case in psychotherapy is that of comparing different texts from the same client, with a view to extracting the underlying discursive matrix common to all of them. Also useful is the possibility of evaluating changes in the discursive organization by analyzing, either throughout or at the close of the therapy, texts that correspond to different points in the therapeutic process. This kind of analysis is known as *intertextual analysis*, given that it is carried out between texts composed by the same subject.

Although the demonstrations of textual analysis that are made here use texts with a narrative structure, the technique is applicable to any kind of text. It is characterized by the search of the representation of the ideological matrix rather than by the narrative dimension that acts as pretext and not as text. An illustration is provided by the analysis of following texts, which all belong to Bill, a 20-year-old man, seriously affected by a preoccupation with personal appearance, focusing on his teeth. These analyses show how it is possible to integrate different types of texts, such as in this case, self-characterizations and dream telling (see Figures 4-20, 4-21, and 4-22).

Bill is an intelligent, educated person of pleasant appearance. He is nice to be with, because it is interesting to hear him explain past or even new experiences lived jointly; he is funny, nothing trivial. When he explains them, he rouses other people's attention. He is funny, but the adjective "ironic" describes him better, given that he never gives the impression of being completely happy although he often makes other people laugh quite a lot.

In general he is a pacific person: He knows how to use the art of diplomacy and often does so when it is convenient. He has always been reserved, but I think that deep down on opening a discussion he is also shy when it comes to criticisms and confrontation, whereas on some issues he does not go into detail or into personal experience.

He is generous when it comes to giving advice and being interested in someone else's problem. Even when he deals with a well-known or stereotyped problem he adopts a position of not reaching a predetermined conclusion but rather starts from scratch in order to analyze everything right from the beginning. In this way, he sometimes reaches a new perspective, which not even he gives the impression of knowing beforehand, but instead discovers it "along the way"; at other times, although no solution is reached, one gets the impression that a well-educated and sometimes even complicated approximation has been made; one that leaves no loose ends.

In school he was considered a charismatic person, but one who did not always accept the confidence others offered him; he accepted it only if he did not have to expose himself; indeed, in such cases he would take the initiative (for example, if a card had to be sent to the Greek teacher; when the class decided to send it to her, he was the one to think what to put on it). On the other hand, he never wanted to be a leader, a role that also implied unpleasant aspects, such as having to expose, on behalf of part of the class, a complaint to a teacher or to make an uncomfortable petition to another teacher.

Summing up then, we are, without doubt, dealing with a youth of uncommon appearance of whom I get the impression that it is not easy to know either the positive or the negative aspects of his personality, but that, for one reason or another, are hidden behind a screen or a veil, which does not allow other people to discover them deep down.

Figure 4-20. Bill's self-characterization.

{0} BILL$_1$ {0/1/2/3/4/5} is an intelligent, educated PERSON$_1$ {0/2/4/5} of PLEASANT {0/1/4} APPEARANCE {0/5}.

{1} HE$_1$ {0/1/2/3/4/5} is NICE {0/1/4} to be with because it is INTERESTING$_2$ {1/3} to hear him$_1$ explain$_3$ past$_4$ or even NEW$_4$ {1/3} EXPERIENCES$_5$ {1/2} lived jointly$_6$; HE$_1$ {0/1/2/3/4/5} is funny$_7$, nothing TRIVIAL$_2$ {1/3}. When HE$_1$ {0/1/2/3/4/5} explains$_3$ them$_5$ HE$_1$ {0/1/2/3/4/5} rouses OTHER PEOPLE'S$_6$ {1/3/4/5} attention$_2$. HE$_1$ {0/1/2/3/4/5} is funny$_7$ but the adjective "ironic"$_7$ describes HIM$_1$ {0/1/2/3/4/5} better, given that HE$_1$ {0/1/2/3/4/5} never gives the impression of being completely happy$_7$ although HE$_1$ {0/1/2/3/4/5} often makes OTHER PEOPLE$_6$ {1/3/4/5} laugh$_7$ quite a lot.

{2} In general HE$_1$ {0/1/2/3/4/5} is a pacific$_2$ PERSON$_3$ {0/2/4/5}: HE$_1$ {0/1/2/3/4/5} knows how to use the art of diplomacy$_2$ and often does so when it$_2$ is convenient. HE$_1$ {0/1/2/3/4/5} has always been reserved$_4$, but I think that DEEP DOWN {2/3/5} on opening a discussion$_5$ HE$_1$ {0/1/2/3/4/5} is also shy$_4$ when it comes to criticisms$_5$ and confrontation$_5$, whereas on some issues HE$_1$ {0/1/2/3/4/5} does not go into detail or into PERSONAL$_3$ {0/2/4/5} EXPERIENCE {1/2}.

{3} HE$_1$ {0/1/2/3/4/5} is generous when it comes to giving advice$_2$ and being interested$_2$ {1/3} in SOMEONE ELSE'S {1/3/4/5} problem$_3$. Even when HE$_1$ {0/1/2/3/4/5} DEALS$_2$ {3/5} with a well KNOWN$_4$ {1/3} or STEREOTYPED$_4$ problem$_3$ HE$_1$ {0/1/2/3/4/5} adopts a position of not reaching$_5$ a predetermined conclusion$_6$ but rather starts from scratch$_7$ in order to analyze$_4$ everything right from the beginning$_7$. In this way, he sometimes$_8$ reaches$_5$ a NEW$_4$ {1/3} perspective$_9$, which not even HE$_1$ {0/1/2/3/4/5} gives the IMPRESSION$_{10}$ {3/5} of knowing beforehand$_{11}$, but instead DISCOVERS$_4$ {3/4/5} it$_9$ "along the way"$_{11}$; at other times$_8$, although no solution$_6$ is reached$_5$, one gets the IMPRESSION$_{10}$ {3/5} that a well-EDUCATED {3/4/5} and sometimes$_8$ even COMPLICATED {3/5} approximatión$_8$ has been made, one that leaves no LOOSE ENDS {2/3/5}.

{4} In school$_1$ HE$_2$ {0/1/2/3/4/5} was considered a charismatic PERSON {0/2/4/5}, but one who did not always accept the confidence$_3$ OTHERS offered {1/3/4/5} HIM$_2$ {0/1/2/3/4/5}; HE$_2$ {0/1/2/3/4/5} accepted it$_3$ only if he did not have to EXPOSE$_4$ {3/4/5} HIMSELF$_2$ {0/1/2/3/4/5}, indeed in such cases$_4$ HE$_2$ {0/1/2/3/4/5} would take the initiative$_5$ (for example, if a card$_6$ had to be sent to the Greek teacher$_7$, when the class$_1$ decided to send it$_6$ to her$_7$, HE$_2$ {0/1/2/3/4/5} was the one$_2$ to think what to put on it$_6$). On the other hand, HE$_2$ {0/1/2/3/4/5} never wanted to be a leader$_5$, a role$_5$ that$_5$ also implied UNPLEASANT$_7$ {0/1/4} ASPECTS {4/5}, such as having to EXPOSE$_4$ {3/4/5}, on behalf of part of the class$_1$, a complaint$_8$ to a teacher$_7$ or to make an UNCOMFORTABLE$_7$ petition$_8$ to another teacher$_7$.

Figure 4-21. Microstructural divisions, redundancy, and coherence analysis of Bill's self-characterization. *(Continues)*

{5} Summing up then, we are, without doubt, DEALING {3/5} with a YOUTH$_1$
{0/1/2/3/4/5} of uncommon APPEARANCE$_2$ {0/5} of WHOM {0/1/2/3/4/5/} I get the
IMPRESSION$_2$ {3/5} that it is not EASY$_3$ {3/5} to know either the positive or the nega-
tive$_5$ ASPECTS$_4$ {4/5} of his$_1$ PERSONALITY {0/2/4/5}, but that$_4$, for one reason or
another, are HIDDEN$_6$ {3/4/5} behind a screen$_7$ or a veil$_7$, which does not allow$_3$
OTHER PEOPLE {1/3/4/5} to DISCOVER$_6$ {3/4/5} THEM$_4$ {4/5} DEEP DOWN {2/3/5}.

Figure 4-21. *Continued.*

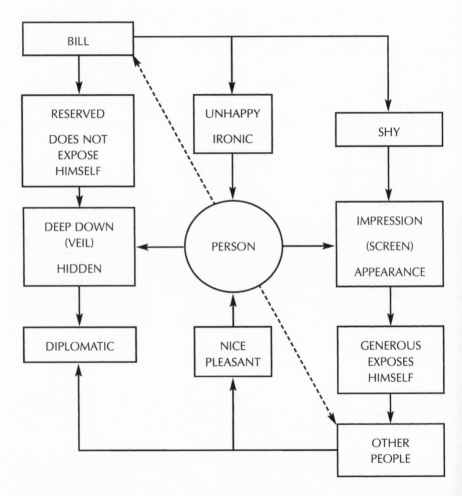

Figure 4-22. Macrostructure of Bill's self-characterization.

Commentary on Macrostructure

The central axis, around which Bill's self-characterization is focused, is defined by the contrast of interior (deep down) versus exterior (appearance), synthesized in the concept of a PERSON, that etymologically refers to the meaning of the mask. Bill tries to hide his shy, reserved, unhappy interior (his real self) from other people with a veil or screen that gives the impression of a nice, generous, pleasant diplomat, providing that all this does not require a personal effort.

The reason for hiding this part of him, as will be divulged in a series of interviews and in the tales of other dreams, lies in the shame and embarrassment caused by his interest in sexual relations with and attraction to girls. An aesthetic complex related to his teeth constitutes an almost insurmountable impediment for the direct satisfaction of his sexual desires, which he tries to balance with an external image that is acceptable and interesting; nothing trivial. However, all this does no more than disguise his fundamental interest in sex, given that even his literary fantasies are in keeping with the desire to impress girls in order to attract them to him. On the other hand, the clandestine fashion in which he attempts to satisfy his sexual needs is made clear in the following dream, which we have called "the television set in the bedroom" (see Figures 4-23, 4-24, and 4-25).

The macrostructure is focused on the meaning of an episode that confuses and embarrasses the patient. Confusion arises because it is his own mother (or so he thinks) who facilitates the solution to his problem of sexual voyeurism when she moves the TV to his bedroom: In this way, he can watch the pornographic films without being watched. Embarrassment arises because this shows that everyone knows the reason for moving the television and in the sense that he is being observed by the women, who are staking him out. With respect to his father and his grandfather he feels freer, given that they are not directly observing him, although they are also up to date on the situation. His reaction is to continue to be vigilant, prepared to disguise the act with a normal cassette which he has placed in the video recorder.

Macroproposition

"I am confused and embarrassed because of a sexual curiosity and attraction that I try to disguise, but I would like to fulfill freely my desires without the feeling that I am being watched."

The joint macrostructural synthesis of these texts allows us to represent the organization of Bill's discourse around the conflict between his sexual urges and aesthetic complex (see Figure 4-26). The strength of his sexual attraction leads him to look for clandestine ways in which to satisfy his urges (Internet, videos, etc.) which are the cause of his shame and embarrassment. Given that the aesthetic complex (the problem of his separated teeth) prevents him from making direct contact with girls, he tries to become closer to them by fantasizing about literary and intellectual success as a way of indirectly attracting their attention.

While I find myself in another part of the house, where my grandparents also are, I return to my bedroom and I observe that my mother (or so I think) has moved the televison and the video from the living room to my bedroom. In the living room my grandfather is watching the television on a minature TV set (which we do not have in the house). I feel very confused and embarrassed, because it is a way of being able to see the television alone at night without being disturbed. I have barely entered the bedroom and closed the door when pictures of women, like the ones on pornographic films, appear on the televison screen. Just in case, I disguise this by placing a normal video in the machine.

Another observation: my sister, my mother, and my grandmother are in the bedroom opposite with the door half open. They know about the television being moved and the reason for moving it: This situation makes me feel a little embarrassed. My grandfather is in the living room. I don't know where my father is, but I take it for granted that he knows the reason for moving it.

Patient's commentary on his own dream:

To be able to understand the dream of the television set in the bedroom I must explain that I do not partake in the exchange of pornographic tapes between friends because it is too embarrassing for me, although in reality I would love to be able to. I do not even go to the newsagent's to buy certain kinds of magazines because I also get too embarrassed. However, I do, for example, entertain myself on the Internet searching for pornographic images, but my father, after having discovered me, says that he is not prepared to spend money on these kinds of telephone calls. Moreover, we have a TV in our apartment, and when I wish to stay up to see something at night, I bother my parents because they always sleep with the door open. However, I cannot deny that these kinds of things attract me. . . . I am greatly interested by the aspects of sexuality.

Figure 4-23. Bill's dream: the television set in the bedroom.

{1} While I_1 {1/2/3/4} FIND {1/4} $MYSELF_1$ in another part of the $HOUSE_2$ {1/3/4}, where $_2 MY_1$ {1/2/3/4} $GRANDPARENTS_3$ {1/4} also are, I_1 {1/2/3/4} return to MY_1 {1/2/3/4} $BEDROOM_2$ {1/3/4} and I_1 {1/2/3/4} OBSERVE {1/4} that MY_1 {1/2/3/4} MOTHER {1/4} (or so I_1 {1/2/3/4} think) has MOVED {1/4} the $TELEVISON_4$ {1/2/3/4} and the $VIDEO_4$ {1/2/3/4} from the LIVING $ROOM_2$ {1/3/4} to MY_1 {1/2/3/4} $BEDROOM_2$ {1/3/4}. In the LIVING $ROOM_2$ {1/3/4} MY_1 {1/2/3/4} $GRANDFATHER_3$ {1/4} is WATCHING {1/2} $TELEVISION_4$ {1/2/3/4} on a minature TV SET_4 {1/2/3/4} (which we do not have in the $HOUSE_2$ {1/3/4}).

{2} I {1/2/3/4} FEEL {2/4}very $CONFUSED_1$ {2/4} and $EMBARRASSED_1$ {2/4} because it is a way of being able to SEE {1/2} the TELEVISION {1/2/3/4} alone at night without being disturbed.

{3} I_1 {1/2/3/4} have barely entered the BEDROOM {1/3/4} and CLOSED {3/4} the DOOR {3/4} when $pictures_2$ of women, like the $ones_2$ on porno-$graphic_3$ $films_2$, appear on the $TELEVISON_4$ {1/2/3/4} screen. Just in case, I_1 {1/2/3/4} disguise this by placing a $normal_3$ $VIDEO_4$ {1/2/3/4} in the MACHINE {1/2/3/4}.

{4} Another OBSERVATION {1/4}: MY_1 {1/2/3/4} $SISTER_2$ {1/4}, MY_1 {1/2/3/4} $MOTHER_2$ {1/4}, and MY_1 {1/2/3/4} $GRANDMOTHER_2$ {1/4} are in the BED-$ROOM_3$ {1/3/4} opposite with the DOOR {3/4} HALF OPEN {3/4}. They $know_4$ about the $TELEVISION_5$ {1/2/3/4} being $MOVED_6$ {1/4} and the $reason_7$ for $MOVING_6$ {1/4} IT_5 {1/2/3/4}: This situation makes ME_1 {1/2/3/4} FEEL {2/4} a little EMBARRASSED {2/4}. My_1 {1/2/3/4} $GRANDFATHER_2$ {1/4} IS IN {1/4} the LIVING $ROOM_3$ {1/3/4}. I_1 {1/2/3/4} don't $know_4$ where MY_1 {1/2/3/4} $FATHER_2$ {1/4} is, but I_1 {1/2/3/4} take it for granted that HE_2 {1/4} $knows_4$ the $reason_7$ for $MOVING_6$ {1/4} IT_5 {1/2/3/4}.

Scenario: The house (the living room, the bedroom itself, the bedroom in front).
Actors: Bill, alone. The rest of the family, divided by gender:
Mother, sister, and grandmother in the bedroom in front.
Grandfather in the living room; father outside.
Actions:
Mother (supposedly) has moved the television set to Bill's bedroom.
Bill closes himself in his bedroom and watches the pornographic films surrep-
titiously.
The women of the house lie in wait in the bedroom opposite with the door
half open.
Father has left the house.
Grandfather watches another TV in the living room.
Reactions:
Concealment and embarrasment (he has normal tapes prepared).

Figure 4-24. Microstructural division redundancy and coherence analysis.

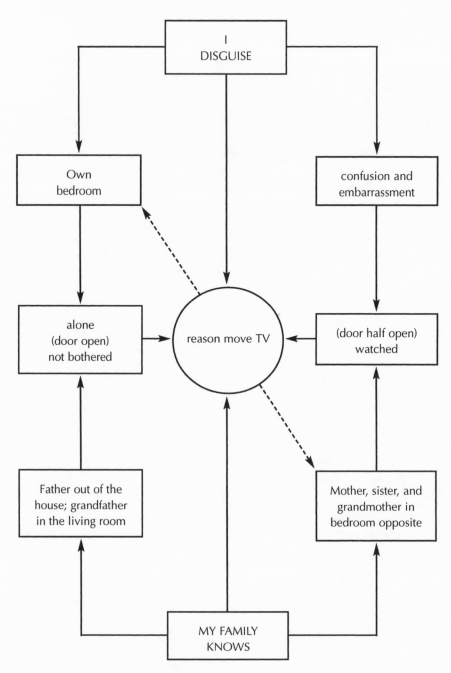

Figure 4-25. Macrostructure of Bill's dream.

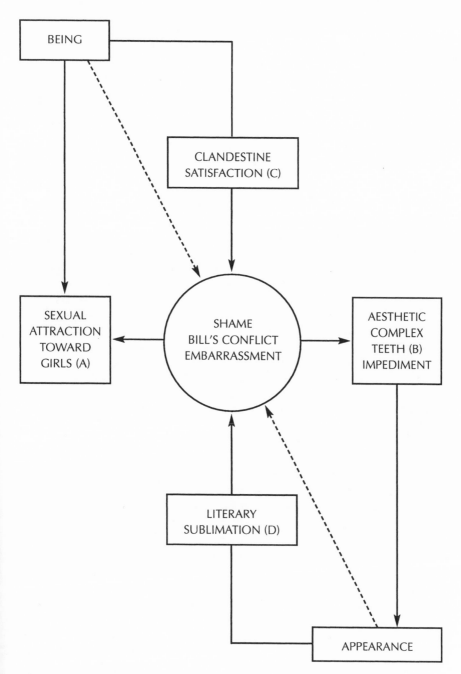

Figure 4-26. Macrostructural discursive synthesis of Bill's texts.

The set of Bill's texts taken from his time in therapy fit perfectly with the four issues incarnate in his dilemma of being and appearance: (A) his attraction to girls and a desire for sexual freedom, (B) his being impeded when it comes to relating to girls because of his aesthetic complex, (C) the search for clandestine satisfaction, and (D) literary sublimation as a way of attracting their attention.

The simultaneous consideration of various texts from the same author, as we have just done with Bill's case, shows that we stand before a coherent and homogenous semantic universe, which emerges from the common discursive matrix. The elicitation of this discursive matrix leads us to a comprehension of the structure of the subject's experiential world. Bill experiences with anxiety his own projection in the world, particularily in relation to the sexual and social dimension. Since adolescence, he has felt a natural attraction toward women; however, he does not find the socially appropriate channels to satisfy this attraction. He believes that in order to please girls he must have an attractive physique, but at the same time considers this to be superficial and that he should have other more profound attributes (e.g., those of a writer or a poet). The perceived discrepancy between the ideal and real images—the teeth problem—reveals the central existential conflict between "being and appearance." The sustained attempt to disguise the nature of the conflict by looking after his appearance unleashes an obsessive external locus of control (focused on his appearance), which, concentrating on the exterior, blocks the process of interior development. The lack of this distinction between *Eigenwelt*—one's own world—and *Mitwelt*—the world with others—only serves to increase disguise, appearances, voyeurism, shame, fear, embarrassment, and so on. These are the consequences of this stance in the inauthenticity of existence, coherent with the family context of hiding, parental absence, and lack of personal commitment.

CONCLUSION

Up until this point, the technique of textual analysis has been described and its application has been demonstrated with a few examples from different texts. As has been mentioned throughout the chapter, the advantage of this approach lies in the possibility of understanding the structural organization of the discourse, which reproduces the ideological matrix from which the discourse originates. Although the immediate origins of many texts are found in concrete or superficial situations, they still shed light on some of the profound discursive organization that sustains them. The possibility of comparing differing texts from the same subject (intertextual analysis) as well as the possibility of establishing the common denominators present in texts produced by different subjects (transtextual analysis) that share the same ideology or vision of the world (*Weltanschauung*) is of particular interest for research in psychotherapy and psychopathology. A recent example of transtextual analysis can be found in the comparison work that we have carried out between the autobiographical texts of three anorexic patients written in different historical moments of the 20th century (Villegas, 1997), in which the discursive matrix typical of a restrictive anorexic is shown to be made up of an existential dilemma of an oppositional nature: "*to be a person or to be a woman (that is the question).*"

The capacity of textual analysis to demonstrate the discursive organization of a text by way of a theoretically uncontaminated analysis, free of *a prioris*, and from that a subject's ideological matrix, or *Weltanschauung*, is extremely interesting for any model of psychotherapy. It is precisely this methodology of analysis that is especially appropriate for the different tendencies within the cognitive and hermeneutic therapies insofar as they are interested in underlining the schemes and construct systems with which subjects organize their experience, and all this from spontaneously produced texts (self-introductions, self-characterizations, dream stories, therapeutic dialog, etc.) as opposed to other more artificial means for obtaining data and personal constructs, such as repertory grids, questionnaires, tests, and so on.

For example, in *Adolphe*'s text by Benjamin Constant, analyzed earlier, we were able to show that "to be free, not to be loved," and to be a "stranger to the entire world" are equivalent terms in the logic of the subject's discourse. The idiosyncratic construction of experience produces semantic equivalencies between concepts that are not equivalent under normal circumstances. This phenomenom can be detected thanks to the redundancy factor, which joins such words in the text so that some of them define the others: Adolphe is free because he is no longer loved, which is the same as being a stranger to the entire world, because only one world exists, that of his beloved Eleonor.

At first sight, the technique of textual analysis is, without doubt, complex; however, it gives us an instrument of exhaustive comprehension free of any prejudice against the texts that the client offers us in psychotherapy. It constitutes a method or technique for qualitative investigation that is in keeping with the most legitimate spirit of the phenomenological approaches to the subject's experience in the world, and with the best constructivist, humanist, and existentialist traditions. Its use complements the attitudes of respect, unconditional acceptance, and empathy with a powerful analytical instrument capable of legitimizing and integrating the different hermeneutic practices that are necessarily carried out in the different psychotherapeutic modalities.

ACKNOWLEDGMENT

Translated from the original Spanish by Martin Hemmings.

REFERENCES

Allport, G. (1942). The use of personal documents in psychological science. *Social Science Research Council Bulletin, 49.*

Belinchón, M. (1991). Comunicación y lenguaje en la esquizofrenia. In C. Castilla del Pino & Ruiz Vargas (Eds.), *Aspectos cognitivos de la esquizofrenia*. Madrid, Spain: Trotta.

Belinchón, M., Rivière, A., & Igoa, J.M. (1992). *Psicología del lenguaje: investigación y teoría*. Madrid, Spain: Trotta.

Brown, G., & Yule, G. (1983). *Discourse analysis*. Cambridge: Cambridge University Press.

Bruner, J. (1990). Acts of meaning. Cambridge: Harvard University Press.

Caro, I. (1994). *La práctica de la terapia lingüística de evaluación*. Salamanca, Spain: Amarú.

Castilla del Pino, C. (1974). *Un estudio sobre la depresión*. Barcelona, Spain: Península.

Castilla del Pino, C. (1993). Análisis del lenguaje: Modelo hermenéutico. Unpublished manuscript.

Clark, H. H., & Havilland, S. E. (1977). Comprehension and the given-new contract. In R. O. Freddle (Ed.), *Discourse production and comprehension*. Norwood, NJ: Ablex.

Constant, B. (1985). *Adolphe*. Madrid, Spain: Cátedra.

De Beaugrande, R. (1979). The pragmatics of discourse planing. *Journal of Pragmatics, 3/6*.

De Beaugrande, R. (1980). *Text, discourse and process. Toward a multidisciplinary science of texts*. Norwood, NJ: Ablex.

Eco, U. (1990). *I limiti dell'interpretazione*. Milan, Italy: Bompiani.

Edmonson, W. (1981). *Spoken discourse: A model for analysis*. London: Longman.

Feixas, G. (1988). *L'anàlisi de construccions personals en textos de significació psicològica*. Doctoral dissertation in microfilm (N. 328). Barcelona, Spain: Publicacions de la Universitat de Barcelona.

Feixas, G., & Villegas, M. (1991). Personal construct analysis of autobiographical texts: A method presentation and case illustration. *International Journal of Personal Construct Psychology*, *4*, 51–83.

Feixas, G., & Villegas, M. (1993). *Constructivismo y psicoterapia*. Barcelona, Spain: PPU.

Goffman, E. (1967). *Interaction ritual. Essays on face-to-face behavior*. Garden City, NY: Doubleday.

Gonçalves, O. (1995). Psicoterapia cognitivo-narrativa: La construcción hermenéutica de los significados alternativos. *Revista de Psicoterapia, 22/23*, 101–122.

Greimas, A. J. (1966). *Sémantique structurale: Recherches de methode*. Paris: Larousse.

Halliday, M. A. K. (1978). *Language as social semiotic. The social interpretation of language and meaning*. London: Arnold.

Halliday, M. A. K., & Hassan, R. (1976). *Cohesion in English*. London: Longman.

Halliday, M. A. K., & Hassan, R. (1980). *Text and context*. Tokyo: Sophia University.

Lakoff, G. (1998). Cómo la metáfora estructura los sueños. *Revista de Psicoterapia, 34/35*, 5–30.

Levelt, W. J. M. (1989). *Speaking: From intention to articulation*. London: Bradford Books.

McTavish, D. G., & Pirro, E. (1990). Contextual content analysis. *Quality and Quantity, 23*, 245–265

Morris, C. (1938). *Foundations of a theory of signs*. Chicago: University of Chicago Press.

Pubill, M. J. (1994). *Anorexia nerviosa y contexto social*. Unpublished doctoral thesis. Universitat de Barcelona, Spain.

Ricoeur, P. (1986). *Du texte a l'action, essais d'herménéutique II*. Paris: Seuil.

Rochester, S. R., & Martin, J. R. (1979). *Crazy talk. A study of the discourse of schizophrenic speakers*. New York: Plenum.

Siguan, M. (1985). La expresión literaria en el lenguaje interior. *Anuario de Psicología, 33*, 117–128.

Sperber, D., & Wilson, D. (1986). *Relevance, communication and cognition.* Oxford, England: Basil Blackwell.

Sperber, D., & Wilson, D. (1987). Précis of "relevance." *The Behavioral and Brain Sciences, 10*, 697–754.

Stiles, W. B. (1992). *Describing talk. A taxonomy of verbal responses modes.* London: Sage.

Stiles, W. B. (1993a). Clasificación de actos ilocutivos intersubjetivos. *Anuario de Psicología, 59(4)*, 79–103.

Stiles, W. B. (1993b). Los modos de respuesta verbal en la investigación del proceso de la psicoterapia. In I. Caro (Ed.), *Psicoterapia e investigación de procesos.* Valencia, Spain: Promolibro.

Van Dijk, T. A. (1977). *Text and context.* London: Longman.

Van Dijk, T. A. (1993). Principles of critical discourse analysis. *Discourse & Society,* 249–283.

Van Dijk, T. (1998). Discourse studies. *Editorial Discourse and Society, 4*, 435–436.

Villegas, M. (1985, May). *Aproximacions de la psicolingüística al llenguaje de l'esquizofrènia.* First International Congress of Applied Psycholinguistics, Barcelona, Spain.

Villegas, M. (1992). Análisis del discurso terapéutico. *Revista de Psicoterapia, 10/11*, 23–66.

Villegas, M. (1997). Psicopatologías de la libertad (II). La anorexia o la restricción de la corporalidad. *Revista de Psicoterapia, 21*, 19–92.

Villegas, M. (1998). El discurso onírico. *Revista de Psicoterapia, 34/35*, 31–94.

Villegas, M., Feixas, G., & López, N. (1990). Phenomenological analysis of autobiographical texts: A design based on personal construct psychology. *Analecta Husserliana, 18*, 405–424.

Vygotsky, L. S. (1934/1962). *Thought and language.* Cambridge: MIT Press.

Werth, P. (1981). *Conversation in discourse: Structure and interpretation.* New York: St. Martin's Press.

Chapter 5

Is There Madness in Our Method? The Effects of Repertory Grid Variations on Measures of Construct System Structure

Greg J. Neimeyer
Robert A. Neimeyer
Chad L. Hagans
David L. Van Brunt

Since its initial presentation in Kelly's (1955) *magnum opus*, the Role Construct Repertory Grid (repgrid) has enjoyed pride of place among methodologies inspired by the parent theory. Utilized in over 90% of the field's empirical research, (Neimeyer, 1985; Neimeyer, Baker, & Neimeyer, 1990), the repgrid has become the primary tool for researchers in personal construct psychology. The reliance of the field on repgrid methodology has triggered a critical reappraisal of this tool at conceptual and operational levels (Adams-Webber, 1989, 1990; Caputi & Reddy, 1999; Epting, Probert, & Pittman, 1993; Probert & Epting, 1990; Soldz & Soldz, 1989; Yorke, 1989a, 1989b). But focused reappraisal has been challenged by the complexity of repgrid methodology, and by the proliferation of conceptual, procedural, and statistical variations associated with the methodology. "Grids are like people," Fransella and Bannister (1977) observed in the opening line of their *Manual for Repertory Grid Technique*, "They come in many shapes and sizes; they ask questions and give answers; they can be studied as a group or individually, on one occasion or successively over time; they can be used well or distorted out of all recognition" (p. v).

This chapter is about that variation and that distortion. Its focus is not on the grotesque disfigurations of the method that are the common cause of alarm. It does not call attention, for example, to those atheoretical adaptations of the method that Bannister (1985) characterized as "a Frankenstein's monster which has rushed away on a statistical and experimental rampage of its own, leaving construct theory neglected, stranded high and dry, far behind" (p. xii). Nor is it concerned with the recent proliferation of computer programs and analytical packages that challenge the fidelity of grid output to the theoretical underpinnings of the methodology (Bringmann, 1992). Instead, this chapter focuses on a range of apparently minor adaptations of the original repgrid as they occur within literatures that are central to the field's scholarship. Many of these are seemingly minor revisions that are borne of convenience, innovation, or accommodation to specific populations, purposes, or procedures. They range from subtle instructional deviations to substantial revisions designed to realign the method with core tenets of the parent theory. The central theme developed in this chapter has to do with the impact of these sometimes subtle adaptations, and the critical role they play in predicating the results and interpretations that follow from them. Even minor variations can register substantial effects, calling attention to the genuinely organic nature of repgrid methodology. The primary purpose of this chapter, then, is to advance our current understandings regarding the nature of specific repertory grid effects and to encourage critical reflection in the application and adaptation of repertory grid technique.

In support of this goal, this chapter consists of three sections. The first section provides an overview, followed by a synoptic review of the literatures surrounding a selected set of repertory grid variations. Broadly speaking, these variations address modifications in the types of constructs and elements that are used, the procedures used for eliciting constructs, and the methods for conducting ratings of elements along constructs. A second section advances this literature by reporting the results of two original studies that were specifically designed to address unresolved issues in these literatures, including the interaction among these variations. The final section translates the implications of the first two sections into a set of recommendations or guidelines for future research using repertory grid technique.

OVERVIEW

In reviewing adaptations of repgrid methodology, the most striking feature is the diversity of its forms, procedures, and instructions. If there is a common denominator among them, it is that "all forms of grid are sorting tasks which enable the person to tell us something of the way in which he sees and orders" the world (Fransella & Bannister, 1977, p. 59). Beyond that, grids vary widely in their design, instructional sets, administration, and analysis. Even a cursory review of the method's development reveals a striking proliferation of mutations over the years, many of them constituting versions distinctly different from the original methodolgy. Exchange Grids (Mendoza, 1985), Family Grids (Procter, 1985), and Dyad Grids (Ryle & Lunghi, 1970), for example, have joined more traditional variations such as Implications Grids (Hinkle, 1965), Resistance-to-Change Grids (Hinkle, 1965), and Dependency Grids (Fransella & Bannister, 1977; Walker, 1997) as modified forms of repertory grid technique. Each of these variations is designed to tap a particular domain, process, or facet of construing, and for that reason has its own focus and range of convenience, as well as design and procedural specifications. And, similar to Kelly's original Role Construct Repertory Grid, each of these modified grids has enjoyed further adaptation to specific purposes, as well, yielding a veritable explosion of repertory grid variation across time and contexts. In this regard, what Fransella and Bannister (1977, p. 59) noted more than 25 years ago is still true today, that "the grid is truly a technique . . . which is only limited by the user's lack of imagination."

This chapter focuses attention on those imagined procedural variations that have particular theoretical value or strong empirical warrant. However, the lessons now being gleaned from these better-studied adaptations may also be useful in understanding other repertory grid modifications that fall outside of the purview of this chapter. These variations and the output to which they give rise are increasingly varied, with a wide variety of computer programs designed to yield a host of different structural scores (Bringmann, 1992; Sewell, Adams-Webber, Mitterer, & Cromwell, 1992). Our major concern in this chapter is on one particular type of structural score: construct system differentiation (or cognitive complexity). The choice of this particular feature was driven by its long-standing role in the empirical literatures deriving from personal construct psychology. Introduced by Bieri in 1955, "cognitive complexity" is understood as the relative number of different dimensions of judgment (personal constructs) available to an individual. Because a personal construct system is composed of a finite number of constructs, the number of different dimensions that it supports should provide a direct gauge of the capacity to generate alternative perspectives. A system composed of few constructs would constrain the individual, limiting him or her to relatively few perspectives, whereas a more multidimensional system would enable the individual to bring to bear a wide variety of differing constructions in interpreting and evaluating experience. This is the fundamental value of a more "cognitively complex" or better differentiated system, and it has been the subject of substantial research over the course of the last 50 years (see Adams-Webber, 1979, 1998).

We chose to concentrate on measures of differentiation because they have been a continuous companion to repertory grid studies since the inception of the method. Because of its centrality to the personal construct literature across time, we know more about the relationship of differentiation to repgrid variations than we do any other single variable. Still, we do not intend to privilege measures of construct system differentiation among the wide range of alternative measures of personal construct organization and structure (indeed, there are cogent critiques of measures of differentiation and their literatures; see Neimeyer, 1992; Soldz & Soldz, 1989). Rather, our hope is to use these more familiar measures as a "case study" to prompt more research into the impact of procedural variations on a wide range of other structural scores, including those yet to be devised by future researchers.

IMPORTANT VARIATIONS IN REPERTORY GRID PROCEDURE

Repertory grids consist of three essential features: a set of elements, a set of constructs, and a series of ratings of those elements along those constructs. This review focuses on selected modifications in each of those three domains. Concerning the constructs, it focuses on the nature of the constructs and the procedures used for eliciting them. A longstanding literature addresses differences in the *type of constructs* used (personal versus provided), and more recent research addresses different procedures for eliciting constructs. These include the use of different *element contexts* for eliciting constructs, as reflected in "triadic" versus "dyadic" procedures. Triadic elicitation procedures present the person with three elements at a time as the context for articulating constructs. Dyadic elicitation procedures, by comparison, present the individual with only two elements at a time, inviting them to consider similarities or differences between them. Recent work has begun to identify the differential impact of dyadic and triadic elicitation procedures on levels of construct system differentiation (Caputi & Reddy, 1999; Hagans, Neimeyer, & Goodholm, 2000).

In addition to triadic versus dyadic elicitation procedures, *the instructional set* for eliciting the constructs has also been varied. One such instructional variation is the distinction between developing constructs based on perceived "differences" (Kelly, 1955), as opposed to specifying contrasts based on perceived "opposites" (Epting, Suchman, & Nickerson, 1971). The differential impact of these two methods was noted in early work nearly 30 years ago (Epting et al., 1971), though its impact on construct system differentiation has only recently begun to receive empirical attention.

In addition to differences concerning constructs and their elicitation, we also draw attention to issues regarding the selection of specific *elements* and the role that this selection plays in structural measures of differentiation. Kelly's original Role Construct Repertory Test provided a range of elements (people) designed to reflect a representative sample of an individual's interpersonal field. For Kelly (1955), "representativeness" included using a range of elements of widely varying valences (positive and negative), and this aspect has been the subject of ongoing experimental attention. *Element valence* (positive, negative, or mixed), has been related to the levels of differentiation derived from the repertory grid, and for that reason it is also included in this review.

The final set of considerations has to do with the ratings of the elements along the constructs. A wide range of rating variations has been reported in the literature. These include specific grid adaptations like the binary grid, the rank-order grid, or a variety of different ratings grids (Fransella & Bannister, 1977). There has also been recent work concerning the *direction of the ratings*; that is, whether the ratings are made down the columns on an *element-by-element basis,* or across the rows in the grid on a *construct-by-construct* basis. Element-by-element ratings require an individual to consider one element at a time and rate that element down each of the constructs in succession. Construct-by-construct ratings, by contrast, require a respondent to consider one construct at a time and rate all elements along that one construct before moving to the next construct. Explicit attention to the differences between these methods is relatively recent (Costigan, Dowling, & Marsh, 1991; Epting, Prichard, Wiggins, Leonard, & Beagle, 1992), although this work has sparked ongoing consideration of this issue and its attendant effects.

This chapter provides a synoptic review of the literature in relation to each of these factors, concentrating on the effects of these variations on measures of construct system differentiation (see Table 5-1). These factors include the nature of the constructs used in the repertory grid (provided versus personal), the context for eliciting constructs (triadic versus dyadic), the instructional set for conducting this elicitation (difference method versus opposite method), the valence of the elements (positive versus mixed) and the direction of ratings (element-by-element versus construct-by-construct). Although each of these variations has received some attention in separate publications, no work to date has provided a single-source review of these variations and their effects. Moreover, no work to

Table 5-1. Repertory Grid Variations Reviewed in This Chapter

Construct Variations	Element Valence Variations
Elicited constructs	Positive
Provided constructs	Negative
	Mixed-valence

Context Variations	Rating Direction Variations
Monadic elicitation	Construct-by-construct ratings
Dyadic elicitation	Element-by-element ratings
Triadic elicitation	

Instructional Variations
Difference method
Opposite method

date has begun to address the *combined* effects of these variations in order to determine how they may interact or to provide guidelines for researchers seeking to make informed choices about the modification of repertory grid procedures in their programs of research. This chapter focuses on all three goals in an effort to integrate, advance, and inform future research using repertory grid technique.

Personal versus Provided Constructs

As Bannister (1985, p. xi) has noted, Kelly "seems to have looked to repertory grid technique to illustrate, in vivid and practical form, what he saw as the primary undertaking of psychology: To develop an understanding of the way in which persons interpret their experience." To this day, many applications of rep-grid methodology have preserved this distinctly phenomenological feature, emphasizing the primacy of personal perceptions by eliciting a set of constructs individually from each person. An alternative to this elicitation procedure, however, was quickly introduced by Bieri (1955), who preferred the use of a standard set of experimentally provided construct dimensions. "The main advantage of supplying constructs . . . is that it permits a higher degree of standardization in administration as a basis for 'nomothetic' comparisons between different populations," noted Adams-Webber (1979, p. 324). "However," he continued, [it does] represent a major departure from Kelly's own emphasis on the personal nature of each individual's construction process."

Differences between the use of personal versus supplied constructs have occupied the attention of the field almost from the outset. Early experimental work on this issue was reviewed in Bannister and Mair (1968) and Adams-Webber (1970a). This work yielded a general consensus that, whereas individuals can effectively use provided constructs, they generally prefer to use their own personal dimensions, and regard them as more meaningful (Adams-Webber, 1970b), relevant (Caine & Smail, 1967), and important (Lemon & Warren, 1974). Isaacson and Landfield (1965) were among the first to demonstrate that personal constructs were not only viewed as more meaningful by their users, but actually used in a more meaningful way, as gauged by the extremity of the ratings they produced. Likewise, Benjafield, Pomeroy, and Jordan (1976) found that individuals tended to distinguish between themselves and others to a greater extent on elicited constructs than on supplied ones. These findings were consistent with earlier work, which further supported the developing consensus regarding the greater meaningfulness and utility of personal over provided constructs (see Adams-Webber, 1979).

Additional data bearing on the issue of personal and provided constructs concern structural differences between them. Metcalfe (1974), for example, found that personally elicited constructs were associated with significantly higher levels of cognitive differentiation than were their experimentally provided counterparts, a finding that has been replicated repeatedly since that time (see Adams-Webber, 1979, and Neimeyer, 1992, for reviews).

One implication of this difference between personal and provided constructs concerns their differential utility or accuracy in perceiving others. As Adams-Webber (1998) has noted, "Whenever one attempts to 'construe the construction processes of another'," which is Kelly's (1955, p. 95) theoretical definition of sociality, "the relative degree of differentiation of that individual's personal construct system also may be a factor in determining accuracy" (p. 499). Specifically, individuals should be more accurate in inferring the psychological perspectives of others when using their own personal constructs than when using provided ones, given that personal constructs are used in more highly differentiated or "cognitively complex" ways (see also Neimeyer, Neimeyer, & Landfield, 1983).

Adams-Webber (1998) recently tested this prediction in a sample of 30 previously unacquainted individuals. Fifteen men and 15 women interacted briefly in randomly assigned pairs and then attempted to infer the self-evaluations of their partners in terms of a set of their own personally elicited constructs and a set of experimentally supplied ones. Overall, the personal constructs were associated with higher levels of construct system differentiation than were the provided ones, and they yielded significantly more accurate inferences, as well. In discussing his results, Adams-Webber (1998, p. 501) emphasized that "individuals' self-evaluations can be inferred more accurately in terms of constructs elicited from themselves than in terms of supplied constructs," a finding that he attributed to the greater relevance and meaningfulness of personal over provided construct dimensions.

Even as investigators continue to document differences between the use of personal and provided constructs, related work has turned toward developing a clearer explanation for them. Neimeyer and Leso (1992) argued that there were at least two competing explanations for these differences, one based on construct content and one based on the process of elicitation itself. On the one hand, consistent with traditional explanations, personal constructs might be used with greater differentiation because they are more meaningful and relevant to their users (Adams-Webber, 1979; Bannister & Mair, 1968). On the other hand, observed differences may stem from the demands of construct elicitation itself, rather than from the nature of the constructs it generates. Provided constructs are simply supplied to individuals in list form and then used to rate the elements (people) in the grid. In contrast, elicited constructs require participants first to articulate a set of personal constructs prior to rating the various elements along them. As a result, elicited forms of repertory grids require considerably more reflection, personal introspection, and time to complete, than do their provided counterparts. It may be that it is this process of review and reflection, rather than the constructs that emerge from them, per se, that accounts for the greater meaning and utility of personal constructs (Neimeyer & Leso, 1992).

This concern is amplified, argue Neimeyer and Leso (1992), by the particular demands that the elicitation procedure places on differentiation. Traditional elicitation procedures specifically pull for differentiation, as is implied in instructions to "indicate how any two of these elements are alike in some way and *different* from the third," a demand not made when constructs are simply given to participants to use in performing their grid ratings. The greater differentiation associated with personal constructs, therefore, may be merely an artifact of the elicitation process, a consequence of the systematic reflection and articulation process used to develop them.

Neimeyer, Leso, Marmarosh, Prichard, and Moore (1992) developed a two-part study to test this possibility. Study 1 attempted to separate out the effects of the elicitation process from the task of rating the elements. To do this, half of the participants were asked to elicit a set of personal constructs and, 1 week later, to either use those personal constructs or a standard set of provided constructs to rate all elements in the grid. The other half were simply given the standard elicited or provided grids, without the 1-week delay prior to performing their element ratings. Neimeyer et al. (1992) reasoned that if the *content* of the constructs is the determining factor, then elicited constructs should show higher levels of differentiation than provided ones, regardless of whether these constructs were separated by 1 week from the process of elicitation that yielded them. On the other hand, if the *process* of elicitation accounts for the higher levels of differentiation, then these higher levels should be associated only with the condition in which the elicitation task directly precedes the rating task; constructs elicited from their users 1 week earlier should show levels of differentiation no different from the provided construct dimensions.

Results were intriguing. As in previous work, personal constructs again showed significantly higher levels of differentiation than did provided constructs. Surprisingly, however, separating the process of construct elicitation from the rating tasks had no effect on levels of differentiation. Personal constructs were used with equally high levels of differentiation whether they were directly preceded by the elicitation process (the usual method), or artificially separated from that process by a 1-week delay. This finding is consistent with the conventional "meaningfulness" interpretation of personal constructs. It suggests that the content of the constructs, rather than the process of elicitation, may be the driving factor in the greater levels of differentiation associated with them.

But Neimeyer et al. (1992) noted an unexpected finding that challenged this interpretation. They found that the *provided* constructs in their study were also substantially influenced by the process of construct elicitation 1 week earlier. Contrary to expectations, when the construct ratings along provided dimensions were preceded 1 week earlier by the elicitation of a set of personal constructs (constructs that were never actually used to make ratings), the provided constructs showed marked increases in differentiation. In other words, the elicitation process rendered the subsequent use of provided constructs more like personally elicited ones, enhancing their capacity to differentiate among elements of experience.

In explaining these effects, the authors interpreted both sets of findings as converging on a meaningfulness hypothesis. According to this reasoning, anything that enhances the personal meaning of a set of constructs would enhance the differentiation with which that system is used. Personally elicited constructs come by this naturally, being forged from within the person's unique experience and idiosyncratic vocabulary. Provided constructs can be made to do this by any manipulation, such as the prior elicitation procedure, that enhances the elaboration or personal relevance of available construct dimensions. This interpretation was speculative, but fueled the development of a study to investigate this possibility directly.

A direct test of this reasoning was conducted in Study 2 of Neimeyer et al. (1992). Arguing that any "manipulations designed to enhance the meaningfulness of provided dimensions should also enhance the subsequent levels of differentiation with which they are used" (p. 125), the researchers tested the effects of a "meaning enhancement" procedure on the levels of construct differentiation. In a mixed-sex sample of 69 individuals, participants were assigned to one of four conditions. Half of the participants completed grids using provided construct dimensions, while the other half used personal construct dimensions. In each condition, half of them completed the grids in the usual fashion, whereas the other half first completed a "meaning enhancement" procedure requiring them "to review each construct individually and to write a short statement about its personal meaning to them" (Neimeyer et al., 1992, p. 126).

Results of the study supported the notion that "differentiation is linked to the personal meaning of the constructs used" (Neimeyer et al., 1992, p. 126). Main effects were found both for construct type (personal versus provided) and for procedural condition (standard versus meaning enhancement). Overall, personal constructs were rated as more meaningful and used with greater differentiation than were provided constructs. Likewise, the participants in the meaning enhancement conditions rated their constructs as more meaningful and used them with greater differentiation, as well. Interestingly, the lack of an interaction between these two factors indicated that the meaning enhancement procedure had the same effect on provided and elicited constructs, in both cases elevating the levels of differentiation associated with them. In concluding their study, Neimeyer and his colleagues (1992) noted that these findings "document, for the first time, the effective manipulation of construct meaningfulness and the impact of that meaningfulness on levels of differentiation" (p. 126). Subsequent work has replicated this effect (Moore & Neimeyer, 1997), again demonstrating the impact of meaning enhancement of levels of construct system differentiation.

In combination, these studies begin to blur the difference between personal and provided constructs as much as distinguish them. Rather than representing two qualitatively distinct classes of construct dimensions, as the history of research in this area would suggest, elicited and provided constructs might simply represent two ends of a continuum of personal meaningfulness (Moore & Neimeyer, 1997; Neimeyer et al., 1992). "More critical than the origin of the construct may be the construct's personal significance or private meaning to the individual who is using it" (Moore & Neimeyer, 1997, p. 93). One implication of this notion is that "individual meaning and relevance may no longer be viewed as the exclusive domain of personally elicited constructs" (Neimeyer et al., 1992, p. 127). Rather, this meaning can be developed by having the individual elaborate the personal significance of a provided set of constructs. Unlike personally elicited constructs that can, by definition, be considered to be personally relevant, the relevance of provided constructs might be expected to vary considerably across individuals (see Neimeyer et al., 1992), depending on their level of involvement, reflection, or elaboration of those dimensions. The irony is that provided constructs were introduced into the literature precisely to reduce the error variance associated with the use of personal (and hence variable) constructs. But it now seems likely that, despite their standardization, they nonetheless introduce greater variability in personal meaning. The relative tradeoff between the level of error variance that is introduced and that which is reduced through the use of provided constructs remains an empirical issue worth addressing in future studies. In the meantime, it is currently clear that (a) provided constructs are on average less meaningful to their users than are personally elicited constructs, (b) this meaningfulness is positively related to levels of construct system differentiation, and (c) as the meaning of provided constructs is enhanced, differences between them and their elicited counterparts vanishes correspondingly.

Elicitation Variations

In addition to variations in the type of constructs used in the grid (elicited versus provided), important differences have been developed in relation to the method of elicitation itself. Two specific modifications concern the *context* and the *instructional set* for construct elicitation. *Context* refers to the number of elements presented to the individual for consideration when generating his or her constructs. *Instructional set* refers to the specific instructions that are given regarding the way in which a construct is formulated, articulated, and conveyed.

Context Variations

Kelly (1955) regarded a personal construct as a perceived basis of comparison and distinction among elements of experience. Accordingly, his original procedure for eliciting construct dimensions relied on the use of three elements (e.g., people) as the context for developing a bipolar construct, asking the person to "identify any way in which two of these people are alike in some way, but different from the third." The way in which two were viewed as alike ("both of these are strong-willed people") anchored one pole of the construct, whereas the difference ("this one is more passive") anchored the other. This elicitation procedure is known as the triadic elicitation method or the "minimum context" form. "Minimum context" refers to the assumption that construing requires the identification of perceived similarity between two or more events in a way that distinguishes them from at least one other event (Kelly's 1955 Construction Corollary). Hence, the minimum context for the creation of a new construct was three elements.

Using three elements as the basis for generating constructs, the original triadic elicitation method has undergone a number of different adaptations and variations. "Even within this basic triad format," Epting, Probert, and Pittman (1993) note, "Kelly started with a very tight procedure and then playfully explored ways to expand the procedure" (p. 81). In fact, Kelly (1955) outlined six different variations on this triadic construct elicitation procedure, as detailed in Epting et al. (1993) and Fransella and Bannister (1977). As Fransella and Bannister (1977) have noted, however, the minimum context only applies to the formulation of a *new* construct, not to the elicitation of a construct already available in the system. This observation has opened the way for a number of further adaptations, including monadic and dyadic elicitation procedures.

Monadic procedures elicit constructs from a single object or element at a time, without demanding an explicit contrast during construct development. Landfield, Stefan, and Dempsey (1990) used a monadic elicitation procedure in their study of self-constructions. They asked participants to consider a single element, themselves, and to list their most positive and negative characteristics. Each of these characteristics served as the "emergent" pole of a construct, and participants were then asked to identify the *opposite* of those characteristics (see Opposite Method, later) to form the "implicit" poles of each dimension. Other adaptations of the monadic elicitation procedure can be found in Leitner (1985) and Epting et al. (1993). In his interview-based procedure, Leitner (1985) invited participants to consider (a) their earliest memories, (b) what they would like to see written on their tombstone, (c) their conception of God, (d) their most significant life events, (e) recurring themes in their important dreams, and (f) some of their most cherished fantasies. In each case, Leitner encouraged participants to identify salient features of their response, and then to articulate the opposite of these features to serve as the implied poles of the construct dimensions. The results of an exploratory study testing this procedure indicated that it yielded significantly more meaningful self-descriptions than did constructs developed through a repertory grid procedure (Leitner, 1985). A final example of a monadic elicitation procedure was provided by Epting et al. (1993), who described a storytelling game involving a series of hypothetical scenarios as contexts for eliciting constructs. Given the name of a person in their lives, for example, the participant might be given the following instructions: "Let's just say this person is in Washington, D.C., and can spend a few hours at one museum. Would they prefer a natural history, history and technology, aerospace, or a fine art museum? Justify your pre-diction" (Epting et al., 1993, p. 93).

The dyadic elicitation procedure bears more similarity to the triadic than to monadic methods, but nonetheless represents a significant departure from Kelly's (1955) original procedure. The first explicit application of the dyadic method can be traced to Landfield (1971), who introduced it in his study of psychotherapy. From a list of significant people in the person's life, the participant was asked to "think about these two people. . . . Are the two people alike in some one way? Or are the two people different in some one way?" (Landfield, 1971 p. 161). If the two were viewed as alike, then the participant was asked to scan the list of remaining elements to find a person who was different, and that difference then anchored the other pole of the construct. On the other hand, if the two people were found to be different, then the description of each anchored the two poles of the construct.

Landfield (1971) noted the potential advantages of this method over the triadic method: "A subject, when restricted to finding a similarity prior to stating a dif-ference, occasionally is unable to respond. However, the subject may perceive all three acquaintances as similar and be able to think of someone outside the triad as being different" (p. 45). The dyadic elicitation method addresses this concern by permitting the participant to report a similarity *or* a difference, without placing the additional demand that the contrast pole applies to either of the elements in the elicitation context. The primary advantage of the dyadic elicitation method is its relative simplicity. Salmon (1976), for example, used the dyadic elicitation proce-dure in her work with children, noting that "the original (triadic) method . . . may do less than justice to the repertoire of constructs which may be pos-sessed by pre-school and junior school children" (p. 27). Although it has been used in a number of studies (Caputi & Reddy, 1999; Keen & Bell, 1980; Landfield, 1971), systematic comparisions of the dyadic method with other elicitation con-texts (i.e., triadic or monadic) have only recently begun to attract attention.

Caputi and Reddy (1999) have provided the first empirical comparison of tri-adic and dyadic elicitation methods. In their study of 24 postgraduate students in counseling psychology, they asked each person to complete one of two repertory grids, using a common set of eight elements. One grid used 12 constructs elicit-ed through the triadic procedure, whereas the other used 12 constructs elicited through the dyadic procedure. The overall purpose of their study was to "exam-ine whether the dyadic elicitation method generates constructs that are different from constructs elicited using the triadic method" (p. 261). Results from a num-ber of different structural measures supported their predictions. In particular, the authors noted that "the triadic method generates construct sets that are cognitive-ly more complex" (p. 261), as indicated by measures of construct system differ-entiation. Caputi and Reddy (1999) attributed this finding to the different tasks involved in the dyadic and triadic procedures. In particular, the triadic procedure demands that all three elements in the context (i.e., those that are "alike" as well as those that are "different") apply to the construct poles (i.e., "two are alike in that they are 'outgoing,' whereas the third one is 'shy'"). By comparison, the dyadic procedure does not have this requirement. When the two elements are viewed as "alike," the difference is implied rather than explicitly formed through the comparison. In interpreting their findings, Caputi and Reddy (1999) noted that "this difference of contrast and comparison in each elicitation method appears to affect the kind and nature of constructs that are generated by the respective approaches" (p. 261).

Although the research literature comparing different contexts for elicitation is still in its infancy, it suggests that the methods are not fully interchangeable. The structural differences in the levels of differentiation between triadic and dyadic methods of elicitation support Caputi and Reddy's (1999) caveat that "personal constructs are elicitation method-dependent" (p. 261).

Instructional Sets

In addition to variations in the contexts of elicitation (monadic, dyadic, triadic), important adaptations have also been made to the instructional set for eliciting constructs. "Difference" methods follow Kelly's (1955) original procedure, encouraging participants to distinguish among elements of experience and use this distinction as the basis for the personal construct. In Kelly's (1955) triadic difference procedure, for example, participants were asked to "identify any two people that are alike in some way, yet different from the third." As an alternative, Epting et al. (1971) devised a procedure in which participants were asked to identify how any two of three elements were alike, and then to nominate its *opposite*, following an early example cited in Kelly (1955). For example, a participant may respond that "Steve and Sue" are both "hard working," the opposite of which is "lazy." The likeness and opposite are recorded on the grid as the two poles of the construct dimension (i.e., "hard working versus lazy"). In comparing this "opposite method" with the original difference method, Epting et al. (1993) found that the opposite method elicited fewer "bent" constructs (nonantonyms), thereby enhancing construct bipolarity.

Hagans et al. (2000) suggested two additional ways in which use of the opposite versus difference method influences the nature of the constructs that are elicited. First, encouraging participants to produce an "opposite," at least on the face of it, would seem to invite more extreme contrasts. Instructions to produce the opposite of the emergent pole "intelligent," for example, might invite extreme contrasts such as "stupid." In contrast, instructions for the difference method ("How are two alike and different from the third?") might invite less extreme characterizations such as "less intelligent." In addition, the opposite method expressly permits the possibility that the contrast pole may apply to *no element on the grid*, a possibility that is specifically precluded by the difference method. In other words, with the difference method, the contrast pole necessarily applies to at least the one element in the sort that is identified as "different" from the others. The opposite method does not impose this requirement; having identified two elements as "intelligent," there is no requirement that opposite ("stupid") applies to any of the elements in the grid.

As Hagans and his colleagues point out, "these differences between the opposite and difference methods of construct elicitation carry direct implications for measures of construct system structure" (2000, p. 158). One common method of calculating construct system differentiation (Landfield's 1971 Functionally Independent Construction score) is directly related to the ways in which elements are placed (or rated) along the constructs. Put simply, any elicitation instructions that demand the distribution of ratings across *both* poles of the constructs will, by definition, *increase* levels of differentiation. By contrast, any method that permits all elements to be assigned to a *single* pole of the construct will reduce levels of differentiation. The difference method does the former, whereas the opposite method does the latter. The result is that the difference method should, by design, yield significantly higher levels of construct system differentiation, whereas opposite methods should yield relatively lower levels. Hagans et al. (2000) explored this possibility, separating out the effects of elicitation context (number of elements) from the effects of elicitation instructions (difference versus opposite methods). They began by noting that it is possible to generate four distinct variations by fully crossing the number of elements (dyadic versus triadic) and the instructional set (difference versus opposite): a Triadic Difference method, Triadic Opposite method, Dyadic Difference method, and Dyadic Opposite method.

The *Triadic Difference* method is Kelly's (1955) original version, and remains the traditional repgrid to this day. It presents participants with three elements (e.g., people) and asks them to report "some way in which any two are alike and thereby different from the third." The two poles identified are recorded on the grid as the construct (outgoing versus shy). The Triadic Difference method requires, by definition, that all three elements fall within the construct's range of convenience, and thus can be rated along both poles, because they have served as the basis for generating them.

The *Triadic Opposite* method (Epting et al., 1971) represents an important departure from this procedure. In the Triadic Opposite method, participants are presented with three elements and asked to identify a way in which any two of the three are alike. Participants are then asked to identify the *opposite* of this likeness. The likeness and the opposite are recorded on the grid as the two poles of the construct dimension. As noted earlier, the Triadic Opposite method may invite more extreme construing, and, unlike the Triadic Difference method, does not require that the contrast pole apply to any of the elements in the repgrid.

The *Dyadic Difference* method (Landfield, 1971) provides yet another variation in repertory grid administration. The method presents participants with only two elements (e.g., people) and asks for a way in which they are alike *or* different. If a difference is reported, (e.g., "he is expressive whereas she is more emotionally reserved"), the two construct poles are recorded (e.g., "expressive versus emotionally reserved") as in the Triadic Difference method. If a likeness is reported, however, the contrasting pole is elicited by asking participants to review the remaining members of the element set and to identify an element (person) that is different. This difference serves as the contrast pole. An important consideration in the Dyadic Difference method is that it requires at least one element in the full element set to fall within the range of convenience of the contrast pole, distinguishing it from the Dyadic Opposite method.

The *Dyadic Opposite* method (Hagans et al., 2000) presents participants with two elements (e.g., people) at a time and asks them to "identify any way in which you view any two of them as alike or different." When participants identify a difference between two elements (e.g., "this one is happy, this one is sad"), this difference serves to define the two poles of the construct (e.g., "happy versus sad"). When a similarity between the two elements is identified (e.g., "they are both outgoing"), then participants are asked to describe the *opposite* of the reported pole (e.g., "quiet"), and these are entered as the two poles of the construct. The Dyadic Opposite method assures the applicability of both poles of the constructs to at least one element in the grid when the constructs develop from perceived differences between elements, but place no such demands when constructs are based on perceived similarities and their opposites. A capsule summary of these four grid variations appears in Table 5-2.

Table 5-2. Variations in Construct Context and Elicitation Instructions

Context Variation	Instructional Variation	Instructional Set
Triadic	Difference	Present three elements at a time and ask, "How are two alike in some way, but different from the third?"
Triadic	Opposite	Present three elements at a time and ask, "How are any two of these alike in some way," and "What is the opposite of that?"
Dyadic	Difference	Present two elements and ask, "How are these two alike or different?" A reported difference specifies the two construct poles; a similarity results in reviewing the remaining list to identify a contrast from among them.
Dyadic	Opposite	Present two elements and ask, "How are these two alike or different?" A reported difference specifies the two poles of the construct; a similarity results in asking for the "opposite" of that similarity to form the contrasting pole of the construct.

Hagans et al. (2000) designed two studies to examine differences among these four variations. The first study addressed differences between the Triadic Difference and the Dyadic Opposite methods, whereas the second study concentrated on Triadic Difference versus Triadic Opposite methods. In study one, 115 participants were randomly assigned to either a Triadic Difference or a Dyadic Opposite condition, in each case eliciting 10 constructs and rating a series of 10 elements (people) along those dimensions. The matrix of 100 ratings (10 constructs x 10 elements) was analyzed for levels of differentiation, using Landfield's (1971) method of Functionally Independent Construction (FIC). In support of their predictions, the Triadic Difference Method yielded higher levels of construct differentiation than did the Dyadic Opposite method, a finding that is consistent with the work of Caputi and Reddy (1999).

In addition to differences in overall levels of construct system differentiation, Hagans et al. (2000) noted that the Dyadic Opposite method also yielded more extreme and "socially undesirable" contrast poles. Correlating these "social undesirability" scores with overall levels of differentiation, the researchers found an inverse relationship ($r = -.22$), suggesting that "higher levels of social undesirability were associated with lower FIC scores" (p. 14). A subsequent analysis of covariance indicated that, when differences in social desirability were removed, differences between the levels of differentiation produced by the two different repertory grid methods were no longer significant. One difficulty with this study, however, was that it compared two grid variation methods that had neither the element context nor the instructional set in common (i.e., Triadic Difference and Dyadic Opposite). As a result, it remained unclear which factor accounted for the observed differences in constructs and construct system structure. Therefore, a second study was designed to hold the context (number of elements) constant, varying only the instructional set for eliciting constructs.

In the second study, Hagans et al. (2000) compared the effects of the two Triadic elicitation methods: the Triadic Difference method and the Triadic Opposite method (see Table 5-2). In order to examine within-subject effects, as well as between-subject effects, participants were brought back to the laboratory 1 week later to complete a second grid. Half of those who completed a Triadic Difference grid the first time, completed another one the second time, whereas the other half completed a Triadic Opposite grid. Likewise, half of those who had initially completed a Triadic Opposite grid completed a second one, whereas the other half completed a Triadic Difference grid. Results of the study again documented the higher differentiation associated with the Triadic Difference over the Triadic Opposite method. As in the first study, the opposite method resulted in more socially undesirable contrast poles, which was inversely related to levels of construct system differentiation ($r = -.43$); the more extreme and negative the contrast poles were, the lower the levels of the construct system differentiation.

An examination of the within-subjects effects was also revealing. Participants who first completed a Triadic Opposite method of elicitation showed a significant increase in their levels of construct system differentiation when they then used the difference procedure, again signaling the impact of the difference method on levels of differentiation. Moreover, participants who first completed a Triadic Difference method showed significant increases in the social undesirability of their contrast poles when they subsequently completed a Triadic Opposite method. This study provided the first controlled, within-subjects investigation of the differential effects of difference and opposite methods of construct elicitation. They provide growing support for "the likelihood that variations in grid methods affect not only the structure of the construct system, but also the nature of the constructs elicited" (Hagans et al., p. 170).

Element Variations

In addition to variations in the type of constructs used in repertory grids (elicited versus provided), and the methods of elicitation (context variations and instructional set variations), changes in the *element sets* constitute yet another significant source of variability in adaptations of repertory grid technique (Bell, Vince, & Costigan, 1999). Kelly's (1955) original Role Construct Repertory Test utilized a set of role titles, asking participants to nominate the names of specific individuals who fit each of a wide range of role descriptions (e.g., best friend, someone who depends on you, your mother, your father, yourself). Kelly (1955) designed the element sets to ensure "that the other people appearing as elements in the test be sufficiently representative of all the people with whom the subject must relate. Representative figures, with respect to whom people seem normally to have formed the most crucial personal role constructs, are incorporated in the list" (p. 230). Empirical work seems to support the importance of Kelly's (1955) early insight in this regard. Mitsos (1958), for example, found that more broadly representative element sets tended to elicit relatively important, superordinate constructions.

Subsequent adaptations have included a broad range of different element sets, varying them according to the specific topic or focus of interest. Element sets have included different aspects of the self, interpersonal relationships, social roles, occupational titles, types of therapy, and a host of different clinical disorders or features of clinical disorders (see Winter, 1992, for a review), as well as a wide range of elements outside the interpersonal or clinical arenas. The effects of these adaptations, however, remain largely unexamined. But even within the original domain of interpersonal role relations, modifications in the element set have been shown to affect the system of constructs that are generated. Stringer (1979) was among the first to vary the element set systematically, studying the effects of these variations on measures of construct system structure. In particular, he examined the differential effects of using the names of specific individuals as elements in the repgrid, versus using more general role titles (e.g., someone you admire; a person in a position of authority). Stringer (1979) predicted that "the construing of roles [as opposed to figures] would be less complex, less differentiated, on the grounds that constructs regarding roles are more consistently validated than constructs about particular individuals" (p. 94). Results indicated that "constructs were not only used in a more differentiated way when construing individuals, but also when constructs were elicited on individuals" (Stringer, 1979, p. 96). Stringer concluded by observing that "different forms of the grid . . . do not elicit the same kinds of construing" (p. 99), and emphasized that "there were considerable alterations in the structure of their personal constructs when they moved from construing roles to construing individuals, or vice versa" (p. 98).

Beyond this early work, the effects of modifying the element sets in repertory grids has received little attention. The single exception to this may be the study of element valence. "Element valence" refers to how positive or negative the element is to the individual who is completing the repertory grid. Early work with "cognitive complexity" established that negatively valenced elements were associated with higher levels of complexity, or construct system differentiation (Turner & Tripodi, 1968), than were positive elements. Explanations focused on a "vigilence hypothesis" that emphasized the adaptive value associated with attending to, understanding, and differentiating potentially threatening elements of experience (Turner & Tripodi, 1968).

It was this reasoning that led Bodden and Klein (1973) to initiate a long-standing program of research concerning the effects of element valence. This research focuses on vocational psychology, and turned to examine the "affective stimulus value" (positivity or negativity) of the occupational set as a determinant of its level of differentiation. They asked 67 male students to complete a modified version of the repgrid, using "liked" and "disliked" occupations as elements. Results indicated that "more independent cognitive constructs were utilized when subjects were judging occupations that evoked negative affect than when the subjects were judging occupations that possessed positive stimulus value" (Bodden & Klein, 1973, p. 78). The authors concluded that "it may be adaptive for a student to examine closely (i.e., become 'vigilant' with) occupations which arouse negative feelings so as not to make a 'wrong' choice in selecting one of these negatively charged occupations" (Bodden & Klein, 1973, p. 78).

A number of subsequent studies have replicated this effect in larger, mixed-sex samples. For example, Moore, Neimeyer, and Marmarosh (1992) systematically varied the valence of the occupational elements in their study of 159 students. They asked participants to select a set of either 12 "liked" or "disliked" occupations from a list of 51 alternatives, and to rate them along a series of personal constructs. Results indicated that disliked occupations were associated with significantly higher levels of construct system differentiation than were "liked" occupations. Likewise, Parr and Neimeyer (1994) studied the effects of three variations in element valence (positive, negative, or mixed-valence) in a mixed-sex sample of 387 undergraduate students. Their results again indicated that negative elements yielded higher levels of differentiation than either positive or mixed-valence elements.

Taken collectively, the results of this work suggest that variations in the valence of the element sets used in repertory grids may exert a significant impact on aspects of construct system structure. This likelihood is consistent with the broader concerns expressed by Bell (1999) concerning the probable impact of the elements, rather than the constructs, in determining structural features of the personal construct system.

Rating Procedures

Repertory grid methods vary substantially in the rating procedures that they employ. Broadly speaking, variations in rating procedures include the use of rankings versus ratings, the size of the scales used, the size of the repgrids themselves, or a variety of other dimensions. In general, little research has been directed toward the effects of various rating procedures on aspects of personal construct structure derived from the grid. Notable exceptions include the effects of different grid sizes, sequences of administration, and data input into analysis programs (Feixas, Moliner, Montes, Mari, & Neimeyer, 1992; Hagans et al., 2000; MacKay, 1992).

One subtle procedural feature of repertory grid ratings that has recently begun to receive attention concerns the ways in which the ratings of elements along constructs are made. One key feature concerns whether or not the participant has access to his or her previous ratings as he or she progresses through the completion of the matrix of grid ratings. The second has to do with the direction of those ratings, rating down constructs on an element-by-element basis versus rating across elements on a construct-by-construct basis. Each of these has received some attention in the recent literature.

The earliest research in this area was the work by Costigan, Dowling, and Marsh (1991), who observed that some researchers apparently "favoured the method of rating elements in grids separately rather than across rows" (p. 2). Citing Kelly's (1955) theoretical support for the elicitation of constructs within the context of multiple elements, they noted the value of making ratings within full view of previous ratings, rather than focusing on one element at a time. Costigan and her colleagues hypothesized differences between two groups of participants who completed a grid using these two different methods. In their study, one group completed a "range" method, rating the whole range of elements across a given construct before moving down to the next construct (construct-by-construct ratings). This method permitted access to the range of previous ratings. By contrast, the "focus" method held a given element constant, instructing the participant to rate that one element down the full set of constructs before turning to the next element (element-by-element ratings). Elements were presented only one at a time, depriving participants of access to their previous evaluations as they completed their matrix of ratings. The researchers reasoned that element-by-element ratings would increase differentiation because participants would be rating each element in isolation, rather than comparing their ratings with their evaluation of other elements on the grid (see also Masgoret, Kernaghan, & Binkley, 1995). However, results indicated no significant differences; "range" and "focus" methods yielded similar levels of construct system differentiation.

A second study bearing on this issue was conducted by Epting, Prichard, Wiggins, Leonard, John, and Beagle (1992). In their exploration of the factor structure of repgrids, they varied the method of ratings and examined its effect on three measures of construct differentiation: the explanatory power of the first factor (EPFF), intensity, and functionally independent constructions (FIC; Landfield, 1971). Like Costigan et al. (1991), they predicted that differentiation would be lower in grid formats where elements were compared (the "range" method). In addition, they also instructed one group of participants to assign preference poles to their constructs in the grid, heightening the evaluative demand of the task.

Results supported predictions; differentiation was lower in the grid formats that involved construct-by-construct ratings than in those completed on an element-by-element basis, and evaluative construct codings were related to reduced differentiation, as well. Unfortunately, this evaluative coding was only performed by participants in the "range" condition, qualifying a more definitive interpretation of the effects. In addition, both the Costigan et al. (1991) and the Epting et al. (1992) studies introduced another confound insofar as neither distinguished *rating direction*, on the one hand, from the *visibility of the previous ratings*, on the other. Thus, effects that were observed could be due to either the direction of the ratings (across constructs or elements) or to the availability of prior ratings. A more definitive test would have to hold one of these factors constant while systematically varying the other.

FURTHER STUDIES IN METHODOLOGICAL VARIATIONS

In an effort to disentangle these and other factors, two original studies were conducted. Study 1 specifically addressed the Costigan and Epting confound, examining the effect of rating down constructs versus across elements. In all cases, participants had access to all previous ratings; only the direction of the ratings was varied. A second study was designed in an effort to replicate the effects of Study 1, and to situate its effects within the context of other procedural variations in repertory grid techniques discussed earlier. That is, Study 2 yielded original data addressing the interactive effects of element context (triadic versus dyadic), instructional set (difference versus opposite method), element valence (positive or mixed valence) and rating direction (down constructs versus across elements) on levels of cognitive differentiation. Our intent was to clarify and integrate previous findings on the impact of methodological factors in repgrid technique, and provide a basis for recommendations to future grid users.

Study 1

Study 1 was designed to clarify the effects of rating direction (down constructs versus across elements) on measures on construct system differentiation. Consistent with previous research, higher levels of differentiation were expected to be associated with element-by-element ratings (i.e., Costigan et al.'s "focus" method) rather than with construct-by-construct ratings (i.e., the "range" method). Unlike previous research, however, all participants had access to their previous ratings; the only modification was in the instructional set, stipulating that they either proceed to go down each column or across each row in stepwise fashion in completing their matrix of ratings (see "Procedure," later).

Subjects and Materials

Participants were 41 undergraduate general psychology students (mean age = 21.6; *SD* = 4.2; 59% female, 41% male) who received credit toward their semester grade for participation. Five of the grids contained unusable data, leaving a total of 36 usable grids for analysis. A standardized paper and pencil grid was used that allowed participants to rate each of 10 elements along a standardized set of 10 provided constructs (see Figure 5-1), using a 4-point rating scale. The GridCor program (Feixas & Cornejo, 1996) was used to obtain multiple measures of construct system differentiation, as well as a variety of other indices. The GridCor program computed values for the measures described below for each grid completed.

Intensity scores (Fransella & Bannister, 1977) indicate the total degree of interrelation among the elements and constructs within the grid. Scores are obtained by summing the absolute values of the Pearson correlations between all possible pairs of ratings, then multiplying them by 100. Higher scores indicate greater conceptual integration, and, therefore, lower levels of construct system differentiation.

Explanatory Power of the First Factor (EPFF) describes the percentage of variance accounted for by the first factor in the grid (O'Keefe & Sypher, 1981). This index assumes that the larger the first factor, the more unidimensional the underlying structure of the construct system. Greater scores reflect lower levels of differentiation.

Cognitive Complexity scores (Bieri, 1955) are computed as the number of perfect matches in ratings of elements on each pair of construct dimensions, divided by the maximum possible score that could be obtained from a grid of the same size. Lower scores (i.e., fewer matches) reflect greater complexity.

Extremity of Ratings represents the percentage of extreme ratings and is related to the degree of meaning of a construct or an element. Higher scores reflect greater meaning (Adams-Webber, 1979).

		Myself	Mother	Father	Best Friend	Least Favorite Teacher	Most Favorite Teacher	Ex Love interest	Authority Figure	Current Love interest	Ideal Self		
1	Dominant	4	3	4	4	0	2	1	2	1	3	Submissive	1
2	Shows feelings	2	4	3	3	4	2	4	0	1	1	Hides feelings	2
3	Depends on others	4	4	4	4	3	4	3	4	4	3	Others depend on him or her	3
4	Good relations with others	4	4	3	1	3	2	4	3	1	2	Poor relations with others	4
5	Attacking	4	4	3	1	3	2	4	3	1	2	Comforting	5
6	Intelligent	4	4	2	3	3	4	4	4	3	4	Unintelligent	6
7	Sincere	4	4	4	4	4	4	4	4	2	1	Insincere	7
8	Mentally Ill	4	3	3	1	3	4	4	4	4	3	Mentally healthy	8
9	Cold	4	4	2	1	3	3	4	4	4	2	Warm	9
10	Vulnerable	1	3	3	3	3	1	4	1	1	4	Not vulnerable	10

Figure 5-1. Row-by-row grid.

The Discriminate Power of the elements and constructs in the grid was originally described as a measure of hierarchical integration of the construct system (Feixas & Cornejo, 1996).

Procedure

Participants were provided with a blank grid and asked to substitute names of personally known figures in their lives for the role titles shown (see Figure 5-1). One half of the participants were instructed to complete the grid in an element-by-element manner, holding the element constant and working down the column of provided constructs, rating each element one at a time. This procedure would be analogous to the "focus" method used by Costigan et al. (1991). The other half of the participants were instructed to complete the grid in a construct-by-construct fashion, working across each row. Holding the construct constant, participants rated "across" all elements before moving on to apply the next construct. This condition was analogous to the "range" condition of Costigan et al. (1991) and would be consistent with the theoretical preference expressed in Kelly's (1955) original Role Construct Repertory Test. As in Figure 5-1, the direction of rating was highlighted by shading either alternate columns or rows as a reminder of the instructional set to participants.

In completing their grids, participants indicated if their use of the midpoint was due to the lack of relevance of either pole, or the equal relevance of each pole. This can be seen in the first two rows of the grid in Figure 5-1, where two different midpoints were used by this individual. Unfortunately, no current analysis packages are able to discriminate different meanings of midpoint ratings, so zero was used in both cases despite the ambiguity of this value (Yorke, 1992).

Following the completion of the first grid, participants performed a filled delay of completing the required forms for receiving their extra credit before receiving a second grid to complete. This delay was approximately 10 minutes in length, and the second grid administration was designed to test the reliability of the effects, as well as the impact of each rating procedure on the other.

On the second administration, participants were instructed to use the same elements and constructs that were used on the first administration. They were then randomly assigned to either follow the same instruction set as for the first grid, or to switch to the other rating method. The result of this counterbalancing was that 10 individuals completed two grids on an element-by-element basis; 9 completed a grid on an element-by-element basis followed by a construct-by-construct grid; 11 completed two grids on a construct-by-construct basis; and 10 completed a grid on a construct-by-construct basis followed by an element-by-element grid.

Results

For between-subject comparisons, grids completed at the first administration were used. Results of comparisons for the two methods are summarized in Table 5-3.

Of the between-subject comparisons, only one of the structural measures proved significantly different due to the direction of ratings. Significant differences were found such that requiring participants to rate down constructs on an element-by-element basis resulted in higher levels of construct system differentiation (as reflected in lower Bieri scores). These results are consistent with the predictions of Costigan et al. (1991) and the findings of Epting et al. (1992), and again document the significant impact of rating direction in determining levels of differentiation.

For within-subject measures, participants were assigned to one of four conditions, depending on the types of grid they completed and the order of their presentation. Scores were analyzed in a 4 (condition) by 2 (time) repeated measures analysis of variance. Differences due to condition were consistent with the between-subjects analysis discussed earlier; the Bieri measure of cognitive complexity and all three measures of cognitive integration showed significant pre–post change, regardless of the order of grid types given. As in previous research (see Feixas et al., 1992), levels of differentiation decreased across time, as reflected in the higher levels of integration, as well as reverse-scored measures of differentiation, suggesting a "tightening" effect upon repeated grid testing. The results of these tests are shown in Table 5-4.

Table 5-3. Between-Subject Differences in Structural Scores by Grid Format, Time 1, Only

| | M (SD) | | |
	Construct-by-Construct	Element-by-Element	
Measures of Cognitive Differentiation			
Explanatory power of first factor (EPFF)	56.17 (11.94)	52.64 (6.44)	1.37
Bieri's cognitive complexity, original grid	0.29 (.09)	0.23 (.06)	6.40**
Measures of Cognitive Integration			
Construct intensity	0.44 (.07)	0.43 (.05)	0.34
Element intensity	0.38 (.05)	0.37 (.05)	0.21
Element discriminate power	2.45 (.54)	2.66 (.60)	1.50
Construct discriminate power	2.79 (.61)	2.66 (.56)	0.49
Other Measures			
Extremity of ratings	33.49 (19.62)	23.11 (14.23)	3.55*

$*p < .1.$ $**p < .05.$

Another issue of interest was how the stability of the measures was affected by rating method. Test-retest reliabilities were obtained for each rating method, although the small number of participants qualified the interpretability of the findings. In general, the structural measures appeared to have fairly high reliability values, in keeping with the findings of Feixas et al. (1992). The mean test-retest reliability for the grids completed on an element-by-element basis (the "focus" method) was .88 for the Bieri (1955) cognitive complexity scores, for example, and the mean for those rated on a construct-by-construct basis (the "range" method) was .91. Individual test-retest reliabilities for each of the structural measures, together with their significance levels, can be found in Table 5-5.[1]

Discussion

Broadly speaking, the results of this study provide a conceptual replication of the effects noted by Epting et al. (1992), despite several differences in the way specific measures performed. For example, unlike the Epting et al. (1992) work, neither the EPFF nor the construct intensity measures showed significant differences as a result of variations in the direction of ratings. However, Bieri's (1955) original measure of cognitive complexity did register differences that support the earlier findings. As with Epting et al. (1992), performing grid ratings on an element-by-element basis resulted in significantly higher levels of construct system differentiation, relative to ratings made on a construct-by-construct basis (i.e., the "range" method).

The failure to provide a strict replication of the Epting et al. (1992) effects could be due to a number of differences between that study and the current one. First,

Table 5-4. Main Effects for Structural Scores Over Time

| | M (SD) | | |
	Pre	Post	F (1, 38)
Measures of Cognitive Differentiation			
Explanatory power of first factor (EPFF)	54.50 (9.71)	55.80 (10.20)	0.72
Bieri's cognitive complexity, original grid	0.26 (.08)	0.28 (.09)	17.00**
Measures of Cognitive Integration			
Construct intensity	0.43 (.06)	0.45 (.08)	1.66
Element intensity	0.38 (.05)	0.39 (.06)	1.25
Element discriminate power	2.56 (.57)	2.29 (.57)	20.66**
Construct discriminate power	2.72 (.58)	2.36 (.60)	21.41**
Other Measures			
Extremity of ratings	28.43 (17.78)	21.03 (17.02)	7.74*

*$p < .01$. **$p < .001$.

Table 5-5. Test-Retest Reliabilities for Structural Measures by Administration Condition

| | Grid Format | |
	Construct-by-Construct ($n = 9$)	Element-by-Element ($n = 10$)
Measures of Cognitive Differentiation		
Explanatory power of first factor (EPFF)	.68*	.57
Bieri's cognitive complexity, original grid	.88**	.91**
Measures of Cognitive Integration		
Construct Intensity	.62	.13
Element Intensity	.87**	.55
Element discriminate power	.82**	.74*
Construct discriminate power	.61	.95**
Other Measures		
Extremity of ratings	.76*	.97**

*$p < .1$. **$p < .05$.

Epting et al. (1992) used personally elicited constructs, whereas the current study relied on a standardized set of provided dimensions. Considerable work has shown that personally elicited constructs are associated with higher levels of differentiation than are provided constructs (see "Personal versus Provided Constructs" earlier), and this difference may account for the differential outcomes between the study by Epting et al. (1992) and the current one. In addition, the current study attempted to eliminate the earlier confound associated with the introduction of an explicitly evaluative set in the Epting et al. (1992) study, and this difference could be related to different outcome. And finally, the current study represents a relatively small-scale exploratory effort, and for that reason may not have had sufficient power to detect differences that would emerge from a larger scale study. Despite these differences, however, both studies converge to suggest that, at least on some measures, instructing respondents to complete grids on an element-by-element basis, rather than a construct-by-construct basis, results in a more complex or differentiated system of personal constructs. Importantly, these results also indicate that these differences are due simply to the direction in which the ratings are performed, rather than to the access to prior ratings. In other words, even when individuals have complete access to all of their prior grid ratings, levels of differentiation are higher when ratings are completed on an element-by-element basis than when they are completed on a construct-by-construct basis. This suggests that these two different rating directions engage somewhat different comparative processes, and that the nature of the comparisons determines the higher differentiation associated with the element-by-element ratings.

In addition, the current study also sheds further light on the stability of structural measures. Feixas et al. (1992) observed very high reliabilities for many structural measures on repeated administrations over varying time intervals. Our results confirmed the overall stability of the structural measures, but also suggested the possible impact of rating direction on these reliabilities. In fact, Bieri's (1955) measure of cognitive complexity may be the only structural score studied that remained unaffected by changes in the direction of ratings. Other measures of cognitive differentiation (e.g., the EPFF), however, may have higher reliability if grids are completed according to Kelly's (1955) preference for rating across constructs (i.e., the "range" method). Likewise, the reliability of intensity, discriminate power, and overall meaningfulness (i.e., rating extremity) may be responsive to changes in rating direction, highlighting the broader impact of this subtle variation on measures of construct system structure. These and other findings should be interpreted cautiously, however, given the relatively small n in the reliability analyses.

Study 2

A second study was conducted to examine further the effects of rating direction, and to situate these effects within the context of other key variations outlined in this chapter. The purpose of this study was to provide the first large-scale attempt to investigate the interactive effects of repertory grid variations. The features included in this study addressed four of the variations reviewed in this chapter. These include *element context* (triadic versus dyadic), *instructional set* (opposite versus difference method), *element valence* (positive versus mixed valence), and *rating direction* (element-by-element versus construct-by-construct). Differences between personally elicited and experimentally provided constructs were not included in this study for two reasons. First, the effects of elicited versus provided constructs on measures of differentiation are already well understood, and have been the continuing focus of work for more than 40 years. And second, the distinction between elicited and provided constructs may be largely artificial, given that the differences between them can be eliminated by directly manipulating the meaningfulness of the dimensions (see "Personal versus Provided Constructs" earlier).

Participants and Procedure

A total of 262 volunteers (87 men, 175 women; mean age = 20.1; *SD* = 4.31) were recruited from university classes to take part in a "study of interpersonal perceptions." Each participant was randomly assigned to 1 of 16 conditions defined by fully crossing the following four factors, each containing two levels: *Element context* (triadic versus dyadic), *instructional set* (difference versus opposite), *element valence* (positive versus mixed valence), and *rating direction* (down constructs versus across elements). This resulted in a 2 x 2 x 2 x 2 completely between-subjects design (see Table 5-6).

Each participant completed one and only one type of repgrid. All repgrids used 10 personally elicited constructs and 10 personally known people as elements. Half of the repgrids used the triadic method for construct elicitation and half used the dyadic method. In each case, half of these used the instructional set specifying that they look for differences, whereas the other half were instructed to specify an opposite, according to the instructions in Table 5-2. In half of these cases, the elements were all positive, whereas they were mixed-valence (i.e., half positive and half negative) in the other half. The valence of the elements was determined by asking individuals to "identify a set of ten individuals that you know personally that you like," versus "a set of ten individuals that you know personally, five of whom you like, and five of whom you dislike." And finally, the fourth factor reflected the direction of ratings; half of each group was instructed to perform the grid ratings by "rating down each column in the grid" before moving on to the next person (i.e., element-by-element), whereas the other half were instructed to perform the grid ratings by "rating across each row in the grid, rating all elements along one construct before moving on to the next construct" (i.e., construct-by-construct). Based on previous literature concerning grid variations, we expected higher levels of differentiation to be associated with the triadic method, with the difference instructional set, with the mixed-valence elements, and with the element-by-element ratings. Any interactions among these factors

Table 5-6. The Sixteen Conditions in Study 2

Element Context	Elicitation Method	Element Valence	Rating Direction	Cell Size
Triadic	Difference	Positive	Element-by-element	17
Triadic	Difference	Positive	Construct-by-construct	18
Triadic	Difference	Mixed	Element-by-element	16
Triadic	Difference	Mixed	Construct-by-construct	22
Triadic	Opposite	Positive	Element-by-element	13
Triadic	Opposite	Positive	Construct-by-construct	11
Triadic	Opposite	Mixed	Element-by-element	13
Triadic	Opposite	Mixed	Construct-by-construct	11
Dyadic	Difference	Positive	Element-by-element	16
Dyadic	Difference	Positive	Construct-by-construct	20
Dyadic	Difference	Mixed	Element-by-element	21
Dyadic	Difference	Mixed	Construct-by-construct	14
Dyadic	Opposite	Positive	Element-by-element	14
Dyadic	Opposite	Positive	Construct-by-construct	16
Dyadic	Opposite	Mixed	Element-by-element	16
Dyadic	Opposite	Mixed	Construct-by-construct	16

were especially important to our interests, although no particular predictions were made regarding the nature of these interactions.

Results

All repgrids were scored for their levels of differentiation, using Landfield's (1971) FIC score. The total differentiation score was used as the measure of differentiation, and consists of the construct differentiation scores and the element differentiation score. The construct differentiation score reflects the total number of functionally independent constructs and, therefore, could range from a low of 1 to a high of 10. The element differentiation score reflects how differently each of the elements on the grid is rated, and also could range from 1 to 10. The total score could therefore range between 2 and 20, with higher scores indicating greater differentiation.

A $2 \times 2 \times 2 \times 2$ between-subjects analysis of variance (ANOVA) was conducted on the measure of total differentiation. Results revealed only one significant main effect, and that was for instructional variations (difference versus opposite), $F(1,246) = 15.07, p < .0001$. As predicted, the direction of this difference indicated that Kelly's (1955) original difference method yielded significantly higher levels of construct system differentiation ($M = 9.14$; $SD = 4.31$) than did the opposite method ($M = 7.25$; $SD = 3.91$) introduced by Epting et al. (1971). No other significant main effects were found.

This main effect for instructional variations, however, was qualified by its significant interaction with element valence, $F(1, 246) = 16.22, p < .0001$. The direction of this interaction was intriguing. When the elements were mixed valence, the levels of differentiation associated with the difference ($M = 7.77$) and opposite ($M = 8.21$) methods were not significantly different from one another. However, when the elements were uniformly positive, higher levels of differentiation were associated with the difference method ($M = 10.42$) than with the opposite method ($M = 6.47$). This interaction is depicted in Figure 5-2. No other two-way interactions reached significance.

Regarding three-way interactions, there was one significant effect. Element context (triadic versus dyadic) interacted with instructional set (difference versus opposite) and rating direction (element-by-element versus construct-by-construct), $F (1, 246) = 3.71, p < .055$. The nature of this effect is depicted in Figure 5-3, and the means and standard deviations for all conditions in the study are depicted in Table 5-7.

Discussion

Results of this study provide the first evidence concerning the interactive effects of different repertory grid variations on measures of construct system differentiation. In addition, they provide a mixture of support for various previous findings, and qualifications regarding the generalizability of those effects.

The main effect found in this study for instructional set (difference versus opposite method) supports a growing body of research in this area (Caputi & Reddy, 1999; Hagans et al., 2000). The developing consensus among this work indicates that Kelly's (1955) original difference method yields consistently higher levels of personal construct system differentiation than does the alternative "opposite" procedure (Epting et al., 1971). Moreover, available evidence suggests that this may be due to one of two factors, or both. One concerns the

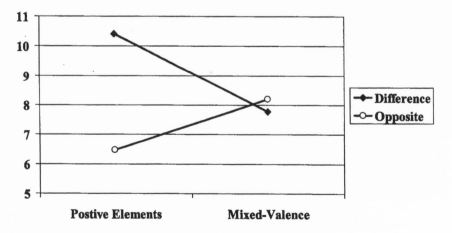

Figure 5-2. Mean differentiation scores as a function of elicitation method and element valence.

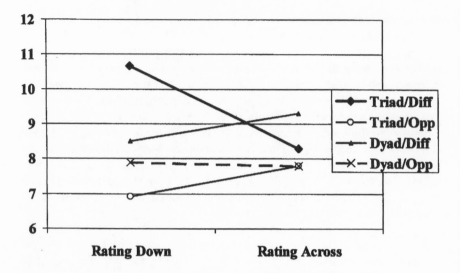

Figure 5-3. Mean differentiation scores as a function of elicitation method, sort technique, and rating direction. *Note:* Triad/Diff = triadic sorts/difference method; Triad/Opp = triadic sorts/opposite method; Dyad/Diff = dyadic sorts/difference method; Dyad/Opp = dyadic sorts/opposite method.

requirement in the difference method that both poles of the construct emerge from among the elements in the grid, thereby assuring that both poles will be used in making construct ratings. By contrast, the opposite method places no such demand, meaning that the "opposite" pole of the construct need not apply to any of the elements in the grid. A related explanation follows from the observation that the opposite method yields more extreme and negative contrast poles, reducing the likelihood that they would be applied as frequently to the field of elements (Hagans et al., 2000).

The results of Study 2, however, place a special qualification on this effect that follows from the interaction of instructional set with element valence. This interaction indicates that the impact of instructional variations (difference versus opposite methods) depends on the valence of the elements used in the grid. This interaction can be understood in relation to the unique situation posed by these two different grid variations. As reflected in Figure 5-2, the effect of the difference versus the opposite method is especially pronounced when the element set is uniformly positive. When the element set is uniformly positive, the difference method is associated with substantial increases in levels of construct system differentiation, whereas the opposite method is associated with substantial decreases in the levels of construct system differentiation. An explanation of this effect follows from the earlier work of Hagans et al. (2000). These researchers found that the use of opposite method tended to generate significantly more extreme and negative contrast poles by calling for the "opposites" of emergent poles based on perceived similarity. They reasoned that the opposite method may yield lower levels of differentiation based on the reluctance of the user to apply these extreme negative poles of their constructs to the people in their grid. The result would be the lopsided use of only the more "positive" construct pole, which would substantially reduce levels of differentiation. It seems especially likely that people would be reluctant to apply these extreme, negative poles to the uniformly well-liked people that form the element set in the positive element condition. In other words, as the element set becomes more positive, the contrast poles generated by the "opposite" method become less and less applicable. The result of this inapplicability is the lopsided use of only one construct pole, which in turn reduces the level of differentiation of the personal construct system.

In contrast to the opposite method, the difference method appears to *increase* levels of differentiation when the element set is uniformly positive. This may reflect the demand to forge distinctions among positive elements, a task that requires developing more subtle discriminations. Because the difference method demands, by design, that both poles of the constructs emerge from the element set in the grid, these elements would then be distributed across both poles of the constructs, increasing the levels of differentiation in the construct system. The critical finding at this point, however, concerns the interactive effects of repgrid modifications. It is now clear that alterations in one feature of the repgrid may have a differential impact on the grid output, depending on the other features of the grid. In other words, the effect of a given repgrid adaptation is not a constant, and may, instead, vary as a function of other adaptations in the grid.

This caution is underscored by the three-way interaction reported in this study. The effect of changes in instructional set (difference versus opposite) and rating direction (element-by-element versus construct-by-construct) varied according to the element context (dyadic versus triadic) used in the grid. As reflected in Figure 5-3, several features of this interaction are noteworthy. First, the opposite method is generally associated with lower levels of differentiation than the difference method (as noted in the main effect reported above). Second, the impact of rat-

Table 5-7. Means (and Standard Deviations) for Differentiation Scores by Conditions ($N = 262$)

	Dyadic				Triadic			
	Opposite		Difference		Opposite		Difference	
	Positive	Mixed	Positive	Mixed	Positive	Mixed	Positive	Mixed
Element-by-Element	6.86	8.75	9.00	8.19	4.85	8.15	11.41	9.88
	(4.67)	(4.02)	(4.44)	(4.46)	(2.64)	(4.36)	(3.37)	(4.62)
Construct-by-Construct	6.88	8.00	10.30	8.00	6.50	8.00	10.32	6.55
	(4.51)	(4.00)	(1.21)	(3.72)	(3.24)	(2.53)	(4.74)	(3.23)

ing direction (element-by-element versus construct-by-construct) is generally less pronounced when the opposite method is used than when the difference method is used. And third, the impact of the rating direction is especially significant with a triadic element procedure with instructions to generate constructs based on perceived differences rather than opposites. Put differently, the highest levels of differentiation are associated with the use of a "triadic difference" method in which the person performs grid ratings on an element-by-element basis. Interestingly, this is the grid form used most frequently by Landfield (1971) and Epting et al. (1992). It is also noteworthy that Study 1 investigated the effects of rating direction in precisely this context (triadic elements, difference instructions), and found precisely the same effects.

On the one hand, the results of Study 2 replicate the findings of Study 1, suggesting the significant impact of rating direction on levels of differentiation. On the other hand, they qualify those findings by suggesting that this effect may be uniquely tied to the use of a triadic difference grid. That being said, the triadic difference grid is the original form of the repgrid (Kelly, 1955), and remains the most common form of the grid in use today. Our results, therefore, raise particular concerns regarding the impact of repertory grid variations in relation to the most prominent versions of the technique. Taken collectively, they suggest that caution should be used when making repertory grid modifications insofar as these modifications can individually, or interactively, influence structural features of the personal construct system. The replication of these effects, and demonstrations of their generalizability to a range of different clinical and non-clinical contexts, are important directions for future research in this area. For now, however, it seems clear that even subtle variations in repertory grid procedures can have a significant impact on aspects of the personal construct system, highlighting the importance of critical reflection in the application and modification of this method.

REPERTORY GRID RECOMMENDATIONS

The use of repertory grids has a long history, but the effects of many modifications have only recently begun to receive empirical attention. Thus, although the effects of personally elicited versus experimentally provided constructs and element valence have been studied systematically, other repgrid modifications remain largely unexplored. Significantly, some of these modifications, such as the use of "difference" versus "opposite" instructions for construct elicitation or varying element context (triadic versus dyadic), are common in the literature, but little empirical work has been directed toward their differential impact. Still other variations, such as rating direction (element-by-element versus construct-by-construct), have largely escaped notice of researchers, and have probably varied idiosyncratically, depending on the approach taken by individual research participants, with an unknown effect on the results of many studies.

Fortunately, the current literature on the effects of repertory grid modifications does permit some provisional observations that may guide future applications, adaptations, and empirical inquiry concerning repertory grid technique. These observations converge to underscore the importance of a critical and reflexive use of repertory grid methodology. It is now clear that even minor variations in repertory grid technique can carry significant implications for the process and outcome of the constructive process that it generates. Perhaps most central to this research is the growing recognition that repertory grid technique does more than enable researchers to gain access to an individual's personal construct system. More fundamentally, it engages that individual in an active process of construction, and the nature of this constructive process may be altered by even minor variations in the application of the technique. The following observations reflect a commitment to appreciating this fundamental feature of repertory grid methodology, and carefully considering the implications of its adaptations.

Assess, Don't Assume, Personal Meaning

Personal construct psychology places a premium on the unique network of meanings that each individual brings to bear in understanding his or her world. The early introduction of experimentally provided constructs into repertory grid methodology naturally invited comparisons of these dimensions with their personally elicited counterparts. It quickly became apparent that these two differ in important respects. In general, compared with provided constructs, personally elicited dimensions were found to be more meaningful (Cromwell & Caldwell, 1962; Isaacson & Landfield, 1965), more useful (Adams-Webber, 1998), and better differentiated (Kuusinen & Nystedt, 1975; Metcalfe, 1974) than provided dimensions (see Adams-Webber, 1979, for a review). These findings soon fueled a growing conviction regarding what came to be viewed as two distinctly different kinds of constructs, with the personally elicited variety considered superior to its more expedient alternative.   ·

Recent work has questioned the fundamental distinction between these two types of constructs, however, emphasizing instead the continuity of meaning that underlies them both. Even within personally elicited constructs, it is clear that individual constructs vary markedly in their meaningfulness, centrality, or importance to the individual (see Kelly's Organization Corollary; Kelly, 1955), and considerable work has addressed this variability (see Crockett, 1982).

Neimeyer and colleagues (1992) have noted that this variability in meaning is a common element that binds, rather than distinguishes, personal and provided construct dimensions. "Rather than being viewed dichotomously as either experimentally contrived or phenomenologically relevant," Neimeyer et al. (1992, pp. 126–127) argued, it seems likely that all constructs "operate along a continuum of meaning" (p. 127). In support for this position, evidence has shown that experimentally provided constructs can be made more personally meaningful through personal review and reflection and that, as their personal meaning increases, so does the level of differentiation with which they are used (Moore & Neimeyer, 1997; Neimeyer et al., 1992). Moreover, the same applies to personally elicited constructs; as methods of personal reflection and elaboration enhance their meaning to the users, they also show increases in differentiation. When levels of meaning converge, personal and provided constructs are used with identical levels of differentiation (Neimeyer et al., 1992).

Personal meaningfulness may provide a critical bridge between two previously distinct research traditions. Adherents to Kelly's (1955) original preference for eliciting personal constructs have maintained strong allegiance to his idiographic tradition, whereas others have maintained an equal adherence to the use of provided constructs. The former traditionally have justified their allegiance to elicitation on the basis of preserving the personal meaning of an individual's constructions, whereas the latter have placed a premium on standardization and control of error variance. Recent research questions both claims and qualifies the utility of both positions. On the one hand, the value of adhering to standardized constructs may be compromised by what now appears to be their widely variable personal meaning. On the other hand, this same finding also compromises the claims of traditionalists insofar as personal meaning and relevance may no longer be viewed as the exclusive domain of personally elicited constructs. For this reason, it may prove equally unwise to abandon prematurely the advantages of provided constructs or to nurture an uncritical adherence to the use of elicited constructs. Instead, future users of repgrid technique might benefit by the following recommendations:

1. Directly measure the perceived meaningfulness of all elicited and provided constructs, as meaningfulness is now clearly linked to the nature and structure of the construct system that emerges.
2. When provided constructs are used in lieu of personally elicited ones, consider using some form of "meaning-enhancement" procedure (see Moore & Neimeyer, 1997) as a way of increasing their personal relevance to the user.
3. Report the relationship between measures of meaningfulness and other aspects of personal construct content or structure. This will contribute to the growing understanding of the relationship between personal meaning and other variables central to personal construct psychology.

Attend to Context

The history of repertory grid research has documented the primacy that has been placed on constructs over elements. Although early work stressed the importance of the element set in generating constructs (Kelly, 1955), until recently this has translated into little empirical attention to the issue (see Bell et al., 1999; Mitsos, 1958; and Stringer, 1979, for exceptions). It is now clear, however, that the choice of elements is a critical determinant of the nature and organizational features of the personal construct system that is generated (Bell et al., 1999).

The heterogeneity of the elements is vital in the generation of representative, meaningful, and well-differentiated construct systems (Mitsos, 1958). One expression of this heterogeneity concerns the valence of the elements. Uniformly favorable elements generate consistently less well-differentiated construct systems than do mixed or negatively valenced elements, for example, an effect that has been well documented across time and different research literatures (Neimeyer & Leso, 1992; Turner & Tripodi, 1968). Although these valence effects are perhaps the single best-studied feature of element variations, it is clear that other, even subtle, modifications in the element sets can influence construct system content and structure (Stringer, 1979), highlighting the need for careful attention to the selection of elements in the construction of repertory grids.

Beyond general heterogeneity in the development of element sets, the selection of a particular procedure for presenting these elements to individuals may merit more careful attention, as well. Dyadic and triadic sorting procedures, for example, may represent fundamentally different processes for generating personal constructs, processes that carry implications for differences in the nature and structure of the construct systems they generate (Caputi & Reddy, 1999; Hagans et al., 2000). In short, both the particular elements that are used, and the way(s) in which they are presented, may be important determinants of the personal construct systems that evolve from them.

The current state of knowledge regarding element effects in repertory grid studies gives rise to at least four general recommendations:

1. Report a complete listing of all elements used. If role titles are used (e.g., a close same-sexed friend; someone you admire, etc.), specify whether or not participants are required to nominate a particular individual to fill that role.
2. Attend to heterogeneity in the development of element sets, including heterogeneity in the valence of the elements. Deviations from this should be based on thoughtful consideration and adaptation to specific contexts where homogeneity is judged to be advantageous or essential.
3. Consider assessing key features of the element set, including its representativeness, personal significance, and/or valence from the perspective of the individual completing the grid.
4. Focus future research on the effects of element variations on the content and structure of personal construct systems.

Consider Subtlety

Several research programs converge to suggest the impact of sometimes-subtle changes in repertory grid procedures. Aside from changes in the type of constructs and the elements that are used, it is clear that even minor variations in elicitation instructions (e.g., difference versus opposite methods) or other repertory grid procedures can carry significant implications. As illustrations of this impact, variations in the instructional set for generating constructs and for rating the elements along those constructs have been shown to have substantial effects on construct system structure.

In eliciting constructs, for instance, two different forms of contrast yield consistently different results. Identifying "differences" among elements, as in Kelly's original procedure, is distinct from specifying a contrast pole by nominating its "opposite" (Epting et al., 1971). Although the opposite technique seems to elicit "cleaner," more genuinely dichotomous (i.e., "unbent") poles, it also generates more extreme and negative contrasts, resulting in significantly less-differentiated personal construct systems (Hagans et al., 2000). This is particularly true as the element set becomes more uniformly positive (as in Study 2), highlighting the interactive effects of various repertory grid modifications in relation to one another.

Just as subtle variations in the elicitation procedure can carry a profound impact, so, too, can changes in the rating procedures. Several independent studies now converge on the finding that rating "element-by-element," rather than "construct-by-construct," increases the level of differentiation within the construct system (Epting et al., 1992; Studies 1 and 2, this chapter). Whether using personally elicited or experimentally provided constructs, a simple shift in the direction of ratings has a substantial impact on aspects of construct system structure, again highlighting the active processes of construction that are engaged by repertory grid procedures. These findings give rise to a number of considerations regarding the future applications of repertory grid technique.

1. "Difference" methods of construct elicitation result in higher levels of construct system differentiation, whereas "opposite" methods result in "clearer," though more negative, contrast poles. These methods are not interchangeable, and should be clearly specified in published reports utilizing repertory grid methodology.

2. Changes in the direction in which grid ratings are made carry important implications for outcomes; "Element-by-element" ratings increase differentiation, whereas "construct-by-construct" ratings reduce it. Research utilizing repertory grid methods should control this feature in the administration of the grids, and report the direction of ratings in published work following from these methods.

3. The active processes of construction that are engaged by repertory grid techniques extend across all aspects of its procedures. From the nomination of specific elements, through the generation and application of the constructs, modifications in process affect outcomes. Simply put, when it comes to repertory grid procedures, processes and outcomes are thoroughly interdependent.

CONCLUSION

Although this chapter has been limited to only a few of the most important variations in repertory grid technique, it nonetheless provides a window onto the effects of these modifications in relation to a variable of long-standing interest to the field: construct system differentiation. The effects of these specific modifications, as well as a host of other adaptations, may well extend more broadly to other aspects of the construct system. Given our current state of knowledge regarding the effects of repertory grid modifications, the conclusions of this chapter should be regarded as provisional and read at a heuristic level. Future work may confirm or qualify their applicability to a wide range of other adaptations and measures as ongoing work continues to clarify the madness in our method.

NOTE

1. In addition to the structural scores discussed here, Study 1 also investigated the responsiveness of the self-ideal discrepancy measure derived by the Feixas and Cornejo (1996) program to variations in rating procedure.. Because of the popularity of this measure in personal construct research on self-esteem (Winter, 1992), it is worth mentioning that the mean value of this index did not vary as a function of rating construct-by-construct ($M = .27$, $SD = .41$) or element-by-element ($M = .40$, $SD = .43$), $F (1, 38) = .34$; n.s. Similarly, self-ideal discrepancy did not change systematically across time; $F (1, 38) = .98$. However, the test-retest reliability of the index was improved in the element-by-element condition (.65) relative to the construct-by-construct condition (.29), where it performed poorly. Such a finding suggests the need for greater attention to the reliability of other grid measures, especially those based on limited data (such as specific element comparisons), under different procedural conditions.

REFERENCES

Adams-Webber, J. (1970a). An analysis of the discriminant validity of several repertory grid indices. *British Journal of Psychology, 61*, 83–90.

Adams-Webber, J. (1970b). Elicited versus provided constructs in repertory grid technique: A review. *British Journal of Medical Psychology, 43*, 349–354.

Adams-Webber, J. R. (1979). Construing persons in social contexts. In P. Stringer & D. Bannister (Eds.), *Constructs of sociality and individuality* (pp. 195–200). London: Academic Press.

Adams-Webber, J. R. (1989). Some reflections on the "meaning" of repertory grid responses. *International Journal of Personal Construct Psychology, 2*, 77–92.

Adams-Webber, J. R. (1990). Some fundamental asymmetries in the structure of personal constructs. In G. J. Neimeyer & R. A. Neimeyer (Eds.), *Advances in personal construct psychology* (Vol. 1, pp. 49–85). Greenwich, CT: JAI Press.

Adams-Webber, J. R. (1998). Differentiation and sociality in terms of elicited and provided constructs. *Psychological Science, 9*, 499–501.

Bannister, D. (1985). Foreword. In N. Beail (Ed.), *Repertory grid technique and personal constructs: Applications in clinical and educational settings* (pp. xi–xiii). Cambridge, MA: Brookline Books.

Bannister, D., & Mair, J. M. M. (1968). *The evaluation of personal constructs*. London: Academic Press.

Bell, R., Vince, J., & Costigan, J. (1999) *Which is more important in repertory grid data: Constructs or elements?* Paper presented at the Thirteenth International Congress on Personal Construct Psychology, Berlin, July 1999.

Benjafield, J., Pomeroy, E., & Jordan, D. (1976). Encounter groups: A return to the fundamental. *Psychotherapy: Theory, Research and Practice, 13*, 387–389.

Bieri, J. (1955). Cognitive complexity-simplicity and predictive behavior. *Journal of Abnormal and Social Psychology, 51*, 263–286.

Bodden, J. L., & Klein, A. J. (1973). Cognitive differentiation and affective stimulus value in vocational judgements. *Journal of Vocational Behavior, 3*, 75–79.

Bringmann, M. W. (1992). Computer-based methods for the analysis and interpretation of personal construct systems. In G. J. Neimeyer & R. A. Neimeyer (Eds.), *Advances in personal construct psychology* (Vol. 2, pp. 57–90). Greenwich, CT: JAI Press.

Caine, T. M., & Smail, D. J. (1967). Personal relevance and the choice of constructs for the repertory grid technique. *British Journal of Psychiatry, 113*, 517–520.

Caputi, P., & Reddy, P. (1999). A comparison of triadic and dyadic methods of personal construct elicitation. *Journal of Constructivist Psychology, 12*, 253–264.

Costigan, J., Dowling, P., & Marsh, M. (1991). *Rating elements: An empirical and theoretical comparison of focusing down columns versus ranging across rows.* Paper presented at Ninth International Personal Construct Psychology Congress, Albany, NY.

Crockett, W. H. (1982). The organization of construct systems: The organization corollary. In J. Mancuso & J. Adams-Webber (Eds.), *The construing person* (pp. 62–95). New York: Praeger.

Cromwell, R. L., & Caldwell, D. F. (1962). A comparison of ratings based on personal constructs of self and others. *Journal of Clinical Psychology, 18*, 42–46.

Epting, F. R., Prichard, S., Wiggins, S. C., Leonard, J. A., John, W., & Beagle, J. (1992). Assessment of the first factor and related measures of construct differentiation. *International Journal of Personal Construct Psychology, 5*, 77–94.

Epting, F. R., Probert, J. S., & Pittman, S. D. (1993). Alternative strategies for construct elicitation: Experimenting with experience. *International Journal of Personal Construct Psychology, 6*, 79–98.

Epting, F. R., Suchman, D. I., & Nickerson, K. J. (1971). An evaluation of elicitation procedures for personal constructs. *British Journal of Psychology, 62*, 513–517.

Feixas, G., & Cornejo, J. M. (1996). *Manual de la técnica de rejilla mediante el programa.* RECORD version 2.0. Barcelona, Spain: Paido's.

Feixas, G., Moliner, J. L., Montes, J. N., Mari, M. T., & Neimeyer, R. A. (1992). The stability of structural measures derived from repertory grids. *International Journal of Personal Construct Psychology, 5*, 25–40.

Fransella, F., & Bannister, D. (1977). *A manual for repertory grid technique.* New York: Academic Press.

Hagans, C. L., Neimeyer, G. J., & Goodholm, R., Jr. (2000). The effect of elicitation methods on personal constuct differentiation and valence. *Journal of Constructivist Psychology, 13*, 155–173.

Hinkle, D. N. (1965). *The change of personal constructs from the viewpoint of a theory of construct implications.* Unpublished doctoral dissertation, Ohio State University, Columbus, OH.

Isaacson, G. I., & Landfield, A.W. (1965). Meaningfulness of personal and common constructs. *Journal of Individual Psychology, 21*, 160–166.

Keen, T. R., & Bell, R. C. (1980). One thing leads to another: A new approach to elicitation in the repertory grid technique. *International Journal of Man-Machine Studies, 13*, 25–38.

Kelly, G. A. (1955). *The psychology of personal constructs.* New York: Norton.

Kuusinen, J. & Nystedt, L. (1975). Individual versus provided constructs, cognitive complexity and extremity of ratings in person perception. *Scandinavian Journal of Psychology, 16,* 137–148.

Landfield, A. W. (1971). *Personal construct systems in psychotherapy.* Chicago: Rand McNally.

Landfield, A. W., Stefan, R., & Dempsey, D. (1990). Single and multiple self implications for change grids: Studies of consistency. *International Journal of Personal Construct Psychology, 3,* 423–436.

Leitner, L. M. (1985). Interview methodologies for construct elicitation: Searching for the core. In F. R. Epting & A. W. Landfield (Eds.), *Anticipating personal construct psychology* (pp. 293–305). Lincoln: University of Nebraska Press.

Lemon, N., & Warren, N. (1974). Salience, centrality, and self-relevance of traits in construing others. *British Journal of Social and Clinical Psychology, 13,* 119–124.

MacKay, N. (1992). Identification, reflection, and correlation: problems in the bases of repertory grid measures. *International Journal of Personal Construct Psychology, 5,* 57–76.

Masgoret, A.-M., Kernaghan, S., & Binkley, D. (1995). *Differential effects of row versus column formats in repertory grids.* Paper presented at the Eleventh International Congress on Personal Construct Psychology, Barcelona, July 1995.

Mendoza, S. (1985). The exchange grid. In N. Beail (Ed.), *Repertory grid technique and personal constructs: Applications in clinical and educational settings* (pp. 173–189). Cambridge, MA: Brookline Books.

Metcalfe, R. J. (1974). Own versus provided constructs in a reptest measure of cognitive complexity. *Psychological Reports, 35,* 1305–1306.

Mitsos, S. B. (1958). Representative elements in role construct technique. *Journal of Consulting Psychology, 22,* 311–313.

Moore, M., & Neimeyer, G. J. (1997). Personal meaning and vocational differentiation: Reversing the decrement effect. *Journal of Career Development, 24,* 83–94.

Moore, M. A., Neimeyer, G. J., & Marmarosh, C. (1992). The effects of informational valence and occupational favorability on vocational differentiation. A test of the disconfirmation hypothesis. *Journal of Counseling Psychology, 39,* 335–341.

Neimeyer, G. J. (1992). Personal constructs and vocational structure: A critique of poor reason. In R. A. Neimeyer & G. J. Neimeyer (Eds.), *Advances in personal construct psychology* (Vol. 2, pp. 91–120). Greenwich, CT: JAI Press.

Neimeyer, G. J. & Leso, J. F. (1992). Effects of occupational information on personal versus provided constructs: A second look. *Journal of Counseling Psychology, 39(3),* 331–334.

Neimeyer, G. J., Leso, J. F., Marmarosh, C., Prichard, S., & Moore, M. (1992). The role of construct type in vocational differentiation: Use of elicited versus provided dimensions. *Journal of Counseling Psychology, 39,* 121–128.

Neimeyer, R. A. (1985). *The development of personal construct psychology.* Lincoln: University of Nebraska Press.

Neimeyer, R. A., Baker, K. D., & Neimeyer, G. J. (1990). The current status of personal construct theory: Some scientometric data. In G. J. Neimeyer & R. A. Neimeyer (Eds.), *Advances in personal construct psychology* (Vol. 1, pp. 3–22). Greenwich, CT: JAI Press.

Neimeyer, R. A., Neimeyer, G. J., & Landfield, A. W. (1983). Conceptual differentiation, integration and empathic prediction. *Journal of Personality, 51*, 185–191.

O'Keefe, D. J., & Sypher, H. E. (1981). Cognitive complexity measures and the relationship of cognitive complexity to communication: A critical review. *Human Communication Research, 8*, 72–92.

Parr, J., & Neimeyer, G. J. (1994). The effects of gender, construct type, occupational information, and career relevance on vocational differentiation. *Journal of Counseling Psychology, 41*, 127–133.

Probert, J. S. & Epting, R. F. (1990). Enhancing repertory grid technique to improve accessibility of familiar constructs. *Constructs, 8*, 10–12.

Procter, H. (1985). Repertory grids in family therapy and research. In N. Beail (Ed.), *Repertory grid technique and personal constructs: Applications in clinical and educational settings* (pp. 218–239). Cambridge, MA: Brookline Books.

Ryle, A., & Lunghi, M. W. (1970). The dyad grid: A modification of repertory grid technique. *British Journal of Psychiatry, 117*, 323–327.

Salmon, P. (1976). Grid measure with child subjects. In P. Slater (Ed.), *Explorations of intrapersonal space* (pp. 15–46). New York: Wiley.

Sewell, K. W., Adams-Webber, J., Mitterer, J., & Cromwell, R. L. (1992). Computerized repertory grids: Review of the literature. *International Journal of Personal Construct Psychology, 5*, 1–24.

Soldz, S., & Soldz, E. (1989). A difficulty with the functionally independent construction measure of cognitive differentiation. *International Journal of Personal Construct Psychology, 2*, 315–322.

Stringer, P. (1979). Individuals, roles, and persons. In P. Stringer & D. Bannister (Eds.), *Constructs of sociality and individuality* (pp. 91–112). New York: Academic Press.

Turner, R., & Tripodi, T. (1968). Cognitive complexity as a function of type of stimulus objects judged and affective stimulus value. *Journal of Consulting and Clinical Psychology, 32*, 182–185.

Walker, B. (1997). Shaking the kaleidoscope: Dispersion of dependency and its relationships. In G. Neimeyer & R. Neimeyer (Eds.), *Advances in personal construct psychology* (Vol. 4, pp. 63–97). Greenwich, CT: JAI Press.

Winter, D. A. (1992). *Personal construct psychology in clinical practice: Theory, research and applications*. London: Routledge.

Yorke, M. (1989a). In the hall of mirrors, or reflections on "reflections." *International Journal of Personal Construct Psychology, 2*, 93–101.

Yorke, M. (1989b). The intolerable wrestle: Words, numbers, and meanings. *International Journal of Personal Construct Psychology, 2*, 65–76.

Yorke, M. (1992). *Multiple interpretations of midpoint repertory grid ratings.* Unpublished manuscript, Manchester, England.

part III

Deconstructing Disorder

Chapter 6

Deconstructing and Reconstructing Substance Use and "Addiction": Constructivist Perspectives

Mark Burrell

"Drug abuse" and "addiction" are frequently cited as major "public health" problems of national and global proportions (e.g., Stares, 1996), and vast resources are devoted to drug-related research, treatment, prevention, and social control. Conventional efforts to understand and address drug-related problems have heretofore been primarily guided by nonconstructivist disorder frameworks. Simply stated, disorder perspectives assume that certain powerful "addictive drugs" cause objectively identifiable and real "substance abuse disorders" that overwhelm or mitigate personal control (Peele, 1989; Schaler, 1998).

Treatments and social policies developed within conventional disorder frameworks have had very mixed results (e.g., Feingold, Carroll, Johnson & Rounsaville, 1998; Peele, 1989, 1997; Trebach & Zeese, 1990). For example, overviews of empirical research on conventional treatments of "drug abusers" that aim to promote abstinence from substance use show that, more often than not, such treatments have no lasting impact on most people's use of substances (Feingold et al., 1998; Peele, 1989, 1997). Interestingly, comparisons of ostensibly distinct conventional treatments such as Twelve-Step/disease approaches and cognitive behavior therapies have shown little or no differences in outcome (e.g., Project MATCH Research Group, 1997). Similarly, conventional social policies in the so-called war on drugs have had little lasting impact on the demand for or use of (illicit) drugs while resulting in an increase in prison populations and related social problems (Szasz, 1992; Trebach & Zeese, 1990).

Moreover, contradictions and inconsistencies abound in conventional approaches to substance use. For example, in disorder-oriented treatments, drug users may be taught that they have little or no control over their drug use while also being required to exercise control by stopping their use. Drug users may be asked to use a drug (e.g., methadone, naltraxone) in order to stop taking another drug (e.g., heroin). Although government, treatment, and educational institutions wage a (selective) "war on [illicit] drugs," pharmaceutical companies and psychiatric professionals promote the use of prescription medications. Thus, people are taught that "drugs don't work" and to "just say no" to "dangerous drugs" such as marijuana and cocaine while being implored to "just say yes" to Ritalin, Prozac, and other "medications" (Breggin, 1998; New Yorker, 1998). Ironically, although the Food and Drug Administration (FDA) approves the use of Ritalin, the U.S. Drug Enforcement Administration (DEA) decries the "abuse" of Ritalin as a street drug (Breggin, 1998). In sum, conventional disorder approaches to substance use have been largely ineffective by their own criteria, and have resulted in numerous conceptual and practical inconsistencies and paradoxes.

In recent years, several theorists and clinicians have argued that constructivist perspectives provide viable alternatives for understanding substance use (Burrell & Jaffe, 1995, 1999; Epstein, 1996; Klion, 1993; Klion & Pfenninger, 1997; Scheibe, 1994; Willutzki & Wiesner, 1996; Winslade & Smith, 1997). Constructivist approaches, which examine substance use in the context of the personal and social construction of meaning, provide illuminating counterpoints to conventional disorder perspectives. Such approaches highlight critical limitations of disorder approaches to drug treatment and social policy and facilitate the creation of promising alternatives for understanding and addressing problems related to substance use. Along these lines, this chapter has three major purposes:

1. To utilize a constructivist perspective as a vantage point for "deconstructing" or critiquing conventional approaches to drug use.
2. To describe constructivist alternatives for understanding substance use.
3. To consider implications of constructivist approaches to substance use for theory, research, and practice.

This chapter first describes the major assumptions and themes of conventional, nonconstructivist disorder approaches to substance use. Then, using constructivism as a general critical vantage point, central problems in disorder perspectives are highlighted. After this brief "deconstruction," an overview is provided of applications of several constructivist theories to substance use, with a particular emphasis on evolutionary constructivism, an integrative perspective. Implications of constructivist perspectives for substance-related theory, research, and practice (including counseling and social policy) are described. This chapter does not aim to describe a constructivist "treatment for drug abuse." Instead, it aims to provide a framework for understanding substance use that can inform and influence our relationships to diverse substances and people who use them.

OVERVIEW OF THE CONVENTIONAL FRAMEWORKS: DISORDER PERSPECTIVES ON SUBSTANCE ABUSE AND ADDICTION

Disorder models of "drug abuse" and "addiction" have been expounded in professional and public circles for at least the last 200 years (Fingarette, 1988, 1991; Musto, 1973; Peele, 1989; Schaler, 1998; Szasz, 1985) although they did not become the dominant views regarding substance use in the United States until about the last quarter of the 20th century. The most common and influential versions of the disorder approach to substances are disease models (Schaler, 1998; Fingarette, 1988, 1991). However, many approaches described as alternatives to disease models such as cognitive-behavior therapy (e.g., Carroll, 1998; Marlatt & Gordon, 1985) and cognitive therapy (Beck, Wright, Newman, & Liese, 1993), actually share a number of central nonconstructivist metatheoretical assumptions with disease perspectives. Although these approaches are not fully equivalent, in the current context they are viewed as being broadly guided by a shared nonconstructivist disorder framework.

Generally speaking, disorder perspectives assume that there are certain dangerous and addictive substances ("psychoactive drugs," "addictive drugs," or "drugs of abuse") that cause specific psychological experiences and behaviors as a function of their inherent properties. Repeated use of such addictive drugs is seen as causing a progressive loss or mitigation of personal control, distortions in perception and judgement (e.g., denial, cognitive dysfunction, unrealistic expectations, etc.), and other negative consequences, often culminating in "addiction" or "drug abuse disorders." Drug abuse disorders are seen as real and objectively definable conditions that occur in individuals. In the conventional view, certain people may be particularly vulnerable to drug disorders as a result of physiological or psychological predispositions or deficiencies, or both.

Disorder perspectives further suggest that substance abuse disorders are "relapsing conditions." This notion of relapse involves two interlocking assumptions. First, that drug abuse disorders are permanent or semipermanent features or characteristics of a human being that can reemerge at any time. Thus, even if a so-called drug addict is not currently using a substance that was seen as problematic, he or she is often viewed as still "having" the disorder in various stages of "remission" (e.g., see the various course qualifiers that can be attached to any of the substance use disorder diagnoses in the Diagnostic and Statistical Manual, 4th edition [DSM-IV], American Psychiatric Association, 1994). Second, owing to the assumption that substance use disorders involve a mitigation or loss of personal control, drug abusers and addicts are seen as continually "at risk" of losing control and "relapsing" (i.e., using a substance) when exposed to various external or internal "triggers" (e.g., environmental cues or subjective "urges" or "cravings"). Consequently, disorder perspectives usually assume that abstinence is the only "realistic" option for presumably impaired or out-of-control drug addicts. From this point of view, certain drugs are seen as so powerful—capable of overwhelming personal control and causing chronic and relapsing disorders—that social controls are considered necessary to prohibit people from using them (e.g., drug prohibitions and the "war on drugs") or to supervise/limit use (e.g., drug schedules, prescriptions, etc.).

Disorder approaches to substance use such as disease models are widely accepted in the United States in both professional and lay circles (Schaler, 1998). For example, surveys suggest that up to 90% of Americans believe that "alcoholism is a disease" (Gallup, 1992; Peele, 1989) and that over 90% of alcohol treatment programs are guided by a disease model (Roman & Blum, 1997). Professional organizations and government agencies almost uniformly explicitly support such notions. For example, the Joint Committee to Study the Definition and Criteria for the Diagnosis of Alcoholism of the National Council on Alcoholism and Drug Dependence and the American Society of Addiction Medicine (1990) describe "alcoholism" as follows:

Alcoholism is a primary, *chronic disease.* . . . The *disease* is often progressive and fatal. It is characterized by continuous or periodic: *impaired control* over drinking, preoccupation with the drug alcohol, use of alcohol despite adverse consequences, and distortions in thinking, most notably denial. . . . *"Disease" means an involuntary disability.* . . . These phenomena are associated with a specified common set of characteristics by which these individuals differ from the norm, and which places them at a disadvantage. . . . *"Impaired control" means the inability to limit alcohol use or to consistently limit on any drinking occasion the duration of the episode, the quantity consumed, and/or the behavioral consequences of drinking.* . . . *"Denial"* is used here . . . to include *a range of psychological maneuvers designed to reduce awareness of the fact that alcohol use is the cause of an individual's problems rather than a solution to those problems. Denial becomes an integral part of the disease and a major obstacle to recovery.* (Joint Committee, 1990; emphasis added)

Similarly, the National Institute of Drug Abuse (NIDA) asserts that "More than two decades of research clearly shows that drug addiction is a chronic relapsing illness that comes about because of the effects of long-term drug use on the brain" (NIDA, 1998).

As noted earlier, disorder assumptions are not limited to disease models of addiction. Most current approaches to research and treatment, including those developed as alternatives to disease models, implicitly or explicitly accept central aspects of the disorder narrative described earlier. For example, although cognitive behavior therapies (e.g., Carroll, 1998; Kadden, Carroll, Donovan, Cooney, Monti, Abrams, Litt, & Hester, 1995; Marlatt & Gordon, 1985) and cognitive therapy of substance abuse (e.g., Beck et al., 1993) suggest nonbiological explanations, they begin by assuming that "substance abuse" and "addiction" are objectively definable and real disorders that "occur" in individuals. Moreover, they presume that the use of certain drugs is a bad, maladaptive, or unhealthy habit that is initiated and maintained primarily because of a person's skill deficiencies, cognitive dysfunctions, and impaired control. Because of such deficiencies and dysfunctions and the power of drugs and triggers, drug abusers/addicts are assumed to be at continued "risk" of "relapsing." Consequently, these approaches promote avoidance or correction of factors that cause "relapse," and view total abstinence from drug use as the most "realistic" goal for "addicts" or "drug abusers."

Such disorder assumptions are apparent in Beck et al.'s (1993) description of cognitive therapy of substance abuse. For example, Beck et al. state (1993) that:

We have written this book in response to the ever-growing need to formulate and test cost-effective treatments for substance abuse disorders, problems that seem to be multiplying in the population despite society's best efforts. . . . (p. ix)

We advocate a program of treatment that strives for abstinence. In this manner we maximize the patients' chances of maintaining an able and responsible lifestyle, reduce the risk of relapse, and avoid giving patients the false impression that we view a mere *reduction* in drug use as the optimal outcome. (p. 2)

Beck et al. (1993) further assert that addicts may continue to use because they "ignore, minimize, or deny the problems or attribute them to something other than the drugs," are "avoiding a true assessment of the disadvantages" of use, and adhere to a "network of *dysfunctional beliefs*" (p. 36). With regard to control over substance use, Beck et al. (1993) note that "many addicted individuals simply have not developed the skills to control temptation" (p. 36). Thus, so-called addicts are viewed as suffering from dysfunctional beliefs, deficient skills, and a failure to understand the "true" disadvantages of use.

Similarly, in Cognitive-Behavioral Coping Skills Treatment for Cocaine Dependence (Carroll, 1998), a recent articulation of an approach also known as Relapse Prevention, attainment of abstinence is the initial single focus of the treatment. This largely didactic approach aims to help cocaine abusers unlearn old habits associated with cocaine abuse and learn or relearn more healthy skills and habits and to enhance self-control in individuals in whom impaired control over cocaine abuse may be a relatively unitary phenomenon or part of a more complex picture of psychiatric disorder or psychosocial disruption. The core of this cognitive-behavioral approach is to teach presumably skill-deficient drug abusers to "recognize, avoid, and cope" with "high risk situations" that may cause relapse to substance abuse.

In sum, conventional approaches construe substance use within a disorder framework that assumes that: there is a class of objectively definable substances known as addictive drugs; these drugs have the inherent power to cause specific psychological experiences and behaviors and to overwhelm personal control; the use of such drugs is maladaptive or unhealthy, often resulting in the occurrence of objectively definable drug disorders in individuals; and so-called drug abusers or addicts are (biologically or psychologically, or both) deficient persons with impaired or no control who are at continued "risk of relapse" due to exposure to drug use "triggers."

Deconstructing Disorder Approaches through Constructivist Lenses

Disorder models of addiction and drug use, particularly disease models, have been the subject of numerous critiques from various empirical and theoretical perspectives (e.g., Fingarette, 1988; Peele, 1989; Schaler, 1998; Szasz, 1985). Rather than review these critical analyses, this chapter outlines a number of central puzzles and problems that emerge when the disorder approach to substance use is examined from a constructivist vantage point. In this context, constructivism refers to a framework that views human beings as actively and proactively constructing meaning and patterns of self-organization (Lyddon, 1992; Mahoney, 1991; Neimeyer, 1993; Neimeyer & Mahoney, 1995). In contrast to objectivist epistemologies, constructivist frameworks assume that individuals have no direct knowledge of an external reality, but instead adapt to changeable, personally and socially constructed realities (Chiari and Nuzzo, 1996; Lyddon, 1995; Neimeyer & Mahoney, 1995). From this perspective, "facts" and notions of objective reality regarding drugs and anything else are viewed as historically changeable human constructions. When we examine critically the coherence and viability of disorder approaches from this perspective, a number of central questions and puzzles come into focus.

What Is a "Drug"? One Person's Meat Is Another Person's Poison

People make a host of meaningful distinctions between substances, including distinguishing between drugs and various nondrug categories (e.g., foods, agricultural products, dietary supplements, etc.), and between numerous subcategories of drugs (e.g., addictive versus nonaddictive, legal versus illegal, good versus bad, "hard" versus "soft," "medications" versus "drugs"). Disorder approaches typically do not explicitly address the distinction between drugs and other substances, as if such distinctions were self-evident and nonproblematic. Differentiation of drugs into various subcategories is ostensibly based on the drugs' inherent biological, psychological, and behavioral properties. For example, the DSM-IV (American Psychiatric Association, 1994) lists a variety of substance use disorders involving the use of different classes of drugs (e.g., stimulants, hallucinogens, etc.). Federal law articulates a "schedule" of drugs, delineating categories of controlled substances based on their "potential for abuse." Such systems presume that substances can be objectively and reliably classified as "drugs" and that drugs can then be reliably distinguished based on objectively definable properties.

In contrast, a constructivist perspective suggests that rather than assuming that drug-related categories necessarily reflect objective distinctions based on substances' inherent properties, we should examine them as human constructions. Simply stated, how do people construe and classify substances? More specifically, how do people determine "what is a drug?" and identify some drugs as "dangerous" and "addictive"? Explored from this point of view, it quickly becomes apparent that despite an appearance of objectivity, the symbolic and practical distinctions people make between so-called drugs are, for the most part, independent of pharmacology (Szasz, 1985; Trebach & Zeese, 1990; Weil & Rosen, 1993). Instead, people make context-sensitive and changeable judgments about substances based on personal and social constructions and strategic considerations.

The social, historical, and strategic variations and inconsistencies in how people classify substances illustrate the context-sensitive and subjective nature of judgments about substances. For example, the same substance may be classified in very different ways depending on who is using it, how it is being used, why it is being used, when it is being used, where it is being used, who is making the judgment, and the strategic purposes of the classifier. For example, is marijuana a "dangerous gateway drug," an agricultural product, a recreational substance, or a "medication"? It is likely that an individual who enjoys smoking marijuana as a means of relaxation, a farmer who grows marijuana as a cash crop, an agent for the DEA, and a cancer patient who smokes marijuana to lessen the side effects of chemotherapy would all provide different answers. Similarly, tobacco may be viewed as a recreational product by cigarette manufacturers, as an agricultural commodity by tobacco farmers, and as an addictive drug by the FDA. In this context, substances that are similar in terms of their physical properties may be construed as being entirely different kinds of substances. Consider, for example, the varied meanings and practices connected to heroin versus methadone in the United States or cocaine versus Prozac or Ritalin. Why are heroin and cocaine viewed as dangerous, addictive, and illegal drugs while substances that are quite similar from a pharmacological perspective—methadone, Prozac, and Ritalin—are construed and promoted as medications or treatments?

In sum, substances do not exist prelabeled in nature as "drugs" or as good and bad drugs. Human beings classify them as such (or not) based on socially and strategically informed perspectives (Heath, 1998; Szasz, 1985).

Conventional disorder approaches to treatment and social policy, while reifying drug-related categories, tend to ignore or minimize the ambiguity, inconsistency, and variability in our classification of substances. With the decisive first step of accepting extant compartmentalizations of substances as matters of fact rather than as strategic and changeable social constructions, substances that have been classified as dangerous or addictive become a focus of social controls and change efforts, whereas others classified as "medications" or "recreational substances" are promoted or accepted.

Good Use, Bad Use: From Social Conflicts to Drug Disorders

Closely connected to the reification of substance-related classifications are the symbolic distinctions that conventional disorder perspectives make between drug abuse and drug use. Drug abuse and its conceptual cousins, drug dependence and drug addiction, are used to label ostensible disorders that "occur" or exist in individuals or that individuals "have" (e.g., see DSM-IV definition of "mental disorder," American Psychiatric Association, 1994). If one accepts the literal existence of such drug disorders, the task then becomes to correct, control, or prevent them through treatment or social policies, or both.

Brief reflection from a constructivist point of view reveals that drug abuse disorders do not refer to objectively definable conditions that exist in or are characteristic of individuals. Consider the following substance use scenarios:

1. Jack uses Substance X on a daily basis to cope with intense feelings of emptiness and sadness. He reports that he feels incomplete and cannot function unless he uses Substance X.

2. Jill uses Substance Y a few times a week with friends to relax.

Imagine the varied social responses that might follow if Jack and Jill were using varied substances in diverse social contexts. For example, if Jack was "taking" Prozac prescribed by a physician, he might simply be labeled as a "good and compliant patient who suffers from depression." On the contrary, if Jack were "using"[1] cocaine, he would most likely be viewed as a "drug abuser" or "addict" who was "self-medicating." If Substance Y was alcohol, Jill would probably be viewed as a "social drinker." If however, Substance Y was heroin, Jill would be viewed (in the United States) as a "heroin addict" in need of treatment or a criminal using an illegal drug. To further complicate these socially constructed distinctions between use and abuse, if Jack was taking Prozac on his own without a physician's prescription, he might be viewed as "abusing prescription medication."

As these examples illustrate, judgments about whether Jack and Jill are using or abusing substances depend on socially informed constructions about the substances they are using and how they are using it. Is a substance judged as socially acceptable within a particular social context? Is a person using a substance for socially acceptable purposes or in the context of sanctioned social roles? Thus, drug abuse disorders are not "in" Jack or Jill or a condition that they "have." They are ambiguous and flexible labels that one person applies to another person when the substance user is perceived as deviating from social rules or roles, or both. In other words, drug disorders reflect social conflicts or deviance. People may be labeled as substance abusers for violating a variety of historically changeable and culturally variable social rules, including those related to which substances one should use (e.g., using a substance that is judged to be unacceptable based on culturally and historically relative rules); the proper purposes or functions of use (e.g., using Ritalin to experience a "rush" or marijuana to "relax"); and how one uses and the context of use (e.g., self-directed use of Prozac; using amounts that someone judges as "excessive"; using alcohol while driving a car). Distinctions between use and abuse often depend on judgments about whether or not a person is violating or adhering to socially defined roles. Thus, a person's use of the substance Prozac to cope with "depression" can be construed either as abuse or as "medication compliance" and good patienthood, depending on whether or not the user is seen as adhering to the patient role as defined by a physician. The curious discrepancies and twists in judgments about use and abuse of diverse substances are well illustrated by a recent statement by Dr. Alan Leschner, the head of the National Institute of Drug Abuse, an agency devoted to the elimination of "drug abuse," concerning the prescription of certain drugs, called selective serotonin reuptake inhibitors (SSRIs): "'My belief is that today, in 1998, you should be put in jail if you refuse to prescribe SSRIs for depression" (*New Yorker,* 1998). Thus, a major general in the war against (illegal) drugs is also a passionate advocate of the use of other drugs, construed as medications.

The DSM-IV (American Psychiatric Association, 1994) criteria for substance abuse highlight the socially defined nature of substance abuse and it's relation to perceived violations of social roles. According to the DSM-IV, substance use can be construed as "abuse" if it is judged to be "maladaptive" or cause a failure to fulfill major role obligations at work, school, or home. Note that the DSM-IV does not ask several important questions. How does one identify "major role obligations"? And who decides what it means to "fulfill" such roles? "Maladaptive" in reference to what? Moreover, the DSM-IV distinguishes between "nonpathological substance use (e.g., 'social drinking')" from the "use of medications for appropriate medical purposes." In this regard, it is interesting to note the DSM-IV describes substance dependence as involving "a pattern of self administration." Thus, two people using similar or the same substance may be viewed quite differently depending on whether or not they are being guided by a physician who judges the use of the substance as "appropriate" or are using the substance independent of a physician's stamp of approval. From this perspective, a person who depends on a substance such as Prozac or lithium and who organizes his or her experience and actions around the use of the substance, cannot be construed as drug dependent if the drug is not "administered" by a physician. Ironically, then, being labeled as drug *dependent* is in part, a function of being *independent* (of a physician's control).

In sum, as the DSM-IV criteria illustrate, "drug abuse" is not an objectively defined individual condition or characteristic. "Drug abuse" is a label referring to socially disapproved patterns of substance use—either using substances socially defined as "bad" or "addictive" or using them in ways that are disapproved of by someone.

The Power of Drugs and the Diminished Powers of Drug Addicts: The Drug or the Disorder Made Me Do It

Disorder approaches assume that the substances known as "addictive drugs" have the inherent power to cause specific psychological experiences and behaviors and to overwhelm or diminish personal control. Along similar lines, they also make the interlocking assumption that the ability of so-called drug addicts or drug abusers to control their own conduct is impaired or weakened.

In regard to the power of drugs to cause specific psychological experiences (e.g., "highs") and behaviors, it is interesting to note that a vast body of literature and anecdotal experience has demonstrated that people's experiences and actions when using substances often has more to do with beliefs, expectations, and context than with the substance itself (Fisher & Greenberg, 1997; Kirsch, 1990; Schaler, 1998; Zinberg, 1984). Research with a wide variety of substances—legal and illegal—has demonstrated that when people believe that a substance will lead to particular changes in their experiences and behaviors, they will often experience and evidence such changes even when they are not actually using the substance. On the other hand, when people are actually using a substance, they may not experience changes in how they feel if they do not believe they are taking the substance (e.g., see Fisher & Greenberg, 1997; Kirsch, 1990; Marlatt, Demming, & Reid, 1973). Similarly, withdrawal experiences (the unpleasant experiences, including drug cravings) that people report when they stop using a substance such as heroin can be ameliorated by the administration of a placebo (Light & Torrance, 1929). Moreover, people commonly report quite varied drug-related experiences when they use substances in different social contexts and when their perspectives on substance use change (Burrell & Jaffe, 1999; Peele, 1997; Weil & Rosen, 1993; Zinberg, 1984). If drugs have the inherent power to cause specific psychological experiences and behaviors, why are people's experiences when using them so varied and changeable as a function of psychological perspective and the social context?

There are numerous puzzles or anomalies related to the ostensible power of substances to overwhelm personal control and the diminished powers of drug addicts. For example, if we examine how people use substances widely construed as "highly addictive," such as cocaine or heroin, we find that the vast majority of users do not do so as a regular and central activity in their lives. (According to results of federal government surveys, only 5% of the people who use crack or other forms of cocaine reported that they used regularly/several times per week. See the results of the Substance Abuse and Mental Health Services Administration [SAMHSA] Household Survey; SAMHSA, 1997). Indeed, people frequently report using such presumably highly "addictive" substances periodically and sporadically without progressing to regular/daily use (Erickson, Adlai, Murray, & Smart, 1987; Erickson & Alexander, 1998; Erickson & Weber, 1998; Robins, Helzer, Hesselbrock, & Wish, 1998). On the other hand, presumably impaired addicts who use the most powerful addictive drugs on a regular basis demonstrate their ability to control and change their drug-related conduct in large and small ways. For example, they frequently change their substance use patterns quite dramatically on their own, shifting to less frequent patterns of use or stopping use (e.g., Biernacki, 1986; Robins et al., 1998). Indeed, the vast majority of people who stop using substances such as nicotine and alcohol, do so on their own (Peele, 1989). Despite the image of the drug addict as an out-of-control automaton who reflexively and involuntarily uses a substance continuously until he or she runs out of the substance or dies, all users of substances evidence the ability to strategically adapt their patterns of use to complex circumstances, as illustrated by the complex behaviors and choices often involved in obtaining and using illegal substances while avoiding discovery. Indeed, even the most ostensibly "out-of-control" substance users will interrupt use in order to address bodily functions and respond to perceived dangers. In other words, use of a substance is far from an automatic consequence of its availability. In this regard, it is interesting to note that in clinical contexts, almost all substance users, including those who view themselves as having been "out of control," acknowledge after some reflection that their use involved multiple momentary choices related to using substances (decisions that cognitive behavioral treatments refer to as "seemingly irrelevant decisions").

Perhaps in response to these anomalies, conventional treatments and self-help groups for drug abusers often adopt a paradoxical stance regarding the powers of drugs and drug addicts. For example, Alcoholics Anonymous (AA) and Narcotics Anonymous (NA) promote the idea that addicts are "powerless" over their disease and their drug use while simultaneously asking people to exercise control by abstaining from drug use (Alcoholics Anonymous, 1955; Narcotics Anonymous, 1983). Similarly, abstinence from drug use is sometimes a precondition for entry into or continuation in drug treatment programs. For example, a recent large treatment outcome study for cocaine abuse funded by the National Institute of Drug Abuse required that cocaine abusers abstain from using cocaine for 3 weeks in order to be admitted into treatment (Crits-Christoph et al., 1999). In other words, if a cocaine abuser (who presumably suffers from "impaired control") wanted to enter treatment to help stop using, he or she had to first stop using cocaine.

Contradictory beliefs about the powers of drugs and drug users are woven into the fabric of current cognitive-behavioral and cognitive approaches. For example, although cognitive-behavioral and cognitive treatment models assert that human decision processes play an important role in substance use (e.g., drug use as a maladaptive effort to cope; the notion of "seemingly irrelevant decisions," etc.), they also assume that people labeled as drug abusers show "impaired control" and that drug use is a "triggered" reaction. The notion of "high-risk situations" implies that the substance user is largely at the mercy of external situations or depersonalized subjective experiences known as "cravings" or "urges." Such factors are seen as potential "triggers" that may impel a person with impaired or absent control to use a substance even if he or she does not want to use. Metaphorically, drug use is thus viewed as a sort of reflex or automatic response that happens to a person, rather than as a strategic choice. Thus, cognitive behavioral and cognitive perspectives concurrently view substance abusers as agents making strategic decisions to use and as impaired victims facing internal and external risks that can impel use.

Interestingly, if we accept the assumption that these approaches make about substance abusers making decisions to use, then the "risk" in "high-risk situations" is not in the situation at all. The "risk" is that a person will decide to use a drug. In this case, the person's own decision is viewed as a potential risk. Because risk usually refers to a potential consequence that may follow our actions or decisions—in other words, something beyond our control that may happen to us—this either requires a reconceptualization of the concept of risk or an implicit oxymoronic suggestion that a person is not in control of his or her own decision processes. In this model, a restaurant that serves fried foods may be considered a "high-risk situation" for a person on a low- fat diet, because the dieter may be impelled (i.e., triggered) to decide to order deep-fried onion rings.

In sum, in contrast to disorder approach assumptions that certain substances have the inherent power to cause specific psychological experiences and behaviors, people's use of and experiences with substances varies as a function of their expectations, perspective, and the social context. In addition, although disorder approaches assume that certain drugs have the power to overwhelm personal control, people, including so-called addicts, demonstrate that they are able to take them or leave them. Paradoxically, although disorder approaches assert that substance abusers suffer from impaired control and are at the mercy of the external environment or depersonalized "impulses" or cravings, they also operate as if they have the power to control themselves and to decide not to use.

Summary

A constructivist perspective highlights a number of central inconsistencies and problems in the disorder approach to substance use. Specifically, such a perspective raises questions about the consistency and viability of objectivist assumptions concerning the properties and powers of substances and the objective existence of drug disorders as conditions that "occur in" or are characteristic of individuals. In contrast, a constructivist perspective suggests that to understand human experiences with and relationships to the substances that we call drugs, it is necessary to consider how people (users, therapists, policy makers, etc.) construe them.

RECONSTRUING SUBSTANCE USE: CONSTRUCTIVIST PERSPECTIVES

A number of constructivist theories have been applied to substance use, including personal construct theory (Klion, 1993; Klion & Pfenninger, 1997), social constructionism (Epstein, 1996; Gergen & Gergen, 1996; Herwig-Lempp, 1996; Scheibe, 1994; Szasz, 1985; Willutzki & Wiesner, 1996; Winslade & Smith, 1997), and evolutionary constructivism (Burrell & Jaffe, 1999). Although these perspectives have diverse foci and somewhat varied epistemological assumptions, they all attempt to understand human experiences with and relationships to substances in the context of the personal and social construction of meaning. This section provides an overview of these constructivist approaches to substance use, with a particular emphasis on evolutionary constructivism, which is considered to be an integrative approach.

Personal Construct Theory and Psychoactive Substance Use

Klion (1993) and Klion and Pfenninger (1997), working from the vantage point of personal construct theory, focused on understanding how and why using a particular substance may become a central activity in a person's life. They argued that addiction is essentially a role—a central pattern of activities and way of relating to the world that emerges from a person's constructions—that can become a central part of a person's "core role" or self. These authors note that as a person begins to focus his or her activities on the use of drugs and to operate in drug-related contexts, the person often explicitly or implicitly elaborates and extends the addict role and decreases his or her ability to reconstrue the self in other terms. Thus, through a person's actions, drug use can become the "primary meaningful event" in a person's life.

From this perspective, substance use is a meaningful activity that a person engages in as part of efforts to articulate and maintain a viable personal construct system, including a viable conception of self. Along these lines, Klion (1993) and Klion and Pfenninger (1997) assert that people may use substances to minimize the impact of invalidating experiences and anticipatory failures related to aspects of personal construct systems (which are reflected by various negative emotional experiences such as sadness and guilt) or to generate experiences of validation (as reflected in emotions such as joy). From this perspective, although drug use may lessen the immediate experiential impact of invalidating experiences, it can also serve to maintain problematic aspects of a person's construct system.

In contrast to disorder approaches, which focus on correcting the cognitive and behavioral deficiencies and dysfunctions of substance abusers or avoiding environmental triggers, Klion (1993) suggests that psychotherapy with a chemically dependent person should be viewed as a form of collaborative experimentation. The personal construct therapist's role is not to educate a deficient drug abuser about the true dangers of drugs, correct dysfunctional beliefs, and teach healthy coping skills. Instead, it is to help clarify how substance use may or may not be a problem from the client's perspective and to facilitate the growth of the person's construct system. Such a stance implies flexibility in terms of treatment goals rather than presuming that drug use is maladaptive with abstinence as the only "realistic" goal.

Social Constructionism and Psychoactive Substance Use

Social constructionist perspectives (Epstein, 1996; Gergen & Gergen, 1996; Herwig-Lempp, 1996; Scheibe, 1994; Szasz, 1985; Willutzki & Wiesner, 1996; Winslade & Smith, 1997) focus primarily on the development, impact, and limitations of social constructions and practices related to substances.

The most comprehensive social constructionist critiques of conventional disorder approaches have been presented by Szasz (1985).[2] Szasz (1985) asserted that the important differences between the substances we call drugs in terms of understanding their use and avoidance, are *ceremonial*—related to social traditions, social rules, and symbolic meanings—not chemical. In other words, just as people's responses to foods are constrained by socially constructed rituals and meanings, people's use or avoidance of the substances we call drugs is primarily a function of the personal and social meanings that they connect to those substances. From this perspective, "drug abuse" is simply a label applied to socially disapproved patterns of substance use. In this sense, "drug abuse" is a socially manufactured problem rather than an existential condition with a literal existence. Consequently, for Szasz, the problem is not to "understand drug abuse." It is to understand the consequences and functions of historically changeable and socially constructed ideas about "drug abuse." In this regard, he argues that drug-related ideas and the social practices that stem from these ideas are developed and promoted because they serve a variety of strategic social functions, including scapegoating, the justification of coercion, and social control.

Along similar lines, several social constructionists have recently critiqued conventional approaches to substance use, particularly disease models and drug prohibition (Epstein, 1996; Gergen & Gergen, 1996; Herwig-Lempp, 1996; Winslade & Smith, 1997), echoing many of Szasz's conjectures about the social construction of "drug abuse" through language and social convention. For example, Epstein (1996) argued that applying the language of disease and medical metaphors to drug use and drug problems has a variety of negative consequences, including isolating drug use from the social context, justifying coercion, foreclosing viewing people who use drugs as making choices, precluding consideration of controlled usage, and so forth. Similarly, Winslade and Smith (1997) argued that disease-based cultural narratives or scripts about alcohol result in "totalizing descriptions" that internalize and reify alcohol problems and make it difficult to reconstrue the self in other terms.

In contrast to disorder perspectives, which tend to reify and decontextualize substance abuse as an existential condition existing in an individual, Epstein (1996), Willutzki and Wiesner (1996), Herwig-Lempp (1996), Gergen and Gergen (1996), and Winslade and Smith (1997) advocate using relational languages for describing substance use that do not isolate drug-using behavior from its social context. They outline alternative approaches to drug problems such as "accepting drug work" (Herwig-Lempp, 1996; Willutzki & Wiesner, 1996), which view drug users as autonomous persons whose choices make sense when considered from their own perspectives. In contrast to disorder models, which promote adoption of addict or abuser identities and abstinence as a universal goal, accepting drug work considers distinctions between "drug abusers" and others as socially constructed and aims to help drug users pursue their own goals. In a similar spirit, Winslade and Smith (1997) describe a narrative approach that invites clients collaboratively to construct nonmedicalized, agency-promoting narratives about the influence of alcohol on their lives.

Personal Construct Theory and Social Constructionism: Contrast and Comparison

Despite differences in focus, personal construct theory and constructionist perspectives on drug use can be viewed as complementary. Both argue that drug use can be understood from the perspective of the user—in other words, drug use is meaningful and goal-directed human action, not a triggered consequence of a disorder or a chemical. Social constructionist approaches, while acknowledging individual choice (or at least individual participation in social processes), focus on understanding drug use from the social to the personal, highlighting the impact of social constructions and social contexts on drug use. Personal construct theory, while acknowledging the impact of the social world on personal constructs and meanings, focuses on understanding drug use from the personal to the social, highlighting personal agency and personal meaning.

EVOLUTIONARY CONSTRUCTIVISM AND SUBSTANCE USE

An evolutionary constructivist perspective (Burrell, 1987) on substance use (Burrell & Jaffe, 1999) reiterates many of the issues highlighted by personal construct theory and social constructionism. However, this particular constructivist approach attempts to further articulate the dynamic interplay over time between the personal and social dimensions of substance use.

Briefly stated, evolutionary constructivism assumes that individuals actively and proactively construct meaning and patterns of self-organization as they attempt to understand and navigate in construed existential circumstances and social contexts. Self-organizational patterns and constructive processes are viewed as primarily tacit (Polanyi, 1966) in that they guide choices and construction of meaning without our being fully aware of or able to articulate their precise nature. An evolutionary perspective suggests that constructive processes develop over time as "the result of human action but not human design" (Hayek, 1978) from our attempts to enhance their viability in the face of discrepancies and existential challenges. Social contexts provide the forums for this evolutionary process, thus functioning as a context of constraint on personal development. In this way, individuals are active participants in the coevolution of themselves and the social orders in which they live. From this point of view, self-organizational patterns are seen as complex, multifaceted, and inherently relational (see Gergen, 1985, 1991; Guidano, 1987, 1991; Mahoney & Moes, 1997).

Meaning and Substance Use

An evolutionary constructivist perspective on substance use suggests that our experiences with and relationships to specific substances are largely a function of the meanings that we actively bring to bear on those substances. Human experiences with substances do not simply happen as a function of the inherent pharmacological properties of those substances. In contrast to disorder models, which tend to depersonalize and objectify drug experience and use, an evolutionary constructivist approach suggests that we actively participate in the construction of substance-related experience in the context of our meaning systems. In other words, how a person feels when using (or not using) a substance will depend largely on what using that substance means to that person in a particular social context. The diverse and changeable subjective experiences that people report when using substances can thus be understood as largely a function of diverse and changeable meanings. When the meanings related to using a substance change— as a function of social evolution (i.e., changes in the social constructions and practices related to the use of particular substances), shifts of social context (e.g., using in the context of different social roles or settings), or personal development (e.g., changes in the relationship between substance use and self organization)—subjective experiences with and relationships to substances will change.

Anticipatory Processes and Substance Use

An evolutionary constructivist perspective (in concordance with personal construct theory) suggests that people use psychoactive substances as part of their efforts to anticipate the future. Consequently, this approach highlights the role of anticipatory processes—ranging from circumscribed drug-related expectations (e.g., Jaffe & Kilbey, 1994; Kirsch, 1990) to self-efficacy expectations (DiClemente, Fairhurst, & Piotrowski, 1995) to complex anticipatory self-narratives—in drug-related experiences and actions.

The simplest illustrations of the role of anticipatory processes are seen in research on drug-related expectancies (see reviews by Fisher & Greenberg, 1997; Goldman, Brown, & Christiansen, 1987; Jaffe, 1992; and Kirsch, 1990) and placebos. Generally speaking, this research has repeatedly demonstrated that people's expectations about drug effects are quite varied (Goldman et al., 1987; Jaffe & Kilbey, 1994; Leigh, 1989) and that substance related expectations can often exert a more powerful influence on subjective experiences and actions than do chemicals (e.g., Fisher & Greenberg, 1997; Kirsch, 1990; Marlatt et al., 1973). Moreover, as highlighted by social constructionist analyses, when anticipatory beliefs about particular substances change historically or vary across social contexts (e.g., cultures)—such as the belief that alcohol will lead to loss of control and aggression—behavior and experience when using those substances varies accordingly (e.g., Critchlow, 1986; MacAndrew & Edgerton, 1969; Peele, 1989; Scheibe, 1994; Weil & Rosen, 1993).

The role of anticipatory processes is further illustrated by shifts in anticipatory focus that people commonly experience before and during substance use. For example, prior to using a substance, a person often constrains his or her anticipatory constructive focus to drug-related contexts and purposes. When using substances, people often constrain their temporal focus to extremely short periods of time (e.g., only looking forward to the next anticipated use and "high") and report alterations in their experience of time (e.g., Hopson, 1993; Lapp, Collins, Zywiak, & Izzo, 1994). For example, one woman reported that when she smokes cocaine, "time stops. I don't think about the past or the future. I just think about the pipe and what I need to do to get the next hit."

Complex Strategic Functions of Substance Use

Disorder approaches tend to compartmentalize substances, assuming that the use of certain substances is maladaptive or "unhealthy." When a labeled substance abuser disagrees about the destructive consequences of using a particular drug, he or she is seen as being "in denial" or as suffering from some sort of cognitive dysfunction. Moreover, substance use is seen largely as a triggered event or consequence of a disorder rather than a purposeful and meaningful action. In this way, substance use is demeaned and depersonalized. In contrast, an evolutionary constructivist perspective suggests that people, including those not labeled as substance abusers, use a variety of substances—legal or illegal, prescribed or nonprescribed—as part of their efforts to construct and maintain viable meanings and self-organizations. Rather than presuming that the use of a particular substance is a "problem" to be eliminated (while the use of another substance, such as a "medication" is presumed to be "therapeutic" or helpful), it is assumed that if a person continues to use a substance, doing so is serving as part of a (fallible) solution to constructive challenges. In this framework, people often continue to use psychoactive substances despite expecting that doing so will cause problems or lead to experiences that they view as negative (e.g., see Jaffe & Kilbey, 1994) because use also serves one or more meaningful functions.

These functions include addressing internally discrepant and disorganizing meanings and constructing alternate meanings. (This includes Klion, 1993, and Klion & Pfenninger's, 1997, notion that people use substances to decrease the impact of "anticipatory failure" of "invalidated" constructs.) For example, Steve, a frequent smoker of cocaine, expressed puzzlement over why he continued to use, noting that he would feel "dirty" and "depressed" after smoking. His experience of himself as "dirty" was connected to his construal of himself within extant social constructions of cocaine addicts as "weak," "low," and morally impure. (See Scheibe, 1994, for a discussion of changing social constructions in the historical career of cocaine.) Interestingly, when the meaning and context of

Steve's cocaine use were explored, he stated that when he didn't use cocaine he felt deeply "depressed," "overwhelmed," and "lost" about his life and relationships. This, along with Steve's continued use of cocaine, suggested that for him, focusing on cocaine use, feeling "depressed" and "dirty" about spending and wasting money on cocaine, and construing himself within a socially deviant cocaine addict role was in some ways preferable to focusing on more encompassing and disorganizing personal meanings that left him feeling "overwhelmed" and "lost." Simply stated, a constrained and socially deviant role as a "cocaine addict" was preferable to general disorganization and ambiguity.

Note that the very same functions may be served when people use prescribed and legal substances in the context of the psychiatric patient role. For example, Alice described herself as feeling "anxious" most of the time, although she found it difficult to understand the origins or focus of these feelings. With great difficulty, she spoke of her concerns about the uncertainty of her future and conflicts in her family relationships, noting that when she contemplated these issues she felt "lost," "frightened," and "paralyzed." She sought the services of a psychiatrist who told her that she "had a generalized anxiety disorder" and prescribed Xanax (an "anti-anxiety medication"). Alice reported feeling a sense of relief that "now I know what I have" and "security" related to being in the psychiatric patient role. Subsequently, when she began to feel "overwhelmed" as she discussed major conflicts and ambiguities in her life (feelings that continued to emerge even though she was taking the medication as prescribed), Alice found some "relief" by taking her pills from her purse, rolling them between her fingers, and thinking about her medication schedule.

Agency and the Tacit Dimension of Substance Use

As implied by the previous examples, an evolutionary constructivist perspective views the use of any substance as strategic action within the context of personal meanings and social contexts/roles. Within this framework, ostensible puzzles and paradoxes related to personal agency and substance use—such as a person continuing to use substances despite explicitly expressing a desire to stop, using substances without apparent volition or plans, and reporting a lack of understanding or control over substance use—can be largely understood by exploring the role of tacit processes and the complex strategic functions of substance use. In this context, in spite of ostensible "lack of control" or understanding, a person using substances is seen as an agent making choices who "knows more than he can tell." As Polanyi (1966) pointed out, when we engage in many if not most complex human skills and activities—driving a car, recognizing human faces, speaking a language, and so forth—we are always following a host of tacit principles that we are not aware of or that we do not fully articulate. However, despite a lack of explicit awareness about the processes guiding our performances, we remain active agents engaging in purposeful and rule-governed action. For example, even though I may not be fully aware of all the tacit principles that I am following when I drive a car, I am still the driver making multiple momentary choices guided by my largely tacit or inarticulate knowledge. Similarly when a person reports "I don't know why I use" substances or "I just ended up using" without apparent volition or plan, an evolutionary constructivist perspective assumes that he or she is still making choices and "knows more than he or she can tell." Along these lines (as noted earlier), regular drug users who initially describe their substance use as "happening" without forethought or control, commonly acknowledge making momentary choices to pursue and use a drug in anticipation of various drug-related consequences.

The Evolution of Substance-Centered Selves in Social Contexts

An evolutionary constructivist perspective highlights relationships between substance use, self-organization, and social constructions/roles. Substance use both influences and is influenced by a person's patterns of self-organization, which are constrained and influenced by substance-related social constructions/roles. Substance-centered self-organizations may be adopted or imposed, or they may evolve as the "result of human action but not human design" in social contexts, or both. In this regard, it is important to note that self- or other labeled "addicts" are not the only people who may operate within substance-centered self-organizations. It is not uncommon, for example, for people in certain psychiatric patient roles to choose or be forced to make the use of substances such as lithium, Ritalin, or other psychiatric drugs a focal point of their self-organizations and their lives.

Owing to the unintended and unforeseen (personal and social) consequences of choices and actions, the influence of tacit constructive processes, and the unpredictable influence of social constraints and contexts, people may reorganize themselves and their lives around the use of psychoactive substances without fully understanding or being explicitly aware of how or why they are doing so. In this way, they participate in the evolution of their own substance-centered self-organization while being influenced by the constraints of their social contexts (e.g., traditions, relationships, laws, cultural narratives about substances, etc.). For example, Sam, who construed himself as a "cocaine addict," described the development of his cocaine-centered identity as the unforeseen consequence of his choices and his social contexts. He described his initial use of cocaine as a response to the "shattering" of his personal dreams for the future, not "fitting in" to his social world, and feeling "alienated" from his family. In contrast, when he used cocaine with new acquaintances, he felt at ease and self-confident. However, in keeping with extant social constructions regarding cocaine users as "low-lifes" and the constrained social pathways available to those who used an illegal substance, as he used cocaine more frequently he began to feel further alienated from people who did not use the substance. Sam's emerging view of himself as a "low-life addict" was further elaborated when his family pressured him to participate in a drug rehabilitation program that aimed to have him accept his "disease" as a lifelong defining characteristic. Thus, despite not having planned to adopt an "addicted identity," Sam's choices and the constraints of his social contexts both contributed to the evolution of drug-centered aspects of self. His personal evolution was a function of the interaction of his strategic efforts to address self-disorganization and existential challenges and the constraints of a variety of social contexts (e.g., family and peer relationships, treatment programs, legal prohibitions) and social constructions (e.g., cocaine users as "low-lifes"; disease narratives).

SELECTED IMPLICATIONS OF CONSTRUCTIVIST PERSPECTIVES ON SUBSTANCE USE

Reconstruing substance use from a constructivist perspective obviously leads to different conceptual pathways than those generated by currently dominant disorder frameworks (see Table 6-1). Some of the major implications of reconstruing substance use from a constructivist perspective are highlighted next.

Going Beyond Categorical/Compartmentalized Thinking About Substances and People Who Use Them

As noted earlier, disorder perspectives tend to construe substances within ostensibly objective categories and to minimize or ignore the impact of social constructions and meanings on our experiences with and relationships to substances. As discussed earlier, this objectivist compartmentalization and segregation of substances lead to numerous theoretical and practical inconsistencies. In contrast, constructivist perspectives assert that substance-related distinctions and classifications are socially constructed for a variety of strategic purposes. This suggests that we should critically reflect on the frequently discrepant meanings we connect to substances and integrate and reorganize our relationships to substances. Thus, rather than promoting some substances (e.g., psychiatric medications) while prohibiting and discouraging the use of others, we should adopt a more conceptually and practically evenhanded approach. For example, in clinical work we should not assume that the use of certain substances is problematic while the use of others is therapeutic. Instead, we should invite clients to reflect on how their use of all sorts of substances is related to their construction of viable meanings, self-organizations, and actions.

Re-Meaning and Recontextualizing Substance Use: Beyond the Reification of Drug Disorders

A disorder approach assumes that drug disorders are objectively defined medical or quasi-medical conditions. This way of construing substance use invites us to locate and reify human problems related to substances within a person and/or

Table 6-1. Summary of Contrasting Assumptions and Consequences of Constructivist and Disorder Approaches

Issue	Disorder Perspectives	Constructivist Perspectives
What is a "drug"?	• Compartmentalize substances ostensibly based on their psychological and physical properties • There are certain substances, known as drugs, that are dangerous and addictive	• Distinctions between substances (drug versus nondrug; good drugs versus bad drugs, etc.) are socially constructed • Substances are construed/classified as "drugs" and as belonging to varied subcategories of drugs for strategic purposes
Use versus abuse and "drug disorders"	• Drug disorders as objectively defined medical or quasi-medical conditions that occur in individuals • Relapsing conditions characterized by lost or impaired control over drug use, and a variety of behavioral and psychological deficiencies/dysfunctions (e.g., denial, cognitive distortions, skill deficiencies)	• One person's meat is another person's poison • "Drug abuse" is a label applied to people who use substances in ways that violate extant social rules or roles • Substance-centered self-organizations may be adopted, be imposed, or evolve as the result of human action but not human design in social contexts
The powers of "drugs" and "drug addicts"	• Particular drugs cause specific short-term bio-chemical changes that, in turn, cause specific psychological experiences and behaviors • Drug addicts suffer from lost or impaired control over drug use • Drug use is triggered or caused by cravings or environmental events • Due to the power of triggers and drugs and the diminished or absent control of drug users, drug addicts are at continued risk of relapse	• People actively participate in the co-construction of their own subjective drug experiences • Experiences with substances are largely a function of the personal and social meanings related to substances • People choose to use or not use substances as part of their efforts to maintain viable self-organizations and meanings • Personal choices about substances are influenced by tacit processes as well as social constructions and constraints

continued

223

Table 6-1 continued

Issue	Disorder Perspectives	Constructivist Perspectives
Social control and policy	• Because addictive drugs have the power to overwhelm personal control and cause drug disorders, legal controls are necessary to stop, minimize, or control use • Substance abuse is both a health and a criminal problem necessitating a dual-focused quasi-medical and legal "war on drugs"	• Legal prohibitions are based on culturally relative, historically changeable, and highly inconsistent social constructions • Social constructions and policies regarding so-called addictive drugs serve strategic social functions, such as scapegoating and the justification of coercion
Therapy/counseling	• Voluntary or mandated (i.e., coerced) treatment of drug disorders and drug addicts • Goal of abstinence from drug use and acceptance of drug addict identity • Focus on identifying triggers and high-risk situations and correcting or changing deficiencies or dysfunctions of drug abusers • Confrontational (to break through denial or cognitive distortion) and didactic (e.g., teaching "healthy" ways of coping)	• Voluntary relationship with focus on dialogs about substance use • Mandated therapy for substance abuse is essentially the forcible imposition of particular social constructions and roles • Goals collaboratively determined through dialog • Explore substance use within a person's meaning system and social context • Focus on understanding relationship between substance use and viability of meaning systems, and considering alternatives. • Invitational, collaborative, and exploratory

the substance itself and directs attention from the subjective and social nature of substance use problems (Szasz, 1985, 1992; Winslade & Smith, 1997). Viewing substance use as a consequence of a "disorder" or depersonalized triggers, or both, thus demeans and depersonalizes the use of substances. In contrast, constructivist perspectives demonstrate that evaluative judgments about substance use are a dynamic function of meanings and social contexts. Constructivist perspectives acknowledge that some individuals may develop lives and self-organizations that revolve around the use of particular substances. However, such self-organizations are not viewed as *disorders*. Instead, they are viewed as reflections of human efforts to construct *order* and meaning. As such, substance-centered self-organizations may be adopted or imposed (e.g., by family, the legal system, etc.), or they may evolve as the result of human action but not human design in social contexts.

Taken together, the deconstruction of drug-related categories and drug disorders invite a reconstruction of social policies (see discussion that follows) and professional discourse about substances, as well as a conceptual integration of areas that heretofore have been treated as distinct (e.g., drugs of abuse versus medications). They also suggest that therapists and policy makers should critically examine how their actions and drug-related social constructions may help generate "drug abuse" problems.

Reconstruing the Powers of Drugs and Drug Users

A constructivist approach consistently assumes that people actively participate in the co-construction of their own subjective drug experiences (as a function of the personal and social meanings that they bring to bear on those substances). Moreover, people are seen as choosing to use or not use substances as part of their efforts to maintain viable self-organizations and meanings. This suggests that we should not relate to substance users as weakened victims who must continually guard against internal and external risks. Instead, we should consistently construe substance users as engaging in strategic action influenced by tacit processes and social constructions.

Reconstruing Social Policies Regarding Substances

Because disorder perspectives assume that addictive drugs have the inherent power to overwhelm personal control and cause drug disorders, these approaches usually advocate social controls as necessary to stop, minimize, or control use. From this traditional perspective, substance abuse is both a health and a criminal problem, necessitating a dual-focused quasi-medical and legal war on drugs. In contrast, a constructivist approach asserts that legal and medical controls and interventions related to the use of particular substances are based on culturally relative, historically changeable, and highly inconsistent social constructions.

Moreover, such social constructions and policies are seen as serving strategic social functions such as scapegoating and the justification of coercion.

By undermining the basic disorder assumptions underlying current legal classifications, prohibitions, and medical controls of various substances, a constructivist approach invites critical reflection and reconstruction of disorder-based social policies. For example, current laws and policies prohibiting the use of certain substances and punishing those who use them, supervising the use of other substances (e.g., in the context of medical relationships and prescriptions), and accepting or promoting the use of other substances are seen as strategic social enactments that forcibly impose particular social constructions. Rather than debating and addressing the inherent powers of substances and the social costs of "drug abuse," we should be closely examining the nature and impact of the social constructions that we bring to bear on substances and debating how we want to address social conflicts and the scope of human freedom in a pluralistic society. We should not use substances as a forum for enacting social conflicts and moral dramas. Along these lines, we should not persecute people who use certain substances or empower others (e.g., physicians) to control access to substances.

Reconstruing Psychotherapy or Counseling Regarding Substance Use

Disorder perspectives advocate voluntary or mandated (i.e., coerced) treatment or "self-help" group participation for drug abusers that aims to foster abstinence from the use of particular drugs and acceptance of a drug addict identity. Disorder-based professional treatments and self-help programs are often confrontational or didactic, focusing largely on identifying and avoiding the ostensible triggers of substance use in the present and correcting or changing the perceived deficiencies or dysfunctions of drug abusers. In contrast, a constructivist approach suggests that mandated therapy for substance abuse is essentially the forcible imposition of particular social constructions and roles. From this perspective, any helping relationship should be a voluntary relationship in which goals are collaboratively determined through dialog. In addition, because constructivist perspectives suggest that substance use is part of fallible solutions to complex constructive difficulties, as well as highlight the limitations of professionals' knowledge, clinicians should be *invitational* rather than *confrontational*, approaching clients with respect for the potential constructive value of substance use. A respectful attitude toward clients (and humility regarding clinicians' knowledge) should be balanced with invitations to critically reflect on relationships between substance use and the construction of viable meanings, self-organizations, and actions within a person's social contexts and to consider potentially viable alternatives. In this respectful and critical exploration, helpers should be critically self-reflective about how social constructions have influenced their own relationships to various substances and the people who use them and how they themselves participate in the social construction of drug problems (collectively and with individual clients).

Broaden and Deepen the Focus on the Relationships Between Substance Use, Self-Organization, and Social Contexts

Constructivist perspectives suggest that we should further explore relationships between substance use and patterns of self-organization in social contexts. Conventional clinical and research approaches to substance use problems often do not directly address self-organization or do so in a very constrained way that is disconnected from the social context. For example, cognitive behavioral/coping approaches attempt to enhance self-efficacy related to abstinence from drug use and situational coping whereas disease models promote acceptance of an "addict" identity. In contrast, constructivist perspectives (particularly evolutionary constructivism) invite collaborative explorations of relationships between substance use and broader patterns of self-organization with the possible goal of facilitating the development of more viable non–substance-centered selves. This approach suggests that such explorations should be attentive to the ways in which social contexts (e.g., relationships with family, therapists and others; social constructions about substance users; and social constraints on substance use) affect the roles/meanings of substance use in a person's evolving self-organization.

A focus on the socially constrained evolution of self-organization as it relates to substance use is seen as a particularly promising focus for research and clinical work. In addition to potentiating a deeper understanding of the meanings and functions of substance use, such a focus may also foster an integration of substance use with other aspects of human action and experience. For example, research from a disorder framework has commonly noted the "comorbidity" of substance abuse, "depression," and "personality disorders." The current framework suggests that socially constrained self-organizational processes may provide a higher-order integrative construct linking these compartmentalized areas of human actions and experience. For example, substance use, depressive experience, and personality styles can be understood not as distinct disorder entities, but as meaningful reflections of how a person organizes his or her experiences of self in social contexts (including both individual relationships and broader sociocultural contexts). Several current approaches to substance-related research and practice seem promising along these lines, including Winslade and Smith's (1997) narrative approach to alcohol counseling; Klion (1993) and Klion and Pfenninger's (1997) applications of personal construct theory; Jaffe and Burrell's (1997) Substance Expectations Therapy (SET), which, in part, invites clients to explore and compare substance and non–substance-related narrative conceptions of current and future selves; and applications of identity theory to addiction (e.g., Biernacki, 1986; Kellogg, 1993).

Proactive Orientation

A constructivist approach invites further exploration of relationships between anticipatory processes and substance use patterns, including and going beyond the cognitive-behavioral focus on substance-related expectations and self-efficacy. In particular, it highlights the role of shifts in anticipatory activities and a person's broader constructions about the future, and suggests that rather than view substance use from a reactive vantage point (e.g., as triggered behavior) we should construe it in the context of proactive constructive processes.

Such a proactive orientation suggests that clinicians should invite individuals attempting to change drug use patterns to expand their temporal focus in a variety of ways, including contemplating the short- and long-term future when making decisions about drug use; exploring the influence of drug-related expectations on substance use and experience; and constructing alternative non–drug-centered anticipatory self-narratives.

SUMMARY AND CONCLUDING COMMENTS

This chapter described and briefly critiqued the major assumptions of the disorder framework guiding conventional approaches to substance use. The disorder approach to substance use was juxtaposed to constructivist perspectives. It was argued that disorder approaches tend to overestimate the inherent powers of substances while underestimating the powers of substance users. Such approaches also tend to reify and objectify drug-related problems while demeaning, depersonalizing, and decontextualizing substance use. In contrast, constructivist perspectives on substance use construe such use as meaningful and strategic action in social contexts. These perspectives argue that "substance abuse" is a label reflecting social conflicts and extant substance-related social constructions. Reconstruing substance use from a constructivist point of view has numerous implications for theory, research, and practice. Most notably, such approaches invite a critical reconstruction of conventional social policies related to substances and noncoercive, integrative, and exploratory relationships to substances and the people who use them.

NOTES

1. Interestingly, we do not usually refer to someone as "using" a prescribed medication, but instead say they are "taking a medication." This appears to reflect our society's ambivalence about autonomy. See Szasz (1985) for a fuller discussion of this ambivalence as it relates to drug use.

2. Szasz does not label his work as "social constructionist," and aspects of his overall framework might not be consistent with social constructionist assumptions. However, his analysis of "addiction" and drugs is generally quite consonant with such an approach.

REFERENCES

Alcoholics Anonymous. (1955). *Alcoholics anonymous*. New York: World Services.

American Psychiatric Association. (1994). *Diagnostic and statistical manual of mental disorders: DSM-IV*. Washington, DC : American Psychiatric Association.

Beck, A. T., Wright, F., Newman, C., & Liese, B. (1993). *Cognitive therapy of substance abuse*. New York: Guilford Press.

Biernacki, P. (1986). *Pathways from heroin addiction: Recovery without treatment*. Philadelphia: Temple University Press.

Breggin, P. (1998). *Talking back to Ritalin: What doctors aren't telling you about stimulants for children*. Monroe, ME: Common Courage Press.

Burrell, M. J. (1987). Cognitive psychology, epistemology, and psychotherapy: A motor-evolutionary perspective. *Psychotherapy, 24*(2), 225–232.

Burrell, M. J. & Jaffe, A. J. (1995). *Constructivism, expectations, and addiction*. Paper presented at the International Congress on Personal Construct Psychology, Barcelona, Spain.

Burrell, M., & Jaffe, A. (1999). Personal meaning, drug use, and addiction: An evolutionary constructivist perspective. *Journal of Constructivist Psychology, 12*(1), 41–63.

Carroll, K. (1998). *Cognitive-behavioral coping skills treatment for cocaine dependence*. New Haven, CT: Yale University Psychotherapy Development Center, Training Series No. 2.

Chiari, G., & Nuzzo, M. L. (1996). Psychological constructivisms: A metatheoretical differentiation. *Journal of Constructivist Psychology, 9*(3), 163–184.

Critchlow, B. (1986). The powers of John Barleycorn: Beliefs about the effects of alcohol on social behavior. *American Psychologist, 41*, 751–764.

Crits-Christoph, P., Siqueland, L., Blaine, J., Frank, A., Luborsky, L., Onken, L., Muenz, L., Thase, M., Weiss, R., Gastfriend, D., Woody, G., Barber, J., Butler, S., Daley, D., Salloum, I., Bishop, S., Najavits, L., Lis, J., Mercer, D., Griffin, M., Moras, K., & Beck, A. T. (1999). Psychosocial treatments for cocaine dependence: National Institute on Drug Abuse Collaborative Cocaine Treatment Study. *Archives of General Psychiatry. 57*(6), 493–502.

DiClemente, C. C., Fairhurst, S. K., & Piotrowski, N. A. (1995). Self efficacy and addictive behaviors. In J.E. Maddux (Ed.), *Self-efficacy, adaptation, and adjustment: Theory, research, and application*. New York: Plenum Press.

Epstein, E. K. (1996). Socially constructing substance use and abuse: Towards a greater diversity and humanity in the theories and practices of drug treatment. *Journal of Systemic Therapies, 15*(2), 1–12.

Erickson, P. G., Adlai, E. M., Murray, G. F., & Smart, R. G. (1987). *The steel drug: Cocaine in perspective*. Lexington, MA: D. C. Heath.

Erickson, P. G., & Alexander, B. K. (1998). Cocaine and addictive liability. In J. Schaler (Ed.), *Drugs: Should we legalize, decriminalize, or deregulate?* New York: Prometheus Books.

Erickson, P. G., & Weber, T. R. (1998). Cocaine careers, control, and consequences: Results from a Canadian Study. In J. Schaler (Ed.), *Drugs: Should we legalize, decriminalize, or deregulate?* New York: Prometheus Books.

Feingold, A., Carroll, K., Johnson, D., & Rounsaville, B. (1998). Efficacy of psychosocial interventions with substance abusers: A meta-analysis. Unpublished manuscript, Yale University.

Fingarette, H. (1988). *Heavy drinking: The myth of alcoholism as a disease.* Berkeley: University of California Press.

Fingarette, H. (1991). Alcoholism: The mythical disease. In D. J. Pittman et al. (Eds.), *Society, culture, and drinking patterns reexamined* (pp. 417–438). Alcohol, culture, and social control monograph series. New Brunswick, NJ: Rutgers Center of Alcohol Studies.

Fisher, S., & Greenberg, R. P. (Eds.). (1997). *From placebo to panacea: Putting psychiatric drugs to the test.* New York: Wiley.

Gallup Poll News Service. (1992). Princeton, NJ, February 7.

Gergen, K. (1985). *The social construction of the person.* New York: Springer-Verlag.

Gergen, K. (1991). *The saturated self: Dilemmas of identity in contemporary life.* New York: Basic Books.

Gergen, M. M., & Gergen, K. J. (1996). Addiction in a polyvocal world. *Journal of Systemic Therapies, 15*(2), 77–81.

Goldman, M., Brown, S. A., & Christiansen, B. A. (1987). Expectancy theory: Thinking about drinking. In H. T. Blane & K. E. Leonard (Eds.), *Psychological theories of drinking and alcoholism* (pp. 181–220). New York: Guilford Press.

Guidano, V. F. (1987). *Complexity of the self: A developmental approach to psychopathology and therapy.* New York: Guilford Press.

Guidano, V. F. (1991). *The self in process: Toward a post-rationalist cognitive therapy.* New York: Guilford Press.

Hayek, F. A. (1978). *New studies in philosophy, politics, economics, and the history of ideas.* Chicago: University of Chicago Press.

Heath, D. B. (1998). The War on Drugs as a metaphor in American culture. In J. Schaler (Ed.), *Drugs: Should we legalize, decriminalize, or deregulate?* New York: Prometheus Books.

Herwig-Lempp, J. (1996). Drug addiction, the systemic approach, and the concept of "acceptance." *Journal of Systemic Therapies,* 15(2), 24–35.

Hopson, R. E. (1993). A thematic analysis of the addictive experience: Implications for psychotherapy. *Psychotherapy,* 30(3), 481–494.

Jaffe, A. J. (1992). Cognitive factors associated with cocaine abuse and its treatment: An analysis of expectancies of use. In H. Kleber & T. Kosten (Eds.), *Clinical handbook on cocaine abuse: Theory, research and treatment* (pp.128–150). New York: Guilford Press.

Jaffe, A. J., & Burrell, M. J. (1997). *Substance Expectations Therapy (SET): Expectations and personal meaning in the treatment of substance abuse.* Unpublished psychotherapy treatment manual. New Haven, CT: Yale University.

Jaffe, A. J., & Kilbey, M. M. (1994). The Cocaine Expectancy Questionnaire (CEQ): Its construction and predictive utility. *Psychological Assessment,* 18–26.

Joint Committee to Study the Definition and Criteria for the Diagnosis of Alcoholism of the National Council on Alcoholism and Drug Dependence and the American Society of Addiction Medicine. (1990). Definition of alcoholism. February 3.

Kadden, R., Carroll, K., Donovan, D., Cooney, N., Monti, P., Abrams, D., Litt, M., & Hester, R. (1995). *Cognitive-behavioral coping skills therapy manual: A clinical research guide for therapists treating individuals with alcohol abuse and dependence.* Washington, DC: National Institute of Alcohol Abuse and Alcoholism Project MATCH Monograph Series, Vol. 3. Washington, DC: National Institute of Alcohol Abuse and Alcoholism.

Kellogg, S. (1993). Identity and recovery. *Psychotherapy, 30*(2), 235–244.

Kirsch, I. (1990). *Changing expectations: A key to effective psychotherapy.* Belmont, CA: Brooks/Cole.

Klion, R.E. (1993). Chemical dependency: A personal construct theory approach. In L. Leitner & G. Dunnett (Eds.), *Critical issues in personal construct psychotherapy* (pp. 279–302). Malabar, FL: Krieger.

Klion, R. E., & Pfenninger, D. T. (1997) Personal construct psychotherapy of addictions. *Journal of Substance Abuse Treatment, 14*(1), 37–43.

Lapp, W. M., Collins, R. L., Zywiak, W. H., & Izzo, C. V. (1994). Psychopharmacological effects of alcohol on time perception: The extended balanced placebo design. *Journal of Studies on Alcohol, 55*(1), 96–112.

Leigh, B. C. (1989). In search of the seven dwarves: Issues of measurement and meaning in alcohol expectancy research. *Psychological Bulletin, 105,* 361–373.

Light, A. B., & Torrance, E. G. (1929). Opiate addiction IV: The effects of abrupt withdrawal followed by readministration of morphine in human addicts, with special reference to the composition of the blood, the circulation, and the metabolism. *Archives of Internal Medicine, 44*(1), 1–16. As cited in S. Peele (1985). *The meaning of addiction: Compulsive experience and its interpretation.* Lexington, MA: Lexington Books.

Lyddon, W. J. (1992). Constructivist psychology: A heuristic framework. *Journal of Mind and Behavior, 13*(1), 89–107.

Lyddon, W. J. (1995). Cognitive therapy and theories of knowing: A social constructionist view. *Journal of Counseling & Development, 73*(6), 579–585.

MacAndrew, C., & Edgerton, B. (1969). *Drunken comportment: A social explanation.* Chicago: Aldine.

Mahoney, M. J. (1991). *Human change processes: The scientific foundations of psychotherapy.* New York: Basic Books.

Mahoney, M. J., & Moes, A. (1997). Complexity and psychotherapy: Promising dialogues and practical issues. In F. Masterpasqua et al. (Eds.), *The psychological meaning of chaos: Translating theory into practice* (pp. 177–198). Washington, DC: American Psychological Association.

Marlatt, G. A., Demming, B., & Reid, J. B. (1973). Loss of control drinking in alcoholics: An experimental analogue. *Journal of Abnormal Psychology, 81,* 223–241.

Marlatt, G. A., & Gordon, J. R. (Eds). (1985). *Relapse prevention: Maintenance strategies in the treatment of addictive behaviors.* New York: Guilford Press.

Musto, D. G. (1973). *The American disease: Origins of narcotic control.* New Haven, CT: Yale University Press.

Narcotics Anonymous. (1983). *Narcotics anonymous.*

National Institute of Drug Abuse. (1998). Media advisory, April 8.

Neimeyer, R. A. (1993). An appraisal of constructivist psychotherapies. *Journal of Consulting and Clinical Psychology, 61*, 221–234.

Neimeyer, R. A., & Mahoney, M. J. (Eds.). (1995). *Constructivism in psychotherapy.* Washington, DC: American Psychological Association.

New Yorker Magazine. (1998). Saying yes to drugs. *New Yorker,* April.

Peele, S. (1989). *Diseasing of America: Addiction treatment out of control.* Lexington, MA: Lexington Books.

Peele, S. (1997). Bait and switch in Project Match: What NIAAA research actually shows about alcohol treatment. *PsychNews International, 2*(3).

Polanyi, M. (1966). *The tacit dimension.* New York: Doubleday.

Project MATCH Research Group. (1997). Matching alcoholism treatments to client heterogeneity: Project MATCH posttreatment drinking outcomes. *Journal of Studies on Alcohol, 58,* 7–29.

Robins, L., Helzer, J., Hesselbrock, M., & Wish, E. (1998). Vietnam veterans three years after Vietnam: How our study changed our view of heroin. In J. Schaler (Ed.), *Drugs: Should we legalize, decriminalize, or deregulate?* New York: Prometheus Books.

Roman, P. M., & Blum, T. C. (1997). National treatment center study. Athens, GA: Institute for Behavioral Research, University of Georgia.

Schaler, J. (Ed.). (1998). *Drugs: Should we legalize, decriminalize, or deregulate?* New York: Prometheus Books.

Scheibe, K. E. (1994). Cocaine careers: Historical and individual constructions. In T. R. Sarbin & J. I. Kitsuse (Eds.), *Constructing the social: Inquiries in social construction series* (pp. 195–212). Thousand Oaks, CA: Sage.

Stares, P. B. (1996). *Global habit: the drug problem in a borderless world.* Washington, DC: Brookings Institution.

Substance Abuse and Mental Health Services Administration. (1997). Preliminary results from the 1996 National Household Survey on drug abuse. Rockville, MD: U.S. Department of Health and Human Services.

Szasz, T. (1985). *Ceremonial chemistry: The ritual persecution of drugs, addicts, and pushers.* Holmes Beach, FL: Learning Publications.

Szasz, T. (1992). *Our right to drugs: The case for a free market.* New York: Praeger.

Trebach, A., & Zeese, K. (1990). *Drug prohibition and the conscience of nations.* Washington, DC: Drug Policy Foundation.

Weil, A., & Rosen, W. (1993). *From chocolate to morphine. Everything you need to know about mind-altering drugs.* New York: Houghton Mifflin.

Willutzki, U., & Weisner, M. (1996). Segregation or cooperation: A social constructivist perspective on drug use and drug work. *Journal of Systemic Therapies, 15*(2), 48–66.

Winslade, J., & Smith, L. (1997). Countering alcoholic narratives. In G. Monk, J. Winslade, K. Crockett, & D. Epton (Eds.), *Narrative therapy in practice.* San Francisco: Jossey-Bass.

Zinberg, N. E. (1984). *Drug, set and setting: The basis for controlled intoxicant use.* New Haven, CT: Yale University Press.

Chapter 7

The Poetic Construction of AD/HD: A Diagnostic Fable

James C. Mancuso
Glenn A. Yelich
Theodore R. Sarbin

In this chapter, we examine the traditional procedure of diagnosing "mental disorders" in order to reframe the diagnostic process as the creation and the telling of a narrative. Our reframing emanates from a strategy designed to demonstrate that traditional psychiatric diagnoses are social constructions that, under the guise of medical practice, serve extrascientific purposes. On this base, we advance our claim that those who have constructed the diagnosis of *attention deficit/hyperactivity disorder* (AD/HD) are engaged, fundamentally, in a moral enterprise.

From all indications, millions of parents and other caretakers have had to guide the development of a child who appears to meet such official diagnostic criteria as "Often does not follow through on instructions and fails to finish school work, chores, or duties in the workplace (not due to oppositional behavior or failure to understand instructions)" (American Psychiatric Association [APA], 1994, p. 84). Observing such a child, a diagnosing clinician can deduce that the child regularly meets other criteria, such as "fails to give close attention to details," "has difficulty sustaining attention in tasks," "often does not seem to listen when spoken to directly," "often avoids, dislikes, or is reluctant to engage in tasks that would require sustained mental effort," "is often easily distracted by extraneous stimuli,"and "is often forgetful in daily activities" (pp. 83–84). Ignoring the medically inspired deductive leaps in the constructive process that influenced his or her data collection, the practitioner makes an even more daring deductive leap and affixes to the child the label *AD/HD*. In short, from the fact that the child had engaged in behavior that is unwanted by significant persons, the clinician infers the presence of a "disordered mental process." In this sequence of events, both the clinician and the child become storied figures in a diagnosis narrative.

It is important to note that numerous professional publications question the very criteria employed to place the target child into the category AD/HD (e.g., see Maag & Reid, 1994; Verhulst & Achenbach, 1995). Informed professionals and laypersons can conclude that the category represents a jerry-built amalgam serving the purpose of justifying pseudomedical intercession, including the administration of potentially damaging drugs; so that "Children appear to be more 'attentive' at home and in the classroom, but objective studies indicate that [the administration of drugs] had virtually no impact on the learning process" (McGuinness, 1989, p. 155).

From an alternative framework, one can propose that the candidate for the AD/HD diagnosis has not yet developed a system of self-defining constructs that would allow him or her to create socially acceptable behavior-guiding anticipatory self-narratives. Holding that medical diagnostic narratives are superfluous and misleading, we, in this chapter, advocate this alternative formulation.

We begin from the postulate that all persons use "goodness of story" as the major truth test in the shared epistemology that guides the knowledge acquisition processes of a community (Freyd, 1983; Griffiths & Mullins, 1972). We then propose that a medical diagnosis formulation is the result of an effort to compose a good narrative. Thereupon, we evaluate the success of using the medical diagnosis narrative as a framework for understanding people who do not adopt socially prescribed anticipatory self-narratives to guide their role enactments in their academic and work ecologies.

In the final section of this chapter, we develop the constructivist view that all person conduct—that of the target of the explanation as well as that of the person attempting the explanation—entails the on-the-spot creation of forward-reaching narratives (anticipatory constructions) that must be validated by the continued flow of ecologically produced inputs.

NARRATIVE AS A GUIDE TO CONDUCT

Very early in life, persons—including future scientists—begin to master a narrative grammar from which they construct the anticipatory narratives that then serve to frame the flow of inputs from the distal and proximal ecologies. The course of the development of the epistemic structures that define the narrative grammar has been addressed by a number of writers (see, e.g., Britton & Pellegrini, 1990; Mancuso, 1986; Mancuso & Sarbin, 1983; Sarbin, 1986; Stein & Glenn, 1979; Sutton-Smith, 1986). Further, as persons adopt the shared, implicit epistemology of the participants in their human community, they accept goodness of narrative as a truth test. ("Goodness" = the condition of being well-formed.)

Narrative grammarians (e.g., Mandler, 1984; Thorndyke, 1977) generally agree that an emplotted story (material in parentheses, following) entails the use of six "parts of speech," as follows:

1. The setting (e.g., Mr. Malfetta attempts to instruct children in his classroom in the use of algorithms that facilitate the adding of numbers);

2. The initiating event; placing the protagonist in a position to react, thus creating a cause (Gabriel engages in unwanted, unrelated behavior each time that the teacher instructs the children to complete the practice items);

3. Goal setting, describing internally set goals and ascribed internal experiences (Mr. Malfetta experiences self-invalidation [disappointment] when he fails to direct Gabriel successfully, and he seeks professional help so he can approach his goal);

4. Descriptions of goal-directed conduct and an outcome of the conduct (A diagnostician classifies Gabriel as an exemplar of the AD/HD category, the boy is placed on a drug regimen, and he shows less unwanted behavior);

5. An ending that locates the outcome in a broader context (Parents and other caretakers are satisfied that Gabriel has been helped);

6. A global ending, particularly if the episode is to be coalesced with other episodes (Data on Gabriel's course of drug ingestion, his classroom conduct, and his performance on other assessments are added to a data bank whose contents, it is hoped, will help to solve the riddles of AD/HD).

Persons who use the social construction that allows the distinction between random text and emplotted story have learned that a "good" story contains, in proper sequence, these six elements (see Mancuso, 1986). A narrator must assure his or her audience that each element of the story can be regarded as credible, within the context of the story.

Sharing this story-building propensity with other humans, builders of diagnostic schemes construct diagnostic narratives, and then tell those narratives, hoping to gain colleagues' agreement that the stories are well-formed stories. When the story plot describes conduct that can be taken as diagnostic signs—symptoms—of a "mental disorder," when a treatment is regarded as having targeted the cause of the symptoms, and when the observed outcome of the treatment repeatedly corresponds to (is not discrepant from) the expected outcome feature of the anticipatory narrative, the observer may conclude that the diagnostic narrative has gained validity. One can say, quite succinctly, that the vaunted hypothetico-deductive methods that lead to repeatedly observed confirmations of cause-and-effect relationships employ *good narrative* as a criterion for testing validity. In the story of Gabriel, outlined earlier, the level of the validity of the narrative is raised by the backward linking of the effect (the reduction of unwanted behaviors) to the drug treatment as cause.

ASSESSING THE FOUNDING AND THE SUCCESS OF AD/HD DIAGNOSIS NARRATIVE

Writers frequently credit G. F. Still (1902) with having produced the first systematic study of children who could be labeled AD/HD. Cross comparisons of Still's founding narrative and the contemporary AD/HD diagnostic narrative illuminates the narrative quality of diagnostic practice.

Establishing the Setting of the AD/HD Diagnosis Narrative

In any well-constructed narrative, the presence of a threat—a dragon, an evil knight, loss of good fortune, a plague, pirates, and so on—provides the setting for the protagonist's motivation and action. Still (1902) introduced a plausible setting element into a diagnosis narrative: "there are children in whom moral control falls so far below this standard that the question may well be raised whether in such cases the defect is not the manifestation of some morbid psychical condition" (p. 1009).

Using his loose category, *moral conduct*, Still believed that children showed "defective moral control" (p. 1009) by engaging in behaviors showing, among other characteristics, "(1) passionateness; (2) spitefulness-cruelty; . . . (8) sexual immorality; and (9) viciousness" (p. 1009). Still warned that, "The serious danger which these children constitute both to themselves and to society calls, I think, for more active recognition" (p. 1167). Misfortune impends; for, "if not protected from themselves . . . [they will] possibly be punished for their acts as criminals in spite of the evidence that their acts are the outcome of a mental state just as morbid as the more generally recognized imbecility or insanity" (p. 1167).

Modern, more mechanistically oriented scientists might show reluctance to follow Still in ascribing general moral functioning to morbidity. Instead, after observing conduct that Still would have taken to be indicative of *passionateness*, a modern diagnostician, using the Diagnostic and Statistical Manual, 4th edition (DSM-IV) as a guide, would speak of hyperactive-impulsive symptoms (APA, 1994, p. 84), or of "temper tantrums" (p. 80). Presaging contemporary AD/HD diagnosticians, Still (1902) claimed that "a notable feature in many of these cases of moral defect . . . is a quite abnormal incapacity for sustained attention" (p. 1166).

Still's (1902) efforts to call attention to the morbid condition underlying children's unwanted behavior echoes through up-to-date professional treatises (e.g., Barkley, 1997; Cantwell, 1996; Szatmari, Offord, &, Boyle, 1989) and popular texts (Hallowell & Ratey, 1994; *Time Magazine,* 1994) that apprise readers of the prevalence of the "mental disorder" AD/HD. Justified alarm might follow from the DSM-IV (APA, 1994) claim that the prevalence of AD/HD "is estimated at 3%–5% in school-age children" (p. 82). But then, one must also take into account Szatmari et al.'s (1989) review of 11 studies in which investigators found great inconsistencies in prevalence rates. The percentages of the studies' samples that could be classed as AD/HD ranged from 0.09% to 14.3%. Dykman, Ackerman, and Raney (1992) summarized 12 epidemiological studies. Reported incidence rates ranged from a high of 27.5% for a sample of second- and third-grade African American children in a midwestern town to a low of 1.72% for a sample of first- to sixth-grade female children attending school in New York City's Chinatown.

Goldstein (1996), providing "current facts" about AD/HD to workshop participants, conveniently cited a study that used a rating scale adapted to assess German teachers' ascribing to children the AD/HD "symptoms" as listed in DSM-IV. In that study the prevalence for AD/HD reached nearly 18% (Baumgaertel, Wolraich, & Dietrich, 1995). Barkley (1994) noted that estimates of prevalence of AD/HD hinges "on how one chooses to define AD/HD, the population studied, the geographic locale of the survey, and even the degree of agreement required among parents, teachers, and professionals. . . . Estimates vary between 1 and 20%" (pp. 56–57).

If concern over the pervasiveness of the disorder is to provide the setting for the AD/HD diagnosis narrative, why would the observed prevalence of the disorder depend on "the geographical locale of the survey"? A response to this question might begin by noting that members of specific cultures or specific socioeconomic classes are often confined to a geographical locus. Then the observation that representatives of different cultures construe different behaviors as symptoms of AD/HD points up the conclusion that the cross-cultural differences in assignment of the diagnosis depends on the cross-cultural differences in the construction of wanted and unwanted conduct (Gittleman, Mannuzza, Shenker, & Bonagura, 1985; Taylor, 1987).

Concomitantly, the differential assignment of the diagnosis to boys in contrast to girls has been a constant source of wonder to those who would warn us of an epidemic of a mental disorder that occurred more frequently in boys. Szatmari et al. (1989), in their analysis of 11 studies of rates of assigning the AD/HD diagnosis, found that the ratios of categorized males to females ranged from 8.3 to 1 to 1.6 to 1. Recently, however, this male-to-female discrepancy has raised concerns about the underdiagnosis of girls (see Greenblatt, 1994). Participants in a U.S. National Institutes of Mental Health (NIMH) study suggested that the underdiagnosis problem might be " . . . 'corrected' by using sex-specific thresholds related to degree of deviance from sex norms . . ." (Arnold, 1996, p. 559). By this simple measurement manipulation, the admission of more females to the AD/HD category would help to establish a suitably alarming setting element in the AD/HD narrative.

Barkley invoked medical metaphors to provide the crisis-laden setting for the action of protagonists in the AD/HD narrative: "The approach taken to the management of this disorder must be the same as is taken in the management of other chronic medical or psychiatric disabilities. I have frequently used the example of diabetes as a condition analogous to AD/HD . . ." (Barkley, 1997, p. 47). Using terms saturated with ambiguity—for example, findings *support or are consistent with, suggest, should be interpreted with some caution*—other scholars (Morgan,

Hynd, Riccio, & Hall, 1996) join the enterprise of identifying AD/HD as the malevolent entity in the setting of the diagnostic narrative. Diagnostic narratives depend on describing a "valid" entity in the setting feature of the story. In the modern scientific canon, validity is established by techniques adapted to epistemologies that specify mechanistically ordered cause-and-effect relationships. The debates are speciously settled by reliance on the rhetoric of scientism: mathematical and statistical terms that evoke images of empiricism, causal relationships, and scientific procedures.

Following their extensive review of such studies, Dykman et al. (1992) state that they had found 42 different scales that had been used to diagnose AD/HD. They summarize 16 validity studies of scales that are variants of the ubiquitous Connors Rating Scales (Connors, 1989a, 1989b). Most commonly, the validity of the ratings on the Connors Scales was assessed by comparing those ratings to raters' responses to other scales, to ratings made during direct observations of behavior, or to the target person's performance on simple tasks that the investigators had assumed to be measures of attention. In that the users of the Connors Scales can assign the diagnosis on the basis of the person's deviation from the scores of an assumed universal average, one would safely conclude that when ratings—by either self or observer—indicate deviantly frequent enactment of certain unwanted behaviors, that person "has AD/HD."

Quite simply, alarm over the presence of AD/HD occurs when significant persons in the social ecology become aroused about persons who deviate from the modal behavior of the population being observed. The mechanist epistemological canon does not unequivocally indicate the presence of a special "mental disorder" labeled AD/HD. Armstrong (1996) may legitimately ask, "ADD: Does it really exist?" The title of his previously published book, *The Myth of the A.D.D. Child* (Armstrong, 1995), suggests his accord with McGuinness (1989) that, "two decades of research have not provided any support for the validity of ADD or ADDH . . ." (p. 151). In short, the tellers of the AD/HD diagnostic narrative have yet to provide a suitable setting for the story.

Initiating Action in an AD/HD Narrative:
The Protagonist's Motivation to Act

One can warily identify certain unwanted behaviors of some children as the event that initiates action in an AD/HD narrative. From the perspective of the diagnostic narrative, such behaviors are labeled symptoms.[1] DSM-IV specifies two broad classes of symptoms: (1) inattention (nine symptoms), and (2) hyperactivity-impulsivity (nine symptoms). If an observer can determine that a person has shown six or more of the symptoms of inattention for at least 6 months, that person is diagnosed *attention deficit/hyperactivity disorder, predominantly inattentive type*. If he or she shows six or more of the symptoms of hyperactivity or impulsivity for at least 6 months, that person can be diagnosed *attention deficit/hyperactivity disorder, predominantly hyperactive-impulsive type.* The diagnostician may award the diagnosis of *attention deficit/hyperactivity disorder, combined type* to a person who shows, for at least 6 months, six or more of the symptoms of inattention and six or more symptoms of hyperactivity/impulsivity. The view that attention problems underlie unwanted behaviors has a venerable history. Still (1902) pointed out "that a notable feature in many of these cases of moral defect without general impairment of intellect is a quite abnormal incapacity for sustained attention" (p. 1902). Tredgold (1908), widely recognized as an authority on mental deficiency (amentia), including the special category *moral deficiency*, helped tie together attention and children's unwanted conduct. Referring to studies available in his day, Tredgold asserted that "in the habitual criminal, stigmata of degeneracy abound just as they do in the ament" (p. 296), and then implicated moral deficiency. Using his crude construction of attention, Tredgold concluded that aments "are quite incapable of concentrating their thoughts upon a particular subject" (p. 104, also see p. 347). Similarly, a modern diagnostician may freely use his or her construction *inattention* when he or she observes a child who "often does not seem to listen when spoken to directly" (APA, 1994, p. 84). Despite nearly a century of reformulation of attention, the creators of DSM-IV appear to follow Still and Tredgold by assuming that their readers consensually share a construction—*attentional problems.*

Shaywitz, Fletcher, and Shaywitz (1994) aptly describe the confused state of affairs resulting from using a fuzzy construction of attention in the AD/HD narrative:

Thus, although the term ADD [attention deficit disorder] had its genesis in the belief that deficits in attention are most fundamental to and underlie the clinical syndrome . . . , this hypothesis has yet to be empirically confirmed. In fact, the demonstration of a deficit in the psychological construct attention is not currently incorporated in the diagnostic criteria for ADD. As a result, we are left with ADD as a paradox: a disorder whose most intimate association—its name—infers a problem with the psychological disorder whose diagnosis depends solely on behavioral manifestations defined on the basis of a rating scale. (p. 4, material in brackets added)

Consider our hypothetical teacher, Mr. Malfetta, being asked to affirm the presence of an initiating event in the AD/HD narrative by telling a professional diagnostician whether or not Gabriel "often fails to give close attention to details or makes careless mistakes in schoolwork, work, or other activities" (APA, 1994, p. 83). He has in his file a sheaf of papers that clearly document Gabriel's frequent errors in spelling and arithmetical calculations. On what basis can he make a decision that those errors derive from the boy's failure to give close attention to details? Even if he observes closely while Gabriel is working on his exercise sheets, how can he determine that the boy's errors are due to a failure of an internal process that can be construed by a vague and multifaceted construction called *attention*? Similarly, how can Mr. Malfetta determine if Gabriel "is often easily distracted by extraneous stimuli" (p. 84), or that he "often had difficulty organizing tasks and activities" (p. 84). If the teacher does offer his perspective on the boy's behavior, using constructions such as *attention* and *distraction*, he does so in terms of his own personal construct system. It is unwarranted to assume that he is using the same constructions used by some mental health professionals who willingly use amorphous constructions that are devoid of consensuality.

The DSM-IV list of symptoms does include some items that describe observable behaviors. For example, one could expect consensual agreement on whether or not the target child "often blurts out answers before questions have been completed," "often leaves seat in classroom and other situations in which remaining seating is expected," "often does not follow through on instructions and fails to finish schoolwork, chores, or duties in the workplace" (p. 84). Nevertheless, should a rater concede to evaluating the presence of such symptoms, assessing the observers' use of the term *often* remains problematic.

Whether or not would-be diagnosticians take these behaviors to be signs of *inattention* or *hyperactivity*, one should not hesitate to regard the behaviors identified as DSM-IV symptoms as representative of *failure to follow rules*. We again recall Still's (1902) foundational narrative, wherein he described the children who embodied morbid moral deficit. He made much of the "lawlessness" of these children; that is, of children who show "a reckless disregard for command and authority in spite of training and discipline as experience shows will render a healthy child law-abiding to a certain roughly definable degree varying with age" (p. 1009). (Still gives a clue to his construction of "training and discipline" in the following sentence: "She is said to have very little sense of obedience and corporal punishment seems to have little or no restraining effect" [p. 1012].)

DSM-IV (APA, 1994) does ask the AD/HD diagnostician to ascertain that failure to comply is "not due to oppositional behavior or failure to understand instructions" (p. 84). It appears that children who persistently show "oppositional behavior" would become actors in a different diagnosis narrative—the oppositional behavior disorder (APA, 1994, pp. 91–94) narrative. Thus arises yet another major issue involved in recounting the AD/HD diagnostic narrative: the "comorbidity" issue. (Space limitations constrain us from discussing the obfuscation arising from a diagnostician's efforts to decide whether or not a person suffers simultaneously from one or more disorders aside from AD/HD [see McKinney, Montague, & Hocutt, 1993, pp. 61–67 for review].)

The Assumptive Leap into Biological Formulations

By borrowing the prestige of medical science, a teller of a diagnostic tale could attempt to convince his or her audience that a physical anomaly is the basic initiating event in the tale. The narrative then can build on statements such as, "More consistent across these studies are the findings of smaller right prefrontal cortical regions and smaller caudate volume, whether on the right or left side. . . . Others reviewing this literature over the last two decades have reached similar conclusions—that abnormalities in the development of prefrontal-striatal

THE POETIC CONSTRUCTION OF AD/HD   241

regions probably underlie the development of AD/HD" (Barkley, 1997, p. 35). Similarly, "dopamine was described as being localized in the limbic areas and assumed to be involved in the expression of ADD" (Quinn, 1997, p. 4).

To support the validity of using biological formulations as the initiating event of the AD/HD narrative, investigators amass data by which to demonstrate a connection between a *bodily structure* and unwanted behaviors. For example, Zametkin et al. (1993), state that, "We *tentatively* argue that our results *support* our original finding on adults and *propose a continuation of the line of investigation*" (p. 338, emphasis on qualifiers added). To parse this equivocating conclusion, a reader must return to the writers' explication of their "original finding in the adults": "A recent study using positron emission tomography (PET) of the brain and fludeoxyglucose F 18 (18Fluorodeoxyglucose [FDG]) demonstrated significant and widespread reductions of glucose metabolism in cortical and sub-cortical regions, specifically in the pre-motor and motor cortices of adults with childhood histories of hyperactivity" (p. 333).

Despite the cover of potentially intimidating, high-tech language, one can focus immediately on the term *significant* to ask, "Significant in what way?" Does this term indicate that any single individual who had been identified by the investigators to have shown a childhood history of hyperactivity would show significant "reduction of glucose metabolism?" Several sentences later, Zametkin, et al. state that "Previous imaging studies have been unable to differentiate individual patients from controls, despite significant group findings" (1993, p. 333). Thus, they point tangentially to the meaning they intended to convey when they used the term "significant change." They referred to statistical significance. To extract statistical significance, investigators analyze data gleaned from a group of putative AD/HD adults and the data gleaned from a group of putative non-AD/HD adults. They derive a statistic—a mean, a correlation coefficient, and so on. They then show, statistically, that the "size" of the difference between the statistic extracted from each group's data allows confidence that the difference would not be attributable to chance. Nevertheless as they state quite clearly, no diagnostician should stake his or her professional reputation on judging that any single person who shows reduction of glucose metabolism would also be judged to have had a childhood history of AD/HD.

Another feature of the Zametkin et al. study must be evaluated before accepting even their equivocating conclusion. They report that "The 10 hyperactive teenagers . . . were included if, upon clinical interview of both parents, subjects met DSM-III-R criteria for AD/HD" (APA, 1987, p. 334). One can then make the appropriately cautioning observation that these investigators were comparing a dependent variable (PET-derived measures of glucose metabolism) to a very low-tech independent variable (presence of AD/HD as determined by interviews and outsider observation of the targets' behavior). The participants were diagnosed as AD/HD on the basis of the disclosure by the parent or by the adolescent that the putative patient had shown patterns of behavior that might be described by language such as the following: "Is easily distracted by extraneous stimuli," or "Often talks excessively" (APA, 1987). The contentious debate about accepting these judgments as indications of the presence of a "disorder" allows one to remain skeptical with respect to the findings of any study that uses such judgments to claim that the independent variable is a "disorder." Instead, it would be more appropriate to construe the independent variable as "a quantification of a judgment, based on vague criteria, that the target fits into a category tentatively labeled AD/HD." In short, articles such as that authored by Zametkin et al. tell us only that an imprecise and barely comprehensible element such as "reduction in glucose metabolism" can be incorporated into the diagnostic narrative. Baxter (1995) cogently concluded that, "Studies of brain morphology . . . , cerebral glucose metabolism . . . , and catecholamine excretion have shown interesting, sometimes contradictory, results that are not conclusive for any one hypothesis" (p. 383).

Another frequently cited report (Beiderman et al., 1995) contains the speculation that 57% of the offspring of persons diagnosed as AD/HD are at risk for the same diagnosis. As with the Zametkin et al. study, the means by which diagnoses are assigned would provide the first grounds to be critical of the results of the study. First, the adults who were diagnosed as AD/HD had come to the attention of the investigators on account of their already having been involved with the medicalization of their life problems. Then, "To be given a diagnosis of adult AD/HD the subject had to 1) have met the DSM-III-R criteria for diagnosis by the age of 7, 2) have at least eight of the DSM-III-R symptoms of the disorder at the time of the assessment, and 3) describe a chronic course of the disorder from child to adulthood" (Beiderman et al., 1995, p. 432). Thus, the independent variable was derived not only from judgments of current behavior, but also from judgments of long-past and continuing conduct of the target participants. To confound further the interpretation of their results, Beiderman et al. had established the dependent variable, AD/HD, in the children of the target adults, by conducting a telephone interview with the children's parents—the putatively AD/HD adult who had self-reported past, continuous, and present behaviors that allowed the investigators to assign the AD/HD diagnosis to those parents.

It is appropriate to raise the issue of the vested interests of the parents who were making the judgments about behaviors that served as initiating events in the AD/HD diagnostic narrative. Many benefits accrue to persons who are assigned to the AD/HD diagnosis (Smelter, Rasch, Fleming, Nazos, & Baronowski, 1996). Special schooling, medical care, and financial benefits can be granted to diagnosed persons (Davila, Williams, & MacDonald, 1991; Latham & Latham, 1992). Widely disseminated, government-supported documents (e.g., Neuwirth, 1997) effusively support the AD/HD diagnostic narrative, advise parents to seek out professionals who can grant the AD/HD diagnosis, define the diagnosed person's "rights," instruct parents and diagnosed persons on the utility and safety of chemical treatments, and encourage them to seek out the support of lobbying groups, such as Children and Adults with Attention Deficit Disorders (CHADD).

Thus, tracing the origins of the unwanted behavior to a biological cause reduces the probability for explanations involving ineffective child-rearing or educational practices. Adults can thereupon attribute to biology their children's unwanted conduct or their disappointments over failures to achieve goals, or both.

To evaluate further the Beiderman et al. study, which showed that 43% of the offspring were not judged to be at risk, one would want to have data to show whether or not those who were diagnosed shared particular biological conditions. Did the 57% of the AD/HD offspring of parents diagnosed with AD/HD share, for example, the biological condition explored by Zametkin et al.—"reduction of glucose metabolism in cortical and subcortical regions"? Did the siblings of the diagnosed children share this same condition?

To their credit, Beiderman et al. showed constraint about using genetic terminology to explain their results. "Our results show that children of parents with AD/HD are at high risk for meeting diagnostic criteria for the disorder. . . . Although preliminary, these findings suggest strong familial underpinnings in adults with AD/HD" (1995, p. 433). Unfortunately, this caution does not prevent the tellers of the diagnostic story from using the Beiderman et al. study to support the conclusion that, "by far, the greatest research evidence suggested AD/HD is a trait which is highly hereditary in nature, making heredity one of the most well-substantiated etiologies for AD/HD" (Barkley, 1997, p. 37).[2]

The Introduction of Flexibility into the AD/HD Diagnostic Narrative

When reports of formal studies to support the AD/HD narrative appeared in the 1950s and 1960s, promoters of the diagnostic narrative wrote equivocating statements such as, "we were able to see that 15 of 21 hyperkinetic subjects can be classified as having probable organic disorders and 6 can be classified as having probable psychogenic disorders" (Knobel, Wolman, & Mason, 1958, p. 315). So confident did the diagnosticians become that they employed the term minimal brain damage to label children judged to be hyperactive (Pincus & Glaser, 1966).

Eventually, commentators acknowledged the illogic of using a term clearly designating damage to a body part in order to discuss overt behaviors that, in the first place, had not been linked to any anatomical function. The replacement term of choice became minimal brain dysfunction (MBD)—a transparently ambiguous term that might be applied even to someone whose mathematical calculations were disrupted by his or her experience of rectal peristalsis. Wender (1971) cogently noted the incorrect logic of using the term minimal brain damage to categorize those children who could be tagged with the MBD label (p. 39). Nevertheless, his use of the confounding term MBD deftly allowed a continuation of hopes for establishing a brain anomaly as the initiating event in the diagnosis narrative.

By 1980, the APA's DSM-III described attention deficit disorder (ADD) solely in terms of unwanted behaviors without reference to etiological factors. The practice continued through two further revisions of the DSM. A small step takes one from the practice of listing this diagnostic category in a medically sponsored catalog to recriminations against those who would withhold medications from those who are the "victims of this disorder" (e.g., Angarola & Minsk, 1996). Indeed, so effective had been efforts to medicalize the initiating event in the diagnostic narrative that adults who show no physical anomalies became the subjects for studies of the efficacy of using drugs to diminish the appearance of behaviors that initiate an AD/HD narrative (Wender, Reimherr, & Wood, 1981), and now physicians can justify prescribing drugs to adults who are classified within the AD/HD rubric (Hallowell & Ratey, 1994; Weiss & Hechtman, 1993).

We are living in an era in which the power centers endorse the practice of medicalizing many behavioral functions, so that describing unwanted behaviors as signs of the presence of a "disorder" is readily taken as a legitimate event for initiating the humanely motivated quest of the protagonist in an AD/HD diagnostic narrative. Concurrently, disbelievers find an ample basis for skepticism about describing a biological anomaly as the narrative's initiating event.

Setting the Goals in an AD/HD Narrative, Including Internally Set Goals and Ascribed Internal Experiences

Working from an uncertainty about the initiating event, a teller of the AD/HD diagnostic narrative would need to conclude that one of several goals might fit into the tale. The storyteller might have the protagonist set a goal of having the target of the diagnosis desist from engaging in unwanted behaviors. From the perspective of the composer of a diagnostic narrative, the narrator might set the protagonists' goals in terms of altering a physiological state that precludes or dampens the development of the unwanted behaviors.

The AD/HD Diagnosis as a Fruitless Evasion of Moral Considerations Involved in Goal Setting

The users of the AD/HD narrative can proceed with greater comfort if the protagonist's goal is the successful treatment of "mental disorder." By claiming to pursue a universally endorsed good—correcting a disorder—the protagonist can evade the responsibility of defending his or her quest from a charge that a questionable moral enterprise has been undertaken.

Nevertheless, the effort to view the unwanted behaviors as symptoms of the AD/HD disorder cannot, by any means, obfuscate the clear facts that the protagonist's action had been initiated by one person having observed another person's unwanted behavior. Moreover, the contents of tens of thousands of pages of research reports have not yet specified an incontrovertible nonbehavioral marker that has been endorsed unequivocally by those who advocate the diagnostic narrative. As Maag and Reid (1994) assert, after reviewing the ways in which the AD/HD diagnosis is assigned, "a label of AD/HD adds little information beyond what should already be readily apparent—a child is demonstrating undesirable behaviors and a robust intervention is required" (p. 8). One must conclude, therefore, that the protagonist in the AD/HD diagnostic narrative would set a goal of eliminating the unwanted behaviors that are specified in officious descriptions of a "disorder." At the same time, one cannot avoid the conclusion that the tellers of diagnostic narrative expect that the unwanted behaviors would be replaced by socially warranted behaviors that reflect the use of anticipatory self-narratives. Upon recognition of this sometimes implicit goal, one also must conclude that the goal in the AD/HD diagnostic narrative is buttressed by social constructions specifying the society's moral positions. Following this assumptive chain, the goal in the AD/HD story turns out to be moral rectitude that has been disguised as "mental well-being."

The user of the AD/HD diagnostic narrative immediately gains assets with regard to setting a course of action. As noted earlier, by pursuing the highly positive goal of "curing a disorder" the protagonist easily evades the moral questions surrounding his or her prerogatives in determining which behaviors the target of the diagnosis is expected to modify. In addition, the use of a diagnostic narrative perpetuates the illusion that the symptoms emerge as a result of an anomalous biological substrate. From this illusion, one may more comfortably specify a goal that appears to correct the anomaly. For example, the protagonist may prescribe stimulant medications with satisfaction, knowing that the target is being relieved of a burden. In addition, the protagonist has consensual assurance that it would be immoral to deprive the target of treatment.

Facing the Moral Issues in a Behavior Change Enterprise

If eliminating unwanted behaviors becomes the goal of the protagonists in the AD/HD narrative, the actor must immediately face ethical questions before choosing to apply one of any number of very effective means of reaching the goal. Extreme confinement in a padded cell would work, as would turning the target person loose in an environment in which no rules are imposed, administering pharmacological agents that interfere with the conduct of selected behaviors, and so on. Then the actor must review the possibility that other implicitly set goals underlie the goal of eliminating unwanted behaviors. If unwanted behavior is eliminated, what kinds of behaviors will the target then perform? Who decides which behaviors are wanted and which are unwanted? Will the target acquire the skill to carry out acceptable behaviors?

If these latter questions are taken seriously, the protagonist in an AD/HD anticipatory narrative should be able to tell a good story about the psychological processes of persons who comply with the expectations of significant others, particularly those processes involved in moral development (Lickona, 1976).

In summary, the setting of the goal in the AD/HD narrative has been seriously obfuscated by attempts to evade the moral issues involved in setting the goal.

Conduct Directed toward a Successful Outcome and the AD/HD Narrative Episode

Administration of Chemical Agents

By setting the goal of ameliorating a biological disorder, the protagonists gain social warrant for prescribing pharmacological treatment. Bradley (1937) was among the first investigators to bring attention to the utility of those drugs that are now most widely prescribed. Subsequently, "The literature suggests that two to six percent of all elementary school-aged children may be treated with stimulant medication, and that from 60 to 90 percent of school-aged children with an ADD diagnosis are treated with stimulant medication for a prolonged period of time" (Swanson, 1992, p. 52). Cantwell (1996) has offered a concise summation of the bases on which to justify the protagonist's use of chemical intervention:

The primary psychopharmacological agents used to treat ADD are the CNS [central nervous system] stimulants. . . . There are a number of amphetamines, including metamphetamine and dextroamphetamine, but dextroamphetamine probably enjoys the greatest use. Methylphenidate is probably used more than any of the other stimulants. At least 70% of children will have a positive response to one of the major stimulants on the first trial. If a clinician conducts a trial of dextroamphetamine, methylphenidate, and pemoline, the response rate to at least one of these is in the 85% to 90% range, depending on how response is defined. (p. 984)

In contrast, Maag and Reid (1994) first state that, "Quite literally, the symptoms constitute the syndrome—no underlying unseen physical or psychological factors are considered in diagnosis," and then go on to assert:

Similarly, treatments, whether medically, behaviorally, or cognitively based, attempt to ameliorate the behaviors exhibited by the child, not "cure" underlying causal factors. In fact, there are no nonmedical treatments specific to ADHD. . . . Therefore . . . the relevance of ADHD as a medical/psychiatric construct for educators and other nonmedical practitioners is greatly reduced. (p. 6)

Psychosocial and Educational Interventions

The specification of a variety of interventions, none of which requires recourse to a diagnostic narrative, would follow from taking seriously the observations of Maag and Reid (1994). These kinds of interventions are variants of techniques that have long been known as *educational practices*. Such practices are pursued on the premise that the target has not yet learned something that he or she "ought" to have learned, and that techniques of instruction will prompt and accelerate his or her acquisition of the required knowledge. The actions of protagonist in this tale are best outlined after clear acknowledgment of a moral stance. They are taken to cause the target to develop the kinds of anticipatory self-narratives that will guide him or her to engage in socially approved conduct.

Fiore, Becker, and Nero (1993) carried out a "review of reviews" of educational interventions to be used in work with children showing the putative AD/HD symptoms. They concluded that studies of the outcomes of the practices of offering rewards for engaging in desired behaviors, setting up contingencies resulting in avoidance of engaging in unwanted behaviors, and using modified combinations of these approaches actually reduce unwanted behaviors. The implementation of these techniques, however, requires a large expenditure of resources. Additionally, the failure to demonstrate that the gains carry into activities other than those directly influenced has discouraged allocating the needed resources to develop further these procedures.

Further, those advocating psychosocial approaches as a recommended course of action should be granted the same concessions as are extended to those promoting the use of the diagnostic narrative. One must acknowledge the theoretical shortcomings of the principles that have guided the administration of rewards for positive behavior and the cognitive-behavioral (essentially, "talk to yourself") approaches. One cannot persuasively dismiss the utility of psychosocial interventions if studies to date have been based primarily on constructions paralleling those used by Still in 1902; constructions from which one regards instruction as "stamping in" approved behavior by a mechanistic process of "adding force" to a tendency for those behaviors to appear. Other constructions are yet to be invented.

Preventing the Development of the AD/HD Syndrome

The research literature related to the AD/HD diagnosis rarely prescribes action that would prevent the development of personal psychological systems that lead to a person's propensity to engage in the behaviors that are assumed to be the symptoms of AD/HD. One can find dismissive statements such as, "Psychosocial factors are not thought to play a primary etiological role" (Cantwell, 1996, p. 979). Such statements are based on the results of studies that focus on long-ago constructed variables such as stress, conditioning, deprivation, and so on.

For a teller of an AD/HD narrative that places biological factors as the foremost initiating event, there would be little reason to consider the possibility that a host of child-rearing variables remain to be constructed and explored. The current interest in the ways in which children develop skills in constructing stories offer a wide range of new variables (see Britton & Pellegrini, 1990, Smith & Thelen, 1993). For example, one might accept that view of emotional life that centers on the ways in which infants and toddlers learn to construct socially warranted narratives (Mancuso & Sarbin, 1998). One would then want to understand the ways in which children learn constructions by which to frame the inputs from the bodily changes that accompany preparation for action in situations of cognitive reorganization. Do they learn to frame the inputs with a construction such as "anxiety state"—a state that one legitimately avoids? Do they learn to recognize such inputs as signals to engage in a successful and satisfying learning experience?

Taking into account the ambiguity of the relationships between the actions and the goals of the protagonists in the AD/HD diagnostic narrative, the narrator must hesitate to specify the actions that will attain desired outcomes—however those outcomes might be defined. One can find good reasons for refusing to endorse the administration of biological suppressants of unwanted behavior: for example, the known adverse effects on the mechanisms of the interactions of those drugs on the neural system (Elia, 1993). Yet, a constructivist could not deny biological scientists the opportunity to invent new constructions of biological functioning on which to base the actions of those who seek to understand the development of particular behaviors. At the same time, behavior scientists must insist on having the opportunity to invent and to promulgate variables that would satisfactorily explain the psychosocial actions that prompt the development of wanted, as well as unwanted, behaviors.

An Ending for a Good (Well-Formed) AD/HD Narrative: The Outcome Is Set into a Broader Context

Lacking the definitive specification of expected outcome, there can be no method by which to assess the success of the actions of a medically inspired protagonist in an AD/HD story. Nevertheless, significant persons in our society have granted to physicians the authority to put thousands of children and adults on a drug regimen.

This authority devolves to physicians because significant persons, even staunch critics of drug use, concede that prescribing drug ingestion does bring about a diminution of the unwanted behaviors. Thus, one observes a repetition of the paradox in the AD/HD narrative. The tellers of the diagnostic narrative have consistently nursed the claim that the initiating events are some kind of biological anomaly, but the outcomes of their actions are evaluated not in terms of the amelioration of the anomaly, but in terms of the elimination of what are assumed to be the results of the putative anomaly—the unwanted behavior. Indeed, because no investigator has identified a biological anomaly, there can be no evaluation of the outcome of the diagnostic narrative in terms of amelioration of a biological anomaly.

The Short-Term Outcome of Administration of Pharmacological Agents

The outcomes of the administration of chemicals to persons who have been diagnosed as AD/HD has evoked a wide variety of reactions. McGuinness (1989) descries the continued use of pharmacological agents, despite "the failure of drug therapy to promote any academic, social, or emotional well-being for the child, and the continuing animosity that is developed between the medical and non-medical communities over this issue, plus the apparent futility of dislodging the medical practitioner from his point of view because of initial impact on behavior" (p. 183). Breggin (1998) reflects his persistent opposition to use of drugs to regulate behavior in his assertion that "there are many other reasons not to give Ritalin to children, including developmental neurotoxicty—the disruption of multiple neurotransmitter systems during their formative stages of growth in the child's brain" (p. 2).

Some endorsements of pharmacological intervention, like that of Quinn (1997), are stated with some caution: "Stimulate medication is one of the most useful tools in dealing with attentional deficits" (p. 107). Klein (1995) offers a much more enthusiastic endorsement: "The efficacy of methylphenidate in ADHD of childhood needs no retelling. In spite of the periodic alarm expressed in the media, it is an unqualified success story for the following reasons, all amply documented: At appropriately high doses of methylphenidate a large proportion of the children with ADHD experience remission of symptoms of ADHD" (p. 429).

In "a review of reviews," Swanson, et al. (1993) extracted the points on which authors of extensive reviews of outcomes of pharmacological treatments have agreed. They concluded that even authors who ended recommending against the use of chemical agents (e.g., McGuinness, 1989) have agreed with drug-supporting reviewers (e.g., Stevenson & Wolraich, 1989) that drug use could be linked to short-term benefits, in terms of cessation of unwanted behaviors.

The Long-Term Outcome of Administering Pharmacological Agents

Agreement on short-term outcomes of drug regimens does not obviate continued concern about their long-term effects, the ethics of drug use, the seriousness of side effects, and the possibility that one could account for much of the ameliorative effect by the "placebo effect" created by the user's belief that his or her behavior was being changed as a result of the drug effects. Assessment of the long-term consequences of action to ameliorate the putative AD/HD symptoms have been complicated by the long-time acceptance of the conclusion that development accompanying adolescent changes led to "remission" (Hill & Schoener, 1996). Additionally, assessments of long-term effects of ameliorative action have been confounded by the repeated changes in the terminology, specification of symptoms, and so on; the issuing of four different official diagnostic manuals; the inability to distinguish outcomes caused by chemical agents from those attributable to social intercessions; attempts to gather data retrospectively; and so forth.

These considerations aside, Swanson's (1992) summary of the review of over 50 years of effort to affirm the utility of drugs as a route to the goal of achieving long-term benefits for those diagnosed as "having" AD/HD, concluded that, "88 percent [of the reviewed reports] acknowledged the lack of demonstrated long term effect" (p. 159). In another report on this "review of reviews," Swanson et al. (1993) indicate that having the protagonist prescribe drugs should not encourage expectations of eventual reduction in antisocial behavior or significant acceleration of development of social skills or academic achievement.

The Global Ending of the AD/HD Narrative:
Coalescing Specific Episodes with Other Episodes

Thousands of publications[3]—reports of studies, review articles, books, commentary, diatribes, and so on—have been written in order to produce a validatable version of the AD/HD narrative. More often than not, a publication includes a variation of the tediously repeated, equivocating global ending, such as:

This operationalization of the anterior-posterior discrepancy model is to be considered a pilot. To be complete, this will require incorporation of certain psychometric considerations, . . . developmental considerations, and the impact of using normative data derived from different samples of children. (Reader, Harris, Schuerholz, & Denckla, 1994, p. 509)

Reader et al. had administered a battery of tests to a sample of young people who had met DSM-III-R criteria for AD/HD. The tests used, of course, were presumed to measure complex cognitive processes showing "executive functioning"[4] (1994, p. 494), and, as such, to reflect the state of the anterior cerebral cortex. They found that many of the AD/HD children do not perform as well on their tests of executive functioning as do nondiagnosed children. Nevertheless, about 94% of the participants scored as well as would the majority of nondiagnosed children on at least one of the tests of executive functioning (EF).

Despite equivocal findings, writers such as Pennington and Ozonoff (1996) enthuse about the possibilities of coalescing the episodes of the AD/HD narrative around the EF variable: "a true test of the primacy [of EF deficit] is available for ADHD because of our knowledge of its neurobiology" (p. 80). "If EF deficits are primary, then reversal of the underlying neurochemical imbalance (dopamine depletion) ought to reverse the EF deficits in ADHD, as well as the behavioral symptoms" (p. 80).

In his influential volume entitled *ADHD and the Nature of Self-Control*, Barkley (1997) further elucidates a construction of EF: "More specifically, it is the conjecturing of the future that arises out of reconstruction of the past and the goal directed behaviors that are predicated on these activities. Such activities, along with other executive functions, permit self-regulation relative to time" (p. 202).

Barkley's discourse prompts a recall of Mr. Malfetta's effort to deal with Gabriel. Malfetta has instructed the children in his class on the use of an algorithm that allows the addition of two-place numbers. Mr. Malfetta, one can say, has given his pupils a *rule*—a socially agreed-upon construction of a particular arithmetical operation that they are to process within their personal construct systems. One can tentatively agree that at this point, Gabriel "must now inhibit responding to preponent stimuli existing in that situation while *adhering to the rule*" (Barkley, 1997, p. 58).

Reaching this agreement, however, does not require that we also agree to invent a neurologically connected special deficit. Nevertheless, to create a narrative in which Gabriel's failure to follow rules becomes the initiating event, the narrator must be able to define, rather elaborately, the ways in which Mr. Malfetta's instructions become a part of the context that includes Gabriel's psychological functioning. Additionally, one would want to have an equally elaborate construction of what is happening when Gabriel is *responding*. In the first place, when one speaks of *response*, is he or she referring only to overt behavior? Would it be useful to apply the term *response* to everything that is happening as Gabriel processes Mr. Malfetta's vocalization; that is, to regard Gabriel's overt behaviors as an extension of Gabriel's cognitive processing of his teacher's instructions? Would Mr. Malfetta find it useful to think of a deficit in EF functioning to explain why Gabriel does not show "behavioral inhibition [which] refers to three inhibitory functions: (1) the *inhibition of prepotent responses*, (2) the *interruption of ongoing responses* that are proving ineffective, and (3) of the protection of the delay created by those forms of inhibition" (Barkley, 1997, p. 158, italics in original).

As Mr. Malfetta attempts to identify a prepotent response that interferes with Gabriel's attempts to work on the assigned practice problems, would a biology-tinged theory of EF deficit be more useful than a sound theory of cognitive development? If one defines response as the entire psychological activity in which Gabriel engages as he processes Mr. Malfetta's instructions, is there reason to assume that other sensory input becomes a source of competition for the processing operations allocated to the inputs that had been provided by the instructor? Is so, why would one assume that such competing sensory input would effectuate a "prepotent response"?

Return again to Barclay's noting that EF involves "the conjecturing of the future that arises out of reconstruction of the past and the goal directed behaviors that are predicated on those activities" (1997, p. 202). This statement evokes our strong endorsement. We would concur fully with an effort to explain Gabriel's conduct in terms of his reconstruction of the past—his reconstruction of Mr. Malfetta's instructions within the context of his already-developed complex personal construct system. That reconstruction would incorporate, of course, the anticipatory self-construction that becomes implicated in the child's goal-directed behavior. We can see no gain from working toward biological reductionism to develop a well-formed theory about the psychological processing of a person's anticipatory self-constructions.

From the propositions stated in the previous paragraph—propositions that we (Mancuso, 1996; Mancuso & Ceeley, 1980; Mancuso & Sarbin, 1983; Sarbin, 1986) and others (Carver & Scheier, 1990) have elaborated elsewhere—we would describe in our theory of anticipatory self constructions the status of Gabriel's system of personal constructs (Mancuso & Adams-Webber, 1982, Neimeyer & Neimeyer, 1992). Has the boy developed a construct system out of which he could build the anticipatory self-construction that would guide his enactment of socially approved overt conduct? Has Gabriel developed sufficiently those numerical constructs upon which to build the number constructions necessary to complete the assignment? Has Gabriel acquired the constructions that would allow him to process the internally instigated inputs that accompany the preparation for effort that occurs under circumstances in which an individual does not have a readily accessible construction of the continued flow of inputs (Mascolo & Mancuso, 1990; Mancuso & Sarbin, 1998)? And, because the term *attention* continuously reappears, what is happening when Gabriel attends to a set of inputs (Mancuso, 1977; Mancuso & Hunter, 1983)?

We would agree that time constructions, indeed, occupy any context in which a person builds and enacts an anticipatory construction (Carver & Scheier, 1990), particularly those anticipatory constructions that guide self-role enactments. To build and to enact an anticipatory self-construction that will gain the approval of the society that placed Gabriel in Mr. Malfetta's charge, the boy must frame the role that he is to enact into a reasonably predictable time sequence. He must be able to see that this arithmetic-learning episode of his anticipatory self-narrative will coalesce with other self-narratives that he will build in the near and far future. Concretely, he would profit from having developed a construct system that allows him to anticipate that his enacting the role of successful learner of arithmetic algorithms will coalesce, in the nearer future, to his role as successful learner of algebra, which anticipates his far-future self role of successful engineer. Essentially, Gabriel does not differ from the theorist trying to build a good narrative for framing children who do not successfully build socially approved self-narratives. Gabriel, too, must go into his arithmetic-learning episode with a construct system by which he can construe all the foundational elements of the story that his social ecology asks him to construct.

DENOUEMENT

Rather than prompting the discovery of an out-there, biologically grounded entity, the epistemological positions guiding this chapter urge a focus on the social constructions of unwanted conduct. We claim that we now have no way of accessing a privileged position from which to make judgments about whether or not the assembled signs in a socially warranted narrative provide an adequate mirror of a putative extant world. The value of a social construction is determined by whether or not a collegial body gives warrant to the claim that a particular anticipatory narrative/construction fits a useful story grammar more adequately than does an alternative story. "The truth of our narratives does not reside in their correspondence to the prior meaning of prenarrative experience; rather, the narrative is the meaning of the prenarrative experience" (Kerby, 1991, p. 84). We cannot now justify attempting to determine the incidence of an "out-there AD/HD disorder." Instead, we believe, greater utility will come from asking questions about the ways in which observers assign the AD/HD diagnosis.

We end this chapter by paraphrasing Sarbin and Mancuso's (1980) ending of their analysis of the diagnostic narrative as applied to those persons called *schizophrenics*.

The concept of [AD/HD] . . . was invented to communicate about certain classes of non-conforming, unacceptable conduct. [ADHD] is but one in a long line of conceptions whose primary purpose was to identify persons whose conduct was contranormative. It was but one way that a society could go in its endless search for solutions to the problem of unwanted conduct.

The findings and arguments [presented here] compel us to examine unwanted conduct from a perspective formed by the basic observation: conduct occurs in social context and these contexts include systems of norms [standards, codes of propriety, group expectations, moral roles]. To say that a person violates norms is to say that he or she has engaged in some overt act and that the act has been judged by another person or persons as inappropriate, improper, immoral, silly, bizarre, dangerous, foolhardy, stupid, and so on. In short, an adequate theory of human conduct must begin at the intersection of action and valuation. (p. 210, bracketed material added or altered from original)

[a socially approved role, such as the *AD/HD person*,] cannot be sustained when behavior scientists move fully into practicing a contextualist science that accounts for both the epistemic or judgmental processes of the diagnostician and those who become the targets of the diagnoses. At this point there is sufficient work in normal science of psychology to show that [constructionist/] contextualist approaches are the most useful in explaining these judgment processes. Furthermore, a strong chain of contextually-based reports demonstrate that the psychological processes of those diagnosed as [ADHD] cannot be differentiated from processes of those who do not bear the diagnoses. (p. 208, bracketed material added or altered from original)

In keeping with this conclusion, we judge the AD/HD diagnostic narrative to be counterproductive. The foregoing text was written to demonstrate that the AD/HD narrative does not qualify as a "good story." Furthermore, because the AD/HD diagnostic narrative influences the target persons (and their families, teachers, and others in their social ecology) to assign to their selves the self-crippling anticipatory self-role construction, "drug-ingesting sick person," "deficient person," and so on, the judgment is appropriate that we have entered the domain of moral discourse. From our perspective, the continuing use of the psychiatric diagnostic narrative must be judged as immoral.

NOTES

1. Though we resist doing so, we shall use the term symptom whenever we discuss the unwanted behaviors listed as "symptoms" in DSM-IV.

2. Restrictions inherent in this short chapter forestall a presentation of our critical analysis of those reports of studies of complex quantitative genetics purporting to show the

extent to which heritability accounts for variation in the presence of the complex behaviors known as symptoms of AD/HD.

3. Swanson (1992) wrote that his research team located more than 9,000 original articles and 300 review articles on the topic of the effects of stimulant medication prescribed for those diagnosed as AD/HD.

4. We find it difficult to imagine any test that could be excluded as a measure of all or some of the vaguely described operations that Reader et al. (1994) describe as components of executive function.

REFERENCES

American Psychiatric Association. (1987). *Diagnostic and statistical manual of mental disorders* (3rd ed., rev.). Washington, DC: American Psychiatric Association.

American Psychiatric Association. (1994). *Diagnostic and statistical manual of mental disorders* (4th ed.). Washington, DC: American Psychiatric Association.

Angarola, R. T., & Minsk, A. G. (1996). In H. I. Schwartz (Ed.), *Psychiatric practice under fire: The influence of government, the media, and special interests on somatic therapies* (pp. 63–84). Washington, DC: American Psychiatric Press.

Armstrong, J. (1995). *The myth of the ADD child: 50 ways to improve . . . without drugs, labels, or coercion.* New York: Dutton.

Armstrong, T. (1996). ADD: Does it really exist? *Phi Delta Kappan, 78,* 424–428.

Arnold, L. E. (1996). Sex differences in AD/HD: Conference summary. *Journal of Abnormal Child Psychology, 24,* 555–569.

Barkley, R. A. (1994). Impaired delayed responding. In D. K. Routh (Ed.), *Disruptive behavior in disorders in childhood* (pp. 11–57). New York: Plenum Press.

Barkley, R. A. (1997). *ADHD and the nature of self-control.* New York: Guilford Press.

Baumgaertel, A., Wolraich, M. L., & Dietrich, M. (1995). Attention deficit disorders in a German elementary school-aged sample. *Journal of the American Academy of Child and Adolescent Psychiatry, 34,* 629–638.

Baxter, P. S. (1995). Attention-deficit hyperactivity disorder in children. *Current Opinion in Pediatrics, 7,* 381–386.

Beiderman, J., Faraone, S. V., Mick, E., Spencer, T., Wilens, T., Kiely, K., Guite, J., Ablon, J. S., Reed, E., & Warburton, R. (1995). High risk for attention deficit hyperactivity disorder among children of parents with childhood onset of the disorder: A pilot study. *American Journal of Psychiatry, 152,* 431–435.

Bradley, C. (1937). The behavior of children receiving benzedrine. *American Journal of Psychiatry, 94,* 577–585.

Breggin, P. (1998). Upcoming government conference on ADHD and psychostimulants asks the wrong questions. [On-line]. Available: www.breggin.com/consensus wrong.html

Britton, B. K., & Pellegrini, A. D. (Eds.). (1990). *Narrative thought and narrative language.* Hillsdale, NJ: Erlbaum.

Cantwell, D. P. (1996). Attention deficit disorder: A review of the past 10 years. *Journal of the American Academy of Child and Adolescent Psychiatry, 35,* 978–987.

Carver, C. S., & Scheier, M. F. (1990). Origins and functions of positive and negative affect: A control-process view. *Psychological Review, 97,* 19–35.

Conners, C. K. (1989a). *Connors' parent rating scales.* North Tonawanda, NY: Multi-Health Systems.

Conners, C. K. (1989b). *Connors' teacher rating scales*. North Tonawanda, NY: Multi-Health Systems.

Davila, R. R., Williams, M. L., & MacDonald, J. T. (1991). Clarification of policy to address the needs of children with attention deficit disorders within general and/or special education. U.S. Department of Education Memorandum. Washington DC: Office of Special Education and Rehabilitative Services.

Dykman, R. A., Ackerman, R. T., & Raney, T. J. (1992). *Assessment and characteristics of children with attention deficit disorder* (ERIC Report). Washington, DC: U.S. Department of Education.

Elia, J. (1993). Drug treatment for hyperactive children. Therapeutic guidelines. *Drugs, 46*, 863–861.

Fiore, T. A., Becker, E. A., & Nero, R. C. (1993). Educational interventions for students with attention deficit disorder. *Exceptional Children, 60*, 163–173.

Freyd, J. (1983). Shareability: The social psychology of epistemology. *Cognitive Science, 7*, 191–210.

Gittleman, R., Mannuzza, S., Shenker, R., & Bonagura, N. (1985). Hyperactive boys grow up: I. Psychiatric status. *Archives of General Psychiatry, 42*, 937–947.

Goldstein, S. (1996). *Advanced training in AD/HD: Conceptual diagnostics and treatment issues through the life span.* Unpublished handout, issued at Brattleboro Retreat, Brattleboro, VT.

Greenblatt, A. P. (1994). Gender and ethnicity bias in the assessment of attention deficit disorder. *Journal of Social Work*, 89–95.

Griffiths, B. C., & Mullins, N. C. (1972). Coherent social groups in scientific change. *Science, 177*, 959–964.

Hallowell, E. M., & Ratey, J. J. (1994). *Driven to distraction*. New York: Pantheon Books.

Hill, J. C., & Schoener, E. P. (1996). Age-dependent decline of attention deficit hyperactivity disorder. *American Journal of Psychiatry, 153*, 1143–1146.

Kerby, A. P. (1991). *Narrative and the self*. Bloomington: Indiana University Press.

Klein, R. (1995). The role of methyl phenidate in psychiatry. *Archives of General Psychiatry, 52*, 429–432.

Knobel, M., Wolman, M. B., & Mason, E. (1958). Hyperkinesis and organicity. *Archives of General Psychiatry, 1*, 310–321.

Latham, P. S., & Latham, P. H. (1992). *Attention deficit disorder and the law: A guide for advocates*. Washington, DC: JKL Communications.

Lickona, T. (Ed.). (1976). *Morality: A handbook of moral development and behavior* (pp. 326–341). New York: Holt, Rinehart, Winston.

Maag, J. W., & Reid, R. (1994). Attention-deficit hyperactivity disorder: A functional approach to assessment and treatment. *Behavior Disorders, 20*, 5–23.

Mancuso, J. C. (1977). Current motivational models in the elaboration of personal construct theory. In A. W. Landfield (Ed.), *Nebraska symposium on motivation: Personal construct psychology* (pp. 43–97). Lincoln: University of Nebraska Press.

Mancuso, J. C. (1986). The acquisition and use of narrative grammar structure. In T. R. Sarbin (Ed.), *Narrative psychology: The storied nature of human conduct* (pp. 91–110). New York: Praeger.

Mancuso, J. C. (1996). Constructionism, personal construct psychology, and narrative psychology. *Theory and Psychology, 6*, 47–70.

Mancuso, J. C., & Adams-Webber, J. R. (Eds.). (1982). *The construing person*. New York: Praeger Press.

Mancuso, J. C., & Ceeley, S. G. (1980) The self as memory processing. *Cognitive Therapy and Research, 4*, 1–25.

Mancuso, J. C., & Hunter, K. V. (1983). Anticipation, motivation, or emotion: The fundamental postulate after 25 years. In J. R. Adams-Webber & J. C. Mancuso (Eds.), *Applications of personal construct theory* (pp. 73–92). Toronto, Canada: Academic Press.

Mancuso, J. C., & Sarbin, T. R. (1983). The self-narrative in the enactment of roles. In T. R. Sarbin & K. Scheibe (Eds.), *Studies in social identity* (pp. 233–253). New York: Praeger.

Mancuso, J. C., & Sarbin, T. R. (1998). The narrative construction of emotional life: Developmental aspects. In M. F. Mascolo, & S. Griffin (Eds.), *What develops in emotional development* (pp. 297–316). New York: Plenum.

Mandler, J. M. (1984). *Scripts, stories, and scenes: Aspects of a schema theory*. Hillsdale, NJ: Erlbaum.

Mascolo, M. F., & Mancuso, J. C. (1990). The functioning of epigenetically evolved emotion systems. *International Journal of Personal Construct Psychology, 3*, 205–220.

McGuinness, D. (1989). Attention deficit disorder: The emperor's clothes, animal "pharm," and other fiction. In S. Fisher & R. P. Greenberg (Eds.), *The limits of biological treatment of psychological distress* (pp. 151–187). Hillsdale, NJ: Erlbaum.

McKinney, J. D., Montague, M., & Hocutt, A. M. (1993). *Synthesis of research on the assessment and identification of students with attention deficit disorder* (ERIC Report). Washington, DC: U.S. Department of Education.

Morgan, A. E., Hynd, G. W., Riccio, C. A., & Hall, J. (1996). Validity of DSM-IV ADHD predominantly inattentive and combined types: Relationship to previous DSM diagnoses/subtype differences. *Journal of the American Academy of Child and Adolescent Psychiatry, 35*, 325–333.

Neimeyer, G. J., & Neimeyer, R. A. (Eds.). (1992). *Advances in personal construct psychology* (Vol. 2). Greenwich, CT: JAI Press.

Neuwirth, S. (1997). Attention Deficit Hyperactivity Disorder: Decade of the brain. [Online]. Available: www.hoptechno.com/adhd.htm

Pennington, B. F., & Ozonoff, S. (1996). Executive function and developmental psychopathology. *Journal of Child Psychology and Psychiatry, 37*, 51–87.

Quinn, P. O. (1997). *Attention deficit disorder: Diagnosis and treatment from infancy to adulthood*. New York: Brunner/Mazel.

Reader, M. J., Harris, E. L., Schuerholz, L. J., & Denckla, M. B. (1994). Attention deficit hyperactivity disorder and executive function. *Developmental Neuropsychology, 10*, 493–512.

Sarbin, T. R. (Ed.). (1986). *Narrative psychology: The storied nature of human conduct*. New York: Praeger.

Sarbin, T. R., & Mancuso, J. C. (1980). *Schizophrenia: Medical diagnosis or moral verdict*. Elmsford, NY: Pergamon Press.

Shaywitz, S. E., Fletcher, J. M., & Shaywitz, B. A. (1994). Issues in the definition and classification of attention deficit disorder. In J. F. Kavanagh (Ed.), *Topics in language disorders* (Vol. 14, pp. 1–25). Gaithersburg, MD: Aspen.

Smelter, R. W., Rasch, B. W., Fleming, J., Nazos, P., & Baronowski, S. (1996). Is attention deficit disorder becoming a desired diagnosis? *Phi Delta Kappan, 77*, 429–432.

Smith, L. B., & Thelen, E. (1993). *A dynamic systems approach to development: Applications*. Cambridge: MIT Press/Bradford Books.

Stein, N. L., & Glenn, C. G. (1979). An analysis of story comprehension in elemetary school children. In R. O. Freedle (Ed.), *New directions in discourse processing* (Vol. 2, pp. 53–120). Norwood, NJ: Ablex

Stevenson, R. D., & Wolraich, M. L. (1989). Stimulant medication in the treatment of children with attention deficit disorders. *Pediatric clinics of North America, 36*, 1183–1196.

Still, G. (1902). The Coulsonian lectures on some abnormal psychical conditions in children. *Lancet, 1*, 1008–1012, 1077–1082, 1163–1168.

Sutton-Smith, B. (1986). Children's fiction making. In T. R. Sarbin (Ed.), *Narrative psychology: The storied nature of human conduct* (pp. 91–110). New York: Praeger.

Swanson, J. M. (1992). Research synthesis on the effects of stimulant medication on children with attention deficit disorder: A review of reviews. In Chesapeake Institute (Ed.), *Executive summaries of research synthesis and promising practices on the education of children with attention deficit disorder* (pp. 52–56) (ERIC Report). Washington, DC: U.S. Department of Education.

Swanson, J. M., McBurnett, K., Wigal, T., Pfiffner, L. J., Lerner, M. A., Williams, L., Christian, D. L., Tamm, L., Willcutt, E., Crowley, K. E., Clevenger, W., Khouzam, N., Woo, C., Crinella, F. M., & Fisher, T. D. (1993). Effect of stimulus medication on children with attention deficit disorder: A "review of reviews." *Exceptional Children, 60*, 154–162.

Szatmari, P., Offord, D. R., & Boyle, M. H. (1989). Ontario child health study: Prevalence of attention deficit disorder with hyperactivity. *Journal of Child Psychology and Psychiatry, 30*, 219–230.

Taylor, E. (1987). Cultural differences in hyperactivity. In M. Wolraich & D. K. Rouyh (Eds.), *Advances in Developmental and Behavioral Pediatrics* (Vol. 8, pp. 125–150). Greenwich, CT: JAI Press.

Thorndyke, P. W. (1977). Cognitive structures in comprehension and memory of narrative discourse. *Cognitive Psychology, 9*, 77–110.

Time Magazine, July 18, 1994, p. 42.

Tredgold, A. F. (1908). *Mental deficiency (Amentia)*. London: Hailliere, Tindall, and Cox.

Verhulst, F. C., & Achenbach, T. M. (1995). Empirically based assessment and taxonomy of psychopathology: Cross-cultural applications, a review. *European Child and Adolescent Psychiatry, 4*, 61–76.

Weiss, G., & Hechtman, L. T. (1993). *Hyperactive children grown up: ADHD in children, adolescents, and adults* (2nd. ed.). New York: Guilford Press.

Wender, P. H. (1971). *Minimal brain dysfunction in children*. New York: Wiley-Interscience.

Wender, P. H., Reimherr, F. W., & Wood, D. R. (1981). Attention deficit disorder ('minimal brain dysfunction') in adults: A replication study of diagnosis and drug treatment. *Archives of General Psychiatry, 38*, 449–456.

Zametkin, A. J., Leibenauer, L. L., Fitzgerald, G. A., King, A. C., Minkunas, D. B., Herscovitch, P., Yamada, E. M., & Cohen, R. M. (1993). Brain metabolism in teenagers with attention-deficit hyperactivity disorder. *Archives of General Psychiatry, 50*, 333–340.

Chapter 8

Evaluating Personal Construct and Psychodynamic Group Work with Adolescent Offenders and Nonoffenders

Linda L. Viney
Rachael M. Henry

Research contrasting the effects of personal construct therapy with those of other therapies is much-needed (Neimeyer, 1993; Winter, 1992). The aim of this research has been to evaluate the effects of two forms of intervention, one of which was personal construct therapy. Psychodynamic psychotherapy, based on an alternative model of psychosocial functioning, was selected by the authors for contrast in its effects. The beneficial impact of psychodynamic therapy has been demonstrated (Laikin, Winston, & McCullough, 1991; Luborsky, Diguer, Luborsky, Singer, Dickter, & Schmidt, 1993). There is another need, also apparent in the literature, for effective interventions with adolescents who are offenders (Fine, Forth, Gilbert, & Haley, 1991; Quay, 1987) as well as nonoffenders (Joanning, Quinn, Thomas, & Mullen 1992; McLennan & Dies, 1992). These interventions should aim to enhance the maturational functioning of the adolescents, and to improve their psychological states. Both personal construct and psychodynamic models should provide sufficient conceptual complexity for developing such interventions with adolescents, and even with offender adolescents, who are particularly responsive to interventions that involve peers. The aim of this research, then, was to evaluate the effects of personal construct and psychodynamic group work on offender and nonoffender adolescents.

GROUP WORK WITH ADOLESCENTS

Group work with adolescent offenders has been recommended because it provides opportunities for its participants to learn how to relate to others, and to experience a positive peer culture and group problem-solving, as well as to acquire information and knowledge (Attwood & Osgood, 1987; Quay, 1987; Zimpfer, 1992). Different types of group work have been conducted with adolescent offenders to achieve therapeutic goals, for example, cognitive behavior group therapy (Becker & Kaplan, 1993) and milieu group therapy (Gautier, 1985). Evaluation studies of group work with such adolescents have provided the following encouraging results. Adolescent offenders who had group work showed higher self-esteem (Fashinger & Harris, 1987; Fine et al., 1991), greater school achievement (Fashinger & Harris, 1987), more empathy with and more support of others (Carpenter, 1984; Fashinger & Harris, 1987; Madonna & Caswell, 1991), and less recidivism (Fashinger & Harris, 1987; Larson, 1990; Leeman, Gibbs, & Fuller, 1993) than adolescent offenders who had no group work.

Group work with nonoffender adolescents has been advocated for many of the same reasons (Dies, 1991; McLennan & Dies, 1992). Aspects of group work with such adolescents, including confidentiality and structure, as well as characteristics of the group leaders, have been discussed (Leader, 1991). A meta-analysis of nine evaluation studies that have compared the effects of individual and group interventions has indicated consistently better effects for group than individual interventions with adolescents (Tillitski, 1990). This differential effect does not occur with children. School-based adolescents who had group work have shown higher self-esteem and less depression (Fine et al., 1991), and better communications with others (Joanning et al., 1992) than school-based adolescents who had no group work.

TWO CONCEPTUAL MODELS OF ADOLESCENT PSYCHOSOCIAL FUNCTIONING AND GROUP WORK

Both personal construct and psychodynamic group work come from therapeutic approaches that pursue the goals of insight and awareness. These approaches also have a wide range of strategies with which to assess clients, the resulting assessment focusing on both the psychological and social processes involved. They also provide the benefits of acknowledging the role of preverbal and unconscious processes in the functioning of adolescents. Both approaches also take the history of the construing of both adolescents and therapists into account, so that the concepts of transference and countertransference are used by both of them. They are also sufficiently distinct to make comparison meaningful, as outlined in the following pages.

Personal Construct Model

The personal construct model (after Berzonsky, 1990; Kelly, 1955; Leitner & Pfennninger, 1994) includes the following features.

1. Adolescents continually try to predict and control their worlds through anticipation, especially those worlds that involve the interaction of self and others. For this purpose, they develop systems of constructs. These constructs are built up by observing the repeated patterns in the events they experience. Constructs that deal with self in relation to others are called core constructs.

2. Constructs develop through individual experiences, but when experiences are shared, so too can the constructs of adolescents be shared. These constructs are also subject to change.

3. Constructs can deal with only a finite range of events. Because of the limited range of convenience of the construct systems of adolescents, others can invalidate core or self-related constructs. Anxiety, anger, and threat then results. This may be especially so for adolescents who have been offenders, whose illegal behavior often seems designed to elicit invalidation of constructions of self from others.

4. Well-functioning adolescents will be able to discriminate, and be flexible, creative, and responsive. They will also be able to be committed, courageous, and forgiving, and to respect their own intimate relationships with others. Poorly functioning adolescents will develop fewer of these capacities.

5. Their problematic constructs can be changed through structured group work. The group work provides a laboratory in which these problematic constructs can be tested, with different types of structure providing different experiments for them. The validating climate of the group minimizes, most importantly, the threat to the most influential core constructs of the members during this experimentation. It also reduces their anxiety and anger, because more of their anticipations are effective in predicting and controlling their worlds.

In sum, the main goal of personal construct group work is to provide opportunities for experimentation by the group members. There is a wider range of controlled conditions in the group in which therapeutic experiments can be conducted than there can be in individual therapy (Viney, 1996).

Personal construct group leaders see three group processes as therapeutic. These processes provide opportunities for the group members to (a) develop better discrimination, (b) examine their preemptive or stereotype-like construing, and (c) add to their ability to understand the thoughts, emotions, and beliefs of a wider range of other people (Winter, 1992). Personal construct group leaders also find the therapeutic processes in group work identified by Yalom (1985) useful. Important processes include hope, the sharing of information and emotions, and recognition of the similarities of the experiences of other group members to their own. These leaders also find the concepts of transference and countertransference, and of preverbal construing, helpful in encouraging group members to test effectively their construing. Therapeutic experiments can also be conducted by using a range of feedback from group members about how each member is perceived. The climate of a personal construct group ensures validation for many of the most central and influential constructs of its members. This uncritical acceptance and understanding of others is the context of experimentation here as it is for individual therapy. Indeed, invalidation has been shown to be more effective when it comes from group members who have provided validation of some of the construing of others in the group (Catina, Tschuschke, & Winter, 1989).

Personal construct psychology has two important corollaries of its main postulate that are central to personal construct group work. The first of these, the Sociality Corollary (Kelly, 1955), states that, "the extent to which one person construes the construction processes of another, he may play a role in the social process involving another." Adolescents interact effectively with others, then, when they behave according to how they understand those others to construe. They understand others best when they see them as fellow construers or creators of personal meanings. For adolescents who have difficulty doing this, enactment and role play can be helpful. The other important personal construct concept is contained in the Commonality Corollary (Kelly, 1955, p.87), which states that, "to the extent that one person construes an event like another, their psychological processes will be similar." There will be some commonality, or sharing, in the construing of people. Such commonality makes communication between them possible. In personal construct group work, such shared construing is of course emphasized. So, too, are the effects of others on the way people construe events (Dalton & Dunnett, 1993).

Personal construct group work can be described as having stages involving sharing of the construing of its members and individualization, or differentiation, of their construing. An account of these stages has been provided by Koch (1985): (a) searching for commonality and confirmation, (b) clarification of differences and reciprocal elaboration and extension of construing, and (c) development of the relationships of individual members to the group, together with recognition of their individuality. Therapeutic experiments in this setting can come from a wide range of other theories. They can include, for example, drawing, playing games, acting written scripts, role playing with role reversal, reflecting on the group process using videos, sharing self-characterizations, and using the dyadic sharing of the Interpersonal Transactional Group (Landfield & Rivers, 1975; Neimeyer, 1988). Details of this last task can be found later in this account of the research.

Further, psychological well-being can be defined, from the perspective of personal construct psychology, as the ability to experiment with shared constructs as well as with personal constructs (Leitner & Pfenninger, 1994). Such well-being also includes the ability to take a perspective on events so as not always to interpret them literally (Koch, 1985). Group work is, therefore, especially useful to adolescents, because it provides opportunities to develop these needed capacities.

Personal construct group work has been effectively used with a wide range of clients (Viney, 1998; Winter, 1992), such as stutterers (Dalton, 1980), depressives (Winter, 1985) and people who are HIV-positive (Viney, Allwood, & Stillson, 1991), as well as with adolescents with problems (Jackson, 1990; Truneckova & Viney, 1997).

Psychodynamic Model

Important considerations for the psychodynamic model of group work with adolescents (after Klein, 1932, 1948, 1957) are outlined next.

1. In adolescence, with the onset of puberty, there is an intensification of sexual impulses, producing a regression to more immature stages of development and return of early infantile impulses. Earlier anxieties and other negative emotions are aroused as earlier unresolved conflicts threaten to reemerge. The defensive processes of projection and splitting are readily apparent. Both of these developments contribute to the struggles of adolescents to achieve their senses of identity, as the central task of adolescence, as do the functional attempts of adolescents to reestablish their disturbed equilibrium. These struggles will be particularly severe for those who commit offenses against the law, because they have more unresolved losses and conflicts and less well-developed ego mechanisms of coping and defense.

2. Individuals can be described as having a range of different selves in relation to different people, situations, and contexts. Well-functioning adolescents understand more the different "groups of selves," and have a greater capacity to maintain identity in different situations, compared with poorly functioning adolescents.

3. The ongoing experiences of adolescents in family and group situations are central determinants of this evolving identity. Group life can aid the process of integration in late adolescence and the achievement of a stable sense of self. Alternatively, peer groups may fail to support their members in the developmental tasks they face, fostering the opposite processes of splitting and ego fragmentation underlying risky acting out. Poorly functioning adolescents will be more vulnerable to those influences than well functioning adolescents.

4. Psychodynamic group work provides opportunities for understanding the complex emotional episodes making up group life. Through interpretation it is possible for group leaders to demonstrate in the here and now, (a) emotional attitudes the group has to individuals, (b) members' perceptions of the attitude of the group to each member, (c) attitude of the individual to the group, and (d) attitude of members to the leader or authority figure. These processes of demonstration and interpretation facilitate integration and reduce splitting and ego fragmentation.

The goal of the psychodynamic group work is to encourage processes of internalization and ego integration within members rather than defensive splitting, externalization, and projection. The purpose is to bring members to acknowledge their warded-off impulses as their own, rather than deny them or evade responsibility for them by attributing them to others or to forces in the environment.

Psychodynamic group work has been developed with children and adolescents over a range of types of clients and settings (Bion, 1961; Foulkes & Anthony, 1957; Ginott, 1961; Hinshelwood, 1989). How the group is used, whether as waste bin or creative container, will determine whether a developmental transformation to a higher level of organization is achieved (Bion, 1970; Zinkin, 1989). The goals of psychodynamic group work are to enhance ego functioning, by increasing the capacity for reality testing, strengthening object relations, and improving regulation of impulses (Buchholz & Mishne, 1994). Peer groups can be an optimum form of intervention with adolescents (Sinason, 1985). Adolescents still engaged in struggles for independence and autonomy often feel freer and more protected in group than in dyadic modes of intervention. Fluctuations between rebellion and submission are allowed in groups, independence and identification with the leader are encouraged, relationship problems not always evident in individual work become clear, distortions in self and other perceptions can be modulated, and members have the opportunity to develop self-directed independent insight and enhanced ego functioning (Buchholz & Mishne, 1994). Group work may also be the preferred intervention for adolescent offenders, because offenders frequently operate in gangs, so that the natural unit of the group approximates situations close to life, fitting with their unique problems and needs. These gangs, in turn, facilitate emotional expression; for example, the strong anger felt toward adults (Macedo, 1955). Positive therapeutic benefits have been shown to flow from the negative transference prominent in psychodynamic offender groups (Truax, 1971).

The psychodynamic group intervention consists of unstructured discussion. It involves (a) establishing the clinical setting, (b) fostering group cohesiveness, (c) fostering individuality, (d) working with group process, and (e) managing a productive termination. These processes are now briefly described. The clinical setting is established primarily through close attention to physical and psychological boundaries. Leaders attend to the physical security of the setting, and protect discussion time and communicate its importance. Psychological structure and continuity are provided fundamentally through creating a space for each member in the leaders' minds. For example, absences from the group are addressed early in the session; attempts by one member to dominate, or another member's low participation are also addressed within the group. In addition, elements of ritual in the beginning and ending of sessions and other procedural matters are designed to moderate the anxiety of members. In this way, feelings, impulses, and thoughts can be expressed in ways not felt to be overwhelming or inhibiting.

When the boundaries are firmly kept, a sense of group cohesiveness is fostered, promoting a feeling of kinship, and optimism about the possibility of change. Establishing helpful group norms is achieved by various means: commenting on constructive events in the group to help them build on positive experiences; helping members reflect on their experiences in the group; establishing a general ethos of group work; enabling members to bring individual experiences of the group into discussion; encouraging members to share a personal view or opinion; supporting individuals by acknowledging expressions of feeling/opinion; reinforcing the giving of feedback to others in the group; acknowledging new accomplishments and understandings; emphasizing important breakthroughs. By discovering that they share concerns and life situations, they can teach each other and have the experience of being a giver and receiver of help, which can itself add to a sense of competence.

Working with the dynamics, process, and emotional aspects of groups, rather than content alone, requires group leaders to be clear about the instrumental purposes of group work. They need to develop and refine their understanding of each person in the group, to keep in touch with their own feelings, to note their own behavior and its consequences, and to see connections between group and individual dynamics. The guidelines for studying and intervening in group processes have been developed from Shapiro's (1968) adaptation for adolescents of Bion's (1961) group work with adults. The group milieu is a powerful tool for eliciting a heightened emotional climate, with less of the distancing and screening out of emotions typical of individual work with adolescents. This provides an opportunity for the group leaders to observe interpersonal interactions and for adolescents to experience and think about interpersonal and intrapersonal dynamics. They can explore personal meanings, such as their own responses to provocations and projections from others, and the impact of themselves (including their own projections) on others. They can explore new behaviors and receive feedback from others. The leaders may initiate changes by first identifying and bringing to light conflictual themes that are then reactivated and enacted in the group interaction. Leaders can then lead members to look for similarities and differences between these themes and situations arising outside the group.

Other accounts of the impact of group work on offenders are available elsewhere (Henry, Viney, & Campbell, 1996; Viney, Henry, & Campbell, 2001). However, this account deals with the effects of group work on nonoffender as well as offender adolescents, and explores the different effects of the personal construct and psychodynamic group work. It identifies, too, adolescents who are likely to benefit from group work, examines personal construct group work processes, and relates those processes to the effects that have been demonstrated.

AIMS AND HYPOTHESES

The *aim* of this research was to evaluate personal construct and psychodynamic group work for school-age adolescents who were offenders and nonoffenders. These *hypotheses* deal with their effects.

1. Adolescents who experienced group work compared with adolescents who had no group work would show more gains, immediately, in terms of the development of:

a. Maturational processes; that is, trust versus mistrust, autonomy versus constraint, initiative versus hesitancy, industry versus inferiority, and affiliation versus isolation;

b. Five psychological states: uncertainty, anxiety, depression, anger, and good feelings; and

c. Six types of anxiety: death, bodily damage, separation, guilt, shame, and diffuse anxiety.

2. Adolescents who experienced group work would show more gains 6 months after group work than adolescents who had no group work.

No predictions were made about the differential effects of personal construct and psychodynamic group work. However, when some effects of the group work were demonstrated, comparisons of the effects for the same outcome measures of the two types of group work were conducted. Other analyses were also carried out to examine the effects of participant and group leader variables on the outcomes.

METHOD

Sampling and Design

Two hundred and three 14- to 18-year-olds volunteered to participate in the research in three juvenile justice centers and three high schools in New South Wales (NSW), Australia. Fifty percent were offenders, and the remaining 50% were nonoffenders based in schools. The offenses with which the juvenile justice center–based adolescents had been successfully charged were all repeated offenses, because such detention was only provided after two or even three such incidents coming to court. The offenses of those participants were as follows: 39% were "breaking and entering"; 34% were "unlawful possession and driving of a vehicle"; 19%, "breaking and entering with a weapon"; and 8%, "attacks against persons."

The sample of adolescents was assigned randomly to the three conditions of the treatment factor of the design. The three conditions were:

1. the personal construct group work,

2. the psychodynamic group work, and

3. the no-group work control condition.

A second factor was type of adolescent: offender and nonoffender. A design consisting of the first two treatment conditions with the type of adolescent was later considered. Table 8-1 shows how the major demographic and other variables were distributed across these three conditions. The similarity of the distributions for age, aboriginal race, use of language other than English in the home, and even for their offender/nonoffender status was apparent, although the no-group-work

Table 8-1. Summary of Demographic Data for Adolescents with Personal Construct, Psychodynamic Group Work, and No Group Work (in Percentages)

	Gender		Age		Aboriginal		Language Other Than English		Legal Status	
	Male	Female	14–15	16–18	Yes	No	Yes	No	O	NO
Personal construct group work	63	37	48	52	11	89	11	89	53	47
Psycho-dynamic group work	69	31	55	45	13	87	14	86	50	50
No group work	54	46	58	42	11	89	13	87	49	51

O = Offender; NO = Nonoffender

condition proved to have somewhat more female adolescents than either of the other two conditions. Dependent variable data were collected on three occasions: before the intervention (Time 1), immediately after it (Time 2), and six months later (Time 3).

Forms of Group Work

Group Sessions and Leaders

The group work occurred weekly for a period of an hour and a half for 10 weeks. Twenty four 10-session groups were run, 12 of personal construct group work and 12 of psychodynamic group work. Two group leaders conducted each group, which had from five to seven participants. The 29 leaders who participated, volunteered for training in the group work of their choice. They were all trained mental health professionals, including registered psychologists and drug and alcohol counselors. Seventeen were women and 12 were men. The ages of the group leaders ranged from 23 to 45 years. Three of the leaders were aboriginal. These leaders attended a 1-day training workshop in the group work of their choice. They read and discussed the training manuals provided by the senior authors, together with selected background material. They also had 14 weeks of 2 hours of peer supervision under the guidance of the authors of this report, dealing with the conceptualization of the group processes and the planning of future group work sessions.

Personal Construct Group Work

The personal construct group work (Viney, Truneckova, Weekes, & Oades, 1996; 1997) used a structured group format for the 10 sessions, because higher structure of such groups has been linked with more therapeutic movement (Neimeyer & Merluzzi, 1981). The tasks that provided structure were selected in order to experiment with the current construing of the group members. The aim was to extend the range of construing of the members a little. The tasks were selected initially by the leaders, but, as the group developed, they were often selected jointly by leaders and group members. One such task included the Interpersonal Transaction Group (Landfield & Rivers, 1975; Neimeyer, 1988). This task involved five steps:

1. Identify mood, write on label, and share with others;

2. Talk with only one other person in a dyad and in response to a question asked;

3. Move to another dyad and share those answers again;

4. Continue to share this response with all the other group members, one at a time; and

5. Identify new mood, write on label, and share with the entire group.

Questions to be answered included: "Who am I?" "How are my expectations of the opposite sex like their expectations of ours, and how are they different?" "How can I give help to others and seek help from them?" "When do I feel safe, and when do I not?" and "What would I most like to say to each group member?" Other structuring tasks were also used.

Psychodynamic Group Work

The psychodynamic group work employed an unstructured discussion/activity group (Henry, 1996; Henry, Wesley, Jones, Cohen, & Fairhall, 1997); and was based on the work of Shapiro (1968) and Bion (1970). This group work evolved over the 10 sessions as follows: (a) rapid establishment of a working collaboration between members and leaders, through providing structure and fostering group cohesiveness; (b) intense, focused work on the carefully delineated problem area; (c) careful, interpretive attention to group process about the problem theme and to processes in the self; and (d) a productive and manageable termination. Although overtly unstructured, subtle but essential forms of structure were supplied. Both physical and psychological boundary control, for example, required attention to be paid to the management of what belonged psychologically inside or outside the group and the relation of the group to the institution. Drawing boundaries also included protecting time and communicating its importance. Working with the dynamics, process, and emotional realm of groups, rather than content alone, required of the leaders to be clear about the instrumental purposes of group work; to develop/refine an understanding of each person in the group; to keep in touch with the dynamics of the group as a whole; to keep in touch with their own feelings; to note their own behavior and its consequences; and to see connections between group and individual dynamics.

A Small Validation Study of the Two Group Interventions

The aim of this small data collection was to provide some supportive evidence that the group work conducted was true to the principles of personal construct and psychodynamic group work, respectively. Given the more overtly active role of the personal construct leader compared with that of the psychodynamic leader, apparent in our accounts of these groups, it was hypothesized that, if this group process were representative of the two different forms of group work, members of the personal construct group would report a higher level of activity for leaders than members of the psychodynamic group, but that there would be no differences for their other contributions. A small subsample of 10 group members was randomly selected from the nonoffender sample and asked to report their impressions of the contributions of leaders and other members to the group process. Five members were involved in personal construct group work and the other five in psychodynamic group work. They used a 3-point ranking scale to report on the activity level (choice of topic and talk) of leaders and members and on the level of their other contributions (their levels of thinking and feeling).

These hypotheses were supported, as can be seen from the mean ranks presented in Table 8-2. There were differences of at least 1 whole rank point, from a range of only 3, for the two aspects of the activity levels of the leaders targeted, but no such differences for the other contributions of the leaders, or for those of the members. Assuming that this sample of group members was representative of those nonoffenders in the full study, it may therefore be concluded that leaders' perceptions of the group work was consistent with the conceptual rationales of the personal construct and psychodynamic group work. There is also considerable supportive evidence from the observations of the two senior authors of their weekly peer supervision of each group therapy session, that the leaders were

Table 8-2. Mean Ranks for Choice of Topic, Talking, Thinking, and Feeling of Leaders and Members in Personal Construct and Psychodynamic Group Work

	Choose Topic	Talk	Think	Feel
Leaders				
Personal construct	2.6	2.2	2.1	2.1
Psychodynamic	1.2	1.2	1.6	1.6
Other Members				
Personal construct	2.0	2.0	2.6	3.0
Psychodynamic	2.4	1.2	2.0	2.2

conducting these two forms of group work, and adhering to the manuals that have been published (Henry, 1996; Henry et al., 1997; Viney et al., 1996, 1997).

Outcome Measures

Content Analysis Scales

The maturational processes and psychological states of these adolescent research participants were the primary dependent variables of this study. They were assessed using content analysis scales, applied to questions, such as: "Now I'd like you to talk for a few minutes about your life at the moment, the good things and the bad, what it's like for you." Any later probes that were needed to elicit sufficient speech from the participants were limited to repetition of the broad themes already introduced in this question. These scales, based on thematic analysis, result in continuous measurement with normalized distributions of scores (Gottschalk, Lolas, & Viney, 1986; Viney, 1983a). Content analysis of free responses overcomes many of the problems of asking adolescents to describe their states, such as the ambivalence of their emotions, and the effects of social desirability on their responses. The results from content analysis scales are less influenced by interviewer characteristics than those from other types of measures (Gottschalk, 1982). Content analysis scales are also conceptually and methodologically compatible with both the personal construct and psychodynamic approaches. Content analysis scales have proved useful in other studies of adolescents (Viney, 1983b, 1987; Wang & Viney, 1996). The 15 content analysis scales selected for this research, and some information about their reliability and validity, are now described.

Maturational Processes

The maturational processes of the participants were measured by applying the Content Analysis Scales of Psychosocial Maturity (CASPM) (Viney & Tyche, 1985) to answers to the open-ended question in the interview schedule. Five of the eight pairs of positive and negative scales making up CASPM were used as appropriate to adolescents. These scales assess the helpful and less helpful maturational processes people use to deal with Erickson's (1950) epigenetic tasks: *trust* and *mistrust, autonomy* and *constraint, initiative* and *hesitancy, industry* and *inferiority,* and *affiliation* and *isolation.* Examples of statements from research participants that would be scored on these scales follow: for the Trust Scale, for example, "I get on good with my mum now," and for the Mistrust Scale, for example, "I try to stay out of the house when my stepfather is home"; for the Autonomy Scale, for example, "I enjoy the weekends because I'm free of school," and for the Constraint Scale, for example, "I'm not allowed to do much at night yet"; for the Initiative Scale, for example, "We are going to organize our own formal," and for the Hesitancy Scale, for example, "I don't know what I am going to do after I leave school"; for the Industry Scale, for example, "Our group is doing well at school this year," and for the Inferiority Scale, for example, "My math is still not up to much"; and for the Affinity Scale, for example, "My friends and I spend a lot of time hanging out at the beach," and for the Isolation Scale, for example, "I don't see much of the old lot, they seem to be changing so fast." A manual to aid in the scoring of these scales has recently become available (Viney, Rudd, Grenyer, & Tyche, 1995).

These Content Analysis Scales of Psychosocial Maturity are based on assumptions about human development and assessment that fit with both the personal construct and psychodynamic conceptual models. These scales measuring psychosocial maturity have appropriate levels of interjudge reliability (with a range of coefficients from .80 to .95 and no significant differences in the sizes of scores) and a good test-retest reliability (ranging from .67 to .71) (Viney & Tyche, 1985). They have shown the expected discriminations between children and adolescents of different ages in Australia, the United States (both white and black youth), and the People's Republic of China (Viney, 1987; Wang & Viney, 1996). These scales have not varied with gender, years of education, socioeconomic class, or academic performance (Viney & Tyche, 1985). They have predicted reactions to illness and to interventions designed to improve those reactions (Viney, 1990), as well as assessed psychotherapy process to predict effectively psychotherapy outcome (Grenyer, Viney, & Luborsky, 1996).

Psychological States

The psychological states of the adolescents were also assessed using content analysis scales applied to answers to the same open-ended interview question. The usefulness of these measures for the assessment of psychological states has been demonstrated elsewhere (Gottschalk et al., 1986), in a range of stages of the lifespan (Viney, 1980) and with a variety of populations, including youth experiencing life stresses (Viney, 1983b), as well as in program evaluation studies with youth (Viney, 1981). The five psychological states assessed consist of *uncertainty, anxiety, depression,* and *anger*, as well as *positive affect*. The scales and subscales measuring these psychological states are described next.

The Cognitive Anxiety Scale (Viney & Westbrook, 1976) is a measure of the uncertainty that occurs when a person has difficulty in making sense of their experiences, as, for example, in a new, unfamiliar situation; for instance, "I was not sure what was happening." The Total Anxiety Scale (Gottschalk, 1982) consists of six subscales, measuring different types of anxiety, examples of which follow: death, for example, "She is scared that I am going to get killed"; bodily damage, for example, "I broke my knuckles trying to belt the crap out of somebody"; separation, for example, "Haven't seen my mum for a while, a couple of years"; guilt, for example, "I ran away and now no one trusts me"; shame, for example, "I feel so embarrassed"; and diffuse anxiety, for example, "I am going mental, going crazy." The Hostility In Scale (Gottschalk, 1982) measures depression, focusing on self-critical responses in which anger is directed to the self, for example, "I am not good at anything"; and the Hostility Out Scale assesses anger directly expressed to others or to the external world, for example, "Most of the kids at school are nerds." The Positive Affect Scale (Westbrook, 1976) taps good, positive feelings associated with happy, enjoyable experiences, which are contrasted with the earlier mentioned disruptive and disconcerting experiences, for example, "I enjoy hanging out with my friends."

The Cognitive Anxiety, Total Anxiety, Hostility In, Hostility Out, and Positive Affect Scales have appropriate levels of interjudge reliability, with a range of reliability coefficients from .71 to .99. Good test-retest reliability would not be appropriate for these measures of transient psychological states. Evidence of their validity has been provided in a number of studies (see Bell, 1991; Gottschalk, 1979; Gottschalk et al., 1986; Nagy, 1995; Viney, 1980, 1983a; Viney, Henry, Walker, & Crooks, 1994; Viney et al., 1994; Viney & Westbrook, 1982). The five scale scores were not found to vary with gender, age, years of education, or academic performance; however, socioeconomic status did have a significant effect on the scores of the Cognitive Anxiety Scale alone, as would be expected (Viney & Westbrook, 1976).

Procedure

The data were collected during standardized individual interviews in the juvenile justice centers, where the offenders were detained, and in the schools, before and after the group work and at 6 month's follow-up. The interviews lasted from half an hour to an hour. Two female interviewers, experienced in working with adolescents, conducted the interviews. These interviewers were independent of the leaders of the group work and blind to the treatment to which the research participants had been assigned.

The responses of the participants to the open-ended question in the interview provided above were transcribed and divided into clauses, each one containing an active verb. The responses were then content analyzed, following the standard scoring instructions for each of the content analysis scales (Viney, 1983a; Viney, Henry, & Campbell, 1995). Each clause was then compared with the sets of content analysis categories, which provided verbal cues for each scorable statement. Clauses matching these verbal cues were then summed. The total score thus calculated was multiplied by a weight representing the verbal productivity of each participant. The final Total Score consisted of the square root of this multiplied score, the square root procedure designed to normalize each distribution of scores. The content analysis was conducted by a trained and experienced coder, who remained blind to the treatment group to which each research participant had been assigned. For a subsample of 30 transcripts, interjudge reliability (Pearson's r) with an independent blind scorer for the 15 content analysis scales varied from .82 to .94. There were no significant differences by t tests between the mean scores of the two judges. The ranges of these scales varied from scale to scale.

Analyses

For the maturational processes (trust, autonomy, initiative, industry, and affiliation on the one hand, and mistrust, constraint, hesitancy, inferiority, and isolation on the other), the psychological states (uncertainty, anxiety, depression, anger, and good feelings), and types of anxiety (death, bodily damage, separation, guilt, shame, and diffuse anxiety), two-factor multivariate analyses of covariance (MANCOVAs) of Time 2 scores, with Time 1 scores as covariate, were used. This procedure made it possible to test for differences according to treatment versus no treatment (Group) and treatment in interaction with type of adolescent (Group x Type), as well as to contrast the two types of interventions (personal construct and psychodynamic group work). Then, in another set of analyses with Time 1 scores as covariates, Time 3 scores were used as dependent variables. Tests of Group x Gender of Participant effects on the same sets of scores and similar comparisons between "stayers" and "dropouts," using MANCOVAs, were also made. Finally, discriminant function analyses (DFA) were conducted to identify the role of level of each one of the sets of psychosocial participant variables at Time 1 in predicting the effects of the group work at Time 2. Because of the large number of comparisons to be made, alpha levels were raised so that $p = .01$.

Retention Rates and Analyses of Bias in the Retained Samples

The retention rate from Time 1 to Time 2 3 months later was quite high for such mobile populations (78%), leaving an N at Time 2 of 156. From Time 1 to Time 3 (9 months later), the retention rate was considerably lower (55%), leaving an N of 110. This retention rate was low, but was not unexpected for a sample of offenders, or even for the sample of low socioeconomic status adolescents. Only 17% of those "dropouts" at Time 3 refused to participate. The other 83% had relocated to distant towns in NSW, Queensland, or Victoria, either with or without their families, moving beyond the range of the research funding. Sixty three percent of these Time 3 "dropouts" were offender adolescents, and 37% were nonoffenders. The number of offender "dropouts" was higher because they were likely, if discharged, to return to distant towns or villages or, if still detained, be moved to distant juvenile justice centers. MANOVAs contrasting "dropouts" with "stayers" at Time 2 for a set of demographic variables, and their two sets of five CASPM scales, the set of five other content analysis scales measuring psychological states, and the set of six anxiety subscales at Time 1 showed no significant differences. The same comparisons were also made for "dropouts" and "stayers" at Time 3, on their Time 1 data, with the same consistent lack of any significant results. The retained samples at both Times 2 and 3 were comparable biographically, then, as well as psychologically.

RESULTS

The results present comparisons of the five sets of dependent variables at Times 1 and 2 in this order: maturational processes, psychological states, and types of anxiety. The findings from these significant analyses are detailed next. However, the results of comparisons of the same variables at Times 1 and 3 showed no significant effects.

Time 1 versus Time 2

Maturational Processes

These results are described in terms of the positive and then the negative CASPM scores. The means and standard deviations for five positive CASPM scale scores dealt with first are available in Table 8-3. Multivariate analysis (MANCOVA) showed significant effects for Group (multivariate $F = 2.99$, $df = 10,282$, $p < .001$) in comparisons of group work and no group work for Time 2 scores, with Time 1 scores controlled. The subsequent univariate analyses for these scores showed group differences in initiative ($F = 4.31$, $df = 2,145$, $p < .01$) and affiliation ($F = 8.08$, $df = 2,145$, $p < .01$). Inspection of the means of Table 8-3 indicated those adolescents who experienced interventions in the treatment condition showed more gains in intitiative and affiliation at Time 2 than those who were in the control condition. Also, significant Group (multivariate $F = 3.83$, $df = 1,98$, $p < .01$) effects were found overall for type of intervention, after the effects of Time 1 scores were removed. The univariate analyses for these scores showed initiative ($F = 3.05$, $df = 1,97$, $p < .01$) and affiliation (univariate $F = 3.17$, $df = 1,97$, $p < .01$) again to make significant contributions to the Group effect. The members of the psychodynamic group showed more gains in initiative and affiliation at Time 2 than the personal construct group members. There were no significant Group x Type effects.

The Group effect proved significant for comparisons of group work with no group work for the five negative CASPM scale scores at Time 2 after the effects of Time 1 scores were removed (multivariate $F = 2.90$, $df = 5,143$, $p < .01$). The means and standard deviations for five negative CASPM scales are available in Table 8-4. Subsequent univariate analyses for the group effect on these scores showed hesitancy ($F = 7.46$, $df = 1,98$, $p < .01$) to make the main significant contribution to this effect. The participants in the treatment condition showed more psychosocial gains in hesitancy (i.e., reduced hesitancy) at Time 2 than those in the control condition. There was no significant Group x Type effect. Also, for type of intervention, significant Group (multivariate $F = 2.54$, $df = 12,182$, $p < .01$) but not Group x Type effects were found overall, after the effects of Time 1 scores were removed. The univariate analyses for these scores showed mistrust ($F = 3.96$, $df = 2,145$, $p < .05$) and hesitancy ($F = 5.00$, $df = 2,145$, $p < .01$) to make significant contributions to the Group effect. Inspection of the means of

Table 8-3. Means and Standard Deviations for Five Positive Psychosocial Maturity Scales for Offender and Nonoffender Adolescents with Personal Construct, Psychodynamic, and No Group Work at Times 1, 2, and 3

			Trust	Psychosocial Maturity Scales Autonomy	Initiative	Industry	Affiliation
Personal Construct	O	Time 1	1.87 (.92)	1.04 (.53)	1.93 (1.18)	1.93 (1.18)	1.35 (.84)
		Time 2	1.68 (.56)	0.88 (.55)	1.22 (.73)	2.51 (1.24)	1.24 (.91)
		Time 3	1.58 (.84)	1.23 (.88)	1.56 (.76)	2.62 (.91)	1.21 (.86)
	NO	Time 1	1.13 (.69)	0.43 (.20)	1.51 (.85)	1.51 (.85)	1.68 (1.13)
		Time 2	0.97 (.50)	0.47 (.13)	1.32 (.58)	1.78 (.99)	2.21 (.82)
		Time 3	1.07 (.45)	0.75 (.45)	1.24 (.65)	1.60 (.72)	1.46 (.91)
Psychodynamic	O	Time 1	1.76 (.55)	1.05 (.65)	1.79 (1.26)	1.79 (1.26)	1.57 (1.07)
		Time 2	1.96 (.66)	0.82 (.37)	1.60 (.78)	2.80 (.99)	1.61 (1.01)
		Time 3	1.41 (.58)	0.67 (.33)	1.66 (.86)	3.42 (1.22)	1.43 (.92)
	NO	Time 1	0.90 (.65)	0.46 (.31)	1.75 (.99)	1.75 (.99)	1.57 (1.13)
		Time 2	0.98 (.53)	0.64 (.28)	1.43 (.67)	1.86 (1.14)	2.08 (.84)
		Time 3	1.12 (.74)	0.63 (.25)	1.02 (.54)	2.33 (1.71)	1.58 (1.14)
No Group Work	O	Time 1	1.79 (.62)	1.18 (.65)	1.93 (.97)	1.93 (.97)	1.99 (1.17)
		Time 2	1.87 (.64)	1.01 (.61)	1.34 (.78)	2.77 (1.04)	2.00 (1.10)
		Time 3	1.55 (.57)	0.81 (.36)	1.28 (.61)	2.61 (1.28)	1.66 (1.15)
	NO	Time 1	1.30 (.73)	0.62 (.39)	2.07 (1.01)	2.01 (.99)	2.59 (1.20)
		Time 2	1.22 (.46)	0.63 (.31)	0.90 (.58)	1.82 (1.01)	2.46 (1.00)
		Time 3	1.43 (.59)	0.68 (.28)	1.58 (.62)	2.42 (1.01)	3.13 (1.39)

Figures in parentheses are standard deviations. O = Offender; NO = Nonoffender

Table 8-4 indicated that the personal construct group members showed more gains in mistrust (i.e., reduced mistrust) at Time 2 than the those experiencing the psychodynamic group work, whereas the psychodynamic group members showed more gains in hesitancy (i.e., reduced hesitancy) at Time 2 than the personal construct group members.

Psychological States

The Group (multivariate $F = 2.02$, $df = 5,143$, $p < .10$) but not the Group x Type effect showed a trend toward significance for comparisons of group work with no group work for the five psychological states. The means and standard deviations for five scales measuring the psychological states are available in Table 8-5. The subsequent univariate analyses for the group effect in these scale scores revealed uncertainty ($F = 8.21$, $df = 1,99$, $p < .01$) to make the main significant contribu-

Table 8-4. Means and Standard Deviations for Five Negative Psychosocial Maturity Scales for Offender and Nonoffender Adolescents with Personal Construct, Psychodynamic, and No Group Work at Times 1, 2, and 3

| | | | Psychosocial Maturity Scales | | | |
			Mistrust	Constraint	Hesitancy	Inferiority	Isolation
Personal Construct	O	Time 1	1.19 (.50)	2.01 (.92)	1.36 (.89)	0.87 (.42)	1.27 (.97)
		Time 2	0.91 (.32)	1.69 (.89)	1.13 (.71)	0.71 (.42)	0.66 (.18)
		Time 3	1.04 (.47)	1.37 (.73)	1.34 (.72)	0.99 (.68)	0.88 (.56)
	NO	Time 1	0.83 (.48)	0.76 (.54)	0.69 (.42)	0.85 (.68)	1.14 (.90)
		Time 2	0.65 (.29)	0.75 (.40)	0.97 (.54)	0.79 (.51)	1.57 (.83)
		Time 3	1.03 (.60)	0.89 (.53)	1.26 (.71)	1.16 (.89)	1.36 (.84)
Psychodynamic	O	Time 1	1.60 (.60)	2.27 (.69)	1.47 (.94)	0.87 (.50)	0.96 (.63)
		Time 2	1.08 (.43)	2.05 (.83)	1.13 (.84)	0.86 (.49)	1.13 (.75)
		Time 3	1.21 (.86)	1.30 (.41)	1.26 (.99)	0.58 (.12)	0.96 (.69)
	NO	Time 1	0.79 (.41)	0.86 (.59)	1.09 (1.04)	0.81 (.78)	0.96 (.81)
		Time 2	0.96 (.37)	0.92 (.57)	1.18 (.70)	1.08 (.95)	1.16 (.81)
		Time 3	0.82 (.45)	1.09 (.61)	1.09 (.58)	1.03 (.93)	0.91 (.81)
No Group Work	O	Time 1	1.31 (.61)	2.07 (1.14)	1.42 (1.03)	0.89 (.61)	1.05 (.64)
		Time 2	1.01 (.39)	1.67 (.63)	1.57 (1.14)	1.02 (.63)	1.05 (.63)
		Time 3	1.07 (.65)	1.23 (.65)	1.13 (.81)	0.69 (.34)	1.16 (.77)
	NO	Time 1	0.81 (.43)	0.93 (.61)	1.41 (.98)	1.02 (.99)	1.16 (.99)
		Time 2	0.85 (.35)	2.89 (1.15)	1.60 (.90)	1.07 (.88)	1.56 (.92)
		Time 3	0.98 (.50)	0.97 (.47)	1.31 (.61)	1.33 (.80)	1.20 (.78)

Figures in parentheses are standard deviations. O = Offender; NO = Nonoffender

tion to this effect. The participants in the treatment condition showed more gains in uncertainty at Time 2 than those in the control condition. In the comparison of the two types of group work, the Group (multivariate $F = 2.97$, $df = 10,282$, $p < .001$) effect, only, was significant overall. The univariate analyses for Group revealed uncertainty ($F = 4.06$, $df = 2,145$, $p < .01$), depression ($F = 3.06$, $df = 2,145$, $p < .01$) and anger ($F = 4.70$, $df = 2,145$, $p < .01$) to make significant contributions. Whereas the psychodynamic group work showed more gains in uncertainty and depression (i.e., reductions in those psychological states) at Time 2 than the personal construct group work, the personal construct group work showed more gains in anger (i.e., reduced anger) at Time 2 than the psychodynamic group work.

Types of Anxiety

For types of anxiety, the Group effect was not significant. In contrast, the Group x Type effect (multivariate $F = 2.90$, $df = 6,141$, $p < .01$) was significant for comparisons of group work with no group work for the six types of anxiety at Time 2. The means and standard deviations for the anxiety types are available in Table 8-6. The univariate analyses for the Group x Type effect in these scores showed mutilation (F =10.20, df = 1,146, p < .01) and separation anxiety (F = 5.88, df = 1,146, p < .01) to make significant contributions. There was less anxiety about mutilation and separation for offenders than nonoffenders immediately after treatment. Also, significant Group x Type (multivariate F = 2.82, df = 12,182, p < .001)—but, again, no Group effects—were found overall for type of intervention. The univariate analyses for the Group x Treatment effects showed mutilation (F = 5.06, df = 2,144, p < .01) and separation anxiety (F = 2.96, df = 2,144, p < .01) to make the significant contributions. The personal construct group work was linked, for the offenders rather than the nonoffenders, with more gains in anxiety about bodily mutilation and separation (i.e., reduced anxiety) at Time 2 than the psychodynamic group work.

Table 8-5. Means and Standard Deviations for Five Scales Measuring Psychological States for Offender and Nonoffender Adolescents with Personal Construct, Psychodynamic, and No Group Work at Times 1, 2, and 3

| | | | Psychological State Scales | | | | |
			Uncertainty	Anxiety	Depression	Anger	Positive Affect
Personal Construct	O	Time 1	1.48 (.91)	2.21 (.96)	2.09 (.84)	1.87 (.74)	1.40 (.74)
		Time 2	1.23 (.66)	1.55 (.83)	1.52 (.84)	1.15 (.51)	1.41 (.56)
		Time 3	1.24 (.69)	1.26 (.78)	1.76 (.78)	1.20 (.54)	1.38 (.61)
	NO	Time 1	0.98 (.74)	1.31 (.82)	1.00 (.60)	1.56 (.76)	1.23 (.55)
		Time 2	1.16 (.69)	1.42 (.64)	1.02 (.48)	1.31 (.60)	1.46 (.56)
		Time 3	1.31 (.65)	1.46 (.69)	1.16 (.60)	1.53 (.74)	1.29 (.51)
Psychodynamic	O	Time 1	1.44 (.81)	1.99 (.88)	2.24 (1.10)	1.94 (.67)	1.09 (.46)
		Time 2	1.29 (.88)	1.51 (.78)	1.02 (.48)	1.52 (.57)	1.36 (.73)
		Time 3	1.26 (.99)	1.41 (.75)	1.53 (.61)	1.51 (.73)	1.20 (.57)
	NO	Time 1	1.63 (.94)	1.15 (.66)	1.01 (.46)	1.48 (.69)	1.15 (.53)
		Time 2	1.21 (.76)	1.29 (.71)	1.22 (.66)	1.77 (.64)	1.36 (.58)
		Time 3	1.13 (.62)	1.23 (.76)	1.03 (.63)	1.82 (.68)	1.32 (.52)
No Group Work	O	Time 1	1.39 (.81)	2.26 (.93)	2.33 (1.17)	1.67 (.87)	1.24 (.53)
		Time 2	1.59 (.93)	1.55 (.77)	1.53 (.65)	1.25 (.66)	1.34 (.68)
		Time 3	1.18 (.81)	1.39 (.91)	1.48 (.84)	1.26 (.63)	1.41 (.51)
	NO	Time 1	1.52 (.96)	1.28 (.66)	1.17 (.58)	1.34 (.88)	1.57 (.65)
		Time 2	1.64 (.87)	1.52 (.76)	1.20 (.53)	1.46 (.71)	1.49 (.50)
		Time 3	1.45 (.86)	1.53 (.93)	1.19 (.63)	1.47 (.65)	1.45 (.65)

Figures in parentheses are standard deviations. O = Offender; NO = Nonoffender

Table 8-6. Means and Standard Deviations for Six Subscales Measuring Types of Anxiety for Offender and Nonoffender Adolescents with Personal Construct, Psychodynamic, and No Group Work at Times 1, 2, and 3

			Death	Anxiety Types Mutilation	Separation	Guilt	Shame	Diffuse
Personal Construct	O	Time 1	.74 (.28)	.74 (.28)	1.68 (.97)	1.24 (.64)	.91 (.48)	.86 (.39)
		Time 2	.61 (.10)	.64 (.14)	1.24 (.80)	0.87 (.47)	.61 (.11)	.76 (.28)
		Time 3	.66 (.26)	.67 (.27)	1.35 (.75)	0.79 (.47)	.79 (.85)	.96 (.55)
	NO	Time 1	.50 (.31)	.56 (.44)	0.73 (.49)	0.61 (.50)	.67 (.37)	.64 (.36)
		Time 2	.52 (.27)	.62 (.87)	0.74 (.32)	0.68 (.52)	.72 (.36)	.78 (.35)
		Time 3	.57 (.33)	.59 (.39)	0.99 (.51)	0.56 (.33)	.81 (.53)	.79 (.52)
Psychodynamic	O	Time 1	.73 (.17)	.73 (.17)	1.56 (.84)	1.27 (.57)	.85 (.55)	.72 (.16)
		Time 2	.67 (.19)	.67 (.19)	1.21 (.66)	1.00 (.57)	.71 (.23)	.77 (.31)
		Time 3	.58 (.12)	.58 (.13)	1.02 (.69)	0.94 (.46)	.58 (.12)	.72 (.36)
	NO	Time 1	.40 (.28)	.53 (.35)	0.76 (.42)	0.73 (.60)	.52 (.24)	.50 (.23)
		Time 2	.57 (.16)	.60 (.30)	0.84 (.45)	0.92 (.51)	.70 (.34)	.59 (.15)
		Time 3	.58 (.13)	.59 (.17)	0.90 (.49)	0.71 (.62)	.69 (.32)	.61 (.19)
No Group Work	O	Time 1	.79 (.34)	.80 (.34)	1.55 (.92)	1.52 (.88)	.89 (.43)	.90 (.36)
		Time 2	.70 (.27)	.84 (.43)	1.20 (.61)	1.06 (.63)	.87 (.56)	.75 (.28)
		Time 3	.61 (.19)	.61 (.18)	1.19 (.69)	0.83 (.46)	.71 (.30)	.75 (.25)
	NO	Time 1	.57 (.30)	.61 (.35)	0.86 (.53)	0.72 (.43)	.72 (.35)	.64 (.37)
		Time 2	.52 (.15)	.54 (.17)	1.09 (.59)	0.82 (.47)	.74 (.39)	.67 (.32)
		Time 3	.64 (.27)	.61 (.32)	0.95 (.64)	0.87 (.50)	.72 (.36)	.94 (.62)

Figures in parentheses are standard deviations. O = Offender; NO = Nonoffender

Prediction of Effects Using Participant Variables

Discriminant Function Analyses were used to predict the effects of the group work using variables descriptive of the participants. High and low levels of Trust, Autonomy, Initiative, Industry, and Affiliation at Time 1 were employed to predict scores on the scales measuring psychological states at Time 2, or the gains achieved from the group work, for participants who had group work only ($N = $ 127). The resulting Discriminant Function Coefficients are to be found in Table 8-7. Level of Trust proved to predict gains in Uncertainty, Anger, and Positive Affect. Level of Autonomy predicted gains in Anxiety, Depression, and Anger. Level of Initiative predicted gains in Anxiety and Depression; and level of Industry predicted gains in Anger and Positive Affect. Level of Affiliation did not successfully predict any of the gains in emotional states. Levels of Trust, Autonomy, Initiative, Industry, and Affiliation were also employed to predict

Table 8-7. Discriminant Function Coefficients from Analyses Using Levels of Content Analysis Scales to Measure Psychosocial Maturity at Time 1 on Content Analysis Scales Measuring Psychological States and Types of Anxiety at Time 2 for Adolescents Who Experienced the Group Work to Predict Their Outcome Gains (N = 97)

	Predictor Psychosocial Maturity Scales (Positive and Negative)								
	Trust	Autonomy	Initiative	Industry affiliation	Mistrust	Constraint	Hesitancy	Inferiority	Isolation
Predicted Psychological States									
Uncertainty	0.54*						0.84		
Anxiety		0.81	0.55		0.76	0.47	0.49		
Depression		0.64	1.00		0.53	0.70	0.39		
Anger	0.63	0.77		0.80	0.81	0.62			0.33
Positive affect	0.53			0.48					1.00
Types of Anxiety									
Death		0.95	1.00		0.62	0.72		1.00	1.00
Mutilation		0.62	0.59						0.45
Separation					0.49	0.81			
Guilt		0.48		1.00	0.67				
Shame		0.50						0.43	
Diffuse							0.49	0.48	

* Only coefficients > .4 provided, and all coefficients were positive.

gains found for the scales measuring types of anxiety (see also Table 8-7 for the Discriminant Function Coefficients). Level of Trust at Time 1 proved to predict gains in anxieties about Death and Mutilation at Time 2. Level of Autonomy predicted gains in anxiety about Death, as well as in Guilt and Shame. Level of Initiative predicted gains for anxieties about Death and Mutilation; and level of Industry predicted gains in Guilt. Level of Affiliation, however, failed to successfully predict any of the types of anxiety.

Levels of Mistrust, Constraint, Hesitancy, Inferiority, and Isolation at Time 1 were employed to predict gains on the scales measuring psychological states at Time 2 (see Table 8-7 for the Discriminant Function Coefficients). Levels of Mistrust, Constraint, and Hesitancy all predicted gains in Anxiety, Depression, and Anger. Level of Inferiority did not successfully predict any of the emotional states. Level of Isolation, however, predicted only gains in Depression and Anger. Finally, levels of Mistrust, Constraint, Hesitancy, Inferiority, and Isolation at Time 1 were employed to predict scores on the subscales measuring anxiety types at Time 2 (see Table 8-7). Level of Mistrust predicted gains in anxieties about Death and Separation, as well as Guilt. Level of Constraint predicted gains in anxieties about Death and Separation. Level of Hesitancy predicted gains in Diffuse Anxiety. Level of Inferiority predicted gains in anxiety about Death, Shame, and Diffuse Anxiety. Level of Isolation predicted gains in anxieties about Death and Mutilation.

SOME GROUP PROCESSES AND CONSTRUCTS IN THE OFFENDER AND NONOFFENDER PERSONAL CONSTRUCT GROUPS

The results of reliable analyses of the major themes, and defined here as constructs, in the group processes for the personal construct group work have been reported elsewhere for offenders (Viney et al., 1996) and for nonoffenders (Viney et al., 1997), and are described briefly here to better inform discussions of the findings of this research. These themes were identified by two independent judges for both types of research participants by reading the reports of the group leaders of each group session. These reports were assessed using the following headings:

1. Themes of interpretation and prediction
2. Group processes
3. Emotions
4. Experiments and the outcomes of experiments, together with
5. Reflections of the leaders on any noteworthy events

Offender Adolescent Group Processes

Six constructs of offender adolescents are described. The first four constructs can be seen as psychologically problematic, and the last two constructs as more helpful. The first four constructs were frequently used in early sessions of the group, and the last two constructs in later sessions.

1. Self As Unknown and Unknowable

Offenders using this construct did not enter group work with the experience of having had their systems of meanings understood or known by another. As a result, they had developed views of themselves as unknown and unknowable. These offenders experienced at times an almost paralyzing threat about the possibility of being known by others, including by their fellow group members. This was because, not only had their construing of themselves not been seen by them to be validated by others, but they had experienced long and extensive invalidation of other possible views of themselves. They lacked intimate relationships, so that their sources of validation and invalidation were, in fact, limited. The threat posed by being known by others in fact meant that they avoided intimate relationships. In terms of bipolar constructs, they seemed to recognize that on one pole they saw themselves as having no relationships with others or even with self, "blocking out" pain, and doing crime. Having relationships, experiencing pain, and not doing crime was at the other pole. They could not see themselves as changing any aspect of this problematic interpretation, but, more seriously, could not even see themselves moving from one pole of that shared, but very polarized meaning, to the other. Establishing relationships within the group was made difficult by their use of this pole of the construct. This interpretation was countered by the group leaders using validation of whatever aspects of themselves the group members were able to share, however socially unacceptable they might be.

2. Action As Constant

Constant action has been described by the offenders as implying addiction to action. Three of the terms they used to describe this construct were "adrenalin rushes," "buzzes," and "greed." The other pole of this bipolar construct involved nonaction, which for these offenders felt intolerably "weird." Their interpretations of the group processes were also of constant action. It required care on the part of the leaders to make the group a safe, validating environment for the more mindful experiments with this construct of the members, when they saw themselves as constantly active, in the mindless, greedy sense. Making the actions in the groups safe and mutually supportive ones helped to encourage a safer environment. This strategy had an impact on both this construct and on group processes, leading to more effective group work.

3. The World As Totally Inconsistent

This construct of the world as constantly in action was based on the assumption of total inconsistency. There was nobody and nothing on which these offenders could rely. They saw everything as changing. This interpretation was applied to themselves as well as to the rest of their interpersonal worlds. Given this belief in inconsistency in the members, the claims of the group leaders that they would return each week for each of the 10 sessions promised was seen by offenders using this meaning as deception. A climate of validation, and therefore of trust, was thus very difficult to establish early in these groups. Careful, constant acting on a series of big and small promises to the group members helped to modify the use of this construct in the groups. Not only changing some, but also keeping other personal meanings, are seen as essential to successful personal construct therapy (Neimeyer & Neimeyer, 1993). Careful and constant validation of what was judged to be their most central and influential interpretations of themselves, so as to avoid the members' experiencing threat, was also used to deal with this construct.

4. The World As Destroyable

The construct of destruction was apparent not only in what these offenders said, but in what they did. This interpretation of the world was also based on that assumption of total inconsistency. In all of the personal construct groups in juvenile justice centers, the members destroyed anything solid. The objects that suffered this fate included pens, crayons, heaters, carpets, and clothing. Needless to say, our group leaders learned very quickly to bring to group sessions only objects that could safely be destroyed. Again, the dominance of this interpretation in early sessions did not provide a climate in which to risk highly personal and precious issues. Consistent lack of destruction by the group leaders of people and things, together with confirmation of the existence of the group members, through, for example, shared massage, helped to modify the use of this meaning in the groups. So, too, did individualization of the interpretations of the members to validate as much of their construing of themselves as they could tolerate.

5. Temporary Intimacy with Others as Possible versus Not Possible

This was the first of the two more helpful constructs revealed by the qualitative analysis of some of the later group work sessions. When working with group members with the preceding intepretations and predictions, the most effective experiment by the leaders proved to be to validate some of those meanings that were more useful for the group members. This validation involved showing that at least some part of their views of the world was both heard and understood. The offenders gave many sad accounts of their deprivation and disconfirmation. There was opportunity for intimate relationships with the group leader, at least temporarily. The main goal of the group leaders then became one of creating more intimate, if momentary, relationships with the other group members, and with themselves. Yet, given their powerful views of themselves as unknowable, intimacy initially could only be transitory. This intimacy occurred firstly through confirmation of their interpretations; that is, through shared understanding of some of their personal meanings.

6. The Group As Ownable by Its Members versus the Group As Not Ownable

The group leaders worked hard to ensure that the group sessions were experienced by the offender members as theirs to be enjoyed and used by them in whatever way they wanted. The only caveat imposed on this ownership was that no harm should come to any of the participants in the groups. This "ownership" of the personal construct group was important because of the confirmation it provided for the abilities, acceptability, and power of each of the members. Because of the interpretations of their worlds as in constant action, inconsistent, and destructive made by these offenders, a sense of ownership of the group was sometimes difficult to achieve for these group members, but did prove possible for most of them.

Nonoffender Adolescent Group Processes

These four constructs were rather different from those of the offenders, underlining the greater ability of these adolescents to relate to others.

1. Trust versus Distrust

This construct wound its way through most group processes, with early group sessions showing more focus on distrust and later sessions on trust. Being able to rely on others is essential to psychosocial maturation. Being able to exhibit trust may lead to greater maturation, and being stuck at the distrust pole in making sense of others may make it difficult to develop.

2. Closeness versus Distance

This theme, too, was important throughout the group process, but differed in its expression from early to late sessions. Distance was more often in focus in earlier sessions and closeness more in focus in later ones. The meaning of this construction had much to do with a choice between togetherness and separateness. Being able to establish closeness with peers may help to promote psychosocial maturation, given the high importance of peer norms to people in this age group. If young people feel close to a group of other young people whose beliefs they share, then this can lead to greater personal development.

3. Sexuality versus Asexuality

The closeness for both young men and young women in these groups was most prized when it involved their own gender. However, the shared group process, with members of both genders present, enabled them to move beyond this position. Such explorations led them into the construct of sexuality, with awareness of bodily desires and frustrations contrasted with avoidance of such awareness. This theme was intrinsic to the developing construing of themselves by these adolescents. Some of these adolescents construed themselves as fundamentally sexual in being, whereas others had not yet included this aspect of their construing of themselves. Adolescents who were more accepting of their sexuality could be said to be showing greater psychosocial maturity than those who were less so.

4. Powerful versus Powerless

This construct was very important to the group process, with much of it, especially early in the sessions, focusing more on powerlessness than power. Feeling powerful had the connotations of being both assertive and aggressive, whereas feeling powerless had the connotations of being both helpless and constrained. Construing of themselves as powerful was more likely to lead to psychosocial maturation for these adolescents, through purposeful action, than viewing themselves as powerless.

DISCUSSION

The finding from this evaluation of the impact of the two types of interventions (personal construct and psychodynamic) for five sets of data immediately after the group work are first considered, together with the results for these data sets 6 months later. Then the somewhat unexpected findings differentiating between the reactions of offender and nonoffender adolescents are described, as are the implications of the findings concerning the identified roles of the psychosocial functioning of the participants on the effects of the group work. Finally, the interesting differences in the effects of the two forms of group work are discussed, and linked, for the personal construct group work, to the construing identified during the group processes. In concluding this account of the research, consideration is also given to possible criticisms of it.

The first set of hypotheses dealt with the immediate impact of the group work on adolescents. The hypothesis that adolescents who had experienced group work compared with no group work would experience gains immediately after was confirmed, overall, for the five positive, helpful, maturational processes of trust, autonomy, initiative, industry, and affiliation. The adolescents showed greatest gains in industry and affiliation with others. The linked hypothesis about immediate reductions in the five negative, less helpful processes of mistrust, constraint, hesitancy, inferiority, and isolation, was also confirmed overall. Adolescents who had group work showed reduced hesitancy, especially. This first hypothesis about the immediate gains of group work was also confirmed overall for the five psychological states of uncertainty, anxiety, depression, anger, and positive affect; in particular, adolescents with group work reported less uncertainty than those who had no group work. However, the hypothesis was not confirmed for the six types of anxiety. Effect sizes (Cohen, 1988) were calculated for the samples with interventions from Time 1 to Time 2 (for Initiative, .55, Affinity, .61, and Hesitancy, .25), showing only small to moderate effects. Of course, effect sizes do not estimate clinically significant gains (Beutler & Crago, 1991). However, these gains were not maintained at follow-up 6 months after the group work was completed. The gains in maturational processes and reductions in immature modes of psychosocial functioning are consistent with and validating of the conceptual underpinnings of the group work. The particular pattern of psychosocial gains following the group work, as compared with preintervention patterns, revealed especially their positive impact on the ability to work at problem solving of the participants and on their peer relationships. At the conclusion of the groups, the adolescents who participated in the groups, compared with those who did not, saw themselves as more self-reliant and less dependent, as enjoying a greater sense of enterprise and less frustration at lack of achievement, as more able to move into a social group on their own initiative, and as better able to work on their relationships. In addition, the group work had a special impact on the participants' sense of fellowship with their peers; on their sense of relationships as spontaneous, warm, and reciprocal; and on their sense of closeness in intimate relationships.

In addition to the group work impact overall, as well as on specific areas of maturational processes, the pattern of results immediately following the group work, as compared with pretest patterns, revealed the impact of the groups on specific psychological states. The biggest gains were in levels and management of uncertainty. This finding indicated the reduced sense of inadequacy and increased confidence of group members in being outspoken about their views. This combination of expressive confidence and responsibility for one's point of view, taken together with the previously mentioned psychosocial gains in active, responsible, and responsive interpersonal functioning immediately after the group work, is encouraging.

Adolescent offenders showed no fewer gains than nonoffenders immediately after the group work. This finding occurred, even though offender adolescents showed higher levels of mistrust, constraint, and hesitancy before the group work, together with all types of anxiety and depression, than those of other previously reported samples of adolescents (Viney, 1983b, 1987). In fact, for the five pairs of positive and negative maturational processes and the five psychological states for which gains from group work had been demonstrated, no differences were found immediately after the group work between the adolescent offenders and nonoffenders. However, when the six types of anxiety—anxieties about death, bodily mutilation and separation, guilt, shame, and diffuse anxiety—were considered, offenders showed especially more gains after group work in their reduced anxieties about bodily damage and separation from others than offenders who had no group work and nonoffender adolescents. That adolescent offenders derived equal and comparable kinds of benefit from group work is consistent with findings that adolescent offenders are responsive to preventive interventions (Fashinger & Harris, 1987; Madonna & Caswell, 1991) and evidence that offenders are more amenable to treatment during adolescence than during adulthood (Oliver, Hall, & Neuhaus, 1993). The results of these short-term group work evaluations are encouraging. It is also possible that the absence of differences between the offender and nonoffender groups may be due, in part, to some overlap in a number of characteristics of the two groups of adolescents. In terms of the measurement made in this research, all of the participants were low in autonomy and high in isolation compared with other previously reported adolescent samples (Viney, 1987). All participants were also high in uncertainty and anger compared with other adolescent samples (Viney, 1983b). It is also noteworthy that both types of group work were immediately effective for members, regardless of their gender, aboriginal status, or use of a language other than English at home.

The complex findings concerning the identified roles of the initial levels of the psychosocial functioning of the participants on the later effects of the group work were of considerable interest. They can be seen as indicating the maturational levels of participants who should be selected for personal construct and psychodynamic group work in order to achieve particular psychological state goals. Those findings for psychological states indicate that, for example, if the goal were to reduce levels of uncertainty of adolescents, then selecting participants who have relatively high levels of trust would be important. If, however, the goal were to reduce levels of anxiety and depression, then selecting participants with relatively high levels of autonomy and inititiative, and low levels of mistrust and constraint would be important, with low levels of isolation also being important for depression. If the goal were to reduce levels of anger, those with high levels of trust and industry but again low levels of mistrust, constraint and isolation would benefit most. If the goal were to raise positive affect, selecting adolescents according to their high levels of industry, only, seems to be important. For gains in these emotional states to occur, especially reducing the more distressing ones, it is apparent that the achievement of early developmental tasks by the participants before the group work, such as trust, is very important.

Comparable recommendations about selecting participants for group work can also be made, if the goal is to reduce the levels of anxiety, for adolescents at different psychosocial maturational levels. Those findings indicate that, if the goal were to reduce levels of anxiety about death, then selecting participants who have relatively high levels of trust, autonomy, and initiative and relatively low levels of mistrust, constraint, and inferiority would be important. If, however, the goal were to reduce levels of anxiety about bodily mutilation, then selecting participants with relatively high levels of trust and initiative, and low levels of isolation, would be important. If the goal were to reduce levels of separation anxiety, selecting those with low levels of constraint would be important. If it were to reduce guilt, then relatively high levels of industry and low levels of mistrust would be important. Similarly, reducing shame using the group work would involve selecting participants according to their relatively high level of autonomy and low level of inferiority. Reducing levels of diffuse anxiety can benefit from selecting participants with low levels of hesitancy. Again, that the participants had achieved early developmental tasks proved important in predicting reduction of a range of anxiety types.

Although the immediate gains for adolescents from the group work were encouraging, the gains in maturational processes and psychological states at the conclusion of the group work were not maintained 6 months after its conclusion. Several possible causes for this finding are considered. The first concerns the match between level of input from the group work and preexisting levels of resources of the populations under investigation. In the case of the detained offenders and in the case of a significant number of the mainstream group (especially those from the two high schools in low socioeconomic areas), adolescents had severe developmental, psychological, educational, family, and social problems, and few employment prospects. So, one possible reason for the failure to maintain gains over the longer term may be that the brief interventions that we were able to offer here simply did not match the level of deprivation of the adolescents. More sustained and longer term input may be needed. That interpretation of the pattern of findings here received informal support from the reflections of group leaders and professionals responsible for the welfare of the adolescents. They welcomed the interventions warmly; they also indicated the need for more ongoing support of the adolescents. A second possible explanation of the absence of long-term gains is that the developmental characteristics of normal adolescence mean that relatively brief group work does not involve enough sessions. There was some support for this explanation from the qualitative analysis of the group work reported elsewhere (Henry, 1996; Viney et al., 1996, 1997). Third, it can be argued that that the absence of gains in the retained samples may have been because those samples were actually less psychosocially mature, in that those who were more autonomous, industrious, and affiliated with peers and less constrained, hesitant, inferior, and isolated from peers, were more likely to refuse to continue to cooperate with the authority figures involved by agreeing to be interviewed. Fourth, a common criticism of outcome measures that demonstrate short-term gains is that selected impact measures tap directly into the content of the interventions, falsely exaggerating their impact. This fourth possibility can be ruled out in the present study, which employed instruments with independent content, validity that was generalizable, and sensitivity to underlying processes rather than surface content, only.

Whereas no predictions were made about the differential impacts of the personal construct and psychodynamic group work, when the gains in sets of outcome measures described earlier were demonstrated, comparisons of the gains in the same measures were made for the two forms of group work. Differences in the impact of the two forms were found for the five positive maturational processes. The adolescents showed greater initiative and affiliation after the psychodynamic than after the personal construct group work. In the case of initiative, the whole sample showed reduced levels at Time 2, so the greater levels of initiative of the psychodynamic group work adolescents needs tempering in this context.

Differences according to type of group work were also found for the five negative maturational processes, with adolescents showing less mistrust after personal construct than psychodynamic group work, and less hesitancy after psychodynamic group work. These differences were found, too, for the five psychological states, with adolescents showing less anger after personal construct than psychodynamic group work but less uncertainty and depression after psychodynamic group work. Differences in the impact of the two forms of group work were not found for the six types of anxiety, although for that set of outcome variables, differences in their impact on offenders and nonoffenders were found. Offenders who had personal construct group work expressed fewer fears of bodily damage and separation from others than those who had the psychodynamic group work. No other indications of differential impact of the two types of group work on offenders and nonoffenders were found after the group work; nor were any found at follow-up 6 months later.

The personal construct group work has proved the more effective of the two forms of group work in reducing the anger, mistrust, and pessimism of the participants in their constructions about themselves in relation to others. Those reductions in levels of anger are important, because they may indicate fewer attempts by the participants to extort validation for problematic constructs of theirs, and so, it is hoped, more openness to changes in those constructs. The reduction of their mistrust and pessimism should also lead them to greater openness to change through interactions with others, also linked with more acceptance of the lack of confirmation from others of some of their problematic constructs. In addition, the personal construct group work was more effective than the psychodynamic groups in reducing anxiety about bodily damage and of separation from others in the offender groups. These are very basic threats, and these gains were achieved in the type of participants most in psychological need. The pattern of differences for the two forms of group work did, however, show the psychodynamic group work to be the more effective in fostering mature psychosocial functioning, increasing active, confident activity and reducing social passivity, frustrated initiative, and feelings of depression. The psychodynamic groups also showed greater gains in the sense of rewarding and reciprocal interpersonal relations of the participants. In summary, it seems that the personal construct group work has proved more effective in reducing developmentally immature modes of psychosocial functioning, and anger directed at others, whereas the psychodynamic group work was more effective in increasing more mature levels of psychosocial functioning and anger directed at the self, in the form of depressive feelings.

It is also interesting to relate these outcomes at Time 2 to the constructs revealed in the personal construct group work. For the offenders, especially, it is striking to relate their gains to some of their highly polarized constructs. Given their self as unknowable, action as constant, the world as inconsistent and destroyable, the gains of these offenders in anger, mistrust, and pessimism were remarkable. This is striking, too, for the gains made especially by offenders in anxieties about bodily mutilation and separation from others. The much less polarized constructs of trust versus distrust, closeness versus distance, sexuality versus asexuality, and powerful versus powerless, of the nonoffender adolescents make their gains less striking but still impressive.

The aim of this research has been to evaluate the effects of two group work interventions, the personal construct and the psychodynamic, for school-age adolescents who are offenders and nonoffenders. This aim was achieved. The findings from the interviews collected immediately after the intervention were encouraging. Both interventions were effective in increasing helpful maturational processes, especially industry and sense of affinity with others, and in reducing the less helpful maturational processes, especially lack of confidence. The interventions were also effective in reducing less helpful psychological states, especially uncertainty. These findings held for both offenders and nonoffenders. There were also some interesting differences in the impact of the interventions on offenders and nonoffenders, with more reductions for offenders in their anxieties about bodily damage and of separation from others than for nonoffenders. The personal construct group work was more effective in reducing immature psychosocial functioning, whereas the psychodynamic group work was more effective in increasing more mature levels of functioning. The encouraging findings can probably be generalized to the adolescent populations, because "dropouts" were not distinguishable from "stayers" demographically or psychologically.

Yet, some criticism of this research must be made. Its sampling has been based on volunteers, limiting the generalizability of the findings only to those adolescents who would choose to be involved in such work. The retention rate immediately after the group work was just 78%, and at follow-up, only 55%. Further research in this field with larger samples, better retention rates, a better nontherapeutic group work condition, better validation of the group work, a wider range of more appropriate outcome measures, and closer examination of group process with these and other models of adolescence is recommended. We have already begun the examination of group processes (Henry, 1996; Henry et al., 1997; Viney et al., 1996, 1997). Promotion of more mature and emotionally comfortable functioning in vulnerable groups, such as offender and school-based adolescents, still remains a very high priority goal, and the findings of this research using both forms of group work make some contribution to achieving that goal. The research also indicates that the personal construct group work has proved an effective intervention for adolescents, resulting in outcomes that are both compatible with and in some cases distinct from those of the psychodynamic group work.

ACKNOWLEDGMENTS

This research was helpfully funded by a grant from the Australian Commonwealth Committee on AIDS Research Grants (CARG) to the two senior authors. Permission was kindly given to conduct the research by the New South

Wales Department of Juvenile Justice and the Illawarra Region, Department of School Education, Australia. The support of administrative and professional staff in these two organizations has been very much appreciated. We would also like to thank the senior staff of the Keelong, Mount Penang, and Reiby Juvenile Justice Centres, and the Albion Park, Shoalhaven, and Warrawong High Schools, New South Wales, for making this work possible. Further, the gifts made to us of time and attention from the busy lives of our adolescent research participants were invaluable.

Joanne Campbell took on the difficult job of coordinating this project, and did it very well, for which we are very grateful. Among the leaders of the preventive group work, the seminal contributions of four should be specially acknowledged: Patricia Weekes, Lindsay Oades, Deborah Truneckova, and Hilary Maitland. The important contributions of the other group leaders who trained in and conducted the group work is also very gratefully acknowledged: Michelle Earle, Craig Perkins, Tony Weaver, Ann Harwood, Keith Burke, Ann Rodum, Hany Gayed, Todd Zemek, Jenny Barton, Annalisa Dezarnaulds, Nasim Wesley, Harry Smith, Monique Cohen, Janet Mulholland, Greg Konza, Nadine Peiser, Chris Fairhall, Renata Kautz, Paul Whetham, Cassandra Mc Naught, Belinda Wall, Ellen Ryan, Peter Bruton, Alexandra Jones, and Tony Hansen. Peter Caputi, Ross Colquhoun, Marilyn Rudd, and Lindsay Oades also aided us in our analyses of the data.

REFERENCES

Attwood, R. O., & Osgood, D.W. (1987). Cooperation in group treatment programs for incarcerated adolescents. *Journal of Applied Social Psychology, 17*, 969–989.

Becker, J. V., & Kaplan, M. S. (1993). Cognitive behavioural treatment of the juvenile sex offender. In A. E. Barbaree, W. L. Marshall, & S. H. Hudson (Eds.), *The juvenile sex offender* (pp. 264–277). New York: Guilford Press.

Bell, P. (1991). *Nurses in transition.* Ph. D. thesis, University of Wollongong, Wollongong, Australia.

Berzonsky, M. D. (1990). Identity systems and self-construct systems: Process and structure interactions. *Journal of Adolescence, 13*, 251–261.

Beutler, L. M., & Crajo, M. (1991). *Psychotherapy research: An international review of programmatic studies.* Washington, DC: American Psychological Association.

Bion, W. R. (1961). *Experiences in groups.* London: Tavistock.

Bion, W. R. (1970). *Attention and interpretation.* London: Tavistock.

Buchholz, E. S., & Mishne, J. M. (Eds.). (1994). *Group interventions with children, adolescents and parents; An ego and self psychological approach.* Northvale, NJ: Jason Aronson.

Carpenter, P. (1984). "Green Therapy" revisited: The evolutions of 12 years of behaviour modification and psychoeducationist techniques with young delinquent boys. *Psychological Report, 54*, 99–111.

Catina, A., Tschuschke, V., & Winter, D. (1989). Self-reconstruction as a result of interaction in analytic group therapy. *Group Analysis, 22*, 59–62.

Cohen, J. (1988). *Statistical power analysis for the behavioural sciences.* Hillsdale, NJ: Erlbaum.

Dalton, P. (Ed.). (1980). *Approaches to the treatment of stuttering.* London: Croom Helm.

Dalton, P., & Dunnett, G. (1993). *Living with personal construct psychology.* Chichester, England: Wiley.

Dies, K. R. (1991). A model for adolescent group therapy. *Journal of Child & Adolescent Therapy, 1,* 59–70.

Erickson, E. (1950). Transactions of the June, 1950 meeting. In M. J. E. Senn (Ed.), *Symposium on the healthy personality.* New York: Macey Foundation.

Fashingar, E., & Harris, L. T. (1987). Social work at 30MPH: Mini-bike rehabilitator groups for juvenile delinquents. *Social Work with Groups, 10,* 33–45.

Fine, S., Forth, A., Gilbert, M., & Haley, G. (1991). Group therapy for adolescent depressive disorder: A comparison of social skills and therapeutic support. *Journal of the Academy of Child and Adolescent Psychiatry, 30,* 79–85.

Foulkes, S. H., & Anthony, E. J. (1957). *Group psychotherapy: The psychoanalytic approach.* Harmondsworth, England: Penguin.

Gautier, F. (1985). Therapie de groupe aupres d'adolescents delinquents. *Revue Canadienne de Psycho-Education, 14,* 107–112.

Ginott, H. (1961). *Group psychotherapy with children.* New York: McGraw-Hill.

Gottschalk, L. A. (Eds.) (1979). *The content analysis of verbal behaviour: Further studies.* New York: Spectrum.

Gottschalk, L. A. (1982). Manual of uses and applications of the Gottschalk-Gleser verbal behaviour scales. *Research Communications in Psychiatry, 7,* 273–327.

Gottschalk, L. A., Lolas, F., & Viney, L. L. (Eds.). (1986). *Content analysis of verbal behaviour in clinical medicine.* Heidelberg, Germany: Springer.

Grenyer, B. F. S., Viney, L. L., & Luborsky, L. (1996). Changes in Eriksonian psychosocial maturity levels over the course of psychotherapy and their relationship to interpersonal mastery and psychological health-sickness. 29th Annual Meeting of the Society for Psychotherapy Research, Amelia Island, Florida.

Henry, R. M. (1996). Psychodynamic group therapy with adolescents: Exploration of HIV-related risk taking. *International Journal of Group Psychotherapy, 46,* 229–253.

Henry, R. M., Wesley, N., Jones, A., Cohen, M., & Fairhall, C. (1997). AIDS and the unconscious: Psychodynamic group work with incarcerated youths. *Journal of Child Psychotherapy, 23.*

Hinshelwood, R. D. (1989). Communication flow in the matrix. *Group Analysis, 22,* 261–269.

Jackson, S. (1990). A personal construct therapy group for adolescents. In P. Maitland (Ed.), *Personal construct theory, deviancy and social work.* London: Centre for Personal Construct Psychology.

Joanning, H., Quinn, W., Thomas, F., & Mullen, R. (1992). Treating adolescent drug abuse: A comparison of family systems theory group therapy and family drug education. *Journal of Marital and Family Therapy, 18,* 345–356.

Kelly, G. A. (1955). *The psychology of personal constructs.* New York: Norton.

Klein, M. (1932). *The psychoanalysis of children.* London: Hogarth Press.

Klein, M. (1948). *Contributions to psychoanalysis.* London: Hogarth Press.

Klein, M. (1957). *Envy and gratitude.* London: Hogarth Press.

Koch, H. C. H. (1985). Group psychotherapy. In E. Button (Ed.), *Personal construct theory and mental health*. Beckenham, England: Croom Helm.

Laikin, M., Winston, A., & McCullough, L. (1991). Intensive short term psychodynamic therapy. In P. Crits-Christoph & J. P. Barber (Eds.), *Handbook of short term dynamic psychotherapy* (pp. 80–109). New York: Basic Books.

Landfield, A. W., & Rivers, P. C. (1975). An introduction to interpersonal transaction and rotating dyads. *Psychotherapy, 12*, 366–374.

Larson, J. D. (1990). Cognitive-behavioural group therapy with delinquent adolescents: A cooperative approach with the Juvenile Courts. *Journal of Offender Rehabilitation, 16*, 47–64.

Leader, F. (1991). Why adolescent group therapy? *Journal of Child and Adolescent Group Therapy, 1*, 81–93.

Leeman, L. W., Gibbs, J. C., & Fuller, D. (1993). Evaluation of a multi-component group treatment program for juvenile delinquents. *Aggressive Behaviour, 19*, 281–292.

Leitner, L. M., & Pfenninger, D. T. (1994). Sociality and optimal functioning. *Journal of Constructivist Psychology, 7*, 119–136.

Luborsky, L., Diguer, L., Luborsky, C., Singer, B., Dickter, S., & Schmidt, K. A. (1993). The efficacy of psychodynamic psychotherapies: Is it true that "Everyone has won, and all must have prizes"? In N. E. Miller, L. Luborsky, J. P. Barber, & J. P. Docherty (Eds.), *Psychodynamic treatment research*. (pp. 497–516). New York: Basic Books.

Macedo, G. (1955). Group psychotherapy in juvenile criminology. *International Journal of Group Psychotherapy, 5*, 54–60.

Madonna, J. M., & Caswell, P. (1991). The utilization of flexible techniques in group therapy with delinquent adolescent boys. *Journal of Child and Adolescent Group Therapy, 1*, 147–157.

McLennan, B. W., & Dies, K. R. (1992). *Group counselling and psychotherapy with adolescents*, New York: Columbia University Press.

Nagy, S. (1995). Nurses' constructions of iatrogenic pain. Wollongong, Australia: University of Wollongong.

Neimeyer, G. J., & Merluzzi, T. V. (1981). Group structure and group process: Explorations in therapeutic sociality. *Small Group Behavior, 13*, 150–164.

Neimeyer, G. J., & Neimeyer, R. A. (Eds.). (1993). Defining the boundaries of constructivist assessment. In *Casebook of constructivist assessment* (pp. 104–142). New York: Sage.

Neimeyer, R. A. (1988). Clinical guide-lines for conducting Interpersonal Transaction Groups. *International Journal of Personal Construct Psychology, 1*, 181–190.

Neimeyer, R. A. (1993). An appraisal of constructivist psychotherapies. *Journal of Consulting and Clinical Psychology, 61*, 221–234.

Oliver, L. L., Hall, G. C. & Neuhaus, S. M. (1993). A comparison of the personality and background characteristics of adolescent sex offenders and other offenders. *Criminal Justice and Behaviour, 20*, 359–370.

Quay, H. C. (1987). *Handbook of juvenile delinquency*. New York: Wiley.

Shapiro, R. (1968). Action and family interaction in adolescence. In J. Marmor (Ed.), *Modern psychoanalysis*. New York: Basic Books.

Sinason, V. (1985). Face values. *Free Associations, 2*, 75–93.

Tillitski, C. J. (1990). A meta-analysis of estimate sizes for group versus individual versus control treatments. *International Journal of Group Therapy, 40*, 215–224.

Truax, C. B. (1971). Degree of negative transference occurring in group psychotherapy and client outcome in juvenile delinquents. *Journal of Clinical Psychology, 27*, 132–136.

Truneckova, D., & Viney, L. L. (1997). Evaluating the effects of personal construct group work with problematic school-based adolescent. Eleventh International Personal Construct Congress, Seattle, WA, July.

Viney, L. L. (1980). *Transitions.* Sydney, Australia: Cassell.

Viney, L. L. (1981). An evaluation of an Australian youth work program. *Australian Psychologist, 16*, 37–47.

Viney, L. L. (1983a). The assessment of psychological states through content analysis of verbal communications. *Psychological Bulletin, 94*, 542–563.

Viney, L. L. (1983b). Psychological reactions of young people to unemployment. *Youth and Society, 14*, 457–474.

Viney, L. L. (1987). A sociophenomenological approach to life span development complementing Erickson's psychodynamic approach. *Human Development, 30*, 125–136.

Viney, L. L. (1990). A constructivist model of psychological reactions to illness and injury. In G. J. Neimeyer & R. A. Neimeyer (Eds.), *Advances in personal construct psychology.* New York: JAI Press.

Viney, L. L. (1996). *Personal construct therapy: A handbook.* Norton, NJ: Ablex .

Viney, L. L. (1998). Should we use personal construct therapy? A paradigm for outcome evaluation. *Psychotherapy, 38*, 366–368.

Viney, L. L., Allwood, K., & Stillson, L. (1991). Reconstructive group therapy for HIV seropositive patients. *Counseling Psychology Quarterly, 4*, 243–254.

Viney, L. L., Crooks, L., & Walker, B. M. (1995). Anxiety in community-based AIDS care givers before and after personal construct counselling. *Journal of Clinical Psychology, 51*, 274–279.

Viney, L. L, Henry, R. M., & Campbell, J. (1995). An evaluation of personal construct and psychodynamic group work with centre-based juvenile offenders and school-based adolescents. International Personal Construct Psychology Congress, Barcelona, Spain.

Viney, L. L, Henry, R. M., & Campbell, J. (2001). The impact of group work on the psychosocial functioning of offender adolescents. *Journal of Counselling and Development, 79*, 373–381.

Viney, L. L., Rudd, M., Grenyer, B., & Tyche, A. M. (1995). *Content analysis scales to measure psychosocial maturity (CASPM): A manual.* Wollongong, Australia: University of Wollongong.

Viney, L. L., Truneckova, D., Weekes, P., & Oades, L. (1996). *Adolescent offenders in personal construct group work: Dealing with their problematic and more helpful meanings.* Unpublished paper, University of Wollongong, Wollongong, Australia.

Viney, L. L., Truneckova, D., Weekes, P., & Oades, L. (1997). Personal construct group work with school-based adolescents: Reduction of risk taking. *Journal of Constructivist Psychology, 10*, 167–186.

Viney, L. L., & Tyche, A. M. (1985). Content analysis scales measuring psychological maturity in the elderly. *Journal of Personality Assessment, 49,* 311–317.

Viney, L. L., Walker, B. M., Robinson, T., Pincombe, J., Tooth, B., Lilley, B., & Ewan, C. (1994). Dying in palliative care units and hospital: Quality of life of terminal cancer patients. *Journal of Consulting and Clinical Psychology, 40,* 157–165.

Viney, L. L, & Westbrook, M. T. (1976). Cognitive anxiety: A method of content analysis for verbal samples. *Journal of Personality Assessment, 40*(2), 140–150.

Viney, L. L, & Westbrook, M. (1982). Patterns of anxiety in the chronically ill. *British Journal of Medical Psychology, 55,* 87–95.

Wang, W., & Viney, L. L. (1996). A cross-cultural comparison of Ericksonian psychosocial development: Chinese and Australian children. *School Psychology International, 17,* 33–48

Westbrook, M. T. (1976). The measurement of positive affect using content analysis scales. *Journal of Consulting and Clinical Psychology, 12,* 85–86.

Winter, D. (1985). Group therapy with depressives: A personal construct theory perspective. *International Journal of Mental Health, 13,* 3–5; 67–85.

Winter, D. (1992). *Personal construct psychology in clinical practice.* London: Routledge.

Yalom, I. (1985). *The theory and practice of group psychotherapy.* New York: Basic Books.

Zimpfer, D. F. (1992). Group work with delinquents. *Journal for Specialisations in Group Work, 17,* 116–126.

Zinkin, L. (1989). The group as container and contained. *Group Analysis, 22,* 227–234.

Index

About the Contributors

Mark Burrell is currently employed in the research division of Sapient, a business information technology consulting firm in Jersey City, New Jersey. He has served on the faculty of the New School for Social Research, and has written extensively on substance abuse problems from a constructivist perspective.

Trevor Butt is Reader in Psychology and Joint Director of the Centre for Constructions and Identity at the University of Huddersfield, England. He is joint author (with Viv Burr) of Invitation to Personal Construct Psychology, and has published in the fields of existential phenomenology and personal and social constructionism.

Chad L. Hagans is a graduate of the University of Florida. His work focuses on aspects of personality, personal construct psychology, and constructivist methodologies, where he has explored qualitative and quantitative measures of personal meaning-making, and the interaction between the instruments and their users.

Rachael M. Henry is a psychodynamic therapist and researcher. Her main areas of expertise and publication are child and adolescent psychology. She also founded and chaired the Graduate Diploma in Psychodyamic Psychotherapy at the University of Wollongong, Australia, prior to her retirement from the university.

Hubert J. M. Hermans is Professor of Psychology at the University of Nijmegen, The Netherlands. His most recent work is on the multivoicedness and dialogicality of the self. Among his books are *The Dialogical Self: Meaning as Movement,* with Harry Kempen, and *Self-Narratives: The Construction of Meaning in Psychotherapy,* with Els Hermans-Jansen. He is "first international associate" of the Society for Personology and director of the Valuation Theory and Self-Confrontation Method Foundation.

James C. Mancuso, now Professor Emeritus, joined the State University of New York at Albany in 1961. Professor Mancuso has published 5 books on personality theory, and over 70 journal articles and book chapters, many of which focus on the emotional and cognitive aspects of reprimand sequences. His recent publications explore the use of anticipatory narrative.

Greg J. Neimeyer is Professor of Psychology and Graduate Coordinator in the Department of Psychology at the University of Florida, where he also serves on the faculty in the Department of Community Health and Family Medicine. A Fellow of the American Psychological Association, Dr. Neimeyer is also the recipient of its award for Outstanding Achievement in Career and Personality Research for his work in the area of constructivism, personality, and counseling psychology.

Robert A. Neimeyer is Dunavant Professor of Psychology and Director of Psychotherapy at the University of Memphis, where he has been presented the Eminent Faculty Award for his scholarly contributions. He is the author or editor of over 200 articles and 18 books, including *Constructions of Disorder* and *Constructivism in Psychotherapy*, and is currently studying grieving as a process of meaning reconstruction.

Theodore R. Sarbin is Emeritus Professor of Psychology and Criminology at the University of California, Santa Cruz. He has received a number of awards including fellowships from the Guggenheim and Fulbright foundations, and Wesleyan University Center for the Humanities. His bibliography lists over 250 items on deviance, narrative psychology, emotional life, metaphor, imagination, clinical inference, contextualism, and constructionism. His present work is aimed at clarifying the narrative quality of emotional life.

Christopher D. Stevens has qualifications in arts, education, religious studies,, and in psychology. He has worked as a teacher, academic, and university counselor. He has specialized research and training interests in the areas of creativity and insight. Chris is currently working full-time in private practice as a therapist and as a psychological consultant in Sydney, Australia.

Dusan Stojnov is Professor of Psychology at the Department of Psychology at the University of Belgrade and Founder and Director of the Serbian Constructivist Association. He edited the book *Psychotherapies* and has published extensively in the fields of constructivist metatheory, personality theory, and psychotherapy.

David L. Van Brunt is currently an assistant professor in the Department of Preventive Medicine at the University of Tennessee Health Science Center. His specialty is in the area of behavioral medicine, focusing on the modification of health behaviors and the interactions between psychological, behavioral, and physical functioning.

Manuel Villegas is Professor of Psychology and Director of a Master's Course on Social Cognitive Therapy at the University of Barcelona (Spain). He is editor of *Revista de Psicoterapia* and former president of the Spanish Association of Cognitive Psychotherapy (ASEPCO). His research interests are in the field of discourse analysis in psychotherapy; he has also published several books and a large number of articles on this subject.

Linda L. Viney is a personal construct therapist who specializes in evaluation research. She has approximately 180 publications in measurement, developmental, clinical, and health psychology, including 6 books. A Fellow of the Australian Psychological Society, she also founded and served as Director of the Clinical Psychology Training Programs at the University of Wollongong, Australia.

Beverly M. Walker is an associate professor in the Department of Psychology at the University of Wollongong, NSW, Australia. She teaches personality theory and research, as well as life span development and individual differences. She has coedited two books on Personal Construct Psychology, The construction of group realities, and Personal construct theory: A psychology for the future. Her main empirical focus in personal construct psychology concerns dependency.

Glenn A. Yelich is a practicing School Psychologist in the Bethlehem Central School District located in Delmar, NY. His interests include the constructional processes underlying learning and behavioral disorders in the social/educational context.